ADHERENCE ISSUES
IN SPORT
AND EXERCISE

Marti
Tel:

1

To be

08

ADHERENCE ISSUES IN SPORT AND EXERCISE

Edited by

Stephen J. Bull

Cheltenham & Gloucester College of Higher Education

JOHN WILEY & SONS, LTD

Chichester · New York · Weinheim · Brisbane · Singapore · Toronto

Paperback edition 2001

Copyright © 1999 by John Wiley & Sons Ltd,
Baffins Lane, Chichester,
West Sussex PO19 1UD, England

National   01243 779777
International   (+44) 1243 779777
e-mail (for orders and customer service enquiries):
cs-books@wiley.co.uk
Visit our Home Page on http://www.wiley.co.uk
                          or http://www.wiley.com

Other Wiley Editorial Offices

John Wiley & Sons, Inc., 605 Third Avenue,
New York, NY 10158-0012, USA

WILEY-VCH Verlag GmbH, Pappelallee 3,
D-69469 Weinheim, Germany

John Wiley & Sons Australia Ltd, 33 Park Road, Milton,
Queensland 4064, Australia

John Wiley & Sons (Asia) Pte Ltd, 2 Clementi Loop #02-01,
Jin Xing Distripark, Singapore 129809

John Wiley & Sons (Canada) Ltd, 22 Worcester Road,
Rexdale, Ontario M9W 1L1, Canada

Library of Congress Cataloging-in-Publication Data

A catalogue record for this book is available from the Library of Congress

British Library Cataloguing in Publication Data

A catalogue record for this book is available from the British Library

ISBN 0-471-560197

Typeset in 10/12pt Times by Dorwyn Ltd, Rowlands Castle, Hants
Printed and bound in Great Britain by Bookcraft (Bath) Ltd, Midsomer Norton, Somerset
This book is printed on acid-free paper responsibly manufactured from sustainable forestry,
in which at least two trees are planted for each one used for paper production.

CONTENTS

ABOUT THE EDITOR

Dr Stephen Bull is an independent sport and business psychology consultant. He is a former section chair, and now Fellow, of the British Association of Sport and Exercise Sciences. He is Chair of the England and Wales Cricket Board Science and Medicine Advisory Group and a World Class Adviser for Sport England. In addition to his many papers in journals and scientific proceedings, Dr Bull has published four other books on applied sport psychology including *Sport Psychology: A self-help guide* and *The Mental Game Plan: Getting psyched for sport.* His expertise in adherence has been acquired through many years of research in addition to consultancy with numerous professional athletes and teams including the England Cricket Team, the British Ski Team and the 1994 and 2000 Great Britain Olympic Teams.

ABOUT THE AUTHORS

Dr Stuart Biddle is Professor of Exercise & Sport Psychology at Loughborough University. He was President of the European Federation of Sport Psychology between 1990 and 1999 and a member of the UK Government's Physical Activity Task Force between 1995 and 1996. In 1998 he was honoured as Distinguished International Scholar by the Association for the Advancement of Applied Sport Psychology. His other many offices include being Chair of the European College of Sport Science Scientific Committee and Psychology Editor for the Journal of Sports Sciences. Dr Biddle has also published over 100 book chapters and academic papers on sport and exercise psychology in addition to several authored and edited books.

Dr Britton Brewer is an Associate Professor of Psychology at Springfield College in Springfield, Massachusetts, USA, where he teaches undergraduate and graduate psychology subjects, conducts research on psychological aspects of sport injury, and coaches the men's cross country team. He is listed in the United States Olympic Committee Sport Psychology Registry, 1996–2000 and is a Certified Consultant with the Association for the Advancement of Applied Sport Psychology.

Dr Albert Carron is a Professor in the Faculty of Health Sciences at the University of Western Ontario. In addition to over 100 research articles, he has been the author of numerous books and chapters including *Motivation: Implications for Coaching and Teaching* and *Group Dynamics in Sport*. Dr Carron is a past president of the Canadian Association of Sport Sciences and a Fellow in both the Association for the Advancement of Applied Sport Psychology and the Canadian Society for Psychomotor Learning and Sport Psychology. He is also a Corresponding Fellow of the American Academy of Physical Education.

Dr Patricia Clarke graduated with a BSc in Psychology from Queens University Belfast, in 1991, following which she completed an MSc in Computer Science & Applications in 1992 at the same institution. After gaining research experience with the Human Nutrition Research Group, University of Ulster and the Rural Development Council for Northern Ireland, Dr Clarke moved to the University of Birmingham where she was awarded a PhD in Sport & Exercise Science in 1997. Currently, she is employed as a researcher by the London Ambulance.

Dr Rod Corban graduated with a BSc in Psychology from the University of Auckland in 1989, following which he completed an MSc in Psychology at the same institution. In 1998 he was awarded a PhD in Sport and Exercise Science from the University of Birmingham. He is currently a lecturer in Sport Psychology at the University of Central Lancashire.

Paul Estabrooks is a doctoral student at the University of Western Ontario. He has been awarded a Canadian Fitness and Lifestyle Research Institute grant and a doctoral fellowship from the Social Sciences and Humanities Research Council of Canada to pursue research associated with social influences in the exercise patterns of older adults. Paul has been involved in sport and exercise psychology as a researcher, fitness instructor, representative rugby player, and as a university rugby coach.

Dr David Gilbourne is a Principal Lecturer in the Centre for Sport and Exercise Science at Liverpool John Moores University. He has a background in physical education and outdoor education and his current research interests include the use of qualitative methods within sport psychology. In an applied context, Dr Gilbourne also specialises in applying psychological skills training within professional soccer.

Dr Heather Hausenblas is an Assistant Professor in sport and exercise psychology in the Department of Exercise and Sport Sciences at the University of Florida. She was the recipient of a doctoral fellowship award from the Social Sciences and Humanities Research Council of Canada for academic scholarship as well as the recipient of the 1996 Young Scientist award from the Canadian Psychomotor Learning and Sport Psychology Association.

Dr Lynne Johnston graduated with a BA in Psychology and Sport Science from Chester College in 1993 and completed her MSc in Investigative Psychology in 1994 at the University of Surrey. She was awarded her PhD from the University of Birmingham in 1998. Dr Johnston is currently a

Research Fellow in the Leisure and Sport Research Unit, Cheltenham and Gloucester College, UK. Her research interests include injury and rehabilitation, and methodology.

Dr Derek Milne is currently Director of the Centre for Applied Psychology at Newcastle University where he also directs the Clinical Psychology programme. He is a member of the Department of Psychological Therapies and Research, Northumberland Mental Health National Health Service Trust. He is qualified as a Clinical Psychologist as well as being a BASES Accredited Sport Psychologist, having a special interest in staff development and in action research. Dr Milne has published widely in the area of training.

Dr Nanette Mutrie is a Professor in the Centre for Exercise Science and Medicine (CESAME) at Glasgow University. She completed her PhD at Penn State University under the supervision of Dorothy Harris who was a pioneer in sport and exercise psychology development. Dr Mutrie is currently chair of the British Association of Sport & Exercise Sciences psychology section. She is co-author of *Psychology of Physical Activity and Exercise* and was the sport psychologist for the Great Britian Women's Curling Team for the Nagano Olympic Games.

Dr Al Petitpas is a Professor in the Psychology Department at Springfield College in the USA, where he directs the graduate training programme in Athletic Counseling. He is a fellow and certified consultant of the Association for the Advancement of Applied Sport Psychology. He has provided consulting services to a wide range of sport organisations including, the US ski team, the Career Assistance Program for Athletes of the US Olympic Committee, and the Transitional Golf Program for the US Ladies Professional Golf Assocation.

Dr Gabrielle Richards Reed graduated in 1995 at the age of 48 from the University of Rhode Island (URI) with a degree in Experimental Psychology. She spent her graduate career as a research assistant at the Cancer Prevention Research Center (CPRC) at the URI. She was then the Director of Grant Funded Research at the CPRC before going to Washington University School of Medicine in St Louis.

Dr Chris Shambrook is a sport psychology consultant working with the Great Britain Rowing Team, with whom he attended the 2000 Olympic Games in Sydney. He is a member of the British Olympic Association's Psychology Advisory Group and the British Association of Sport and

Exercise Sciences Education and Training Committee. He has published in the scientific and popular sport psychology literature and is co-author of *The Mental Game Plan: Getting psyched for sport.*

Dr Adrian Taylor is a Professor in the Faculty of Education and Sport Science at De Montfort University in Bedford. He has presented and published in academic and professional circles in North America, New Zealand, Israel, mainland Europe and the UK on a variety of psychological topics related to leisure, sport, exercise and health, over the past 18 years. He is acknowledged as an international expert on issues relating to public sector exercise promotion schemes and regularly represents the British Association of Sport & Exercise Sciences. He has co-authored a national quality assurance framework for exercise referral systems in England for the Department of Health.

FOREWORD

The topic of adherence has never been more important. Having been rightfully chastised in a review of *Advances in Exercise Adherence* for not including a chapter from the United Kingdom, it is fitting and proper that I offer this foreword. Steve Bull has ably assembled a broad-based book, designed to expand research and application to new areas in exercise and sport. The following chapters usher out the millennium with some new views on an old problem—namely, keeping people active. As many questions as answers are given, which is what a good book does.

Athens, Georgia, USA
March 8, 1999   Rod K. Dishman

ACKNOWLEDGEMENTS

Many thanks to:

John Albinson for getting me interested in the adherence area a long time ago!

Britt Brewer for organising the APA symposium in Toronto which stimulated the idea for the book.

The contributing authors for their willingness, expertise and effort.

Melanie Phillips and all at Wiley for their notable efficiency.

Donna for her support and encouragement.

Alexa and Morgan . . . for their smiles.

PREFACE

At the 1996 Annual Conference of the American Psychological Association in Toronto, a symposium was organised under the auspices of Division 47 (Exercise and Sport Psychology) by Britton Brewer which addressed adherence issues in sport and exercise. I was an invited presenter at that symposium which, in part, stimulated the idea for this book. Issues of adherence and compliance have long been of interest to psychologists in a variety of domains. As Meichenbaum and Turk (1987) pointed out, 'Ever since Hippocrates noted that patients often lie when they say they have taken their medicine, health care providers have been concerned with issues of patient compliance and nonadherence to treatment' (p. 11). Recent research has examined adherence/compliance concerns in relation to a variety of health behaviours such as depression (Frank, 1997), bulimic disorders (Waller, 1997), anger management (Mammen et al., 1997), post-myocardial infarction stress management (Trzcieniecka-Green and Steptoe, 1994), social phobia (Edelman and Chambless, 1995), sexual hypoactivity (Hulbert et al., 1995), medical controls in psychiatric disorders (Ruscher et al., 1997) and psychatric aftercare (Owen et al., 1997). Within this varied research, adherence concerns have been identified in relation to a variety of treatment modalities such as medication compliance, appointment keeping, homework completion, record keeping, and individual or group therapy programmes. The overriding message from the research is that adherence to these different modalities is a problem and that a wide range of personal and situational variables impinge on the adherence process.

In sport and exercise, academic and professional interest in the last 20 years has been focused very much on the problem of adherence to exercise and physical activity. Dishman (1988) published a landmark text which provided a state of the art review of theoretical models relating to exercise adherence, methods and strategies for behaviour intervention and various methodogical issues. In the preface, Dishman (1988) stated, 'It has been gratifying to see exercise adherence become a common topic of symposia and original research sessions at the meetings of scientific and professional organisations, as well as an increasingly popular topic for graduate student research. The interest expressed in this area by scholars, professionals, and graduate students has grown exponentially. . . . Exercise adherence is now an established area of study with clearly defined questions and developing methods. Emerging theoretical models will soon begin to keep pace with the pragmatic problems of promoting physical activity in the population, delivering exercise programs in supervised settings, and studying the efficacy and effectiveness of exercise adherence among the many segments of the population that might benefit' (p. xii). Six years later Dishman (1994) published another high-quality text confirming that interest in exercise adherence had remained high and had continued to grow in Europe and Australia, as well as the United States.

However, a further development in these intervening years, has been the emergence of academic, and professional, interest in other sport/exercise adherence behaviours such as injury rehabilitation (Brewer, 1998), primary health care exercise referral schemes (Taylor, 1996), psychological skills training (Bull, 1991), cohesion in sports teams (Brawley et al., 1988) and fitness training in elite performers (Palmer et al., 1999). Whilst research attention has spread far beyond the original focus on exercise adherence, the theoretical models arising from the work of Dishman and others have been instrumental in steering these new research initiatives.

This broadening focus of adherence research is not surprising. We have known for many years now that adherence to treatment programmes in the health care setting is often very poor indeed. Meichenbaum and Turk (1987) summarised evidence for non-adherence to a wide variety treatments and identified over 50 different causal related factors. They also described over 20 different illustrative patient beliefs that can undermine adherence. More than 20 different health care provider behaviours were identified as having the potential to interfere with effective patient communication and hence contribute to non-adherence. Towards the end of their book, Meichenbaum and Turk (1987) even present a chapter suggesting that many health care providers (HCPs) will not adhere to the recommendations they have read and that certain literature has 'indicated that HCPs often do not follow clinical procedures that they know should be implemented' (p. 254). They go on to suggest that attempts to modify the behaviour of HCPs have not generally proved successful. 'The same factors that contribute to patient non-adherence are likely to influence HCP non-adherence' (Meichenbaum & Turk, 1987, p. 257). In concluding their excellent text, Meichenbaum and Turk (1987) suggest that although it is necessary for good intentions and attitudinal change to be present, they are not enough to produce desired behavioural change. This assertion is equally applicable in all sorts of other sport and exercise domains. Despite high levels of commitment by competitive athletes, we know that adherence to training advice and sports science recommendations is often poor. Recognition of the range of potentially influential variables is essential in understanding the adherence process in any context. These variables generally fall into categories relating to the client (athlete/exercise participant), the setting, the practitioner (e.g., physiotherapist, sport scientist, exercise leader) and the client–practitioner relationship.

I felt that the time was now right to pull these new lines of research together into a consolidated text book examining theoretical developments, empirical findings, and research/practice recommendations in each of the emerging areas. This book is not, therefore, another exercise adherence text. It is a thematic collection of review articles which address much broader adherence issues from different perspectives. It is intended to be an addition to the existing literature in the exercise adherence domain rather than an alternative. Each chapter examines theoretical, definitional and practical issues and attempts to identify recommendations for researcher and practitioner.

In Chapter 1, Albert Carron and colleagues examine social influence and exercise involvement. They review research evidence relating to the influence of other exercisers, the class leader and the family. They explain how the impact of social influence is manifested via cognitions about exercise, attittudes towards exercise, and exercise behaviour. In Chapter 2, Gabe Reed reviews the development of the Transtheoretical Model of Behaviour Change and presents lessons learned from using the model to measure regular exercise. Gabe has been an integral part of the Rhode Island research team developing this model and her chapter opens the way for investigators to utilise the Transtheoretical Model in other adherence research domains. Adrian Taylor then presents a review of primary health care exercise promotion schemes in Chapter 3. The chapter examines barriers to exercise promotion activity, exercise counselling, the effects of interventions on patient activity levels and factors influencing adherence. The chapter should prove useful to the burgeoning group of scholars with an interest in referral exercise schemes in primary health care. In Chapter 4, Nanette Mutrie reviews exercise adherence in clinical populations. The chapter examines the general theoretical issues before addressing specific issues for various categories of clinical population—cardiovascular and pulmonary diseases, metabolic diseases, immunological and hematological disorders, orthopaedic diseases and disabilities, and mental health issues. One of the conclusions of this chapter is that researchers and academics should try to form links with medical teams dealing with specific conditions. This suggestion applies equally in many other sport and physical activity contexts. Stuart Biddle examines adherence to sport and physical activity in children and youth in Chapter 5. After providing evidence on adherence using descriptive approaches, Stuart examines various theoretical approaches to understanding children's adherence. Attitude–behaviour relationships, goal orientation, motivational climate, intrinsic motivation, self-determination and emotion as a determinant are all examined before a number of future directions are suggested. These include investigation into physical activity as personal transport—an issue of notable interest to politicians as well as sport and exercise science researchers! In Chapter 6, Britt Brewer reviews the current state of knowledge in adherence to sport injury rehabilitation regimens. Britt begins by addressing the challenges involved in defining and measuring adherence. Similar challenges still occur in most adherence domains despite being highlighted for many years (Dishman, 1988). In reviewing theory and research on sport injury rehabilitation adherence, Britt examines personal investment theory, protection motivation theory and cognitive appraisal models. The chapter concludes with some useful recommendations relating to methodology and measurement. Chris Shambrook and I examine the under-researched area of adherence to psychological preparation in sport in Chapter 7. The chapter reviews our conceptual framework for understanding adherence and presents a number of practical suggestions for both researchers and applied sport psychologists. Chapter 8 focuses on environmental determinants of adherence in applied sport psychology. Derek Milne examines the important role of coaches and parents in the adherence process in addition to highlighting the influence of the sport psychologist. Derek also raises the issue of manipulation checks and provides a helpful illustration to show how one can operationalise relevant interventions and measure them reliably. The final three chapters of the book address issues relating to methodology. In Chapter 9, Al Petitpas examines the client–practitioner interaction and its relationship to adherence and treatment outcomes. The chapter reviews the counselling relationship and specifically examines the facilitative conditions and working alliance models which are deemed to have clear implications for sport and exercise psychology interventions. Al calls for the integration of counselling psychology research paradigms into sport and exercise psychology research. He claims that this integration would have the potential to advance knowledge and provide information which would assist practitioners in promoting adherence to successful interventions. The chapter concludes by addressing implications for the training of sport and exercise psychology professionals and the specific importance of self-awareness promotion. In Chapter 10, David Gilbourne reviews the process of adopting action research themes to promote adherence to changing practice. This chapter provides some fascinating insights for those researchers seeking a radical departure from the dominant paradigm of positivist or natural science. The chapter links the theme of adherence to action research and the processes of collaboration and reflection. It demonstrates how action research procedures seem to provide an ideal framework from which researchers can facilitate reflection and encourage adherence to change. Finally, Chapter 11 presents an overview of two exploratory approaches that have been used to study adherence in sport and exercise settings, and suggests a confirmatory procedure which may be applied in future adherence research. Grounded Theory and Multidimensional Scalogram Analysis are reviewed and the chapter argues that both methodologies can be used to produce a holistic (multi-method) approach to the study of adherence.

This book is intended for all those interested in the theory and practicalities of adherence issues in sport and exercise. It is hoped that the contents will stimulate further research initiatives in this fascinating aspect of human behaviour as well as providing guidance for practitioners seeking to improve their understanding of the variables which influence adherence processes.

REFERENCES

Brawley, L.R., Carron, A.V. & Widmeyer, W.N. (1988). Exploring the relationship between cohesion and group resistance to disruption. *Journal of Sport & Exercise Psychology*, **10**, 199–213.

Brewer, B. (1998). Adherence to sport injury rehabilitation programs. *Journal of Applied Sport Psychology*, **10**, 70–82.

Bull, S.J. (1991). Personal and situational influences on adherence to mental skills training. *Journal of Sport & Exercise Psychology*, **13**, 121–132.

Dishman, R.K. (1988). *Exercise adherence: Its impact on public health.* Champaign, IL: Human Kinetics.

Dishman, R.K. (1994). *Advances in exercise adherence.* Champaign, IL: Human Kinetics.

Edelman, R.E. & Chambless, D.L. (1995). Adherence during sessions and homework in cognitive-behavioural groups treatment of social phobia. *Behavior Research and Therapy*, **33**, 573–577.

Frank, E. (1997). Enhancing patient outcomes: Treatment adherence. *Journal of Clinical Psychiatry*, **58** (supplement), 11–14.

Hulbert, D., Apt, C. & Hylbert, M.K. (1995). Sexual characteristics, treatment compliance and the effectiveness of orgasm consistency training in the treatment of women reporting hypoactive sexual desire. *Canadian Journal of Human Sexuality*, **4**, 15–23.

Mammen, O., Shear, K., Greeno, C., & Wheeler, S. (1997). Anger attacks and treatment non-adherence in a perinatal psychiatric clinic. *Psychopharmocology—Bulletin*, **33**(1), 105–108.

Meichenbaum, D. and Turk, D.C. (1987). *Facilitating treatment adherence: A practitioner's guidebook*. New York: Plenum.

Owen, C., Rutherford, V., Jones, M., Tenant, C. & Smallman, A. (1997). Non-compliance in psychiatric aftercare. *Community Mental Health Journal*, **33**, 25–34.

Palmer, C., Burwitz, L. & Smith, N. (1999). Fitness training adherence of elite junior netball players: Comparing the Theory of Planned Behaviour and Social Cognitive Theory. *Journal of Sports Sciences* (Abstract), **17**, 68–69.

Ruscher, S.M., deWit, R., & Mazmanian, D. (1997). Psychiatric patients' attitudes about medication and factors affecting non-compliance. *Psychiatric Services*, **48**, 82–85.

Taylor, A. (1996). *Evaluating GP referral schemes: Findings from a randomised controlled study*. Brighton, UK: Chelsea School Research Centre.

Trzcieniecka-Green, A. & Steptoe, A. (1994). Stress management in cardiac patients: A preliminary study of the predictors of improvement in quality of life. *Journal of Psychosomatic Research*, **38**, 267–280.

Waller, G. (1997). Dropout and failure to engage in individual outpatient cognitive behaviour therapy for bulimic disorders. *International Journal of Eating Disorders*, **22**, 35–41.

Chapter 1

Social Influence and Exercise Involvement

Albert V. Carron, Heather A. Hausenblas,
and Paul A. Estabrooks

An adherent has been defined as one who sticks, holds fast or is attached; a supporter or follower (Collins Concise English Dictionary, 1992). Increasingly, researchers, health professionals, and governments have shown an interest in increasing the numbers of adherents—people who stick to, hold fast, and stay attached to, become supporters or followers—in regular exercise and physical activity. For example, Dishman (1994) noted that:

> Since 1988 several scientific and professional consensus meetings sponsored by governments in Great Britain, Canada, and the United States have focused on the problem of understanding increasing leisure-time physical activity. Interest in exercise and adherence continues to grow in Europe and Australia. (p. vii)

As a second example, Biddle (1995) noted that an interest in exercise has been growing even in countries where traditionally the national emphasis has been on elite sport. As he stated:

Adherence Issues in Sport and Exercise. Edited by Stephen J. Bull.
© 1999 John Wiley & Sons Ltd.

> The change in political conditions in East European countries has led to greater interest in 'sport for all' and exercises promotion. This is consistent with the World Health Organization's Health for All targets for the year 2000 for European countries. (Biddle, 1995, p. 1)

The interest shown by governments and their agencies is not surprising given the well-documented benefits of regular exercise or physical activity. For example, among the physical and physiological benefits observed are decreased blood pressure, lowered resting heart rate, reduced body weight, decreased per cent body fat, increased maximal oxygen uptake, improved flexibility, and decreased levels of stress-related indices such as cholesterol and triglyceride (Hill, Glassford, Burgess, & Rudnicki, 1988).

The benefits of sustained activity are not limited to physical and/or physiological function, however. Recent meta-analyses have shown that numerous psychological changes also follow regular involvement in exercise or physical activity[1]. As Table 1.1 shows, exercise has a medium-sized effect on depression, reactivity to stress, anxiety (whether it is assessed through physiological or psychological indices), and cognitive functioning.

Table 1.1   The impact of exercise on psychological states and traits: An overview of various meta-analyses

Psychological factor	Effect size	Reference
State Anxiety	0.24	Petruzzello, Landers, Hatfield, Kubitz, & Salazar (1991)
Trait Anxiety	0.34	Petruzzello, Landers, Hatfield, Kubitz, & Salazar (1991)
Psychophysiological Indices of Anxiety	0.56	Petruzzello, Landers, Hatfield, Kubitz, & Salazar (1991)
Various indices of Anxiety	0.47	McDonald & Hodgdon (1991)
Reactivity to Stress	0.48	Crews & Landers (1987)
Depression	0.53	North, McCullagh, & Tran (1990)
Depression	0.55	McDonald & Hodgdon (1991)
Cognitive Functioning	0.25	Etnier, Salazar, Landers, Petruzzello, Han, Nowell (1997)

---

1. Meta-analysis is a statistical technique that provides a way of combining the results from a large number of studies to determine the overall size of an effect. Cohen (1969, 1992) has suggested that 0.20, 0.50, and 0.80 represent small, medium, and large effect sizes (ES) respectively.

In spite of these physiological, physical, and psychological benefits, the number of adherents in regular exercise programmes remains problematic. For example, epidemiological studies have shown that as few as 30% of all adult North Americans exercise at a moderate intensity on a regular basis—a participation rate that decreases with age (Lee, 1993; Stephens & Caspersen, 1993). Moreover, when individuals begin an exercise programme, 20–50% withdraw within the first 6 months (Dishman, 1988; Robison & Rogers, 1994).

Not surprisingly, health professionals have been interested in not only determining how to increase the numbers of individuals who exercise but also how to improve their adherence. There is no single solution, of course, as evidenced by the large number of articles and position papers written on this issue (cf. Godin, 1993; Smith & Biddle, 1995; Wankel & Mummery, 1993). In the present chapter, we propose an approach that is based on our understanding of the principles of social influence. Social influence exerted by groups and/or people important to the exerciser can play an important role in, first, stimulating interest in exercise and physical activity, and, second, improving adherence after individuals become more active.

Therefore, one main objective in this chapter is to define social influence and outline how its various forms might be expected to play a role in exercise adherence. A second is to review research in which social influence, operating in the exercise environment, has led to increased involvement. A third objective of the chapter is to present possible intervention strategies—drawing on our understanding of social influence—that might be expected to improve individual involvement in exercise. Finally, the last objective of the chapter is to provide suggestions for future research.

SOCIAL INFLUENCE DEFINED

Social influence may be defined as an individual's perceptions of comfort/ discomfort, assistance, information, approval/disapproval, and/or pressure from formal or informal contacts with individuals, groups, or collective others (cf. Wallston, Alagna, DeVellis, & DeVellis, 1983). Hence, social influence has a tremendous impact on individual and group cognitions, attitudes, and/or behaviours. As Baron and Byrne (1991) have pointed out, 'perceptions, attitudes, and actions are strongly affected by other persons, either individually or collectively. In short, our behaviour and thoughts are very different from what they would be if we lived in total isolation' (p. 311).

We don't live in total isolation, of course. We are strongly influenced by the social context in which we live. Consequently, as Courneya and

McAuley (1995) observed, a number of 'social cognitive theories applied in the exercise domain hypothesize various social constructs to be important determinants of behavior' (p. 325). As an extension of this point, Courneya and McAuley went on to say that 'social constructs are particularly import- ant in the exercise domain because intervention strategies are often based on changing the social milieu within a group setting' (p. 325). The three primary social constructs assumed to play a major role in exercise involve- ment are subjective norm, social support and group cohesion (Courneya & McAuley, 1995). Each of these is defined and measured in quite distinct ways.

Subjective norm, a cornerstone in the theories of reason action and planned behavior (Ajzen, 1991; Ajzen & Fishbein, 1980), reflects the social pressure thought to be exerted by important others. Thus, Ajzen (1991) has defined it as 'the perceived social pressure to perform or not to perform the behavior' (p. 188).

Social support, on the other hand, represents the behavioral and func- tional benefits derived from interpersonal relationships. A definition which serves to capture the nature of social support is 'the comfort, assistance, and/or information one receives through formal or informal contacts with individuals or groups' (Wallston, Alagna, DeVellis, & DeVellis, 1983, p. 369).

Finally, group cohesion is considered to be 'a dynamic process that is reflected in the tendency for a group to stick together and remain united in the pursuit of its instrumental objectives and/or for the satisfaction of member affective needs' (Carron, Brawley, & Widmeyer, 1998, p. 213). In its simplest form, cohesion can be assumed to represent the degree of bonding that is present around the task and social aspects of the group.

There is little doubt that social influence has an impact on exercise involvement. This impact is manifested via cognitions about exercise (e.g., confidence, intention), attitudes toward exercise, and exercise behavior.

SOCIAL INFLUENCE AND EXERCISE INVOLVEMENT

The Influence of Other Exercisers

Research evidence

The need for interpersonal attachment is a fundamental human motive (Baumeister & Leary, 1995)—a fact that has important implications for promoting adherence in exercise and physical activity. Individuals naturally form into groups. In general, research has shown that compared to exercising alone, exercising in a group results in increased adherence and more positive attitudes (e.g., Heinzelman & Bagley, 1970; Massie & Shephard, 1971). In their meta-analysis, Carron, Hausenblas, and Mack (1996) found a small to moderate relationship for increased exercise adherence for individuals exercising in a group versus alone ($ES = 0.32$). An example of one study that illustrates the impact of groups was undertaken by Massie and Shephard (1971). They found better adherence in sedentary middle-aged business men who had exercised in a group setting (a drop out rate of 18.2%) compared to those who has exercise alone (a drop out rate of 52.6%). As another example, Bravo, Gauthier, Roy, Payette, Dubois, Harvey, and Gaulin (1996) reported that osteopenic women in a group exercise program showed greater improvement in self-rated health in comparison to those enrolled in a home program. Further, women in the home program used significantly more health services during the 12-month follow-up than women in the group program. Bravo et al. suggested that:

> the greater flexibility offered by a home-based program does not seem to be sufficiently attractive to compensate for the disadvantages associated with such a program. One of the disadvantages concerns the high degree of motivation that a home-based program requires from a participant. Another disadvantage is that a home-based program does not promote bonds between the participants, who have little opportunity to get together. (p. 159)

Attitude and mood states are also enhanced in group-based exercise programs. For example, Gauvin and Rejeski (1993) observed that participants in group exercise programs experienced more positive changes in their feeling states than those involved in isolated, controlled laboratory programs. Also, when Heinzelman and Bagley (1970) assessed attitudes toward an exercise program, they found that sedentary men rated the social benefits among the least important in influencing their decision to participate. However, at the end of the program, more than one-fourth of the respondents listed the social aspects among the best-liked features of the program and a factor which had an influence on their adherence. Thus, the social reinforcement and companionship characteristic of group programs can facilitate increased exercise adherence (Franklin, 1988; Wankel, 1985; Wankel, Yardley, & Graham, 1985) through increased enjoyment, a sense of social support, personal commitment to continue, and the opportunity to compare progress and fitness level with group members (Heinzelmann & Bagley, 1970).

If being in a group is beneficial, being in a highly cohesive group is doubly so. This conclusion emanates from a series of investigations carried out by Carron and his colleagues, which focused on the role played by cohesion in exercise classes. In the first study, which was retrospective in nature, former exercisers were asked to recall the level of cohesiveness that had been present in their class (Carron, Widmeyer, & Brawley, 1988, Study 1). In contrast to individuals actively involved in exercise programs, the former exercisers rated their class as substantially lower in both task and social cohesion.

Two later studies carried out by Spink and Carron (1994) used a prospective design. In Study 1, perceptions of class cohesiveness were assessed in Week 3 of a 13-week exercise program that was held in a university setting. It was found that adherence in the exercise program could be reliably predicted; individuals who dropped out during the 13-week session possessed lower perceptions of their class's task cohesion as early as Week 3. Spink and Carron (1994, Study 2) then carried out a second, identical study with exercisers from private fitness clubs. Almost identical results were obtained except that dropouts from the program had held lower perceptions of the class's social cohesion in Week 3.

There are a number of other aspects of adherence aside from drop out behaviour; all of these are associated with cohesion. For example, Spink and Carron (1992) found that exercise class participants who perceive that their class was lower in cohesion, were also absent and late more frequently. As another example, Brawley, Carron, and Widmeyer (1988, Study 2) showed that cohesion is related to a belief by class members that their exercise class can better withstand the negative impact of potentially disruptive events—for example a poor instructor or overcrowding.

When Carron, Hausenblas, & Mack (1996) summarized the research on cohesion and adherence using meta-analysis, they found that the size of the effect was 0.62 for the adherence and task cohesion relationship and 0.25 for the adherence and social cohesion relationship. Developing a sense of community in an exercise class (i.e., greater class cohesion) can pay important dividends for exercise behaviour.

Implications for the practitioner

Fitness classes typically possess only a few of the group processes, structural elements, and outcomes that are considered to be essential before a collection of individuals is viewed as a group. For example, exercise classes do not possess a group goal. Unlike true groups, exercise classes do not have a stable social structure characterized by role expectations, task and social interactions, and status differences. Further, as Zander (1982) pointed out, 'a body of people is not a group if members are primarily interested in individual accomplishments, are not concerned with the activities of other members . . . and are often absent (pp. 1–2). Zander's description certainly applies to exercise classes. Consequently, it would be difficult from a theoretical perspective to consider an exercise class to be a true group. Nonetheless, as Carron and Spink (1993) pointed out, however:

> fitness class participants—because of their need for social bonding and social identity—probably come to view their classes in terms of 'we', develop an evaluation bias about those classes . . . and possesses some degree of cohesiveness. In short, social categorization likely occurs. And, in turn, it is the strength of these perceptions of social collective, a 'we' (i.e., group cohesiveness) that contributes to the enhanced adherence behaviour reported in previous research.' (pp. 9–10)

Fitness instructors should capitalize on what is known about the beneficial effects of group involvement on adherence to develop a stronger sense of community within their classes—to develop a more cohesive class. A programme emphasizing group dynamics principles will increase the perceptions of cohesion, produce exercise classes in which the participants are more satisfied, and increase adherence behaviour (Carron & Spink, 1993; Spink & Carron, 1993).

Table 1.2 contains selected group dynamics principles, which were used in an intervention program carried out by Carron and Spink (1993). A greater perception that the class is distinctive leads to greater perceptions of cohesiveness. Increasing feelings of distinctiveness stimulate the development of feelings of 'we' and 'us' and promote better class cohesion. When Carron and Spink (1993) had fitness instructors engage in a brainstorming exercise to develop specific strategies to make their classes feel more distinctive, a number of options were suggested (see Table 1.2). These included having a class name (e.g., 'The Fit Bunch'), making up a class T-shirt, providing distinctive headbands and/or shoelaces, and having posters and slogans for the class.

Collections of individuals also develop stronger feelings of 'we' when their collective develops a stable structure—when members consistently occupy the same position. This is another group dynamics principle that could be used to develop a more cohesive class. As Table 1.2 shows, stability in class structure might be achieved by having members consistently exercise in specific areas of the gym or pool depending on their level of fitness, or by having them pick a personal spot and encouraging them to remain in it for the year.

The perception of being in a cohesive group is increased when members hold common expectations (i.e., when group norms are established). As Table 1.2 shows, common perceptions might be achieved by having class members establish a group goal either to lose weight together, reduce absenteeism, or promote a smart work ethic as a class characteristic.

A fourth group dynamics principle is that feelings of cohesiveness are increased when individuals make sacrifices for the group; when individuals

Table 1.2 Examples of principles to promote group cohesion and specific strategies for the implementation of those principles in fitness classes (Adapted from Carron & Spink, 1993)

Principle	Specific strategies for fitness classes
Distinctiveness: A perception that the group is distinctive increases feelings of cohesion	Have a class T-shirt Provide class members with neon headbands and/or shoelaces Make up posters/slogans for the class
Positions: When individuals consistently occupy the same position, the group develops a stable structure and feelings of cohesion increase	Have members pick a spot to exercise and encourage them to remain in it throughout the year Use specific locations for low, medium, and high impact exercisers
Group norms: When members hold common expectations, feelings of cohesion increase	Establish a goal to lose weight together Establish a goal to reduce absenteeism Promote a smart work ethic as a class characteristic
Sacrifices: When members of cohesion are increased	Ask different individuals establish the class goal for the day Ask regular exercisers assist new people
Interaction and communication: When interaction and communication among members increases, feelings of cohesion are increased	Have members introduce themselves to each other Use more partner activities

make contributions to the group, their sense of ownership of that group is enhanced. The fitness instructors in the Carron and Spink study suggested a variety of strategies designed to have class members make sacrifices including asking different class members to establish a goal for the day and asking regular exercisers to assist new people.

The fifth group dynamics principle illustrated in Table 1.2 that can be applied to exercise classes is that feelings of cohesion are increased when interaction and communication among members increases. A variety of approaches can be used to capitalize on this principle, including having members introduce themselves to each other and using more partner activities.

Class Leader

Research evidence

Researchers also have been interested in the role that exercise leaders play in participants' attitudes toward exercise as well as their adherence in exercise programs (e.g., Heinzelman & Bagley, 1970; King, Barr Taylor, Haskell, & DeBusk, 1990; Martin, Dubbert, Katell, Thompson, Raczynski, Lake, Smith, Webster, Sikora & Cohen, 1984; McAuley & Jacobson, 1991; Wankel, 1985; Wankel, Yardley, & Graham, 1985). The results of that literature is unequivocal—and well summarized by Oldridge (1977) who concluded that the exercise leader is 'the pivot on which the success or failure of a program will depend' (p. 86). When Franklin (1984, 1988) compiled a list of over thirty variables that influence exercise dropout and adherence behaviour, he identified the exercise leader as 'the single most important variable affecting exercise compliance' (p. 238). In their meta-analysis, Carron, Hausenblas and Mack (1996) reported a small to moderate effect ($ES = 0.31$) for the influence that exercise leaders have on adherence behaviour.

Although the effect of the instructor on adherence is small to moderate, it is important for at least two reasons. First, when research is typically carried out with intact classes, some special treatment focusing on the instructor or mode of instruction is given to half the groups; the other groups are simply taught in the normal manner. In short, that research does not generally compare good versus poor instruction (or teaching approaches) but rather good versus better instruction (or teaching approaches). Showing any effect under those conditions shows the potential of the instructor to have a positive impact. Also, it is important to keep in mind that exercise adherence rates for the general public are low. Moreover, adherence among those who initiate programs is problematic. Therefore, any factor that can make a positive difference is important; the exercise class instructor can make a difference.

There is also evidence that exercise leaders can influence both the self-efficacy and mood of their class (McAuley & Jacobson, 1991; Turner, Rejeski, & Brawley, 1997). At the completion of an exercise program, McAuley and Jacobson (1991) had formerly sedentary females respond to a self-efficacy question pertaining to their continued exercise over the next eight weeks and a question indicating the degree to which they felt the instructor had influenced their adherence to the program. The results showed that an instructor could influence participants' confidence in their personal capabilities for exercise.

Turner, Rejeski, and Brawley (1997) examined the influence of leadership behaviour on self efficacy and the exercise-induced feeling states of revitalization, positive engagement, tranquillity, and physical exhaustion. College women were assigned to classes structured to be either socially enriched or socially bland (i.e., not irritating, stimulating, or invigorating) in terms of interactions from the exercise leader. The participants in the socially enriched classes reported more enhanced mood states from involvement in the exercise than those in the bland classes. Further, the socially enriched leadership style had a greater impact on self-efficacy beliefs.

Implications for the practitioner

Oldridge (1977) has suggested that 'the stimulus for continuing or adhering to the program grows from the participants' response to the environment set up by the exercise leader' (p. 86). One potential method for stimulating increased adherence in instructor-led fitness programs is to use instructors that are of similar age to the participants—especially in classes composed of older adults. Lee (1993) found that 56% of middle-aged women (an average age of 56.5 years) preferred an instructor close to their own age. Lee proposed that providing specialized classes with older instructors may make the environment less threatening and, therefore, may make it easier for older women to begin an exercise program.

Second, according to social cognitive theory (Bandura, 1986), self-efficacy cognitions influence the tasks that a person chooses, the amount of effort he or she expends, and the persistence he or she shows in accomplishing that task. It is no surprise that efficacy cognitions play a major role in exercise initiation and adherence (McAuley & Courneya, 1993; McAuley, Wraith, & Duncan, 1991). According to Turner et al. (1997), instructors should develop a socially enriched leadership style (i.e., a high frequency of technical instruction, specific technical support, and positive skill-related feedback) in order to enhance participants' self efficacy beliefs, and adherence. A socially enriched leadership style will maximise the learning of skilled behaviour. Table 1.3 provides some examples of how instructors can use a socially enriched leadership style (Turner et al., 1997).

Third, both verbal and nonverbal communications from the instructor play an important role in participant adherence. For example, Chaikin, Gillen, Derlega, Heinen and Wilson (1978) found that teacher attractiveness and the use of nonverbal cues such as more direct eye contact, smiling, and head nods influenced student motivation.

Family and Important Others

Research evidence

In the previous two sections, we discussed the important role that other exercisers and the class leaders can play in improving exercise adherence. Social influences outside the exercise class itself—from family and

Table 1.3 Strategies for using a socially enriched leadership style (adapted from Turner, Rejeski, & Brawley, 1997)

Leader behaviour	Example
Use participants names	Hi Carrie.
Provide specific reinforcement for positive behaviour	Thanks for attending the class Bill
Give encouragement before and after an exercise and after a mistake	You can do this; you'll do fine
Focus on positive comments during instruction	Make sure you bend your knees
Be specific in feedback	You did 20 sit-ups
Give ability feedback	This is one of your better exercises
Ignoring mistakes	
Reward effort and ability immediately after the activity	Excellent effort in the cardio workout
Engage in general communication and conversation with participants before and after class	Wasn't it a beautiful day?

important others, for example—also can play a role improving exercise involvement[2].

Historically, much of the earliest research investigating the influence of family and important others was carried out in cardiac rehabilitation and/or weight control centres. The fundamental concern of health professionals was 'how can we improve compliance to the exercise programmes we have prescribed?' When Carron et al. summarized that research using meta-analysis, they found that compliance to exercise programs is strongly influenced by family and friends (ES = 0.69).

Recent research has produced findings consistent with the above. For example, Dew, Roth, Thompson, and Kormos (1996) examined compliance to a number of modalities of rehabilitation including exercise following heart transplant. One hundred and one heart recipients were tracked for a year following the transplant. The results showed that pre-operative psychosocial status—bolstered by family support—was a strong predictor of compliance. Dew, Roth, Thompson, & Kormos (1996) concluded that strategies to improve compliance to exercise and other

2. Important others are any individuals who have a meaningful relationship with the exercise participant, but are not family members; e.g., close friends, physicians, and co-workers.

treatment modalities should focus on educational and supportive interventions that improve the quality of family relations.

Researchers have also suspected that family and important others might influence the adherence of participants who independently choose to become involved in exercise programs (i.e., participants who elect to become involved in exercise and are not simply complying with the prescription of a health care professional). Summarizing 53 studies which included over 13 000 participants, Carron et al. found that family influence and important others produced a small to moderated effect ($ES = 0.36$ and 0.44 respectively) on exercise adherence.

As was pointed out previously, subjective norm (Ajzen & Fishbein, 1980) is a social construct that has been frequently examined in research examining the correlates of exercise adherence. Hausenblas, Carron and Mack (1997) reported a small effect for the relationship between subjective norm and exercise behavior ($ES = 0.18$) and a moderate effect for the relationship between subjective norm and intention to exercise ($ES = 0.56$).

Recently, Shropshire and Carroll (1997) assessed the involvement by 924 Grade 6 school children in physical activity over the previous week and their perceptions of their parent's exercise involvement was completed. The physical activity of the child was strongly associated with the exercise habits of the father. As another example, Hopper et al. (1996) completed two studies which examined the effectiveness of school-based exercise and nutrition programs associated with parental participation. They also found that parental involvement improved the effectiveness of the programs.

The exerciser's family doesn't just have an impact on adherence behaviour. As the Carron et al. meta-analysis shows, it also influences the satisfaction the participant obtains from exercise ($ES = 0.59$), the strength of the participant's intentions to exercise ($ES = 0.49$), and even the participant's level of efficacy for exercise (ES = 0.40).

The nature of these various relationships is illustrated in a study by Martin and Mushett (1996) concerning the relationships between social support mechanisms (family members and friends), self-efficacy, and affect of swimmers with disabilities. They found that mothers were important providers of primary support in non-sport related knowledge whereas fathers provided secondary support in both sport expertise and nonsport expertise. The Martin and Mushett results support the suggestion that family support is related to improved self-efficacy of the participants. Further, increased participant satisfaction was related to increased support from family and friends. Martin and Mushett (1996) concluded that by utilizing the support mechanisms available from family, confidence in swimming ability and enjoyment of swimming could be increased for youths with disabilities.

Implications for the practitioner

The studies cited above support the view that if an intervention programme has the support of family and friends, it will produce exercisers who plan to attend, are confident in their ability, and will enjoy the participation once they are involved. To develop such a programme, a three-step intervention process could be effective. In Step one, the health care professional should promote family or spousal exercise programmes that are designed to include options for friendly interaction. At Step two, the health care professional should outline the importance of exercise including its benefits to the participant and the family. It is important for supportive others to understand the benefits of exercise (Hopper et al., 1996); if they don't, then it is unlikely that the necessary support will be provided.

In Step three, a common goal or goals should be established for both the participant and the supportive other. A good way to develop this common goal could be to prepare the exercise regimen in such a way that both supportive others and the participant can complete the programme together.

FUTURE DIRECTIONS

After conducting their meta-analysis which focused on the impact of various types of social influence on exercise involvement, Carron, Hausenblas, & Mack (1996) observed that their 'search for empirical data . . . showed that there are still numerous unexplored issues and unexplained findings' (p.9). Although the pattern is changing, a considerable number of issues remain unexamined. For example, given Franklin's (1988) assertion that the exercise leader is 'the single most important variable affecting exercise compliance' (p. 238), it is surprising that so few studies have examined the impact of the leader. The Turner et al. research discussed above was an excellent beginning. But, we need to know more about factors such as the age of the instructor (i.e., relative to the average age of class members). Similarly, does the size and weight of the instructor have an impact on his/her perceived effectiveness? For example, anecdotal testimony and even common sense might contribute to a suggestion that elderly exercise participants would prefer an instructor of similar age and physical condition. However, there is no evidence bearing on this question.

Summary

We are by our very nature social. One consequence of this fact is that our lives are characterized by the reciprocal exchange of influence. That is, our attitudes, cognitions, and behaviours are influenced by other people; in turn we exert an influence on those around us. Exercise professionals can capitalize on the power of social influence to improve exercise adherence. In the present chapter, three dominant sources of social influence were discussed—the group, the exercise leader, and family and important others.

REFERENCES

Ajzen, I. (1991). The theory of planned behavior. *Organizational Behavior and Human Decision Processes*, **50**, 179–211.

Ajzen, I., & Fishbein, M. (1980). *Understanding attitudes and predicting social behavior*. Englewood Cliffs, NJ: Prentice-Hall.

Bandura, A. (1986). *Social foundations of thought and action*. Englewood Cliffs, NJ: Prentice Hall.

Baron, R.A., & Byrne, D. (1991). *Social psychology: Understanding human interaction* (6th edn, Instructor's edn). Boston, MA: Allyn & Bacon.

Baumeister, R.F., & Leary, M.R. (1995). The need to belong: Desire for interpersonal attachment as a fundamental human motivation. *Psychological Bulletin*, **117**, 497–529.

Biddle, S.J.H. (1995). Exercise motivation across the life span. In S.J.H. Biddle (ed.), *European perspectives on exercise and sport psychology* (pp. 3–25). Champaign, IL: Human Kinetics.

Bravo, G., Gauthier, P., Roy, P.-M., Payette, H., Dubois, M., Harvey, M., & Gaulin, P. (1996). Comparison of a group- versus a home-based exercise program in osteopenic women. *Journal of Aging and Physical Activity*, **4**, 151–164.

Brawley, L. R., Carron, A. V., & Widmeyer, W. N. (1988). Exploring the relationship between cohesion and group resistance to disruption. *Journal of Sport and Exercise Psychology*, **10**, 199–213.

Carron, A.V., Brawley, L.R., & Widmeyer, W.N. (1998). The measurement of cohesiveness in sport groups. In J.L. Duda (ed.), *Advances in sport and exercise psychology measurement* (pp. 213–226). Morgantown, WV: Fitness Information Technology.

Carron, A.V., Hausenblas, H.A., & Mack, D.E. (1996). Social influence and exercise: A meta-analysis. *Journal of Sport and Exercise Psychology*, **18**, 1–16.

Carron, A.V., & Spink, K.S. (1993). Team building in an exercise setting. *The Sport Psychologist*, **7**, 8–18.

Carron, A.V., Widmeyer, W.N., & Brawley, L.R. (1988). Group cohesion and individual adherence to physical activity. *Journal of Sport and Exercise Psychology*, **10**, 119–126.

Chaikin, A. L., Gillen, B., Derlega, V. J., Heinen, J., & Wilson, M. (1978). Students' reaction to teacher's physical attractiveness and non-verbal behavior. *Psychology in the Schools*, **15**, 588–595.

Cohen, J. (1969). *Statistical power analysis for the behavioral sciences*. New York: Academic Press.

Cohen, J. (1992). A power primer. *Psychological Bulletin*, **112**, 155–159.

Collins Concise English Dictionary (3rd ed). (1992). Glasgow: Harper-Collins.

Courneya, K.S., & McAuley, E. (1995). Reliability and discriminant validity of subjective norm, social support, and cohesion in an exercise setting. *Journal of Sport and Exercise Psychology*, **17**, 325, 337.

Crews, D.J., & Landers, D.M. (1987). A meta analytic review of aerobic fitness and reactivity to psychosocial stressors. *Medicine and Science in Sports and Exercise*, **19**, (Suppl. 5), S114–S120).

Dew M.A., Roth, L.H., Thompson, M.E., & Kormos, R.L. (1996). Medical compliance and its predictors in the first year after heart transplantation. *Journal of Heart and Lung Transplantation*, **15**, 631–645.

Dishman, R.K. (1988). Exercise adherence research: Future directions. *American Journal of Health Promotion*, **3**, 52–56.

Dishman, R.K. (1994). Epilogue and future direction. In R.K. Dishman (ed.), *Exercise adherence: Its impact on public health* (pp. 417–426). Champaign, IL: Human Kinetics.

Etnier, J.L., Salazar, W., Landers, D.M., Petruzzello, S.J., Han, M., & Nowell, P. (1997). The influence of physical fitness and exercise upon cognitive functioning: A meta-analysis. *Journal of Sport and Exercise Psychology*, **19**, 249–277.

Franklin, B. (1984). Exercise program compliance: Improvement strategies. In J. Storlie & H. Jordan (eds.), *Behavioral management of obesity* (pp. 105–135). New York: Spectrum.

Franklin, B. (1988). Program factors that influence exercise adherence: Practical adherence skills for the clinical staff. In R.K. Dishman (ed.), *Exercise adherence: Its impact on public health* (pp. 417–426). Champaign, IL: Human Kinetics.

Gauvin, L. & Rejeski, W.J. (1993). The exercise induced feeling inventory: Development and initial validation. *Journal of Sport and Exercise Psychology*, **15**, 403–423.

Godin, G. (1993). The theories of reasoned action and planned behavior: Overview of findings, emerging research problems, and usefulness for exercise promotion. *Journal of Applied Sport Psychology*, **5**, 141–157.

Hausenblas, H.A., Carron, A.V., & Mack, D. (1997). Application of the theories of reasoned action and planned behavior to exercise behavior: A meta-analysis. *Journal of Sport and Exercise Psychology*, **19**, 36–51.

Heinzelmann, F., & Bagley, R.W. (1970). Response to physical activity programs and their effects on health behavior. *Public Health Reports*, **85**, 905–911.

Hill, R., Glassford, G., Burgess, A., & Rudnicki, J. (1988). Employee fitness and lifestyle programs, Part One: Introduction, rationale, and benefits. *Journal of the Canadian Association for Health Physical Education, and Recreation,* **54**, 10–14.

Hopper, C.A., Munoz, K.D., Gruber, M.B., MacConnie, S., et al. (1996). A school-based cardiovascular exercise and nutrition program with parent participation: an evaluation study. *Children's Health Care,* **25**, 221–235.

King, A.C., Barr Taylor, C., Haskell, W.L., & DeBusk, R.F. (1990). Identifying strategies for increasing employee physical activity levels: Findings from the Stanford/Lockheed exercise survey. *Health Education Quarterly,* **17**, 269–285.

Lee, C. (1993). Attitudes, knowledge, and stages of change: A survey of exercise patterns in older Australian women. *Health Psychology,* **6**, 476–480.

McAuley, E., & Courneya, K. S. (1993). Adherence to exercise and physical activity as health-promoting behaviors: Attitudinal and self-efficacy influences. *Applied and Preventive Psychology,* **2**, 65–77.

McAuley, E., & Jacobson, L. (1991). Self-efficacy and exercise participation in sedentary adult females. *American Journal of Health Promotion,* **5**, 185–207.

McAuley, E., Wraith, S., & Duncan, T. E. (1991). Self-efficacy, perceptions of success, and intrinsic motivation for exercise. *Journal of Applied Psychology,* **21**, 139–155.

McDonald, D.G., & Hodgdon, J.A. (1991). *Psychological effects of aerobic fitness training: Research and theory.* New York: Springer-Verlag.

Martin, J.J. & Mushett, C.A. (1996). Social support mechanisms among athletes with disabilities. *Adapted Physical Activity Quarterly,* **13**, 74–83.

Martin, J.T., Dubbert, P.M., Katell, A.D., Thompson, J.R., Raczynski, J.R., Lake, M., Smith, P.O., Webster, J.S., Sikora, T. & Cohen, R.T. (1984). The behavioral control of exercise in sedentary adults: Studies 1 through 6. *Journal of Consulting and Clinical Psychology,* **52**, 795–811.

Massie, J.F., & Shephard, R.J. (1971).Physiological and psychological effects of training: A comparison of individual and gymnasium programs, with a characterization of the exercise 'dropout'. *Medicine and Science in Sport,* **3**, 110–117.

North, T.C., McCullagh, P., & Tran, Z.V. (1990). Effects of exercise on depression. *Exercise and Sport Science Reviews,* **18**, 379–415.

Oldridge, N. (1977). What to look for in an exercise leader. *The Physician and Sportsmedicine,* **5**, 85–88.

Petruzzello, S.J., Landers, D.M., Hatfield, B.D., Kubitz, K.A., & Salazar, W. (1991). A meta-analysis on the anxiety-reducing effects of acute and chronic exercise: Outcomes and mechanisms. *Sports Medicine,* **11**, 143–182.

Robison, J.I., & Rogers, M.A. (1994). Adherence to exercise programs: Recommendations. *Sports Medicine*, **17**, 39–52.

Shropshire, J. & Carroll, B. (1997). Family variables and children's physical activity: Influence of parental exercise and socio-economic status. *Sport, Education and Society*, **2**, 95–116.

Smith, R.A., & Biddle, S.J.H. (1995). Psychological factors in the promotion of physical activity. In S.J.H. Biddle (ed.), *European perspectives on exercise and sport psychology* (pp. 85–108). Champaign, IL: Human Kinetics.

Spink, K.S., & Carron, A.V. (1992). Group cohesion and adherence in exercise classes. *Journal of Sport and Exercise Psychology*, **14**, 78–86.

Spink, K.S., & Carron, A.V. (1993). The effects of team building on the adherence patterns of female exercise participants. *Journal of Sport and Exercise Psychology*, **15**, 39–49.

Spink, K.S., & Carron, A.V. (1994). Group cohesion effects in exercise groups. *Small Group Research*, **25**, 26–42.

Stephens, T. & Caspersen, L.J. (1993). The demography of physical activity. In Bouchard, C., Shephard, R.J., & Stephens, T. (eds), *Physical activity, fitness, and health: Consensus statement* (pp. 204–213). Champagne, IL: Human Kinetics Publishing.

Turner, E.E., Rejeski, W.J., & Brawley, L.R. (1997). Psychological benefits of physical activity are influenced by the social environment. *Journal of Sport and Exercise Psychology*, 19, 119–130.

Wallston, B., Alagna, S., DeVellis, B., & DeVellis, R.F. (1983). Social support and physical health. *Health Psychology*, **2**, 367–391.

Wankel, L.M. (1985). Personal and situational factors affecting exercise involvement: The importance of enjoyment. *Research Quarterly for Exercise and Sport*, **56**, 275–282.

Wankel, L.M., & Mummery, W.K. (1993). Using national survey data incorporating the theory of planned behavior: Implications for social marketing strategies in physical activity. *Journal of Applied Sport Psychology*, **5**, 158–177.

Wankel, L., Yardley, J., & Graham, J. (1985). The effects of motivational interventions upon exercise adherence in high and low self-motivational adults. *Canadian Journal of Applied Sport Sciences*, **10**, 147–146.

Zander, A. (1982). *Making groups effective*. San Francisco: Jossey-Bass.

Chapter 2

Adherence to Exercise and the Transtheoretical Model of Behavior Change

Gabrielle Richards Reed

This chapter will (1) introduce the constructs that make up the Trans-theoretical Model of Behavior Change (TTM), (2) present the series of studies that developed the TTM for smoking cessation, (3) delineate the unique advantages of using Stage as an organizing concept, (4) explain the instruments developed to measure the TTM constructs for engaging in regular exercise, and (5) present lessons learned from using the TTM to measure regular exercise.

CONSTRUCTS OF THE TRANSTHEORETICAL MODEL

The Transtheoretical Model of Behavior Change (TTM) (Prochaska & DiClemente, 1983) (Prochaska, DiClemente, Velicer, & Rossi, 1993)

Adherence Issues in Sport and Exercise. Edited by Stephen J. Bull.
© 1999 John Wiley & Sons Ltd.

(Prochaska, Velicer, DiClemente, & Fava, 1988) is a blueprint for effecting self change of health behaviors. The model describes the general area of behavior change by first categorizing Stage of readiness to engage in a behavior and then measuring the use of key variables that have been found to promote behavior change. The four key variables measured by the model are: (1) stage of change, (2) decisional balance, (3) self-efficacy, and (4) processes of change.

Stage of Change

The core organizing concept of the TTM is the temporal dimension represented by the Stages of Change. The TTM, in early work and in more recent work, conceptualizes five Stages of readiness to cease an unhealthy or adopt a healthy behavior (DiClemente, Prochaska, Fairhurst, Velicer, Velasques, & Rossi, 1991; Velicer, Prochaska, Rossi, & Snow, 1992). These Stages are named: Precontemplation, where no change in behavior is thought of for at least the next 6 months; Contemplation, where change is thought of within the next 6 months; Preparation, where change is planned in the next 30 days and some type of approximate behavior has been attempted in the last year; Action, where change has begun and has been sustained for less than 6 months; and Maintenance, where change has been maintained for longer than 6 months.

Precontemplation

Within the TTM, if you state that you have no intention of making a behavior change in the foreseeable future (approximately 6 months), you are categorized into the Precontemplation Stage. The hallmark of Precontemplation is the lack of intention to take action, regardless of the reason. Reasons may run the gamut from not thinking the behavior is valuable to believing in the behavior but being overwhelmed by barriers. Historically for smoking cessation with adults, 6 months has been used to quantify the term 'foreseeable future'. Six months may not always be the appropriate time span for all populations and behaviors. This has been called the 'I WON'T' or 'I CAN'T' Stage.

Contemplation

If you are thinking of making a change (i.e. starting a healthy behavior or stopping an unhealthy one) sometime in the next 6 months, you are placed in Contemplation. Contemplators are only thinking about making a change. They are generally open to new information, willing and interested to know more about the benefits of change. They can also become stuck and never move beyond the information-gathering phase and become chronic contemplators. This has been called the 'I MIGHT' Stage.

Preparation

If your plans to change are more imminent (within approximately 30 days) and you have tried some type of approximate behavior (e.g., having bought a pair of athletic shoes, having signed up for an exercise program, or having engaged in some type of exercise on an irregular basis) you are put in the Preparation Stage. Preparation has both a behavioral and an intentional component. Behaviorally oriented interventions are most appropriate for those in Preparation. Those in Preparation are nearly ready to take on the many action-oriented tasks of changing a behavior. It could be called the 'I WILL' Stage.

Action

If you have made a change in behavior recently (i.e. within the last 6 months) you are categorized into the Action Stage. This change in behavior must meet *an established criterion* to equal the hallmark of Action. People in Action are extremely busy learning many behavioral techniques, including relapse prevention strategies. Because the person in Action has only recently established a new habit, vigilance and attentiveness are necessary. There are many fine action-oriented interventions (i.e. programs) that are well-matched to the needs of persons in the Action Stage. It can be thought of as the 'I AM' Stage.

Maintenance

If you have engaged in the new behavior for more than 6 months, you are placed in the Maintenance Stage. People in Maintenance have a different set of problems and needs than those in Action. Most programs are oriented to those who are trying to establish a habit (Preparation and Action people) and do not deal with the difficulties of maintaining a behavior over the long term. Although in Maintenance, the new habit has become better established, boredom and shifting focus can become a real danger. The constant vigilance initially required to establish a new habit is exhausting and difficult to sustain. Routines become boring and reinforcement is needed. Despite this, it could be called the 'I HAVE' Stage.

Decisional Balance

The second construct of the TTM contains two scales articulated in the
Decisional Balance Measure as the Pros and Cons (Velicer, DiClemente,
Prochaska, & Brandenburg, 1985). These instruments are based on Janis
and Mann's (Janis & Mann, 1977) concept of Decisional Balance. The
construct incorporates four underlying dimensions for the Pros of changing
a behavior: (1) utilitarian gains for self, (2) utilitarian gains for others, (3)
self-approval, and (4) the approval of others. The construct also incorporates four underlying dimensions for the Cons of changing a behavior: (1)
utilitarian losses for self, (2) utilitarian losses for others, (3) self-
disapproval, and (4) the disapproval of others. The instruments are written
to incorporate these eight underlying dimensions in order to assure the
breadth of the constructs. Despite this, Principal Component Analysis of
the Decisional Balance instruments has consistently produced only the two
separate constructs, the Pros and the Cons. The Pros and Cons are particularly important for moving early Stage subjects (in Precontemplation,
Contemplation and Preparation) to Action.

Self-efficacy

The third construct of the TTM is measured as the scales of Confidence/
Temptation or Self-efficacy instruments (Velicer, DiClemente, Rossi, &
Prochaska, 1990). These measures are based on Bandura's work (Bandura,
1977). The Self-efficacy construct involves the degree of confidence subjects have that they will not engage in a problem behavior in tempting
situations or conversely, the confidence that they will engage in a positive
behavior in challenging situations. The underlying situations for the Self-
efficacy measure may vary according to the particular behavior of interest.
   In the area of smoking cessation, three underlying dimensions have been
measured. The situations that are found to be the most challenging for
subjects can be grouped as (1) those situations where the subject displays
negative affect, (2) those situations which are social and positive, and (3)
those situations that are controlled by habit. Examples of situations where
negative affect can be a challenge for the newly quit smoker can include
times that the subject has had a bad day, has had a fight with a significant
coworker or family member, or when they are particularly tired. Examples
of social/positive situations that can be a test of the newly quit smoker's
resolve can include going to a favorite restaurant with a group of friends to
relax, or celebrating at the holidays with lots of food and drink. Examples
of situations controlled by habit include times that are triggered by a frequent event, for instance, lighting up a cigarette whenever on the phone or

driving a car. They are done automatically and are often paired to a frequent occurrence.

In the area of exercise, the underlying dimensions are still being clarified. Negative affect can produce situations that challenge adherence to regular exercise. Feeling tired, depressed, or angry can keep you from your routine. The paradox is that exercise is an excellent intervention for dissipating tiredness, mitigating depression, and dispersing anger. These states of negative affect should be a reinforcing cue to exercise. For regular exercise, social/positive situations are less of a challenge and more of an incentive. The more pleasurable and fun the exercise experience, the better the adherence. Cardiac rehabilitation groups often bond together and can be found still exercising many years after their original class because of camaraderie and the positive social experience they provide. Situations that disturb the routine are particularly challenging to adherence. Things such as experiencing bad weather, going on vacation, sustaining an injury, contracting an illness, or even finding the exercise facilities closed for renovation or cleaning can be very disruptive to maintaining a habit. Reestablishing a routine can be very difficult. Self-efficacy is particularly important to help late Stage subjects (those in Action and Maintenance) avoid relapsing. ✧

Processes of Change

The ten Processes of Change (Prochaska et al., 1988) measured in the TTM were chosen after reviewing the most commonly used psychotherapy techniques (Prochaska, 1984) and represent the behaviors, cognition, and emotions which the subjects engage in during the course of changing a behavior. They can be divided into five experiential processes and five behavioral processes. The five experiential or cognitive processes are Consciousness Raising, Dramatic Relief, Environmental Reevaluation, Self Reevaluation, and Social Liberation. The five behavioral processes are Counterconditioning, Helping Relationship, Reinforcement Management, Self Liberation, and Stimulus Control. People in different Stages of Change have been found to use the Processes differently. For example, Consciousness Raising (i.e. learning about the benefits of a behavior), which is so important for people in Contemplation, is not necessary by the time a person reaches Action and has already begun engaging in the behavior.

Behavior Specific Measures

In addition to the four constructs of the TTM, instruments are always included to measure the behaviors appropriate for a specific problem area. For instance, for regular exercise an important outcome to measure is the number of minutes of vigorous exercise a subject engaged in over the last week.

In summary, the TTM uses instruments that measure the four constructs (Stage, Decisional Balance, Self-efficacy, and the Processes of Change) in order to assess and intervene upon a population's self-change behavior. The smoking cessation measures are a good example of TTM assessment instruments.

THE SERIES OF STUDIES THAT DEVELOPED THE TTM

The TTM was first fully developed in the area of smoking cessation. Over more than fifteen years, James O. Prochaska, Ph.D., Wayne F. Velicer, Ph.D. and many graduate students at the Cancer Prevention Research Center at the University of Rhode Island, worked, first, to pick the most important and strongest variables that influence behavior change; second, to develop valid and reliable instruments to measure these variables and rigorous methods to test the relationships between them; and third, to develop a completely empirically driven, expert-type system intervention based on the subject's responses to the instruments which generates feedback for the subject.

Expert-type Systems: Normative Feedback

An expert-type system is a computer-based decision-making system designed to utilize client information (the answers to TTM questionnaires) to produce individualized feedback (on how to change a specific behavior). A normative database is drawn from the population of interest and is used to arrive at a criterion for each of the constructs of the TTM. This criterion discriminates those who have progressed through the Stages of Change from those who have not. The normative database also shows which Processes of Change and techniques are used effectively in which Stages of Change. The expert system is programmed to deliver positive feedback in response to a participant's scores that are above the criterion and corrective feedback in response to scores below the criterion on Processes judged to be important to the participant's Stage of Change.

The expert system compares the participant's answers to the battery of TTM questions to the criterion scores from the normative database. If the score for a particular variable (e.g. the Pros), is higher than the criterion, the participant will receive congratulatory feedback. If the score is lower than the criterion, the participant will receive feedback that suggests additional strategies to make progress. In an expert feedback system, the topic areas to be addressed are established for each Stage of Change based on the analysis of the normative data. Thus, if people in the normative database who progressed from Precontemplation to Contemplation had high scores on Environmental Reevaluation, feedback on this Process would be given in the intervention designed for Precontemplators. Similarly, if people who reached Maintenance in the normative database showed high scores on Reinforcement Management, this process would be emphasized in interventions for those in Maintenance. When participants answer their personal questionnaire, the Stage that they choose will determine the content areas on which they get feedback. For example based on a normative database for smoking, people in Action always get feedback on their answers to questions about Self-efficacy, Helping Relationship, Counterconditioning, and Stimulus Control; whereas a person in Contemplation gets feedback on their responses to items measuring Pros, Consciousness Raising, and Social Liberation. Whether the feedback is positive or corrective depends on the subject's score and how it compares to successful changers.

Expert-type Systems: Ipsative Feedback

The questionnaires that implement the expert-type system are administered at regular intervals. The most common timing is baseline, 3 months, and 6 months. When participants answer a questionnaire at 3 months and 6 months, their answers are not just compared to the normative database, but they are also compared to how they answered the same question the previous time. This ipsative (i.e. comparison to oneself) feedback will offer positive praise for improving a score or draw attention to a negative trend in those who have moved in the opposite direction or have not changed.

Expert-type Systems: Benefits

Expert-type systems allow interactive, Stage-based, individualized feedback. Interactive, because it is empirically based on the subject's response to a questionnaire; Stage-based because Stage determines which content areas are given as feedback; and individualized because of the level of detail upon which the feedback is personalized. When a participant's behavior is examined this closely, there are many opportunities to give encouragement. If participants have not exercised regularly according to the definition, they may have at least moved from not thinking about exercising to thinking about it (i.e. from Precontemplation to Contemplation). This can be praised. Even if unable to move out of a Stage, participants may have managed to use one of the Processes (e.g. enlisting a helping relationship) to a greater extent than the norm. This can be praised. Even if unable to progress and not exceeding the norm, a participant may have improved their Helping Relationship score since baseline. This small ipsative improvement can be acknowledged. Recognition of improvement reinforces the positive direction and shows the subject how to proceed. Between normative and ipsative feedback, there are some 16 368 potential unique feedback reports that can be generated (Velicer, Prochaska, Bellis, DiClemente, Rossi, Fava, & Steiger, 1993).

Study one

The first study used to develop the TTM was a smoking study (DiClemente et al., 1991) in Rhode Island and Texas. The study followed 1466 current and ex smokers recruited through newspaper advertisements. The two-year study examined how people in different Stages answered the Processes of Change, Decisional Balance, and Self-efficacy questions differently. From the normative database gathered in this study, a first generation expert-type system intervention was created as well as the first generation of Staged-matched self-help manuals.

Study two

The second study was a three-year intervention study (Prochaska et al., 1993), again using newspaper ads targeted at current and recently quit smokers. The study compared generic educational materials (American Lung Association fliers) (ALA) against Stage-matched manuals (SMM), interactive three expert-type system generated feedback reports at baseline, 3 and 6 months plus Stage matched manuals (3R+M) against interactive three expert-type-system generated feedback reports plus Stage matched manuals and telephone counselors (3R+M+C). At 18 months the interactive three expert-type system generated feedback reports plus Stage matched manuals (3R+M) outperformed the same intervention with the addition of a phone counselor (3R+M+C). The intervention with the counselors (3R+M+C), in turn, out performed the Stage-matched manuals (SMM) which outperformed the generic educational materials (ALA).

Study three

The third large study (Velicer, Prochaska, Fava, Laforge, & Rossi, 1999; Prochaska, Velicer, Fava, Ruggiero, Laforge, Rossi, 1998; Velicer, Prochaska,

Fava, Laforge, Rossi, in press) followed members of a New England HMO and compared dose and timing of the intervention. Dose could consist of : (a) manuals alone (M), (b) manuals with expert-type system reports (MR), (c) a counselor in addition to manuals with expert-type system reports (MRC) or (d) a hand-held computer in addition to the manuals with expert-type system reports (MRH). Timing could consist of: (a) a single delivery of manuals (M1), (b) two deliveries (M2), (c) three (M3), or (d) six (M6). In the other condition of manuals with expert-type system reports, the same variation occurred: MR1, MR2, MR3, and MR6, as well as MR3C and MR3H.

The clearest finding was that individualized feedback reports outperformed Stage-based manuals alone. Three deliveries of manuals and reports supplemented by a phone counselor (MR3C) outperformed everyone with a 40% point prevalence quit rate at 6 months, but drastically fell off by 18 months, possibly due to the counselors having been stopped at 6 months and the subjects feeling some type of abandonment.

Study four

The fourth study (Fava, Velicer, & Prochaska, 1995) was a random digit dial of 12 000 Rhode Islanders. The study proactively recruited 4144 current smokers and followed them for 3 years. The study had three groups: immediate treatment, delayed treatment, and a control group that was only assessed. The study subjects were recruited from three sites: physician's offices, schools, and worksites. A representative sample was able to be recruited and retained by using an initial phone call to enroll subjects. Follow-up was through the mail, unless the questionnaire was not returned, in which case the Telephone Survey Center called until they reached the subject. The intervention produced quit rates comparable to clinic-based rates (24%).

Study five

Study five has recently begun and is an extension of study three which examines tailoring interventions dose to Stage of Change and compares this to a step care approach, and other enhancements added to the classic 'manuals plus three expert-type system reports'.

Study six

Study six is an expansion of study four to risks other than smoking. In the worksites, dietary fat, sun exposure, and exercise are added to smoking. In the physician's offices, dietary fat, sun exposure, and mammography-screening are added to smoking. In the schools, dietary fat and sun exposure are added to smoking. Each of the sites has an on-site intervention and a home-based intervention (expert-type system feedback reports).

In summary, a series of studies over 18 years, involving more than 10 000 subjects, has systematically developed the assessment tools, the expert-type system intervention, and the optimum delivery techniques that presently make up a TTM intervention. Present studies continue to hone the delivery techniques using another 7000 subjects.

THE UNIQUE ADVANTAGES OF USING STAGE OF CHANGE

There are five advantages to breaking a population up into separate Stages. The first benefit is the ability to match interventions to the very different needs of each of the Stages. This allows you to work with the total population (i.e. those who have not yet made a behavior change and are at risk and those who have changed, but may be at risk of relapse). The second advantage is being able to subdivide the at-risk population into Precontemplation, Contemplation and Preparation. An examination of these subgroups shows far fewer people to be in the Preparation Stage compared to Precontemplation and Contemplation. This identification of the three types of people at risk allows you to proactively go out after those who need you the most but are least likely to react to a program call (i.e. the Precontemplators and Contemplators). The third benefit comes from an in-depth examination of recruitment and retention patterns. Stage of readiness to change can predict the likelihood of being successfully recruited and retained in a study. The fourth advantage comes through a study of progression by Stage. This can influence intervention development. The fifth advantage is illustrated by examining the intervention curve of a TTM study as compared to a classic intervention curve which drops off after the intervention.

Advantage One: Working with Total Populations

The TTM is particularly pertinent for studying adherence to exercise in general populations. General populations are composed of people from all the Stages of Change (Precontemplation, Contemplation, Preparation, Action, and Maintenance). Interventions in the exercise area so often consist of attendance at a program. Programs are an appropriate intervention for only two (Preparation and Action) of the five Stages. It is necessary to think in terms of having five different interventions to match the unique needs of each Stage of Change.

Advantage Two: Distribution of the Population by Stage

Research shows that the percentage of people in Preparation to be relatively small compared to the number who stage themselves into the earlier Stages of Precontemplation and Contemplation. For smoking cessation, in four different samples, 20% or less were in the Preparation Stage (Velicer, Fava, Prochaska, Abrams, Emmons, & Pierce, 1995). A screener sent to 25,000 members of a New England HMO (Rossi, 1992) looked at a number of variables including Exercise, Smoking, Dietary Fat, Fiber, Weight Control, and Stress. The percentage of people in Preparation for these behaviors ranged from a low of 14% being in Preparation for working on stress to a high of 28% being in Preparation for Weight Control. The exercise algorithm used in that study had a very incomplete definition of exercise that did not specify what intensity would meet the criterion. Even this brief definition of exercise only produced 37% being in Preparation. What this means is that for smoking 80% were in the early Stages of Precontemplation and Contemplation, for dietary fat, 77% , for fiber, 83%, for weight control, 72%, for stress, 86% , and for exercise, 63%. Bess Marcus also used a variety of different algorithms to stage subjects in a worksite study. One of the algorithms staged 58% of the subjects into Precontemplation and Contemplation and only 10% into Preparation (Marcus, Rossi, Selby, Niaura, & Abrams, 1992).

For the most part Precontemplators and Contemplators will not come to programs, but they can be proactively recruited to interventions that are appropriate to their Stage of Change.

Recruitment and Retention by Stage

Recruitment of early Stage subjects can be successful if (1) you proactively go out after them and (2) you offer them an intervention matched to their Stage of Change, rather than force them into an Action-oriented program. Proactive recruitment by either telephone or personal letter coupled with Stage matched interventions have been able to generate participation rates of 82% to 85% (Prochaska Velicer, Fava, Rossi, & Tsoh, 1998; Prochaska, Velicer, Fava, Ruggiero, Laforge, Rossi, 1998; Velicer, Prochaska, Fava, Laforge, Rossi, 1999).

Lichtenstein and Hollis (1992) used an intensive proactive recruitment technique for a one size fits all, action-oriented smoking cessation program. If 5 minutes with the physician did not convince the subject to sign up for a smoking cessation clinic, then 10 minutes was spent with a nurse. If this did not accomplish the goal of signing up, then it was followed by 12 minutes with a video and a health educator. The final push was a proactive counselor call. All this effort produced only 1% base-rate participation. As was seen, trying to force early Stage subjects to engage in an action-oriented intervention was not successful. The people who did sign up were staged. Of those that did sign up, 35% staged themselves as being in Precontemplation. The other 65% were split between Contemplation and Preparation. Only 3% of the 35% showed up for the actual program and only 2% actually completed it, whereas 15% of the 65% showed up and 11% actually completed the program. This says that there is five times the chance of getting Contemplation and Preparation people to come than Precontemplators (15% compared to 3%) and that subjects in Contemplation and Preparation are more than five times more likely to complete the program than those in Precontemplation (11% to 2%).

Progression by Stage

Progress is also related to Stage of change at enrollment. When you examine the percent of subjects from Texas and Rhode Island (DiClemente et al., 1991) that were quit at six months, you see variable results dependent on Stage of Change at enrollment and whether or not change was made in their first month. (Prochaska, DiClemente, & Norcross, 1992; Prochaska & DiClemente, 1992). Of subjects that started in Precontemplation and remained there for one month, 3% had quit at six months compared to 7% that moved from Precontemplation at enrollment to Contemplation at one month. Moving one Stage doubled the chance of success. Even more dramatic were the results for those starting in Contemplation. Of subjects that started in Contemplation and remained there for one month, 20% had quit at six months, compared to 41% that moved from Contemplation at enrollment to Preparation at one month. Again we see the doubling of the chance of success with Stage movement.

Rate of Progression by Stage

Early Stage people take longer to change. The classic spike during intervention and drop-off post intervention does not occur when you match your intervention to Stage of Change. Preparation people will move most rapidly followed by Contemplation and finally by Precontemplation (Prochaska, Norcross et al., 1992). Quit rates at 12 months will look better than at 6 months and 18 months will look better than 12 months.

To summarize, the five main advantages to using the Stages of Change to subdivide a population are (1) it allows matching of intervention to the total population, (2) it locates the larger, more at-risk segment of the population (those in Precontemplation and Contemplation), (3) it enhances successful recruitment and retention of subjects, (4) it increases the chances of making progress through the Stages, and (5) it extends the intervention curve beyond the normally expected drop-off.

TTM INSTRUMENTS FOR REGULAR EXERCISE

Bess Marcus, Ph.D. and Joe Rossi, Ph.D. developed the first generation instruments to measure regular exercise based on the four constructs of the TTM: Stage of Change, Decisional Balance, Self-efficacy, and the Processes of Change. The present author analyzed some of those instruments and extended the process of developing TTM exercise instruments by refining and adapting the first generation instruments. Ongoing instrument development is an iterative process. In particular, adaptations will continue to be made as we turn our attention to more select populations, for example, to older adults. The TTM instruments for regular exercise include instruments to measure Stage (an algorithm and a continuous measure), Decisional Balance, Self-efficacy, and the Processes of Change.

Measuring Stage of Change for Exercise

Stage can be measured in two ways: by means of an algorithm and by a continuous measure. An algorithm is a short measure that categorizes a subject into a single, discrete Stage (Precontemplation, Contemplation, Preparation, Action or Maintenance). A continuous measure, on the other hand, gathers information on each of the Stages of Change for a subject giving the individual a score for Precontemplation, Contemplation, Preparation, Action and Maintenance. Individuals are then classified into Profiles based on the set of Stage scale scores. An in-depth examination of a continuous measure for regular exercise (Reed, Velicer, Prochaska, & Sonstroem, manuscript in preparation) and an extensive comparison of a series of different algorithms for regular exercise (Reed, Velicer, Prochaska, Rossi, & Marcus, 1997) have been made.

Staging Algorithms: Two Variations

The state of the science presently recommends two long definitions of vigorous regular exercise that include frequency, duration, and in place of intensity, a list of examples of what is and what is not considered meeting the criterion.

Version A. The first uses the following definition:

'Exercise includes activities such as brisk walking, jogging, swimming, aerobic dancing, biking, rowing, etc. Activities that are primarily sedentary, such as bowling, or playing golf with a cart, would not be considered exercise.'

Regular exercise = 3 times or more per week for 20 minutes or longer.

This definition is followed by the question 'Do you exercise *regularly*?' This single question is followed by a five choice format:

    Yes, and I have for more than 6 months   (Maintenance)
    Yes but for less than 6 months   (Action)
    No, but I intend to start in the next 30 days   (Preparation)
    No, but I intend to start in the next 6 months   (Contemplation)
    No, and I don't intend to start in the next 6 months   (Precontemplation)

This question is followed by a second question about an approximate behavior (Do you have a pair of athletic shoes?) which is answered with a Yes or a No. Subjects who say they intend to start exercising in the next 30 days (Preparation) must also say that they have gotten athletic shoes or they will be dropped back to Contemplation. This allows for Preparation to have an intentional and a behavioral component which is the classic representation of Preparation.

Another algorithm is currently being tested for use with older adults. It presents a vigorous exercise definition with a simplified response format.

Version B. The second definition is as follows:

'Any planned physical activity (e.g. brisk walking, aerobics, jogging, bicycling, swimming, rowing, etc.) *performed to increase physical fitness. Such activity must be performed 3 to 5 times per week* for *20 to 60 minutes per session* to meet criterion. Exercise must be done at a level that *increases your breathing rate or causes you to break a sweat* to meet criterion.'

Do you exercise REGULARLY according to the criterion?

NO	YES
____ I WON'T ever (Precontemplation Nonbeliever)	____ I AM (Action)
____ I CAN'T in the next 6 months (Precontemplation Bel)	____ I HAVE for the last 6 months (Maintenance)
____ I MAY in the next 6 months (Contemplation)	
____ I WILL in the next 30 days (Preparation)	

Continuous Measure of Stage

This author developed a second generation continuous measure of Stage of Change for regular exercise, The University of Rhode Island Change Assessment for Exercise—Version 2 (URICA-E2). This was done in order: (1) to more fully understand what it means to be a member of a Stage (by having a series of items represent each Stage of Change); (2) to discover the most common patterns or types of regular exercisers (by using Cluster Analysis); and (3) to study the relationships between the Stages of Change (by comparing a variety of models using Structural Equation Modeling).

The original continuous measure is the University of Rhode Island Change Assessment (URICA) (McConnaughy,Prochaska, & Velicer, 1983; McConnaughy,DiClemente,Prochaska, & Velicer, 1989). The URICA was adapted for exercise by Bess Marcus, Ph.D. and Joe Rossi, Ph.D. to measure the Stage of Change of participants in a worksite study. The adapted instrument was named URICA-E1 and it was analyzed by this author (Reed, Velicer, Rossi, & Marcus, 1993, 1994). The URICA and the URICA-E1 both measured four Stages of Change: Precontemplation, Contemplation, Action, and Maintenance. Only four Stages were measured because the analysis of the original URICA could not identify a fifth Stage that had been conceptualized as Decision Making. The items written originally to measure the middle Stage were very different in content from the current definition of Preparation. When the URICA-E1 was adapted from the original URICA, it was done as a strict translation with the substitution of the word 'exercise' for the word 'problem' in the original measure.

Based on the results of the analysis of the URICA-E1, this author developed the next generation instrument. The author wrote items to represent five Stages of Change (Precontemplation, Contemplation, Preparation,

Action, and Maintenance). Principal Component Analysis, confirmed by Confirmatory Factor Analysis, actually found six correlated constructs: Contemplation, Preparation, Action, and Maintenance, as anticipated, and two types of Precontemplation (Precontemplation-Nonbelievers in Exercise and Precontemplation-Believer in Exercise). The Alpha reliability for each scale was: Precontemplation Nonbeliever (0.81), Precontemplation Believer (0.91) Contemplation (0.91), Preparation (0.88), Action (0.92), and Maintenance (0.94).

In order to discover groups of subjects who had the same pattern of answers across the six Stages a cluster analysis was done. For the cluster analysis, each subject's six standardized (Mean = 50, SD = 10) scale scores were entered into the analysis. Seven clusters were retained. The seven Profiles, that were named, corresponded to the six Stages of Precontemplation (Nonbeliever, Precontemplation Believer, Contemplation, Preparation, Action, and Maintenance) plus a Profile named Ambivalent/Action. See Figure 2.1.

Measuring Decisional Balance for Regular Exercise

The Decisional Balance for Regular Exercise instrument has 14 items using a five point Likert scale from 'Not Important' to 'Extremely Important'. The instrument presents the definition of vigorous regular exercise and asks subjects to indicate *how important* are each of the statements in their decision to exercise according to the definition. Seven of the items are Pros of regular exercise (alpha = 0.94) and seven of the items are the Cons of regular exercise (alpha = 0.77) It is an adaptation of the Pros and Cons of regular exercise (Marcus, Rakowski, & Rossi, 1992) which was based on the Decisional Balance measure for smoking (Velicer et al., 1985).

An adaptation of the Decisional Balance for regular exercise measure is currently being tested in a population of older adults. It is a 24 item version with 12 each, Pro and Con items.

Persons in the early Stages of Precontemplation and Contemplation have been found to have low scores for the Pros and high scores for the Cons of exercising regularly. These early Stage people can not see beyond the difficult aspects of exercising regularly. Persons in the Action and Maintenance Stages have been found to have high Pro scores and medium to low Con scores. Action Stage people have the highest Pro scores. These people in Action appreciate the benefits of regular exercise. Subjects in the Preparation Stage have balanced Pro and Con scores. The difficult things that get in the way of exercising are just as important as the beneficial reasons for exercising. If you plot a graph of the Pro and Con scores across

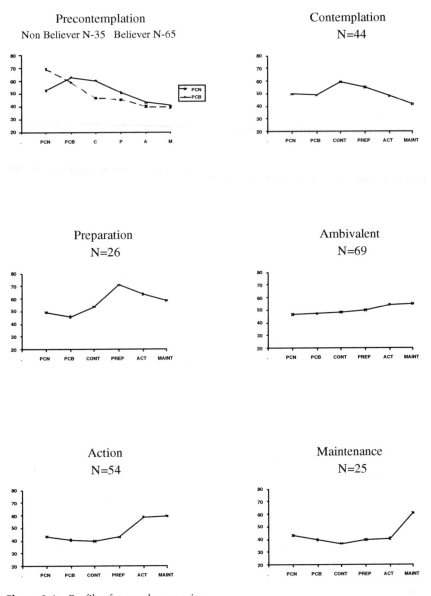

Figure 2.1 Profiles for regular exercise

the Stages, the pattern resembles an X. The Pros rise from low to high across the continuum of Stages (Precontemplation, Contemplation, Preparation, Action) then dip slightly to Maintenance. The Cons fall from high to medium across the Stage continuum.

Measuring Confidence for Regular Exercise

This is a seven-item instrument using a five-point Likert scale from 'Not at all confident' to 'Very confident'. The instrument presents the definition of vigorous regular exercise and asks subjects to indicate how confident they are that they will exercise regularly according to the definition in particular situations. The situations represent the domains of negative affective, social/positive, and difficult situations. This instrument was discovered to represent a single dimension rather than the three underlying concepts that it had been written to capture. It is an adaptation of the confidence instrument for regular exercise (Marcus, Selby, Niaura, & Rossi, 1992; Marcus & Owen, 1992); Marcus, Eaton, Rossi, & Harlow, 1994) which was based on a self-efficacy smoking measure (Velicer et al., 1990).

A further developed version of the Confidence instrument for regular exercise is currently being administered to an older adult population. It is a 16-item instrument with four items that measure the influence of negative affect, six representing difficult situations, three asking about adverse weather conditions, and three looking at the effect of health problems on confidence to exercise.

Self-efficacy theory holds that confidence in one's ability to perform a behavior, in this case, regular exercise, is strongly related to one's actual ability to perform the behavior (Bandura, 1977). A linear relationship has been found for the confidence instrument across the continuum of Stages. Precontemplation has the lowest scores and they rise progressively to Maintenance which has the highest.

Measuring the Processes of Change for Regular Exercise

This is a 40-item instrument using a 5-point Likert scale (Never to Repeatedly). It is composed of four items each representing ten Processes of Change. The Processes are the variables that assess how people go about changing their problem behaviors. These are covert and overt activities that individuals attempt to modify behaviors they consider a problem (Prochaska et al., 1988). The present author has renamed the processes to facilitate their being more readily understood by the older adults with which she works. The classic title will appear in parenthesis following the revised name. The five experiential processes that seem to be more important in the early Stages of Change with their alpha reliability and a definition are: (i) gathering information (Consciousness Raising) (0.85)—the process of gathering information about regular exercise, in particular learning about the Pros and Cons of doing regular exercise; (ii) being moved emotionally (Dramatic Relief) (0.73)—the process of taking advantage of being moved to action by emotional stories or events that depict the virtues of regular exercise or the dire consequences of inactivity; (iii) being a role model (Environmental Reevaluation) (0.71)—the process of realizing that whether you exercise or not has an effect on your family, friends, associates, and fellow citizens of the world; (iv) developing a healthy self-image (Self Reevaluation) (0.79)—the process of appraising one's self-image as a healthy, vigorous regular exerciser; (v) taking advantage of social mores (Social Liberation) (0.59)—the process of taking advantage of social policy, custom and mores which enhance or promote regular exercise. The five behavioral processes which have more importance in the later Stages of Change with their alpha reliability and definitions are: (i) making substitutions (Counterconditioning) (0.59)—the processes of substituting exercise for unhealthy activities or of engaging in an activity instead of being sedentary; (ii) getting social support (Helping Relationship) (0.70)—the process of seeking out or enlisting people to support your intention to exercise; (iii) being rewarded (Reinforcement Management) (0.84)—the process of getting others to reward you for exercising or establishing a self-reward system for regularly exercising; (iv) making a commitment (Self-Liberation) (0.84)—the process of committing oneself to becoming or staying a regular exerciser; (v) using cues (Stimulus-Control) (0.58)—the process of using cues to remember to exercise. This instrument is descended from the Smoking Processes of Change scale (SPC) (DiClemente & Prochaska, 1985) (Prochaska et al., 1988) (DiClemente et al., 1991). The SPC was the model for a first generation exercise instrument, the Process of Change Questionnaire (PCQ) (Marcus, Rossi et al., 1992) (Marcus,Simpkin,Rossi, & Pinto, 1996). This present instrument was built on both the SPC and the PCQ.

A version of the Processes of Change for regular exercise is currently being administered to a population of older adults. It is a 50-item instrument with six items measuring gathering information, six being moved emotionally, six being a role model, six developing a healthy self image, four taking advantage of social mores, four making substitutions, four getting social support, four being rewarded, six making a commitment, and four using cues.

In summary, the instruments to measure regular exercise based on the TTM and presented here are multigenerational. They trace their roots to the smoking cessation instruments developed through the previously described series of smoking studies. These instruments are most directly related to the generation of instruments developed by Bess Marcus, Ph.D. and Joe Rossi, Ph.D.

LESSONS LEARNED FROM USING THE TTM TO MEASURE REGULAR EXERCISE

Measuring each of the TTM constructs has given us insight into the process of adopting and maintaining the behavior of exercising regularly.

Lessons from Measuring Stage of Change

Algorithms. From comparing a series of exercise algorithms (Prochaska, Norcross, Fowler, Follick, & Abrams, 1992), we learned that algorithms can better stage subjects when the criterion definition of exercise includes frequency (how often you need to do it), duration (for how long each time) and intensity (enough to increase breathing rate or make you sweat) or some proxy of intensity (examples of what would be vigorous enough).

Continuous Measure (URICA-E2): Instrument Development. From developing the URICA-E2 we were able to (1) confirm the presence of Contemplation, Action and Maintenance as Stages of Change, (2) affirm a strong Preparation Stage which this instrument had not previously been able to isolate, and (3) tease apart two types of Precontemplation (i.e. the Stage when people are not thinking of starting to exercise in the next 6 months).

The two types of Precontemplators have very different reasons for not planning to exercise. The Precontemplation Nonbelievers do not believe in regular exercise, or do not see the value of engaging in it. The Precontemplation Believers do believe that exercise is a worthwhile behavior, but they can not see their way clear to being able to exercise regularly. The Precontemplation Nonbelievers need to become aware of and learn to appreciate the Pros of exercising. The Precontemplation Believers need help overcoming the Cons of exercising. These two different types of Precontemplators demand different intervention strategies.

Continuous Measure (URICA-E2): Cluster Analysis. From the cluster analysis, we replicated and confirmed the six Stages of Changes (Precontemplation Nonbeliever, Precontemplation Believer, Contemplation, Preparation, Action, and Maintenance). We also revealed a seventh Profile (Ambivalent/Action) which had t-scores for all the Stages close to the mean but rising in a linear progression (46.3 for Precontemplation Nonbeliever, 47.1 for Precontemplation Believer, 48.0 for Contemplation, 50.1 for Preparation, 54.6 for Action, to 55.3 for Maintenance).

We can characterize this Ambivalent/Action group in terms of the classic Stages of Change. Of people who staged themselves into Action using the single question algorithm, 42% were found in the Ambivalent/Action Profile. Of those who staged themselves into Maintenance, 33% were in the Ambivalent/Action Profile. Only 3% of those who staged themselves as Preparation and 2% of those who staged themselves as Contemplation were in the Ambivalent/Action Profile. No one who staged themselves into Precontemplation was in the Ambivalent/Action Profile. So, the Ambivalent/Action Profile is mainly composed of people who exercise regularly. This is confirmed by the fact that 74% of those with this Profile exceeded the criterion for number of hours exercised per week. The Profile averaged 3.6 h/wk (SD 3.4). Table 2.1 gives a sense of how the Ambivalent/ Action Profile compares to the other Profiles on the Pros, Cons, Confidence, and Hours of Exercise measures.

To summarize, on Pros, the Ambivalent/Action subjects are equal to Maintenance subjects as well as Precontemplation Believer, Contemplation, and Preparation subjects. This is the middle of three groups between the Precontemplation Nonbelievers who have the lowest scores for the Pros of exercising and those in Action who have the highest. In Maintenance the importance of appreciating the Pros of a behavior becomes less important as the habit becomes stronger and more automatic.

On the Cons, the Ambivalent/Action subjects are equal to Action subjects. This is also the middle of three groups and between Maintenance with the lowest scores on the Cons and a grouping of Precontemplation Nonbeliever, Precontemplation Believer, Contemplation and Preparation with the highest scores on the Cons.

Table 2.1 Standardized means and standard deviations of pros, cons, and confidence by profile for regular exercise

Profile	Pros Mean (SD)	Cons Mean (SD)	Confidence Mean (SD)	Hrs of Exerc Mean (SD)
PCN	39.60 (10.1)	56.00 (10.2)	42.57 (8.8)	2.13 (3.0)
PCB	52.51 (7.0)	53.60 (8.4)	44.04 (6.8)	1.44 (2.4)
C	50.60 (8.0)	54.05 (9.2)	48.02 (6.5)	2.12 (3.3)
P	51.72 (8.3)	53.83 (11.6)	52.42 (10.5)	4.00 (4.1)
Ambivalent/ Action	50.58 (7.6)	48.88 (7.5)	52.34 (7.3)	3.60 (3.4)
A	55.75 (5.4)	46.43 (6.9)	57.17 (7.2)	4.36 (3.9)
M	51.52 (10.5)	42.32 (2.6)	58.44 (7.1)	4.08 (3.9)

Pattern of differences:

Pros   PCN < ABVA=C=M=P=PCB < A
Cons   < A=ABVA < PCB=P=C=PCN
Confidence   PCN < PCB < C < ABVA=P < A=M
Hours of Exercise   PCB=P < PCN=C < ABVA=M=A

On Confidence, the Ambivalent/Action subjects are equal to Preparation. Of five groupings, Ambivalent/Action falls second from the highest. It is only exceeded by a group of Action and Maintenance.

On Hours of Exercise, the Ambivalent/Action subjects are equal to Maintenance and Action subjects which is the highest of three groups.

Ambivalent/Action could be interpreted as a group of current exercisers who instead of being clear on the Pros of exercise are more similar to those who are still trying to learn about the virtues of exercise. They are also a group for whom the Cons of exercising are still somewhat an issue, and who are only as confident about continuing to exercise as people in Preparation who have as yet succeeded in starting to exercise regularly.

Lessons from Decisional Balance

From examining the Decisional Balance instrument across the Profiles (Precontemplation Nonbeliever, Precontemplation Believer, Contemplation, Preparation, Ambivalent/Action, Action, and Maintenance), we have learned that four of the Profiles (Precontemplation Believer, Contemplation, Preparation, and Ambivalent/Action) have their Pro and Con scores closer than a half standard deviation apart. This means that their conviction about the value of exercising is nearly balanced by the amount of difficulty they perceive impeding their ability to exercise. Only the Action and Maintenance groups appear convinced that the Pros clearly outweigh the Cons. This suggests to me that a more personalized Decisional Balance exercise might be effective. Presently a subject answers a small number of universal questions that represent the domains of Pros of exercising and the Cons of exercising. In the classic expert-type system intervention feedback is given only on these representative Pros.

As a more personalized Decisional Balance exercise, I would suggest working with both the Pros and the Cons. For the Pros, I would suggest that the subject be given a comprehensive list of many of the documented Pros of exercising regularly. More than sixty benefits of regular exercise have been documented (Reed, 1995). The list could include instructions to the participants to pick the three benefits that are the most important to them in their decision to exercise. These are the three most salient Pros for these participants and as such are unique to them. This allows a finer degree of personalization than with the universal items of the present Pros questionnaire. The exercise would then suggest to the participants, as an intervention, that they should attempt to prove to themselves, in a very personal fashion, the saliency of the three Pros that were chosen. This requires being willing to take the time to experience the Pros on a personal level.

For the Cons, I would again suggest a move away from the universal to the personal. The particular Cons or barriers that impede a subject from exercising regularly are often readily apparent to participants. It is usually not difficult to get participants to articulate what stands in the way of their being able to exercise regularly. The most frequently cited barrier is lack of time. I propose that subjects be asked to write down their three greatest barriers to regular exercise. I would also suggest that the three Cons be examined for which are true barriers, which are excuses, and what possible solutions can be found to overcome them. Three are suggested as a discrete set on which to work. This prevents the participants from being over-whelmed by a large array of Cons. There is an old adage about always being able to do what we want to do badly enough. When the Pros of exercising become real to participants, they will find a way to overcome the Cons.

Lessons from Self-efficacy

A fundamental lesson that we have learned from trying to measure Self-efficacy is that we need to move beyond the subdimensions used in smoking cessation (negative affect, social/positive, and habit strength). To more adequately measure the breadth of the construct of self-efficacy for regular exercise in addition to measuring the effect of negative affect, we are presently exploring how other variables may influence self-efficacy. We are testing to see how the effect of health problems, inclement weather, lack of time, travel, and the absence of support persons may affect a subject's confidence that they will be able to exercise regularly.

Lessons from the Processes of Change

The most basic lesson we have learned from measuring the Processes of Change is that we need to either improve the measurement of or discard the Processes of using cues, taking advantage of social mores, and making sub-stitutions. More research needs to be done to understand which Processes are most important in each of the Stages. A normative, longitudinal database is presently being collected on older adults which will show which Processes are used the most in each of the Stages. This information will inform an exercise expert-type system for older adults that is being developed.

In summary, the lessons we have learned have (1) expanded our idea of Stage to include two types of Precontemplation (Precontemplation Non-believer & Precontemplation Believer) and the Profile named Ambivalent/ Action, (2) suggested new ways of intervening (New Decisional Balance

Exercise), and (3) pointed out areas that need more research (Self-efficacy and the Processes of Change).

CONCLUSIONS

There are seven major conclusions from this review of using the TTM to study regular exercise behavior.

1. The constructs of the TTM can, if measured correctly, match behavior change intervention techniques to a subject's Stage of Change.
2. The series of smoking cessation studies gives a solid basis of experience on which to rest the development of the instruments for regular exercise.
3. The TTM instruments to measure regular exercise were all based on smoking instruments that have had more than 15 years of development. The exercise instruments being presently tested are the third generation from the original instruments.
4. Using Stage of Change gives a unique advantage to recruiting, and retaining subjects as well as influences progression through the Stages.
5. The regular exercise instruments points us to further refinement of all of the instruments especially Self-efficacy and Processes of Change, and creation of new intervention tools like the New Decisional Balance Intervention Exercise.
6. The teasing apart of Precontemplation into Precontemplation Non-believer and Precontemplation Believer has major implications for intervening upon this most difficult group of people who have no intention of changing in the next 6 months.
7. The Profile labeled Ambivalent/Action seems to be a group possibly at risk for relapse and consequently in need of a focused intervention strategy.

In summary the Transtheoretical Model of Behavior Change is a useful tool for attempting to engage full populations of subjects who are in all five Stages of Change from Precontemplation, through Contemplation, and Preparation, and on to Action and Maintenance. It is also a useful tool to deliver interventions matched to Stage. But in order to be a really effective change agent for regular exercise, the TTM needs more research, particularly on Self-efficacy and the Processes of Change. This is an ongoing process of students at the Cancer Prevention Research Center, University of Rhode Island, of Bess Marcus, Ph.D., at Miriam Hospital, Providence, Rhode Island, and of the present author at Washington University School of Medicine, Division of Health Behavior Research.

REFERENCES

Bandura, A. (1977). Self-Efficacy: Toward unifying theory of behavioral change. *Psychological Review*, **84**, 191–215.

DiClemente, C., & Prochaska, J. (1985). Processes and stages of change: Coping and competence in smoking behavior change. In S. Shiffman & T. Wills (eds.), *Coping and Substance Abuse* (pp. 319–343). San Diego, CA: Academic Press.

DiClemente, C., Prochaska, J., Fairhurst, S., Velicer, W., Velasques, M., & Rossi, J. (1991). The process of smoking cessation: An analysis of pre-contemplation, contemplation, and preparation stages of change. *Journal of Consulting and Clinical Psychology*, **59**, 295–304.

Fava, J., Velicer, W., & Prochaska, J. (1995). Applying the Transtheoretical Model to a representative sample of smokers. *Addictive Behaviors*, **20**(2), 189–203.

Janis, I., & Mann, L. (1977). *Decision Making: A Psychological Analysis of Conflict, Choice and Commitment*. New York: Collier Macmillan.

Lichtenstein, E., & Hollis, J. (1992). Patient referral to smoking cessation programs: Who follow through? *The Journal of Family Practice*, **34**(6), 739–44.

Marcus, B., Eaton, C., Rossi, J., & Harlow, L. (1994). Self-efficacy, decision making, and stages of change: A model of physical exercise. *Journal of Applied Social Psychology*, **24**, 489–508.

McConnaughy, E., DiClemente, C., Prochaska, J., & Velicer, W. (1989). Stages of change in psychotherapy: A follow-up report. *Psychotherapy*, **26**, 494–503.

McConnaughy, E., Prochaska, J., & Velicer, W. (1983). Stages of change in psychotherapy: Measurement and sample profiles. *Psychotherapy: Theory, Research, and Practice*, **20**, 368–375.

Marcus, B., & Owen, N. (1992). Motivational readiness, self-efficacy, and decision making for exercise. *Journal of Applied Social Psychology*, **22**, 3–16.

Marcus, B., Rakowski, W., & Rossi, J. (1992). Assessing motivational readiness and decision making for exercise. *Health Psychology*, **11**, 257–61.

Marcus, B., Rossi, J., Selby, V., Niaura, R., & Abrams, D. (1992). The stages and processes of exercise adoption and maintenance in a work site sample. *Health Psychology*, **11**, 386–95.

Marcus, B., Selby, V., Niaura, R., & Rossi, J. (1992). Self-efficacy and the stages of exercise behavior. *Research Quarterly for Exercise and Sport*, **63**, 60–6.

Marcus, B., Simpkin, L., Rossi, J., & Pinto, B. (1996). Longitudinal shifts in employees' stages and processes of exercise behavior change. *American Journal of Health Promotion*, **10**, 195–200.

Prochaska, J. (1984). *Systems of Psychotherapy: A Transtheoretical Analyses* (2nd edn). Homewood, IL: The Dorsey Press.

Prochaska, J., & DiClemente, C. (1983). Stages and process of self-change of smoking: Toward an integrative model of change. *Journal of Consulting and Clinical Psychology*, **51**(3), 390–5.

Prochaska, J., & DiClemente, C. (1992). Stages of change in the modification of problem behaviors. In M. Hersen, R. Eisler, & P. Miller (eds.), *Progress in Behavior Modifications* (pp. 184–214). Sycamore, IL: Sycamore Press.

Prochaska, J., DiClemente, C., & Norcross, J. (1992). In search of how people change: Application to addictive behaviors. *American Psychologist*, **47**(9), 1102–14.

Prochaska, J., DiClemente, C., Velicer, W., & Rossi, J. (1993). Standardized, individualized, interactive and personalized self help programs for smoking cessation. *Health Psychology*, **12**, 399–405.

Prochaska, J., Norcross, J., Fowler, J., Follick, M., & Abrams, D. (1992). Attendance and outcome in a work-site weight control program: Processes and stages of change as process and predictor variables. *Addictive Behaviors*, **17**, 35–45.

Prochaska, J., Velicer, W., DiClemente, C., & Fava, J. (1988). Measuring processes of change: Applications to the cessation of smoking. *Journal of Consulting and Clinical Psychology*, **56**, 520–8.

Prochaska, J., Velicer, W., Fava, J., Rossi, J.S., & Tsoh, J.Y. (1998). Stage matched expert systems for a total population of smokers. Submitted for publication.

Prochaska, JO, Velicer, WF, Fava, JL Ruggiero, L, Laforge, RG, Rossi, JS. (1999). Counselor and stimulus control enhancements of a stage-matched expert system intervention for smokers in a managed care setting. Submitted for publication.

Reed, G. R. (1995). Measuring Stage of Change for Exercise. (Doctoral Dissertation, University of Rhode Island, 1995) Dissertation Abstracts International, 56–09B, Page 5220, 00183 Pages.

Reed, G., Velicer, W., Prochaska, J., Rossi, J., & Marcus, B. (1997). What makes a good staging algorithm: Examples from regular exercise. *American Journal of Health Promotion*, **12**, 57–66.

Reed, G., Velicer, W., Prochaska, J., & Sonstroem, R. (manuscript in preparation). The development of a continuous measure of stage of change for regular exercise.

Reed, G., Velicer, W., Rossi, J., & Marcus, B. (1993). Profiles from the URICA-E: A continuous measure of the stages of change for exercise.

Paper presented at the Annual Meeting of the American Psychological Association. Washington, DC.

Reed, G., Velicer, W., Rossi, J., & Marcus, B. (1994). Stages of change for exercise: A comparison of an algorithm and a continuous measure. In Paper presented at the Annual Meeting of the Society For Behavioral Medicine. Boston, MA.

Rossi, J. (1992). Stages of change for 15 Health Risk Behaviors in an HMO Population. In 13th Annual Scientific Session of the Society of Behavioral Medicine. New York, NY.

Velicer, W., DiClemente, C., Prochaska, J., & Brandenburg, N. (1985). Decisional balance measure for assessing and predicting smoking status. *Journal of Personality and Social Psychology*, **48**, 1279–89.

Velicer, W., DiClemente, C., Rossi, J., & Prochaska, J. (1990). Relapse situations and self-efficacy: An integrative model. *Addictive Behaviors*, **15**, 271–83.

Velicer, W., Fava, J., Prochaska, J., Abrams, D., Emmons, K., & Pierce, J. (1995). Distribution of smokers by stage in three representative samples. *Preventive Medicine*, **24**, 401–411.

Velicer, W., Prochaska, J., Bellis, J., DiClemente, C., Rossi, J., Fava, J., & Steiger, J. (1993). An expert system intervention for smoking cessation. *Addictive Behaviors*, **18**, 269–90.

Velicer, W.F., Prochaska, J.O., Fava, J.L., Laforge, R.G., Rossi, J.S. (1999) Interactive versus non-interactive interventions and dose-response relationships for stage-matched smoking cessation programs in a managed care setting. *Health Psychology*, **18**, 21–28.

Velicer, W., Prochaska, J., Rossi, J., & Snow, M. (1992). Assessing outcome in smoking cessation studies. *Psychological Bulletin*, **111**, 23–41.

Chapter 3

Adherence in Primary Health Care Exercise Promotion Schemes

Adrian Taylor

Growing evidence within developed nations suggests that a large proportion of the population is at risk of developing health problems associated
with sedentary lifestyles (Bouchard et al, 1994). The proportion increases
with age (Young et al., 1997). For example, the Allied Dunbar National
Fitness Survey (ADNFS, 1992) revealed that 39% of males and 42% of
females, over 50 years of age, did less than 30 minutes of moderate
intensity activity, less than once a week. James (1995) and others have
also identified rapidly increasing obesity in the UK, similar to other western countries, largely explained by reduced energy expenditure rather
than increases in energy consumption. While technology facilitates a less
physically demanding existence, it becomes increasing necessary to develop strategies and design interventions to counter such change across
the whole population. A variety of intervention levels exist, including
mass media campaigns (Reid, 1996), the modification of fiscal policies,
the design of facilitating environments and community schemes,

Adherence Issues in Sport and Exercise. Edited by Stephen J. Bull.
© 1999 John Wiley & Sons Ltd.

modification of professional practice, and individual behavioural counselling and change strategies (Dishman, 1994; King, 1994; Leith & Taylor, 1992). The present chapter will focus on strategies originating within primary health care (PHC).

Over 70% of the population in the UK see their GP at least once a year and almost 95% do so over a 3 year period (Office of Population Concensuses and Surveys, 1995). Given the high esteem generally attached to GPs and health professionals working in PHC one may speculate that an opportunity exists for promoting healthy lifestyles and in particular, physical activity, to a large proportion of the population, across all age, gender, race, socio-economic status, and mental and physical health status levels. This approach may well have a significant impact on public health if patients both adopt and maintain a more active lifestyle.

Initially this chapter will examine the extent to which exercise promotion in PHC settings is occurring, and in what forms. This will be followed by an analysis of the factors which appear to influence the attempts to encourage behaviour change among patients. A critical review of the effectiveness of these interventions in PHC, for increasing physical activity and maintaining it, will then be presented. This will be followed by some implications for the practitioner, and finally some conclusions. The question of exercise adherence is therefore considered in terms of both adoption and initial increases, followed by maintenance.

HEALTH AND EXERCISE PROMOTION ACTIVITY IN PHC

Calnan & Williams (1993) reported a generally low status of health promotion activity among GPs in the UK. In the USA fewer than 50% of patients were routinely asked by their GP about their exercise habits (Henry, et al., 1987) though a variation from 15% to 84% was reported (Pender et al., 1994) with very few spending more than 3 to 5 minutes engaged in promoting physical activity. In the UK, Taylor (1994) reported that in a sample of 310 over 35 year olds, of whom 52% had done no moderate or vigorous intensity activity in the previous week, only 13% claimed to have been advised to exercise more by their GP. Nevertheless, a growing interest in promoting physical activity in PHC has occurred (Browne, 1997; Campbell, Browne & Waters, 1985; Godin & Shephard, 1990; Hammond, Brodie & Bundred, 1997; Patrick et al, 1997; P. Smith et al., 1996b; F. Smith & Iliffe, 1997).

Barriers to Exercise Promotion Activity

A variety of barriers exist for those working in PHC, particularly general practitioners, which appear to influence the decision to promote physical activity (Bull et al., 1995; Harsha et al., 1996; Long et al., 1996; Swinburn et al., 1997; Williford et al., 1992). Perhaps the most consistently reported has been that of time, within average GP-patient consultations of 7 to 15 minutes. Clearly time costs money. In an attempt to financially reward health promotion activity and merge public health interests with PHC in the UK, a new funding formula was introduced in 1989 (Department of Health and the Welsh Office, 1989; Williams et al, 1993). This innovation recently ceased to operate, though new funding arrangements look set to facilitate exercise promotion activity (e.g., lottery funding and 'healthy living centres'). Nevertheless, with GPs in the UK likely to gain even greater control over PHC budgets there may be little incentive for such activity when the benefits are more long-term. Pender et al., (1994) also noted that little remuneration exists in the USA for health promotion activities.

In addition to financial issues, prioritising attempts to influence a patient's lifestyle has several other important determinants including the moral views of the practitioner (e.g., 'it is the patient's decision to live how they wish'), and socio-economic perceptions (e.g., 'it isn't worth trying to change an old person's lifestyle'). A multidimensional examination of the determinants of why a member of the PHC team will or will not focus on health and exercise promotion is clearly important and a range of characteristics associated with the health professional and also the patient have been identified.

Findings from a study of nurses and GPs by McDowell et al. (1997) and McKenna et al. (1998) supported a review by Pender et al. (1994) which suggested that those PHC workers who exercised and held more positive attitudes towards exercise were up to four times more proactive in raising issues concerned with physical activity. In addition to personal habits, a PHC professional's self-efficacy, with respect to counselling patients, may also be an important determinant of exercise promotion activity (Williford et al., 1992). GPs are less likely to counsel about physical activity than other health behaviours (Long et al., 1996; Mullen & Tabak, 1989). Advice about smoking cessation or dietary fat control may be perceived to be easier to give than suggestions about adopting a safe and appropriate form of exercise, since early exercise guidelines focused on enhancing fitness through vigorous activity . This obviously raised important safety issues, necessitating rigorous screening. Concern about the appropriateness of vigorous activity for the majority of the population led the Active for Life Campaign, in the UK, to focus on providing those working in PHC with simpler messages about moderate intensity activity such as walking (Health Ecucation Authority, 1995a; 1996). Nevertheless, issues remain about the appropriate type, frequency, duration and intensity of activity for both 'healthy' and 'unhealthy' populations, in order to maximise physical and psychological benefits and reduce the risk of exercise-related morbidity and mortality (Gould, et al., 1995).

In terms of health professionals' attitudes towards health and exercise promotion, there are also differences in the extent to which inactivity and other facets of lifestyle are identified as important risk factors. For example, Steptoe and Wardle (1993) reported differences between countries within Europe, with health experts in the UK and Ireland less likely to endorse lifestyle–disease links than those from other countries. In a rare theoretically driven investigation of health professionals (excluding GPs), R.A. Smith (1998) identified perceived behaviour control and personal attitudes towards physical activity as the only components from the Theory of Planned Behaviour (Ajzen 1989) to predict intentions to promote physical activity.

The decision to offer opportunistic advice and/or provide health promotion literature is likely to be also dependent on the real or perceived receptiveness of the patient and the perceived benefits to the patient (Swinburn et al., 1997). Wallace et al. (1987) reported that 72% thought their doctor should be interested in their patients' exercise habits though doctors were more pessimistic in their appraisal of patient interest (Henry et al., 1987). For example, Reed et al. (1991) reported that 83% of a sample of family physicians in the USA believed that less than 50% of their patients would adhere to an exercise programme even if encouraged to do so. If patients seem unlikely to respond to advice or counselling one may expect that such practice will be less favoured by GPs in their busy caseload (i.e., the self-fulfilling prophecy; Rosenthal, 1974). In addition, GPs with a low belief in their own effectiveness when exercise counselling (outcome expectancy) limited the use of counselling (Mullen and Tabak, 1989). It may also seem inappropriate to advise patients, attending for diagnosis and treatment of an illness, to initiate an exercise programme, with perhaps only long-term benefits. Lifestyle change may simply not be on a patient's agenda at that time.

The shifting emphasis towards greater health promotion activity (Department of Health and the Welsh Office, 1989; Department of Health, 1995, 1998) has led to a change in roles and team membership within PHC. While GPs remain central to the initial diagnostic process and gatekeepers to some health promotion interventions and secondary health care, their opportunistic advice-giving role in promoting health may be somewhat limited (Stott et al., 1994). Other PHC professionals (e.g., practice nurses, health visitors, and specialist counsellors) may play a more effective role in behaviour change, with appropriate training and time to work with patients (McDowell et al., 1997).

There have been few studies designed to test the effectiveness of strategies to influence advice giving, among PHC workers. In one such study, Lewis and Lynch (1993) described research in which normative advice giving was monitored, followed by a period during which intervention doctors (trained to give a 2–3 minute protocol of advice on exercise) and control doctors (not trained) were compared. The simple protocol involved three steps of patient interaction, 'ASK', 'ASSESS', and 'ADVISE'. Training about the protocol involved just 15 minutes. Doctors in the intervention group increased advice giving from 21% to 80% while those in the control group increased from 30% to 40%.

Exercise Counselling

In reviewing the literature, or indeed in practice, it is not easy to differentiate between what is simply advice giving and what constitutes counselling. In terms of time, counselling may well involve a longer interaction although the example above, involving a 2–3 minute protocol of advice giving was not described as counselling by the authors. The two terms (advice and counselling) may also be differentiated by the locus of power within the practitioner–patient relationship. Advice giving is likely to be more authoritarian in nature, while counselling may imply a mutual alliance or client centred focus.

A significant initiative has emerged in the USA which involves a carefully designed exercise counselling strategy in PHC (Patrick et al, 1994a; 1994b). Physician-based Assessment and Counselling for Exercise (PACE) attempts to focus the practitioner on specific behaviour-change strategies using a simple client-centred approach, which takes only 3–5 minutes of interaction, in order to overcome many of the barriers previously highlighted. Prior to the consultation, a patient completes a brief assessment form (taking less than 1 minute) to identify 'stage of readiness to change' (Marcus et al., 1992; Prochaska & Di Clemente, 1983) and the PAR-Q (Shephard, 1988). The practitioner then negotiates behaviour change by systematically exploring perceived barriers to, and benefits from exercise, support from family and friends, and self-efficacy towards exercising. Three specific counselling protocol are used, matched to the stages of change (i.e., precontemplators, contemplators, and actives). At the end of the consultation patients may be given a prescription for exercise and a booklet on physical activity. This is followed by inexpensive brief communication by phone and/or postcard.

In a study of the effectiveness of training practitioners to conduct physical activity counselling, four physicians were selected to receive training (Marcus, et al., 1997). Prior to this, 25 patients (control group) were asked about their physicians exercise advice giving/counselling. After a 2 hour training session on using PACE with these physicians, a further 19 patients (experimental group) were asked about exercise-related physician counselling. Comparisons between the groups revealed that all patients in the experimental group had been spoken to about exercise and two-thirds had been given a prescription and written materials, whereas 32% of the controls had been spoken to about exercise and none had been given a prescription or written materials. Practitioners confirmed the acceptability of the intervention and reported a considerable increase in their counselling self-efficacy. The average time spent counselling was 5 minutes and was described as relatively brief. However, even this would serve as a significant barrier in the UK where average NHS consultations are only 7 minutes. It may also be difficult to entice GPs to attend a 2 hour training session.

In a much larger study, at ten locations across the USA with a diverse range of patients, the acceptability of Project PACE was assessed (Long et al., 1996). Once again, this involved an evaluation of a training programme, the PACE programme and materials, and 107 patients' perceptions of PACE. There were notable improvements in knowledge about physical activity, perceived counselling ability (self-efficacy), and use of exercise counselling. The PACE materials and programme materials were rated highly, although a major barrier to their use was identified as a lack of staff support. The researchers examined this organisational aspect in more detail and revealed that office staff, in practices where the PACE Programme worked effectively, were instrumental in ensuring that physicians engaged in exercise counselling. In particular, office staff ensured that forms were kept in convenient places, office staff had clear responsibilities for handing out PACE forms, and completed protocols were consistently placed in patient records. It was concluded that for successful implementation of the PACE programme training of office staff was essential. The patients were largely in favour of the PACE approach to counselling and the materials. Although the study revealed a favourable response from PHC staff and patients, the authors were rightly aware of the bias inherent in the research due to the self-selected sample of practitioners.

The use of client-centred counselling within PHC is becoming widely accepted in the UK and elsewhere (Calfas et al., 1996; Kohl et al., 1998). For example, the idea of matching strategies for behavioural change to the patient's stage of readiness to change has received widespread attention through the Helping People Change training programme (Health Education Authority, 1994). Further research on the effects of client-centred counselling such as brief motivational interviewing, originating in the field of addiction counselling (Miller & Rollnick, 1991; Rollnick et al., 1992, 1993), is necessary.

Exercise Prescription Schemes

Other professionals, outside the PHC setting, may also play an important role in promoting exercise (Health Education Authority, 1995b, 1996). In a review of physical activity promotion in PHC, in the UK, commissioned by the Health Education Authority (Biddle et al., 1994; Fox et al., 1997), 157 schemes were identified in April 1994. Only 32% involved management by the PHC team and the remaining 68% involved referral by a member of the PHC team to a public or private leisure centre. A further 35 schemes, all involving referral to leisure centres, were planned for initiation at that time, indicating the degree of interest in this approach. A UK audit by Chichester Institute of Higher Education in 1995/1996 identified over 300 leisure centre-based schemes (personal communication, 1997). Despite this rapidly growing popularity, Fox et al. (1997) noted that leisure centre-based schemes could only have very limited impact on public health since no scheme involved more than 1% of a general practice caseload. However, one may speculate that such an intervention may have a multiplier effect through referees advocating exercise in the community to friends and relatives.

Biddle et al. (1994) provided a useful series of case studies which identified the variety of, and most common, schemes. Those schemes managed by the PHC team usually involved specific exercise promotion clinics or exercise sessions within the health centre, plus advice about free-living physical activity. In contrast, those schemes involving referral outside the PHC setting most frequently involved sending low to moderate risk patients, with an exercise prescription, to a local authority operated leisure centre in the community. This intervention may well be restricted to only a few countries who have an extensive provision of publicly operated facilities. As an example, one of the first such schemes emerged in Hailsham, East Sussex in 1990, with the enthusiasm of a GP and a conveniently sited adjacent leisure centre. Following the appointment of a nurse by the local Leisure Services (rather than by the Health Services), to co-ordinate the scheme, within 4 years, 83 GPs were referring about 30 new patients per week from within a 20 mile radius to the centre. By the end of 1996 approximately 3000 patients had been referred, which is over 5% of the population of Hailsham and surrounding areas.

Regular workshops attended by health and leisure centre professionals from across the UK, led by the Hailsham scheme personnel, provided a significant catalyst to the growth of such schemes, nationally. As such, many schemes follow similar protocol to those described in the operations manual (Wealden District Council., 1993). Typically, a patient is identified by a member of the PHC team, but usually the GP, and given a card which indicates various physical indices (e.g., blood pressure) and reason(s) for referral. Various health problems, similar to those identified on the PAR-Q (Shephard, 1988) are listed as criteria for non-referral. Upon presentation of the prescription card at the leisure centre, an initial appointment is arranged. This then involves further screening, an interview about past exercise history, future goals with respect to exercise and specific outcomes, and the design of a tailored exercise programme, lasting 20 sessions over 10 weeks. The programme is based on a submaximal test and consideration of health status. Exercise sessions of up to an hour typically involve aerobic activity on treadmills, cycle ergometers, rowing machines and stairs. Patients pay at a subsidised rate each time they attend. Specially trained exercise leaders are available at the centre to offer advice, encouragement and to facilitate the self-monitoring process. Mid-point and end-point assessments are also conducted, with the final evaluation being returned to the GP.

In contrast, the Stockport scheme (Stockport Leisure Services, 1994) allows patients to select and join 15 different community-based activities. Monitoring a patient's progress at the health centre is an important feature. Free admittance is given to patients receiving social benefits.

A number of peer reviewed and in-house reports have been published which refer to the appeal that leisure centre-based schemes generate among patients. For example, in the Stockport scheme, Lord and Green (1995) reported that 60% of those given prescriptions attended an initial consultation at the health centre, although initial attendance at the 15 activities in different locations was lower. Taylor (1996) reported that 87% attended the leisure centre for their initial appointment, although patients were referred as part of a study, following a mailed invitation and one hour assessment at the health centre. Many schemes do not enable such analysis since records of referees are not maintained at the health centre. Davey and Cochrane (1998) reported difficulty in recruitment to a community-based, multi-centre programme. Only 20% ($n = 600$) of those recommended to attend one session per week responded. It is very likely that the recruitment strategy into such schemes will influence patient responses (Fielder, Shorney & Wright, 1995; King, Harris & Haskell, 1994), although it would appear from numbers of referrals and qualitative reports that patients are generally quite positive about being referred (Taylor, 1996; Fox et al., 1997).

Reports by Wealden District Council (1995, 1996) provided detailed information from two audits in the period from January 1994 to May 1996 about the characteristics of patients referred (which is partly indicative of those attracted to the scheme). These involved 729 and 627 successive patients, respectively. The most common reasons for referral were for weight management, hypertension, and mental health. From the second audit, 66% were females, the mean age was 52 (with 80% between the ages of 30–70 years), and the mean body mass index was 29.3 (with 38% greater than 30, i.e., obese). Mean blood pressure was 135/83 mm Hg (systolic/ diastolic) for the whole sample (with 40% greater than 140 mm Hg SBP, and 30% greater than 90 mm Hg DBP). From a submaximal treadmill test, predicted VO_2 max. was 28.7 ml $kg^{-1}min^{-1}$ for males and 24.1 for females.

FACTORS INFLUENCING THE DEVELOPMENT OF EXERCISE PROMOTION SCHEMES IN PHC

In the next section, attention will turn briefly to the factors contributing to the establishment of exercise promotion schemes in both the PHC setting and also at leisure centres. Biddle et al. (1994) reported that a key factor was the presence of at least one enthusiastic person to promote physical activity since schemes were rarely part of a strategic plan within PHC. A variety of other factors seem to also be important and are listed under the headings, staffing, facilities and processes in Table 3.1.

Table 3.1 Advantages and disadvantages of primary health care-based and leisure centre-based exercise programmes

Intervention	Factor	Advantages	Disadvantages
PHC based	Staffing	Counselling skills Ethical awareness Safety skills Exercise and health knowledge	Not exercise focused Competing demands Mixed interest by staff
	Facilities	Can serve groups Sessions run when needed	Limited equipment and facility flexibility
	Process	Liaison within PHC Tailored to need	Limited social support Limited post-programme Competing resources
Leisure-centre-based	Staffing	Exercise testing and prescription skills Motivational skills	Narrow focus on fitness Low skill base with 'unhealthy' clients Mixed safety skills Low credibility with GPs
	Facilities	Existing facilities Various options	Off-peak availability 'Sporty' environment
	Process	Community-link Inter-agency sharing Empowerment	Limited PHC liaison Uni-risk approach Funding issues

A PHC-managed scheme may be able to employ trained health professionals or counsellors familiar with behaviour change strategies, though such skills may not readily be transferable to modifying physical activity (cf. adoption versus cessation of behaviours). Where exercise specialists are employed, an understanding of the risks associated with a variety of disease states is likely to be beneficial. It may be more acceptable to pay salaries commensurate with this level of training in a PHC setting than in a leisure centre.

Health professionals are very aware of ethical issues such as confidentiality of patient records and treatment plans, which may not always be the case in leisure centres. Violation of routine ethical procedures may well limit the referral of patients to exercise programmes outside the jurisdiction of the PHC team. Similarly, GPs and health professionals are particularly concerned about the safety of patients in a leisure centre. This may be one of the key barriers to the establishment of such schemes. The current minefield of exercise-related qualifications in the UK provides little comfort for the cautious GP. This has prompted some schemes, subsidised by Health Authorities, to develop, in partnership with Institutes of Higher Education, training courses for staff intending to work with referred patients (e.g., East Sussex, GP Referral Training Programme, University of Brighton). While exercise specialists may well have greater understanding and knowledge of the processes involved in initiating and maintaining a programme of exercise, they may lack the broader skills and knowledge to counsel on other lifestyle facets such as stress, diet and smoking.

In a study of PHC staff involved in referring patients to a leisure centre, interviews were conducted to determine why they had decided to join the scheme, what benefits they thought patients would accrue and how they were selected (Smith et al., 1996). Twenty-three respondents (16 GPs, 4 practice managers, 2 practice nurses, and 1 receptionist) from 10 referring practices in inner London took part. Respondents had been attracted to the scheme largely due to the potential for health benefits of exercise among their patients. However, restrictions, imposed by the health service managers, on the type of patient who could be referred (i.e., 'low risk' due to concerns about safety at the leisure centre) frustrated the PHC referrers. They believed that those at greater risk (not being referred) had most to gain from an exercise prescription. Psycho-social gain and relaxation were identified as the main benefits of the scheme. This study offers an example of how some of the advantages and disadvantages, identified in Table 3.1, influenced PHC staff within the referral process.

Fox et al. (1997) identified only a few schemes in the UK in which exercise sessions took place within a PHC setting. In these circumstances there was an opportunity to run classes for groups with specific needs, though the environment may not have encouraged social interaction and community integration, often observed in leisure centres. In contrast, patients referred to leisure centres are usually limited to attending only during off-peak hours, and even then they compete for space with non-referred patients. Leisure centres with swimming pools and other facilities do have the opportunity to run sessions in groups and offer a choice of activity but this requires greater organisation.

EFFECTS OF INTERVENTIONS ON PATIENT ACTIVITY LEVELS

Multi-factorial Studies

Recent large randomised controlled trials have reported on the effects of multifactorial health promotion interventions in PHC, within which exercise advice/counselling was incorporated (Cupples & McKnight, 1994; Imperial Cancer Research Fund OXCHECK Study Group, 1994, 1995). The former involved angina patients and the latter selected patients from the general population. Both studies examined change in a wide range of outcomes including physical (e.g., cholesterol, blood pressure, body mass index) and behavioural self-report measures (e.g., smoking, diet, alcohol intake, and exercise).

In the Northern Ireland study (Cupples & McKnight, 1994) only the intervention group ($n = 342$) were 'given practical relevant advice regarding cardiovascular risk factors' by a health visitor in the patient's health centre or own home. Clearly this was not seen as an important factor as data were not reported for each site of the intervention. The length of consultation was also not reported, making an estimation of cost-effectiveness impossible. Intervention patients were 'reviewed at four monthly intervals and given appropriate health education.' A researcher assessed change after two years. The findings revealed that the proportion doing less than five sessions of at least 20 min exercise per week dropped from 48% to 40% in the intervention group and increased from 42% to 54% in the control group. A significant difference was also reported for change with the proportion increasing activity in the intervention group and control group being 34% and 21%, respectively. In contrast, 28% and 54% decreased the amount of activity they did in the intervention and control groups, respectively.

In the Bedfordshire OXCHECK study (Imperial Cancer Research Fund OXCHECK Study Group, 1994, 1995) results were presented for a one year and three year follow-up, respectively. Comparisons were made between subjects attending a follow-up health check (intervention group) and those attending their first health check. Health checks by nurses in a health centre involved an introduction (3 minutes), information gathering (14 min), clinical measurement (12 min), and target negotiation and health education (15 min). Findings revealed that 5.1% fewer patients (7.1% males and 3.6% females) in the intervention group ($n = 2136$), compared with the control group ($n = 3988$), were doing less than one vigorous intensity session per month, after one year. At the 3 year follow-up, the statistically significant difference was 3.3% (5.6% males and 1.4% females), still in favour of the intervention group. The new public health message about increasing moderate activity (Killoran, Fentem & Casperson, 1994; Wimbush, 1994), which has been promoted since this study, means that both the advice given by the nurses and the data collected in this study is rather meaningless and redundant. If other physical activity data were collected within the study it would be useful to conduct further analyses on the number of 30 minute sessions of moderate exercise per week, for example.

Findings from the INSURE Project (Lodgson et al., 1989) in the USA, with 4500 subjects, suggested that 15 minutes of education and counselling on risk reduction (not just through exercise) could have a small effect on activity one year later. Following the physicians' intervention, 35.9% of patients began a programme of vigorous activity (at least once a week), compared with 28.2% of a matched control group (with no trained physicians). It was not clear whether the small increases in activity would have any clinical significance, in terms of health outcomes. Also, the findings are based on only a 28% response rate at follow-up. It is very likely that non-respondents changed to a lesser extent (see Taylor, 1996).

The Johns Hopkins Medicare Preventive Services Demonstration Project (Burton et al., 1995) involved a well-conducted large randomised controlled trial, with good generalisability. Over 3000 sedentary older patients were involved. One year after discussion with a physician about smoking, alcohol or exercise (89%), no effects of the intervention were observed.

In a Swedish randomised controlled trial, change over 18 months following either 'usual health advice' ($n = 342$) or 'intensive health care advice' ($n = 339$) was compared (Lindholm et al., 1995). The latter involved six group sessions (including about eight patients per group) with a trained health care professional (doctor or nurse) in a health centre. Sessions involved discussion following a video dealing with myocardial infarction risk factors (with one on exercise). Subjects were selected on the basis of high CHD risk. In contrast to the previous two studies there was no difference between the two groups in change in physical activity, categorized on a five-point scale from doing more than 30 minutes of daily moderate activity to doing none.

Most of the above studies involved huge financial commitment to deliver the interventions, which is not typically allocated by health service managers. The OXCHECK Study Group concluded 'The benefits of systematic health promotion in primary health care are real, but must be weighed against the costs in relation to other priorities' (p. 1099, 1995). Also, the multi-faceted approach may have led to watered-down effects on any single behavioural change target. Such studies also leave an uncertainty about what actually caused the change and how much time was devoted to changing specific behaviours. For example, in the Swedish study weight management counselling may or may not have included an exercise promotion element, in addition to the exercise session.

Other multifaceted studies also had important methodological limitations. Kelly (1988) reported a significant increase in physical activity following lifestyle education, but after only 6 weeks, and this was based on an unvalidated telephone survey. In a UK study, Dowell et al. (1996) reported that 2 years after a health check, a largely sedentary group of over 1500 patients actually decreased their exercise. The study was limited in that the focus was only on vigorous intensity exercise, assessed by a mailed survey.

Exercise-only Advice and Counselling

Harris et al. (1989) reviewed the evidence for the effectiveness of exercise counselling in PHC on change in physical activity and concluded that little evidence existed. The few studies had a variety of methodological limitations which made interpretation difficult. More recently, Hillsdon and Thorogood (1996; and Hillsdon et al., 1995), in a review of randomised controlled trials to specifically evaluate free-living exercise promotion schemes, reported no studies in which the intervention was PHC-based. In contrast, Eaton and Menard (1998) conducted a systematic review of clinical trials (three of which involved randomised assignment to intervention or control group) in which the efficacy of primary care office-based exercise promotion was investigated, and reviewed the findings from eight trials (and 13 981 patients). Five of these were mentioned above, but a further three involved an exercise intervention in isolation.

Lewis and Lynch (1993) examined the change in activity of patients consulting with a physician trained to offer advice in a specific way or not, in Colorado (see earlier discussion). Those receiving 2–3 minutes of exercise advice from trained physicians increased their weekly minutes of exercising by 132 minutes more than the patients not consulting a trained physician. Training also led to an 8% greater increase in patients doing some exercise. Interestingly, the increase was due to longer exercise sessions rather than more sessions.

Swinburn et al. (1997) reported how GPs in New Zealand had enthusiastically adopted the idea of a written 'Green prescription' for exercise (mainly free-living walking). They reported on a randomised controlled trial to comparing the effectiveness of GPs' giving verbal advice to 239 patients against written advice (a Green Prescription) ($n = 252$) in New Zealand (Swinburn et al., 1998). Sedentary patients were opportunistically selected by the GP and 79% were advised to walk. The intervention took an average of 5.1 minutes. Follow-up telephone interviews after 6 weeks revealed that for both groups in combination, the proportion of patients doing some recreational physical activity increased from 54% to 81%. There was a significant difference between the groups with a 14% greater increase among the written advice group. Similar changes were observed among both males and females. No differences were observed between the two groups in terms of change in minutes of walking, sport or other activity. One limitation with this study was the relatively brief follow-up period, although the authors do have limited data to show that almost half those initially exercising more were still maintaining it after 11 months (personal communication, 1997).

However, the cost to the health practice/GP for the time to 'quantify, discuss and prescribe exercise for each patient' was remunerated as part of the study. In focus group interviews, GPs were sceptical about whether they would find the time to prescribe without an incentive. Clearly, research needs to focus on strategies which have ecological validity, although contrived interventions, if carefully costed, can lead the way to policy formation, strategic planning and wider implementation. The idea of a 'Green Prescription' in New Zealand looks set to become common practice following this pilot research.

The PACE intervention has been previously described. Calfas et al. (1996) reported the effects of counselling on sedentary patients' walking levels after 4–6 weeks. The intervention group increased their walking by an average of just over 4 minutes per day more than the control group. However, the average of 11 minutes per day would seem of limited health benefit. Long-term change would likely be even less, and the health practice staff involved in the study all volunteered, thereby suggesting limited efficacy and generalisability.

In conclusion, there appears to be some short-term, but minimal long-term, exercise adherence, across studies using a wide range of measures, research designs, and interventions.

Exercise Prescription Schemes

A number of in-house audits of the effectiveness of GP referral schemes emerged in the early 1990s (e.g., Stockport Leisure Services, 1994) and even more anecdotal claims about the success of these innovations. The media grasped this information indiscriminately with little understanding of the likely confounds associated with such research protocols. It seemed that the onus was on leisure centres to 'show that such schemes worked' in order to attract health service subsidies for referred patients. No doubt, some centres also wished to maintain financial support for such schemes, from within their own leisure services, even though there was growing concern that the resources needed to operate a scheme were greater than initially believed. Also, patient adherence and subsequent membership of leisure centres was not as high as originally claimed. Leisure centre audits also focused on adherence to the 20 session scheme over 10 weeks, whereas health services were more interested in long-term change in all forms of physical activity. This led Iliffe et al. (1994) to caution PHC staff to consider effectiveness before setting up or entering partnerships with leisure centres.

Biddle et al. (1994) identified only one randomised controlled trial underway which has since been completed (Taylor, 1996, 1998). A large randomised controlled trial in Sheffield, funded by the HEA, is due to report its findings shortly (Cochrane & Davey, 1998).

The study by Taylor et al. (1998), examined both adherence to the 10 week exercise programme at the Hailsham Lagoon leisure centre, East Sussex, and also moderate and vigorous activity (using a 7-day recall measure; Blair, 1984) at baseline, 8, 16, 26 and 37 weeks. 345 patients were mailed an invitation to enter the study from the GP and researcher team on the basis of having at least one CHD risk factor (from hypertension, smoking or overweight) identified in their computerised records. Sixty smokers (35% of the 174 invited smokers, cf. 48% of non-smokers invited), 71 hypertensives (38% of the 188 invited hypertensives, cf. 45% of non-hypertensives invited), and 107 overweight patients (45% of the 239 invited overweight patients, cf. 33% of non-overweight patients invited) were randomised. After attending an initial assessment, 142 patients were randomly assigned to a referral ($n = 97$) or non-referral group ($n = 45$). At the above weeks, all patients were invited back to the health centre for assessments. 40 (41%) completed the study in the exercise group and 31 (69%) in the control group. Of those randomized, 27 (45%) smokers, 52 (48%) overweight and 43 (61%) hypertensive patients completed the study. 87% of referees used the prescription and 28% (45% of obese patients) did at least 15 sessions. The mean attendance rate was 9.1 sessions. Referees only did significantly more moderate and vigorous activity at week 8, and more vigorous activity at week 16, and the percentage doing some moderate or vigorous activity at 37 weeks had returned to baseline. There were no changes in the control group. On the basis of the stages of change measure of exercise, the proportion describing themselves as in the active or maintenance stage increased from 36% at baseline to 97% and 61% at 8 and 37 weeks, respectively, compared with 23%, 35%, and 23% at the three assessments in the control group.

Adherence levels from this study did not therefore match previously claimed figures. It may have been the case that, because patients were actually referred by the researcher immediately following the baseline assessment at the health centre, rather than the GP, this led to reduced adherence. However, concurrent data (which did not include patients referred through the study), from a previously described large audit with 729 patients, revealed a 22% completion rate (a slightly different criterion measure but one which enables some comparison) (Wealden District Council, 1995). In the second Wealden audit (1996) of 627 referred patients, conducted after the study by Taylor (1996), completion rates had increased to 43%.

In a recent study in the UK, Stevens et al. (1998) conducted a randomised controlled trial to compare the effects of a GP sending an invitation to patients (45–74 year olds) to visit an 'exercise development officer' at a leisure centre, versus mailing information about local leisure centres. Of the 126 (35%) in the invitation group who attended the first consultation, 91 returned for a follow-up session with the exercise officer, after a 10 week personalised exercise programme. Eight months later, patients in both groups received a mailed questionnaire to assess activity change. There was a net 10% reduction in the proportion of people classified as sedentary in the intervention group compared with the control group. Also, the intervention group increased the number of exercise sessions per week by 1.5 more than the control group. Clearly, there were some major limitations with the study, particularly concerning non-response bias and the use of a self-administered one month recall physical activity survey.

Factors Influencing Adherence

Within the controlled trial (Taylor, 1996), quantitative analyses revealed that those at baseline who were smokers, were not overweight (BMI < 25), had lower body fat, and were less active, had lower adherence levels. Smokers attended 6.7 of the 20 sessions compared with 10.8 for non-smokers. The finding that overweight, particularly obese referees, and those with greater body fat, attended more sessions was somewhat surprising in light of previous reports of a negative relationship between weight/body fat and adherence (Dishman, 1994). The progressive, tailored exercise programme offered at the leisure centre demonstrates the possibilities for using diagnosed health risk as a motivational source for exercising. Surprisingly, there was no relationship between measures on the four abbreviated subscales of Physical Self-Perception Profile (Fox,

1997) at baseline, and subsequent adherence to the prescribed programme. Similarly, initial perceived barriers to exercise were not related to adherence (Taylor, 1996).

Qualitative attributions for not attending the prescribed exercise sessions included lack of time and conflicts with other roles, programme factors, including a busy, noisy and hot environment at the gym, with sometimes limited support from staff and boredom with the equipment. Personal attributions included injury or illness, fatigue and embarrassment. These largely confirmed independent interviews in the first Wealden audit (Wealden District Council, 1995). Interestingly, analysis of individual exercise profiles during the study revealed that a number of referees initially reduced their normal physical activity patterns (e.g., walking to town) and replaced that with gym sessions. At the end of the referral period they returned to their initial activity patterns.

In Wealden's 1996 audit, a number of factors appeared to be related to programme completion though reporting of statistical analyses were insufficient to enable any conclusions to be drawn. Completion rates varied between referring GPs from less than 30% to over 50%. Because many patients are referred for more than one reason it was somewhat difficult to interpret differences in completion rates between single referral categories. Nevertheless, those referred for hypertension ($n = 73$), asthma ($n = 22$), arthritis ($n = 61$) had completion rates above 53%, whereas those referred for psychological/stress ($n = 90$), general fitness ($n = 92$), weight loss ($n = 121$) and injury rehabilitation ($n = 40$) had completion rates below 39%.

Taylor's evaluation (1996) involved a snapshot of the Hailsham GP referral scheme, with patients being referred over an 18 month period. Changes in the operation of the scheme took place soon afterwards, in a number of ways, in response to some of the observations and findings reported above. These are shown in Table 3.2

Hillsdon & Thorogood (1996) were critical of GP exercise prescription schemes on several counts. Firstly, from a review of a broad range of exercise promotion schemes they suggested that adherence rates would be

Table 3.2 Revised programme characteristics of a leisure-centre-based exercise prescription scheme

1. Exercise leaders attended health authority/university training programme
2. Training programme incorporated counselling workshop
3. New referees cut from 30 to 10 per week
4. New agenda set to encourage free-living activity (not just gym-based)
5. Financial incentive offered to leisure centre for every patient completing programme
6. GPs better trained on inclusion and exclusion criteria for referees

highest if exercise were not dependent on a facility and involved personal instruction and continued brief support. Clearly, leisure-centre-based schemes are facility based, and support may end at the end of the programme. The idea of exercising in a leisure centre is also novel to most referees and can not automatically be included in a person's lifestyle. Secondly, the words 'exercise prescription' suggest a power base in the hands of a GP, rather than an alliance or shared decision-making process between the GP and patient to initiate exercise. There is general agreement in health promotion that dictating behaviour change may be ineffective (Hunt & Hillsdon, 1996), and yet referred patients are generally positive about the idea of being referred and GPs/health professionals have been shown to be enthusiastic towards them. Thirdly, GP exercise referral schemes have tended to focus on fitness gain through more vigorous activity, which may not facilitate long-term adherence. Hillsdon et al. (1995) provided evidence for better adherence to moderate rather than vigorous intensity exercise.

As adherence rates appear to increase in GP referral schemes, due to better training and refined patient selection procedures, there may well be an argument that behaviour change can be made in the short term. The challenge though is for schemes to demonstrate that their programmes facilitate long-term change before health service managers are more enthused about offering financial support. Within the 10 operational schemes in East Sussex, adherence rates are highest where a smaller number of patients are referred, and yet these schemes are less likely to have any impact on public health. Carefully conducted research is necessary to evaluate the effects of modifying a variety of factors on long-term behaviour change.

These factors may include:

1. Health and leisure professional counselling skills.
2. Exercise protocol such as varying intensity and duration of prescriptions.
3. Establish a more formalised social support process during exercise programmes, which links into other community-based exercise opportunities after the programme.
4. The use of a wide range of cognitive, stimulus control, reinforcement control, and relapse-prevention strategies within the leisure centre, delivered by trained exercise counsellors.
5. The matching of counselling strategy to patient's stage of readiness to change a wide range of daily physical activity opportunities, during the exercise programme. The stages of change model has been limited by defining exercise as a singular behaviour, rather than a wide range of cumulative activity opportunities.
6. Offering exercise prescription schemes at times when full-time workers can attend.

PRACTICAL IMPLICATIONS

In summarising the text so far, in the form of practical implications, it may be useful to adopt Green and Kreuter's (1991) Precede–Proceed Model for Health Promotion. Within phase 4 of the Model they suggest three important targets for change, preceding increases in health behaviours (physical activity), namely, predisposing factors (e.g., knowledge, attitudes, beliefs, values and perceptions), reinforcing factors (e.g., attitudes and behaviours of health professionals and others), and enabling factors (e.g., availability of resources, referrals, and rules or protocol, and service structures).

Patient's Predisposing Factors

Earlier reference to the self-fulfilling prophecy (Rosenthal, 1974) served to identify a key process which would appear to be prevalent in PHC. That is, patients may bring verbal and non-verbal cues (beliefs, attitudes, values, perceptions) to the PHC setting (in single consultations or from a series of interactions) which provide the health professional with a low expectation for successful change in health and exercise behaviours. The research evidence suggests that this low expectancy of change influences the emphasis placed on health and exercise promotion activity. Awareness and understanding of this process is essential for health professionals.

Health Professional as Reinforcer

There is clearly a need to enhance the health professionals' personal attitudes towards healthy lifestyles. In particular, GPs are important figureheads from whom patients expect to receive advice and counselling on health-promoting behaviours. Further work is necessary to raise exercise promoting activity up the agenda of health professionals.

Interestingly, Cohen et al. (1994) reported on the methods being employed within a large randomised controlled trial in the USA. This study was designed to examine the effectiveness of matching strategies to increase health promotion activity among physicians to their stage of readiness to counsel patients on cancer-related health behaviours. There was no mention by Cohen and colleagues about changing physicians' exercise-related interventions, but clearly, within continuing medical education, this approach may be useful to further the promotion of exercise in PHC.

One further approach in changing health professional's practice has involved action research and is increasingly being reported in the literature and other forums (Hart & Bond, 1996; Gilbourne & Taylor, 1996). Indeed,

Chapter 10 provides a detailed examination of this area. While many forms of action research exist, one underlying principle is to avoid imposing external wishes for change on a practitioner. Through phases of external observation, and encouraged self-reflection, a practitioner may initiate behaviour change (in this case, a greater emphasis on appropriate exercise promotion activities within PHC) without feeling that a researcher or health service manager is dictating the change. In some ways the principles of client-centred counselling parallel those of action research.

Enabling Factors

The Health Education Authority (1995b, 1996) have made important contributions to understanding the role of structural and strategic changes necessary to enable exercise promotion to occur within the UK. Indeed, GP exercise prescription schemes have been a good example of how multi-agency (i.e., Health and Leisure Services) approaches can work. Expansion of further partnerships between Social Services, local government, and PHC offer exciting possibilities for the promotion of physical activity. Perhaps the most important need within health authorities is to establish a physical activity policy, which may serve to influence funding decisions made at a variety of levels, but particularly within PHC.

With increasing emphasis on evidence-based medicine, it has become harder rather than easier to attract PHC money into exercise promotion activity (e.g., time spent on counselling, or subsidising GP exercise referral schemes). There is simply a lack of well-conducted evaluations of exercise promotions schemes which provides evidence of best practice (Biddle et al., 1994; See Tai et al., 1997). Without 'seed corn' money to conduct such research, the situation seems unlikely to change dramatically in the near future. On a more positive note, the opportunity to use lottery money in the UK to establish and evaluate the effectiveness of 'healthy living centres' may open up new opportunities for promoting physical activity within PHC.

CONCLUSIONS

1. A greater proportion of health professionals in PHC can become more receptive to the promotion of physical activity through training.
2. Strategic planning is necessary to facilitate the promotion of physical activity by PHC staff and remove some of the real and perceived structural barriers (Owen, 1996).

3. PHC-based counselling interventions which are simple to use, brief, and have good administrative support can be effective in increasing patients' physical activity levels. Simple support materials which allow quick assessment of patients' physical activity level and stage of readiness to change are likely to be well received by health professionals (Buxton et al., 1996).
4. GP exercise on prescription schemes can provide an important exercise experience for sedentary patients. However, strategies need to be implemented which maximise the likelihood of long-term behaviour change.
5. The greatest health benefits may be possible among patients who are at higher risk. It is therefore essential for leisure centre staff (exercise professionals) to be adequately trained to work with both the physical and psychological characteristics of moderate-risk referred patients.
6. The focus has largely been on the physical benefits of GP exercise referral schemes. Such schemes offer great potential in the treatment of mental health problems, enhancing psychological wellness and quality of life among patients of all ages. Separate adherence issues exist for patients with different needs.
6. Further research is needed which addresses the cost-effectiveness of different approaches to exercise promotion in primary health care, including simple advice giving with written supportive literature, phone calls, mailed reminders, brief and longer exercise counselling, PHC-based exercise programmes, leisure-centre-based exercise programmes, and community-based more flexible schemes.

REFERENCES

Ajzen, I. (1989). *Attitudes, Personality, and Behaviour*. Milton Keynes, UK: Open University Press.

Allied Dunbar National Fitness Survey: A Summary Report (1992). Sports Council and Health Education Authority.

Biddle, S. Fox, K. & Edmunds, L. (1994). *Physical Activity Promotion in Primary Health Care in England*. London: Health Education Authority.

Blair, S. N. (1984). How to assess exercise habits and physical fitness. In J.D. Matarazzo, S. M. Weiss, A.A. Herd, N.E. Miller, & S. M. Weiss (eds.) *Behavioural Health: A Handbook of Health Enhancement and Disease Prevention*. New York: J. Wiley (pp. 424–47).

Bouchard, C., Shephard, R.J. & Stephens, T. (eds.) (1994). *Physical Activity, Fitness & Health: International Proceedings and Consensus Statement*. Champaign, IL: Human Kinetics.

Browne, D. (1997). Exercise by prescription. *Journal of the Royal Society of Health*, **117**(1), 52–55.

Bull, F.C., Schipper, E.C., Jamrozik, K. & Blanksby, B.A. (1995). Beliefs and behaviour of general practitioners regarding promotion of physical activity. *Australian Journal of Public Health*, **19**, 300–4.

Burton, L.C., Paglia, M.J., German, P.S., Shapiro, S., & Damiano, A.M. (1995). The effect among older persons of a general preventive visit on three health behaviours: smoking, excessive alcohol drinking, and sedentary lifestyle. *Preventive Medicine*, **24**, 492–7.

Buxton, K., Wyse, J., & Mercer, T. (1996). How applicable is the stages of change model to exercise behaviour? A review. *Health Education Journal*, **55**, 239–57.

Calfas, K.J., Long, B.J. & Sallis, J.F. (1996). A controlled trial of physician counselling to promote the adoption of physical activity. *Preventive Medicine*, **25**(3), 225–233.

Calnan, M. & Williams, S. (1993). Coronary heart disease prevention in general practice: the practices and views of a national sample of general practitioners, *Health Education Journal*, **52**, 197–203.

Campbell, M.J., Browne, D. & Waters, W.E. (1985). Can GPs influence exercise habits? A controlled trial. *British Medical Journal*, **290**, 1043–6.

Cochrane, T. & Davey, R. (1998). Evaluation of exercise prescription for 25 general practices and a large leisure complex in Sheffield. *Journal of Sport Science*, **16**, 17–18.

Cohen, S.J., Halvorson, H.W., & Gosselink, C. A. (1994). Changing physician behaviour to improve disease prevention. *Preventive Medicine*, **23**, 284–291.

Cupples, M.E. & McKnight, A. (1994). Randomised controlled trial of health promotion in general practice for patients at high cardiovacular risk. *British Medical Journal*, **309**, 993–996.

Davey, R. & Cochrane, T. (1998). General practice community-based exercise programmes for sedentary adults over 65 years of age. *Journal of Sport Science*, **16**, 18.

Department of Health (1995). *The Health of the Nation: More People, More Active, More Often. Physical Activity in England, a Consultation Paper.* London: DoH.

Department of Health (1998). *Our Healthier Nation. Consultative Green Paper.* London: HMSO.

Department of Health and the Welsh Office (1989). *General Practice in the National Health Service: a New Contract.* London: DoH and Welsh Office.

Dishman R. K. (Ed.) (1994). *Advances in Exercise Adherence.* Champaign, IL: Human Kinetics.

Dowell, A.C., Ochera, J.J., Hilton, S.R., Bland, J.M., Harris, T., Jones, D.R., & Katbamna, S. (1996). Prevention in practice: results of a 2-year follow-up of routine health promotion interventions in general practice. *Family Practice*, **13**, 357–362.

Eaton, C.B. & Menard, L.M. (1998). A systematic review of physical activity promotion in primary care office settings. *British Journal of Sports Medicine*, **32**, 11–16.

Fielder H, Shorney S, Wright D. (1995). Lessons from a pilot study on prescribing exercise. *Health Education Journal*, **54**, 445–52.

Fox, K. (1997). *The Physical Self: From Motivation to Well-being*. Champaign, IL: Human Kinetics.

Fox, K., Biddle, S., Edmunds, L. & Bowler, I. (1997). Physical activity promotion through primary health care in England. *British Journal of General Practice*, **47**, 367–9.

Gilbourne, D. & Taylor, A.H. (1996). Rehabilitation experiences of injured athletes and their perceptions of a task oriented goal-setting programme: The application of an action research design. *Journal of Sports Sciences*, **13**, 54–5.

Godin, G. & Shephard, R.J. (1990). An evaluation of the potential role of the physician in influencing community exercise behaviour. *American Journal of Health Promotion*, **4**, 225–9.

Gould, M.N., Thorogood, M. Iliffe, S. & Morris, J.N. (1995). Promoting exercise in primary care: measuring the knowledge gap. *Health Education Journal*, **54**, 304–11.

Green, L.W. & Kreuter, M.W. (1991). *Health Promotion Planning: An Educational and Environmental Approach*. London: Mayfield.

Hammond, J.M., Brodie, D.A., & Bundred, P.E. (1997). Exercise on prescription: guidelines for health professionals. *Health Promotion International*, **12**(1), 33–41.

Harris, S.S., Caspersen, C.J., DeFries, G.H., & Estes, E. H. (1989). Physical activity counseling for healthy adults as a primary preventive intervention in the clinical setting: Report from the US Preventive Services Task Force, *Journal of the American Medical Association*, **261**(24), 3590–8.

Harsha, D.M., Saywell, R.M., Thygerson, S., & Panozzo, J. (1996). Physician factors affecting patient willingness to comply with exercise recommendations. *Clinical Journal of Sports Medicine*, **6**, 112–118.

Hart, E. & Bond, M., (1996). *Action Research for Health and Social Care: a Guide to Practice*. Milton Keynes: Open University.

Health Education Authority. (1994). *Helping People Change*. London: Health Education Authority.

Health Education Authority. (1995a). *Health Update 5: Physical Activity*. London: Health Education Authority.

Health Education Authority. (1995b). *Promoting Physical Activity: Guidance for Commissioners, Purchasers and Providers.* London: Health Education Authority.

Health Education Authority. (1996). *Promoting Physical Activity in Primary Care: Guidance for Primary Health Care Teams.* London: Health Eduation Authority.

Henry, R.C., Ogle, K.S. & Snellman, L.A. (1987). Preventive medicine: Physician practices, beliefs, and perceived barriers for implementation. *Family Medicine*, **19**, 110–113.

Hillsdon, M., & Thorogood, M. (1996). A systematic review of physical activity promotion strategies. *British Journal of Sports Medicine*, **30**, 84–9.

Hillsdon, M., Thorogood, M., Anstiss, T.A., & Morris, J. (1995). Randomised controlled trials of physical activity promotion in free living populations: a review. *Journal of Epidemiology and Community Health*, **49**, 448–53.

Hunt, P. & Hillsdon, M. (1996). *Changing Eating and Exercise Behaviours.* London: Blackwell.

Iliffe S., See Tai, S., Gould, M., Thorogood, M., & Hillsdon, M. (1994). Prescribing exercise in general practice. *British Medical Journal*, **309**, 20–27.

Imperial Cancer Research Fund OXCHECK Study Group (1994). Effectiveness of health checks conducted by nurses in primary care: results of the OXCHECK study after one year. *British Medical Journal*, 308, 308–12.

Imperial Cancer Research Fund OXCHECK Study Group (1995). Effectiveness of health checks conducted by nurses in primary care: final results of the OXCHECK study. *British Medical Journal*, **310**, 1099–104.

James, W.P.T. (1995). A public health approach to the problem of obesity. *International Journal of Obesity*, **19**: Suppl 3, S37–45.

Kelly, R.B. (1988). Controlled trial of a time-efficient method of health promotion. *American Journal of Preventive Medicine*, **4**, 200–7.

Killoran, A.J., Fentem, P., & Casperson, C. (eds.) 1994. *Moving on: International Perspectives on Promoting Physical Activity.* London: Health Eduation Authority.

King, A.C. (1994). Clinical and community interventions to promote and support physical activity participation. In R. K. Dishman (Ed.). *Advances in Exercise Adherence* (pp. 183–212) Champaign, IL: Human Kinetics.

King, A.C., Harris, R.B. & Haskell, W.L. (1994). Effect of recruitment strategy on types of subjects entered into a primary prevention clinical trial. *Annals of Epidemiology*, **4**, 312–20.

Kohl, H.W., Dunn, A.L., Marcus, B.H. & Blair, S.N. (1998). A randomised trial of physical activity interventions: design and baseline data from Project Active. *Medicine and Science in Sport and Exercise*, 30, 275–83.

Leith, L.M., & Taylor, A.H. (1992). Behavior modification and exercise adherence: A literature review. *Journal of Sport Behavior*, 15(1), 60–74

Lewis, B.S. & Lynch, W.D. (1993). The effect of physician advice on exercise behaviour. *Preventive Medicine*, 22, 110–21.

Lindholm, L.H., Ekbom, T., Dash, C., Eriksson, M., Tibblin, G., Schersten, B. on behalf of the CELL Study Group (1995). *British Medical Journal*, 310, 1105–09.

Lodgson, D.N., Lazaro, C.M. & Meier, R.V. (1989). The feasibility of behavioural risk reduction in primary medical care. *American Journal of Preventive Medicine*, 5, 249–56.

Long, B.J., Calfas, K.J., Wooten, W., Sallis, J.F., Patrick, K., Goldstein, M., Marcus, B.H., Schwenk, T.L., Chenoweth, J., Carter, R., Torres, T., Palinkas, L.A., & Heath, G. (1996). A multisite field test of the acceptability of physical activity counseling in primary care: project PACE. *American Journal of Preventive Medicine*, 12(2), 73–81.

Lord J.C., & Green, F. (1995). Exercise on prescription: does it work? *Health Education Journal*, 54(4), 453–64.

McDowell, N., McKenna, J. & Naylor, P.J. (1997). Factors that influence practice nurses to promote physical activity. *British Journal of Sports Medicine*, 31, 308–313.

McKenna, J., Naylor, P.J., & McDowell, N. (1998). Barriers to physical activity promotion by general practitioners and practice nurses. *British Journal of Sports Medicine*, 32, 242–247.

Marcus, B.H., Banspach, S.W., Lefebvre, R.C., Rossi, J.S., Carleton, R.A., & Abrams, D.B. (1992). Using the stages of change model to increase the adoption of phsyical activity among community participants. *American Journal of Health Promotion*, 6, 424–9.

Marcus, B.H., Goldstein, M. G., Jette, A., Simkin-Silverman, L., Pinto, B.M., Milan, F., Wahburn, R., Smith, K., Radowski, W., & Dube, C.E. (1997). Training physicians to conduct physical activity counselling. *Preventive Medicine*, 26, 382–8.

Miller, W.R. & Rollnick, S. (1991). *Motivational Interviewing: Preparing People to Change Addictive Behaviour*. New York: Guilford.

Mullen, P. & Tabak, G.R. (1989). Patterns of counselling techniques used by family practice physicians for smoking, weight control,exercise and stress. *Medical Care*, 27, 694–704.

Office of Population Censuses and Surveys (1995). *The health survey for England 1993*. HMSO.

Owen, N. (1996). Strategic initiatives to promote participation in physical activity. *Health Promotion International*, 11, 213–18.

Patrick, K., Sallis, J.F., Long, B.J., Calfas, K.J., Wooten, W.J., Heath, G., & Pratt, M. (1994a). A new tool for encouraging activity: *Project PACE. Physician and Sports Medicine,* **22**(11), 45–55.

Patrick, K., Sallis, J.F., Long, B.J., Calfas, K.J., Wooten, W.J., & Heath, G. (1994b). PACE: physician-based assessment and counseling for exercise, background and development. *Physician and Sports Medicine,* **22**, 245–255.

Patrick, K., Calfas, K.J., Wooten, W.J. Long, B.J., & Sallis, J.F. (1997). The impact of health-care providers on physical activity. In A.S. Leon (ed.) *Physical Activity and Cardiovascular Health.* Champaign, IL: Human Kinetics

Pender, N.J., Sallis, J.F., Long, B.J. & Calfas, K.J. (1994). Health-care provider counseling to promote physical activity. In R. K. Dishman (ed.). *Advances in Exercise Adherence* (pp. 213–235) Champaign, IL: Human Kinetics.

Prochaska, J.O. & Di Clemente, C.C. (1983). Stages and processes of self-change of smoking: toward an integrative model of change. *Journal of Consulting Clinical Psychology,* **51**, 390–5.

Reed, B.D., Jensen, J.D. & Gorenflo, (1991). Physicians and exercise promotion. *American Journal of Preventive Medicine,* **7**(6), 410–15.

Reid, D. (1996). How effective is health education via mass communications? *Health Education Journal,* **55**(3), 332–344.

Rollnick, S., Heather, N., & Bell, A. (1992). Negotiating behaviour change in medical settings: the development of brief motivational interviewing. *Journal of Mental Health,* **1**, 25–37.

Rollnick, S., Kinnersley, P. & Stott, N. (1993). Methods of helping patients with behaviour change. *British Medical Journal,* **307**, 188–90.

Rosenthal, R. (1974). *On the Social Psychology of the Self-fulfilling Prophecy: Further Evidence of the Pygmalion Effects and their Mediating Mechanisms.* New York: MSS Modular.

See Tai, S., Gould, M. & Iliffe, S. (1997). Promoting healthy exercise among older people in general practice: issues in designing and evaluating therapeutic interventions. *British Journal of General Practice,* February, 119–22.

Shephard, R.J. (1988). PAR-Q, Canadian Home FItness Test and exercise screening alternative. *Sports medicine,* **5**(3), 282–91.

Smith, F. & Iliffe, S. (1997). Exercise prescription in primary care. *British Journal of General Practice,* May, 272–3.

Smith, P., Gould, M., See Tai, S. & Iliffe, S. (1996a). Exercise as therapy? Results from group interviews with general practice teams involved in an inner-London 'prescription for exercise' scheme. *Health Education Journal,* **55**(4), 439–46.

Smith, P., Iliffe, S., Gould, M. & See Tai, S. (1996b). Prescription for exercise in primary care: is it worth it? *British Journal of Health Care Management*, **2**(6), 324–7.

Smith, R.A. (1998). Health professionals' attitudes towards promoting physical activity. *Journal of Sport Science*, **16**, 104.

Steptoe,A. & Wardle, J. (1993). What the experts think: A survey of expert opinion in Europe about the influence of lifestyle on health. Paper presented at the 7th Conference of the European Health Psychology Society, Brussels.

Stevens, W., Hillsdon, M., Thorogood, M. & McArdle, D. (1998). The cost of a primary care-based physical activity intervention in 45–74 year old men and women: A randomised controlled trial. *British Journal of Sports Medicine*, **32**, 236–241.

Stockport Leisure Services (1994). *Stockport Exercise on Prescription: Evaluation Report*. Stockport, UK: Stockport Leisure Services Division.

Stott, N.C.H., Kinnersley, P. & Rollnick, S. (1994). The limits to health promotion. *British Medical Journal*, **309**, 971–2.

Swinburn, B.A., Walter, L.G., Arroll, B., Tilyard, M.W., & Russell, D.G. (1997). Green Prescriptions: attitudes and perceptions of general practitioners towards prescribing exercise. *British Journal of General Practice*, **47**, 567–9.

Swinburn, B.A., Walter, L.G., Arroll, B., Tilyard, M.W., & Russell, D.G. (1998). The Green Prescription Study: A randomised controlled trial of written exercise advice in general practice. *American Journal of Public Health*, **88**, 288–291.

Taylor, A.H. (1994). Evaluating the efficacy of exercise promotion signs on Eastbourne seafront: observations and perceptions of over 35 year olds. *British Journal of Physical Education: Research Supplement*, **14**, 17–22.

Taylor A.H. (1996). Evaluating GP referral schemes: findings from a randomised controlled study. *Chelsea School Topic Report* No. 6, University of Brighton.

Taylor A.H., Doust J. & Webborn A.D.J. (1998). Randomised controlled trial to examine the effects of a GP exercise referral programme in East Sussex, UK, on modifiable coronary heart disease risk factors. *Journal of Epidemiology and Community Health*, **52**, 595–601.

Wallace, P.G., Brennan, P.J. & Haines, A.P. (1987). Are general practitioners doing enough to promote healthy lifestyles? Findings of the Medical Research Council's general practice research framework study on lifestyle and health. *British Medical Journal*, **294**, 940–942.

Wealden District Council (1993). *The Oasis Programme Operation Manual*. Hailsham, E. Sussex, UK: Wealden District Council Leisure Services.

Wealden District Council (1995). *The Oasis Programme Evaluation Report 1995*. Hailsham, E. Sussex, UK: Wealden District Council Leisure Services.

Wealden District Council (1996). *The Oasis Programme Evaluation Report 1996*. Hailsham, E. Sussex, UK: Wealden District Council Leisure Services.

Williams, S.J., Calnan, M., Cant, S. & Coyle, J. (1993). All change in the NHS? implications of the NHS reforms for primary care prevention. *Sociology of Health and Illness*, **15**, 107–12.

Williford, H.N., Barfield, B.R., Lazenby, R.B., & Olson, M.S. (1992). A survey of physicians' attitudes and practices related to exercise prescription. *Preventive Medicine*, **21**, 630–6.

Wimbush, E. (1994). A moderate approach to promoting physical activity: the evidence and implications. *Health Education Journal*, **53**, 322–36.

Young, A., Skelton, D., Walker, A., & Hoinville, L. (1997). *Physical Activity in Later Life*. London: Health Education Authority.

Chapter 4

Exercise Adherence and Clinical Populations

Nanette Mutrie

This chapter focuses on exercise adherence issues for clinical populations, that is populations who have sought help for a particular medical condition, who are under medical supervision or who have been diagnosed by a relevant clinical specialist. Structured or supervised exercise has been promoted for a host of medical conditions for some time. Bouchard, Shephard and Stephens (1994) listed 24 medical conditions for which exercise has a potential therapeutic role. Research on the efficacy of exercise for these clinical groups grew out of the knowledge which had been accumulated on the prevention and treatment of cardiovascular disease through exercise and activity (Pate et al., 1995). Initial interest in the role of exercise for clinical populations came from physicians and exercise physiologists who used exercise tests as part of a medical diagnosis or who sought physical improvements and decreased morbidity and mortality for their patients. More recently it has been recognised that longevity is perhaps not the key issue for exercise with these patients groups, and that quality of life and the ability to function in everyday activities are more salient issues, both of which can benefit from regular exercise. The American College of Sports Medicine (ACSM) has produced a very comprehensive text on managing

Adherence Issues in Sport and Exercise. Edited by Stephen J. Bull.
© 1999 John Wiley & Sons Ltd.

exercise programmes for clinical populations to assist the increasing number of exercise specialists in this area (1997a). Moore (1997), in the introductory chapter of this text summarised the short history of the rationale for exercise programmes with clinical populations as follows:

> . . . in the 1980s, research and clinical applications for exercise expanded to populations with a variety of chronic diseases and disabilities, for whom exercise is perhaps more fundamentally related to *quality* of life rather than *quantity* of life. Perhaps the greatest potential benefit of exercise is its ability to preserve functional capacity, freedom and independence. (p. 3).

If exercise is to be beneficial to patients we must be able to keep them involved in activity over the longest time possible and thus psychologists clearly have a role to play. It is, therefore, surprising to note that the topic of adherence (starting and maintaining exercise) was not covered in the text from which the quotation in the preceding paragraph is taken (American College of Sports Medicine, 1997). The process of keeping people involved in beneficial activity has been under-researched in comparison to the outcomes from such activities. In order to promote exercise adherence for patients who have a defined medical condition, an understanding of the psychological factors which affect adherence, along with an understanding of the particular challenges to exercise which the various medical conditions create, is required. The prescribed exercise treatment may present problems because patients are not confident of their physical abilities or the medical conditions themselves may present difficulties for the intending exerciser. The focus of this chapter will be the psychology of starting and maintaining exercise for these patient groups. The aims of this chapter are to explore what is known about starting exercise for various clinical populations and what hinders or helps the process of long-term adherence. Guidelines for good practice in promoting and studying adherence are also provided.

WORKING WITH CLINICAL POPULATIONS

It is likely that exercise specialists working with clinical populations will be part of a team of clinicians and paramedical staff such as physiotherapists. Exercise is one part of a multi-treatment package designed to help the patients. It is clear that such exercise specialists need an understanding of the physiological demands of exercise and the adaptations and limitations which various conditions will require. Such specialists may be in charge of exercise testing for diagnostic or exercise prescription purposes. Therefore a solid background in exercise physiology is required. However, it is clear that knowledge of exercise psychology is also very important. Exercise psychology will provide an understanding of the psychosocial issues which will affect test results (e.g. anxiety will affect tests which involve voluntary termination) and the ability to undertake the prescription of exercise (e.g. the patient may not believe exercise will help and is thus unlikely to adhere to the programme). In addition, exercise psychology suggests that there are beneficial psychological outcomes from exercise participation which may play an important motivational role (Fox, 1997). Some hospitals now employ exercise therapists who work alongside physiotherapists providing appropriate exercise prescriptions. Some specialists groups, such as the British Association of Cardiac Rehabilitation (BACR) provide their own training courses for exercise specialists working in cardiac rehabilitation and this training includes exercise psychology. The British Association of Sport and Exercise Science (BASES) provides an accreditation system to ensure quality control. It would seem that this is an expanding field of application.

THEORETICAL ISSUES

No one theoretical model has been accepted as a guide to research or practice. Many researchers have tried to use models such as the Health Belief Model or Theory of Reasoned Action to predict exercise behaviour and have met with varying degrees of success (cf. Biddle & Mutrie, 1991). Similarly models which explain relapse into unhealthy behaviours, such as Marlatt and Gordon's (1985) relapse model, have been used as a basis for understanding why people return to sedentary lifestyles. One major issue is that many of the models which have proved useful in other health promotion research do not readily apply to exercise for two reasons. Firstly, exercise adherence is a lifelong process and not a single behaviour such as visiting the dentist or attending a screening clinic. Sallis and Hovell's (1990) model of adherence as a process, which involves the concepts of initiating, maintaining, dropping-out and resuming exercise, is therefore a fundamental starting point in this area. The second reason that models established in other areas of health behaviour may not apply, is that exercise is a positive behaviour which people have to start and continue rather than (as with most other health behaviours) a negative behaviour which has to be stopped. It is likely that exercise specific models will evolve as a basis for guiding research and practice.

One model which is generating considerable interest in the world of exercise is Proshaska and DiClemente's Transtheoretical model (1983), which was originally developed in a effort to understand stages which people went through in attempting to give up smoking. Marcus et al. (1992) provided a translation of this model into exercise behaviour and that application has been well received. As described in Chapter 2, this model classifies people into stages of readiness for exercise behaviour starting with those who have no intention to exercise (*pre-contemplators*), those who are thinking about starting some exercise (*contemplators*), those who have started a bit of exercise (*preparers*) and those who are doing regular exercise (*actioners* if they have been regular exercisers for less than six months and *maintainers* if they have been regular exercisers for more than six months). Along with this description of the stage of readiness comes a suggestion that people use various behavioural processes (such as giving themselves rewards) and experiential processes (such as being exposed to something which raises awareness) to move through the stages. The Transtheoretical model provides a framework for various agencies involved in the promotion of physical activity because each stage requires a different intervention strategy. For example, national agencies are probably best placed to provide information and raise awareness through media campaigns and thus the target audience should be precontemplators and contemplators. Local public and private organisations can provide much more individualised opportunities and are therefore best suited to targeting preparers and actioners.

What is perhaps surprising is that very few studies have attempted to study adherence to exercise for clinical populations from a theoretical framework. Descriptions of motivations and barriers are often provided, but without a theoretical underpinning it is hard for practitioners to understand how to improve adherence or for researchers to understand the processes which patients will go through. A strong recommendation is that all studies which report adherence have a theoretical model on which to base the study.

It is likely that the prevailing ethos in clinical settings is a medical model which focuses more on diagnosis and prescription of treatment than on the person. However, with regard to exercise adherence, a person centred approach should be considered. This implies that the same exercise prescription is not suitable for all people. Instead the exercise prescription must be tailored to each person's circumstances and provide them with control over their exercise rather than maintaining control with the hospital setting. The long-term goal must be independent exercisers and not exercisers who are dependent on hospital supervision. This idea fits very well with the current Active Living recommendations for increasing activity which suggests that sedentary people should aim to accumulate around 30 minutes of moderate intensity activity, such as walking, most days of the week (Pate et al. 1995). Dunn, Marcus, Kampert, Garcia, Kohl, & Blair (1997) have shown that the Active Living approach produces similar fitness and health gains over 6 months to a more traditional exercise prescripton of at least 20 minutes of vigorous activity three times each week. Loughlan and Mutrie (1995) have advocated a counselling approach to maximise adherence to recommendations. This counselling approach was shown to be equally effective to a high-tech fitness assessment approach for a group of NHS employees who were contemplating increasing activity levels (Loughlan & Mutrie, 1997). Lowther and Mutrie (1999) have shown that the counselling approach is more appealing to sedentary people and that fitness assessment is more appealing to more active people. It is likely that patients are not active and therefore a counselling approach may be more appealing to them. This approach includes getting an understanding of the person's exercise and activity history, allowing them to say what they feel are the benefits and drawbacks of increasing activity levels, helping them see ways to overcome stated barriers to activity, looking for ways to assist motivation like finding an exercise 'buddy', going to a class, getting support from family and friends and finally helping them set realistic short- and long-terms goals about their activity levels. This approach has been piloted with type 1 diabetic patients and was seen to be more successful that standard literature about exercise for diabetic patients (Hasler & Fisher, 1997).

EXERCISE ADHERENCE ISSUES FOR VARIOUS CATEGORIES OF CLINICAL POPULATIONS

The framework suggested by the American College of Sports Medicine (1997a), which is shown in Table 4.1, classified 40 separate medical conditions into six categories of disease or disability.

This framework has been adapted for use in this chapter. The major adaptation is that some sections of the categorisation, such as neurological disorders, have not been mentioned due to lack of literature on adherence issues. Within each category a brief mention will be made of the known physical and psychological benefits of exercise, special challenges for adherence will be outlined and what is known about motivations, barriers and adherence rates discussed. The inclusion of certain conditions within each category was based on current literature searches which used adherence (and associated words) as key terms, and this may have resulted in omissions of work which does have information on adherence but did not list any of the associated key words. It is hoped that readers will note (and even research) the topic of exercise adherence in other conditions which may have been missed.

Table 4.1   The American College of Sports Medicine's classification of diseases and disabilities (American College of Sports Medicine, 1997a)

Major category of disease/disability	Sub-categories
1. Cardiovascular and pulmonary diseases	Myocardial infarction Coronary artery bypass grafting and angioplasty Angina and silent ischemia Pacemakers and implantable cardioverter defibrillators Valvular heart disease Congestive heart failure Cardiac transplant Hypertension Peripheral arterial disease Aneurysms and marfan syndrome Pulmonary disease Cystic fibrosis
2. Metabolic diseases	Renal failure Diabetes Hyperlipidemia Obesity Frailty
3. Immunological/haematological disorders	Cancer Anaemia Bleeding disorders Acquired immune deficiency syndrome Organ transplant Chronic fatigue syndrome
4. Orthopaedic diseases and disabilities	Arthritis Low back pain syndrome Osteoporosis
5. Neuromuscular disorders	Stroke and head injury Spinal cord injury Muscular dystrophy Epilepsy Multiple sclerosis Polio and post-polio syndrome Amyotrophic lateral sclerosis Cerebral palsy Parkinson's disease
6. Cognitive, emotional and sensory disorders	Mental retardation Alzheimer's disease Mental illness Deaf and hard of hearing Visual impairment

CARDIOVASCULAR AND PULMONARY DISEASES

Chronic Obstructive Pulmonary Disorders (COPD)

COPD is a title which includes asthma, chronic bronchitis and emphysema (Higgins, 1989). As much as 10% of the world's population suffer from asthma and the incidence of asthma is increasing, particularly for children. In the UK, asthma is the most frequent reason for children being off sick form school and for repeated visits to their GP (Holgate, 1993). Adherence to exercise programmes for people with COPD has certainly been studied (Atkins, Kaplan, Timms, Reinsch & Lofback, 1984) and the results have enhanced the knowledge on the effectiveness of various adherence strategies. These studies show that cognitive behaviour modification strategies will work with this patient group, with simple techniques such as goal-setting increasing the number of minutes walked in an eleven week programme almost four times as much as the control group. These results are shown in Figure 4.1.

Special challenges for COPD patients and exercise include the issue that for some asthmatics exercise is a double-edged sword. On the one hand it can improve overall functional capacity and reduce breathlessness, but on the other hand it can also induce an asthmatic attack (Belman, 1989). Exercise programmes must be tailored to avoid breathlessness and there

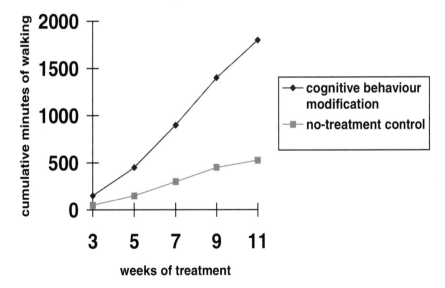

Figure 4.1 The effect of cognitive behaviour modification strategies on walking for COPD patients (adapted from Atkins, Kaplan, Timms, Reinsch & Lofback, 1984)

may be the need to overcome a belief from such patients that they should not exercise. Special advice on how and when to use medication in conjunction with exercise is usually required (Gordon, 1993b).

Cardiac Rehabilitation

Exercise-based cardiac rehabilitation programmes are in widespread use in the USA (Naughton, 1985) but their introduction has been relatively slow in the UK (Gloag, 1985), despite the greater percentage of the UK population who will suffer a myocardial infarction (MI) (Tunstall-Pedoe and Smith, 1986). The reasons for this caution in the UK are unclear. Perhaps the reason is as simple as finding the extra cost of mounting these programmes within an already stretched National Health Service budget. Perhaps the reason is the more complex point that medical consultants review success in medical treatment of MI in terms of decreased mortality and the early evidence for that via exercise was equivocal (Naughton, 1985). However, Oldridge, Guyat, Fischer & Rimm (1988) conducted a meta-analysis of available studies and concluded that MI patients who had a cardiac rehabilitation programme which included exercise had a 25% reduction in mortality compared to controls.

Given the need to heal infarcted heart tissue and improve the efficiency of the cardiovascular system, it is not surprising to note that most research on the effect of exercise during cardiac rehabilitation has focused on physiological and cardiovascular parameters (Dugmore, 1992), although Oldridge et al. (1988) suggested that improvements in psychological well-being and quality of life may be more beneficial than changes in exercise tolerance.

Anxiety and depression are perhaps the most frequently measured psychological outcomes. Milani, Lavie & Cassidy (1996) estimated that 20% of cardiac patients exhibit symptoms of depression 4–6 weeks after a cardiac event. There has been more work in the area of psychological outcome for this group of patients than any other clinical group. Kugler, Seelbach & Kruskemper (1994) completed a meta-analysis of 15 studies which had investigated anxiety and/or depression as outcomes of exercise-based cardiac rehabilitation programmes. These authors found low to moderate effect sizes of 0.31 for anxiety and 0.46 for depression as a result of exercise-based cardiac rehabilitation. These effects are perhaps underestimates of the true effects of exercise on anxiety and depression because not all the subjects in the studies reported will have symptoms of anxiety or depression. Thus there appear to be both physiological and psychological benefits associated with exercise in cardiac rehabilitation.

The field of exercise adherence has benefited greatly from all the research conducted in cardiac rehabilitation settings. Considering adherence itself, Oldridge, Donner & Buck (1983) report that 40–50% of Canadian patients drop out of cardiac rehabilitation programmes 6–12 months after referral. In the UK Pell, Pell, Morrison, Blatchford & Dargie (1996) report a 58% completion rate for Glasgow hospital-based rehabilitation programmes. Quaglietti and Froelicher (1994) noted that adherence drops over time with perhaps only 30–55% of patients continuing to exercise 4 years after the initial cardiac event.

An example of a study which highlights the issue of long-term adherence was completed by Rovario, Holmes, & Holmsten (1984). They randomly assigned cardiac patients to either a three times per week supervised exercise programme ($n = 27$) or a routine care programme which included exercise advice but no supervised sessions ($n = 19$). After three months of supervised training and at a follow-up four months later, the patients in the exercise-based rehabilitation had improved more than those in routine care on measures of cardiovascular functioning, self-perceptions and psychosocial functioning, including reduced employment-related stress, more frequent sexual activity and increased household activities. However, when these patients were followed up six years later (Holmes, 1993) the advantages for the original exercise-based groups had disappeared. The authors suggest that the explanation lay in the increased level of activity in the routine care group and the decreased level in the group who initially had supervised exercise. This issue raises the question of how the exercise classes within a hospital setting might achieve the long-term goal of creating independent exercisers who can find ways of continuing exercise after the initial supervision.

Thus there is a concern that many patients do not get the benefits from the exercise programmes because they do not complete it. There have been some excellent studies of the factors associated with such drop-out (e.g. Oldridge, Donner & Buck, 1983) and there is a general conclusion that individual factors and factors related to the programme itself provide reasons for drop-out. Given the concern over adherence levels in cardiac rehabilitation it is surprising that very few studies have sought patient viewpoints on the content of the programme. In the UK, Campbell, Grimshaw, Rawles and Ritchie (1994) interviewed 29 patients who had recently suffered a myocardial infarction. The most frequently suggested element for the cardiac rehabilitation programme was exercise, but it was also clearly noted that the hospital was not the most suitable location. Programmes in more local centres with supervision were requested. It was also noted by a majority of patients that bad weather was off-putting for walking programmes and other imaginative alternatives must be considered such as walking round large DIY stores (about as close as we come to a mall in the UK).

A variety of exercise programmes have been tried including hospital-based and home-based, aerobic- and strength-based programmes and differing exercise intensities. In the long run home-based programmes which encourage walking seem to have the best chance of long-term adherence. For those managing cardiac rehabilitation programmes Quaglietti and Froelicher (1994) offer the following suggestions:

> . . . reduce the waiting time, provide expert supervision, tailor the exercise to avoid physical discomfort and frustration, use variable activities including games, incorporate social event, recall absent patients, involve the patient's family or spouse in the program, and involve the patient in monitoring his or her progress (p. 599).

Special challenges for this patient group include fear of another myocardial infarction, and the possible interaction of exercise with commonly prescribed drugs such as beta-blockers. Beta-blockers will attenuate heart rate response and thus exercise intensity is best introduced to the patient via rating of perceived exertion. Perhaps because of the fear of a further infarction there is a concern that patients become dependent on the hospital environment and it is a challenge to assist patients to become independent exercisers and to sustain this. The British Association of Cardiac Rehabilitation is addressing the problem directly by providing training for exercise leaders and physiotherapists in what is described as Phase IV (i.e. in the community) cardiac rehabilitation. The issue of long-term adherence is addressed in the training.

METABOLIC DISEASES

Diabetes

Both Type 1 (insulin dependent, IDDM) and Type 2 (non-insulin dependent, NIDDM) diabetics are usually advised to exercise as part of their treatment along with medication, modification of diet and monitoring of glucose levels (Wing, Epstein, Nowalk & Lamparski, 1986). A joint position statement by the American College of Sports Medicine (ACSM) and the American Diabetes Association (1997b), provides anyone involved with either Type 1 or 2 diabetic patients with a comprehensive set of guidelines concerning exercise. In this position statement benefits to cardiovascular, peripheral arterial and metabolic systems from exercise are described and preparing the diabetic patient for exercise is discussed. Interestingly, from the point of view of exercise adherence, no reference is made to maintenance of exercise or psychological outcomes. The psychological effects of facing a lifetime of dealing with diabetes, and the consequent emotional and social adjustments are very well documented by health psychologists, as is the need for patient education about treatment (Dunn, 1993). Given the wealth of literature on these psychological issues in diabetes, and the standard recommendation that exercise should be part of treatment, it is surprising that neither the psychological benefits of exercise for diabetics nor patient education in appropriate exercise have received much attention from researchers. Literature searches suggest that no experimental work has been carried out on the psychological effects of exercise on IDDM or NIDDM. Two articles based on anecdotal evidence suggest that there are psychological effects of exercise for diabetics such as a sense of control and a reduction in stress (Vasterling, Sementilli & Burish, 1988; Norstrom, 1988). It is possible that central to these reported benefits is a changing view of the physical self from one which is compromised by the need to monitor food intake and blood sugar levels to one coping with exercise and feeling improvements in physical condition. Berg (1986) suggested that:

> The psychological effects of exercise may be just as important as the more readily measured physical and physiological effects. The realisation that participation in physical activity, including vigorous sport, can be engaged in safely and even beneficially may do much to create a positive feeling about life. Physically active diabetics may even be encouraged to maintain a higher degree of control of their condition so that they can maintain a vigorous lifestyle. (Berg, 1986, p. 428).

Some recent work (Swift, Armstrong, Beerman, Campbell & Pond-Smith, 1995) has shown that among NIDDM patients, who regularly participated in exercise, over half of them selected diabetes control as the main reason for starting and continuing with exercise. Barriers to exercise included physical discomfort from exercise, fear of reactions from low blood sugar, being too overweight to exercise and lack of family support. A large-scale survey ($n = 1030$) of IDDM patients' motivations and barriers to exercise (Marsden, 1996) suggested that fear of a hypoglycaemic event was not seen as a major barrier. Instead, and similar to the non-diabetic populations, time constraints were listed as the major barrier. Motivations to exercise were to avoid future diabetic complications and to improve physical health. This suggests that IDDM patients need similar exercise counselling (Loughlan & Mutrie, 1995) to non-clinical populations. A recent pilot study of the use of exercise counselling in a diabetic hospital clinic suggested that this kind of intervention could increase exercise over a short time span (3 weeks) in comparison to a randomly assigned control group who received the British Diabetic Association's exercise leaflet (Hasler & Fisher, 1997).

Marsden's work (1996) also revealed that less than a third of IDDM patients took regular exercise, but that at least another third are contemplating starting or doing some irregular exercise. This work high-lights the need for exercise education to be part of diabetic patient care because the majority of patients had not received advice about exercise from their hospital clinic.

The special challenge to Type 1 diabetics is to balance insulin control, glucose and exercise bouts. Patients need adequate knowledge of how to do this including the knowledge that exercise should not be undertaken with high levels (>250 mg/dl) of blood glucose. Blood glucose monitoring should therefore be encouraged before and after exercise. Type 2 patients may have different challenges which include being overweight and perhaps less motivated to deal with their condition. The special challenge in work-ing with overweight individuals is to find activities which do not increase the stress on joints and which avoid potential embarrassment. Swimming might seem like an obvious non-weight bearing activity, but swimsuits and public swimming pools may be too threatening for many obese people. Cycle and rowing ergometers may therefore be more realistic exercise modes.

IMMUNOLOGICAL AND HAEMATOLOGICAL DISORDERS

Cancer

It has long been recognised that coping with the diagnosis and treatment of cancer may require assistance in the form of psychological interventions (Anderson, 1992). It is also recognised that exercise as part of treatment has the potential to improve both physical (e.g. fatigue, nausea, weight change) and psychological functioning, although exercise is unlikely to have positive effects on the cancer itself. Simon (1990) concludes his dis-cussion of an excellent review of exercise immunity, cancer and infection by Calabrese (1990) by stating:

> There is little systematic information dealing with the role of exercise in the functional or psychological rehabilitation of cancer patients. There is little reason to expect that exercise training will help induce remissions in these patients, but there is good reason to expect that exercise may improve their quality of life. (p. 586)

Friedenreich and Courneya (1996) reviewed the use of exercise with cancer patients and found only nine studies on this topic and all of them related to breast cancer; the results of this review are never the less encour-aging since the overall conclusion was that exercise resulted in both physical and psychological improvements. Friedenreich and Courneya (1996) report that the issues of recruitment and adherence to exercise have been poorly studied (or reported) in the existing literature and that all of the exercise interventions were supervised.

Clear objectives for future research with exercise and cancer patients are to investigate different types of exercise including home-based and non-supervised programmes, to understand motivations and barriers, and to estimate adherence rates at various stages of the disease including treatment and long-term follow-up.

Special challenges for exercise prescription with cancer patients include exercising whilst recovering from intensive treatment such as chemotherapy, muscle weakness and perhaps embarrassment in public facilities because of hair loss due to treatment or fear of what people might think of a mastectomy scar.

HIV/AIDS

There is increasing interest in the use of exercise as part of a treatment schedule for people who have contracted Human Immunodeficiency Virus (HIV) (Rigsby, Dishman, Jackson, McLean and Rowen, 1992; Lawless, Jackson and Greenleaf, 1995). These initial studies focused on the immune system response to exercise and they found that there were no adverse effects (Berk, 1996). Indeed, LaPerriere, Fletcher, Antoni, Klimas, Ironson and Schneiderman (1991) suggested that physical training can increase CD4 cell counts (the helper cells which are important in immune response) by around 50 cells per cubic millimetre, which is comparable to the effect of certain AIDS drugs with none of the side effects.

Other studies show the potential for exercise to have positive psychological effects for the HIV population, such as increased ability to cope with HIV+ status (LaPerriere, Antoni, Schneiderman, Ironside, Klimas, Caralis & Fletcher, 1990), increased perception of well-being (Lox, McAuley & Tucker, 1995) and improved quality of life (Stringer, Berezovskaya, O'Brien, Beck & Casaburi, 1998).

There are clearly some special concerns for adherence to exercise for this population since 75% of subjects dropped out of one 24 week study of the effects of exercise on HIV (McArthur, Levine & Berk, 1993). However, a recent study which compared the effects of high and moderate intensity aerobic training to a control group, had more optimistic adherence results. Stringer et al. (1998) reported a study in which 34 HIV+ subjects were enrolled and 77% completed the 6 week programme. In addition, the authors report 91% adherence to the two exercise regimes which included three sessions of cycle ergometry per week for 6 weeks. There was no discussion from the authors of these excellent adherence results about how the programme compared to previous exercise programmes with this population. This was unfortunate since future researchers have no guidance about how to structure an exercise programme to maximise adherence. Clearly a 6 week programme is much less of an adherence challenge than the 24 week programme of McArthur et al. (1993). Nevertheless to get good adherence at 24 weeks, there must be good adherence earlier and we clearly need to know more about the time course, modalities and intensities of activity which provide the best adherence.

Special challenges in working with this population include obtaining ethical approval for studies which involve laboratory testing, protection of confidentiality of subjects, public prejudice against this group if exercise is conducted in public facilities, poor muscle mass and muscle weakness.

ORTHOPAEDIC DISEASES AND DISABILITIES

Arthritis

Sharratt and Sharratt (1994) present an excellent summary of the role of exercise in both rheumatoid arthritis (inflammation of membrane surrounding the joint) and osteoarthritis (degeneration of cartilage within the joint). It would seem that in this particular disease there is a consensus that exercise can enhance the quality of life by maintaining range of movement and functional capacities connected with daily living (Stenstrom, 1994), and yet there is still a paucity of research which can contribute to our understanding of how to promote exercise to this patient group to maximise long-term adherence.

In one of the few studies addressing motivations and barriers for this patient group, Neuberger, Kasal, Smith and Hassanein (1994) surveyed 100 patients with either rheumatoid or osteoarthritis to determine perceptions about exercise. They established that perceiving benefits from exercise was a significant predictor of exercise participation; those with less formal education and a longer duration of arthritis perceived fewer benefits from exercise. In addition, subjects who exercised in their youth reported more benefits of exercise.

The major challenge for arthritis sufferers who are exercising is the issue of joint pain and the type of activity which should be undertaken. Exercise should be undertaken at the time of day at which inflammation is at its lowest and non-weight bearing activities such as swimming and cycling are probably best. If inflammation or increased pain occurs as a result of exercise, then the exercise may have to be adjusted so that the affected joint is not so stressed. Gordon (1993a) has written a very good guide to exercise for those suffering from arthritis which deals directly with the issue of pain and is essential reading for anyone constructing exercise opportunities for this patient group.

Osteoporosis

Osteoporosis is the medical term for a condition in which there is a decrease in absolute amount of bone which renders the skeleton susceptible to breakage and fractures. Osteoporosis can affect both sexes as there is a gradual decline in bone density with age. However, the loss of bone mass accelerates for women when ovarian function decreases during and after menopause. Thus postmenopausal women are more susceptible to osteoporosis than any other segment of the population (Kanis et al., 1990) In addition, osteoporosis sufferers often have to contend with pain, disability, depression and decreased confidence in their physical abilities (Rickli & McManus, 1990; Vaughn, 1976).

A variety of treatments have been tested but none are without controversy. Hormone replacement therapy slows down the process of bone loss (Gannon, 1988) but if treatment ceases, this effect will be sustained for only up to three years (Lindsay et al., 1976). The role of calcium and vitamin D supplementation is not yet clear (Smith, 1982). Several reviews have suggested that physical activity can enhance bone density and therefore should be considered as part of the treatment for osteoporosis (Marcus et al., 1992; Gannon, 1988). Clinical trials suggest that appropriate weight bearing activity can enhance bone density by around 4%, which is similar to improvements noted from drug therapies (Smith, Smith & Gilligan, 1990; Simkin, Ayalon & Leichter, 1987; Chow, Harrison & Notarius, 1987).

Kriska et al. (1986) have noted that adherence to the exercise programmes has been the major problem in most studies evaluating the effect of exercise on bone, but very few studies have attempted to study adherence issues. Mitchell, Grant and Aitchison (1998) reported very high adherence to a 12 week class-based programme of exercise for osteoporotic women. On average, the 16 exercisers in this study attended 87% of the target of 24 classes. However, very little is known about exercise behaviour over a longer period of time for this patient group, including what are perceived as motivations and barriers, how patients view activity and the benefits it may provide, or what strategies the medical professions might adopt to increase or maintain adherence for a period of time which would allow bone measurements to alter as a result of exercise (9–12 months). One study which has attempted to shed light on this issue used a postal questionnaire to a local branch of the National Osteoporosis Society to establish current activity patterns and attitudes towards activity (Paton,

1993). A response rate of 55% was achieved (74 out of 140) but no follow-up of non-respondents was possible because the society required that responses were anonymous. Thus the results may not be representative of the larger group of osteoporotic patients. All of the respondents had been diagnosed as osteoporotic for at least five years. Twenty-six percent of this group were sedentary and of the 74% who reported that they were physically active more than half were participating in three exercise bouts each week. The most popular activity was walking. The three most commonly noted motivations for exercise were 'to feel better physically', 'to prevent further osteoporosis' and 'to feel better mentally'. The three most commonly perceived barriers to exercise were, 'no facilities nearby', 'no knowledge of how to exercise' and 'not fit enough'. It is interesting to note that only 24% of these respondents reported that they had been advised to begin exercise on diagnosis of the condition. Clearly further studies on this population are required to enhance the understanding of motivations and barriers to exercise, but based on these results it would seem that exercise is perceived to have benefits and that barriers could be overcome by education of how to undertake exercise.

Special challenges for this population include finding enjoyable weight bearing activity which will influence bone density, the need for both aerobic and strength-enhancing components in the exercise programme, overcoming fear of falling or worsening the condition by undertaking exercise, decreased mobility and low fitness levels, and the need to modify programmes depending on limitations imposed by the disease.

Chronic Low Back Pain

Managing chronic low back pain (i.e. pain which is almost always present in area of lower spine) is a serious problem for health services. In the UK, low back pain as a reason for being off work has increased by 104% in the last decade (Klaber Moffett, Richardson, Sheldon & Maynard, 1995) and is the most common reason for attendance at out patient physiotherapy clinics (Jette, Smith, Haley & Davis, 1994). There appears to be no consensus as to the most effective treatment (Waddell, 1992) although both general and isokinetic exercise (Timm, 1991) have been suggested as effective treatments. Frost, Klaber Moffett, Moser & Fairbank (1995) showed that a 4 week supervised fitness programme was more effective than a home-based programme in reducing perceived disability and pain and in increasing self-efficacy for daily living tasks. The difference in perceived disability between the two groups was maintained at a 6-month follow-up. These authors suggested that the changes in self-efficacy may be due to endorphins released during exercise decreasing pain perception or increasing feelings of well-being, although the two groups did not differ in psychological change as measured by the General Health Questionnaire. What is becoming evident in this area of research is that the patient's psychological state (including pain perception, depression, self-efficacy) may be very important in determining recovery. In this sense the psychological outcomes of exercise programmes designed to manage low back pain may be just as important as the physiological responses such as increased strength, flexibility or aerobic performance.

Frost, Klaber Moffett, Moser & Fairbank (1995) described a teaching style used by the physiotherapist conducting the fitness programme, which incorporated psychological principles such as increasing self-efficacy for exercise, and reinforced positive physical self perceptions (e.g. I am a regular exerciser) rather than negative perceptions (e.g. I am a disabled patient). This suggestion emphasises the important role of exercise psychology in exercise programmes designed to manage low back pain. It is very important to note that this teaching approach produced very high adherence levels over four weeks, with a mean attendance rate of 87% of all possible sessions (8). However, it is presumably easier to attend for a short duration, and the authors do not report adherence to exercise in the 6 month follow-up results. No other adherence statistics for exercise as part of back pain management could be found.

Special challenges for this group include overcoming the fear that movement will cause further injury. Perhaps what is therefore required in the early stages is not an exercise programme but a movement education programme. Once patients realise that movement does not necessarily involve pain then gentle exercise can begin. There is also the challenge of finding enjoyable and interesting low impact activity.

MENTAL HEALTH ISSUES

Mental Health

Exercise has been shown to be an effective adjunctive treatment for several mental health problems including depression, anxiety and schizophrenia (Biddle & Mutrie, 1991). The best evidence is in the area of depression. There is now a growing body of evidence, both from meta-analysis (North, McCullagh & Tran, 1990) and randomised control trials (Klein, Griest, Gurman, Neirneyer, Lesser, Bushnall, & Smith, 1985; Fremont & Craighead, 1987), to show that exercise is beneficial in the treatment of mild to moderate depression and may also be of use in more chronic and severe depression (Martinsen, Hoffart & Solberg, 1989). It is also known that people with mental illness exercise less that the general population

(Tsuang, Perkins & Simpson, 1983) and thus it is possible that exercise may also serve a protective function. In addition both European (Weyerer, 1992) and North American (Dishman, 1995) prospective studies show that low activity increases the risk of depression. Surprisingly, there have been no full-scale randomised controlled trials of the use of exercise as a treatment for depression in a primary care setting in the UK. Furthermore, no studies have directly compared the effects of standard drug treatment with exercise. Exercise has relatively few adverse side effects, compared to many drug treatments. Patients are often cited as saying that they do not want drug treatment (Scott, 1996) and exercise is therefore a reasonable option. There may also be a cost-effectiveness advantage to exercise since it is relatively cheap to put in place. Mutrie (in press) reviewed all available randomised controlled trials ($n = 10$) in which exercise had been used as treatment for depression and concluded that the anti-depressant effect of exercise was a robust finding. The exercise programmes ranged from 8 weeks to 12 weeks in length with follow-ups of 6 months to 1 year, but adherence was rarely discussed or reported in these studies.

Special challenges include motivation, as lethargy is a common symptom of depression. This is perhaps best dealt with by using a very graduated exercise programme which may start with 5 minute bouts of activity. Using goal setting to increase the length of activity and reinforcing successful completion of early goals may assist motivation. Asking the patient to notice whether or not energy levels rise or fall immediately after exercise may also assist in overcoming lethargy and understanding that exercise can be used to boost energy levels. There is another challenge for exercise programming for this patient group in the potential interaction of exercise and drugs. Beta-blockers attenuate heart-rate response and thus exercise intensity is best introduced to the patient via rating of perceived exertion. Some anti-psychotic medications cause dehydration and frequent drinking of water before and during exercise may be necessary. These potential interactions of drugs and exercise should be discussed with the medical team.

Alcohol Abuse

The topic of appropriate treatment for alcohol abuse has received much discussion with no one method showing distinct advantages (Heather, Robertson & Davies, 1985). Rehabilitation from an addictive behaviour involves establishing self-control strategies and finding coping strategies for the emotions involved with withdrawal and continued abstinence (Marlatt & Gordon, 1985). Self-esteem is often at a very low level as the problem drinker faces the need for treatment and realises the physical and mental

damage that alcohol may have caused (Beck, Weissman & Kovacs, 1976; Donaghy & Mutrie, 1997). It is intriguing to note that one of the earliest documented pieces of research in exercise psychology was in the area of alcohol rehabilitation (Cowles, 1898) although several decades passed before the research was replicated. Cowles' (1898) conclusion provides a challenge to current researchers to provide experimental evidence of the declared benefits of exercise:

> The benefits accruing to the patients from the well-directed use of exercise and baths is indicated by the following observed symptoms: increase in weight, greater firmness of muscles, better colour of skin, larger lung capacity, more regular and stronger action of the heart, clearer action of the mind, brighter and more expressive eye, improved carriage, quicker responses of nerves, and through them of muscle and limb to stimuli. All this has become so evident to them that only a very few are unwilling to attend the classes and many speak freely of the great benefits derived. (p. 108)

Problem drinkers often have low levels of cardiorespiratory fitness and muscle strength and appropriate programmes of exercise have been shown to be effective in improving these physical parameters (Tsukue & Shohoji, 1981; Donaghy, Ralston & Mutrie, 1991). Since regular exercise has been associated with improved mental health (cf. Biddle & Mutrie, 1991), decreased levels of depression and anxiety, and increased self-esteem (Fox, 1997) which are commonly reported problems in alcohol rehabilitation, the use of exercise as part of the treatment for alcohol rehabilitation has been piloted in several locations (Gary & Guthrie, 1972; Frankel & Murphy, 1974; Sinyor, Brown, Rostant & Seraganion, 1982; Murphy, Pagano & Marlatt, 1986; Palmer,Vacc & Epstein, 1988; Donaghy, Ralston & Mutrie, 1991). In these studies the exercise programmes can be considered to be lifestyle interventions which provide the problem drinker with the skills to undertake a positive health-promoting behaviour (exercise) which simultaneously may provide self-control strategies, coping strategies and an alternative to drinking (Marlatt & Gordon, 1985; Murphy et al., 1986).

Donaghy & Mutrie (1998) reported a randomised control trial in which 117 problem drinkers were assigned to either a 3 week supervised exercise programme, which was followed by a 12 week home-based programme, or a placebo group which received a stretching programme for 3 weeks and advice to continue exercising for the next 12 weeks. The exercise group improved scores on physical self-worth and perceptions of strength and condition at 1 month and 2 months after entry to the programme. The between-groups difference in physical self-perceptions was not evident at 5 months, but this may be due to drop off in exercise adherence (Donaghy & Mutrie, 1999). Thus there is good evidence that a structured exercise programme added to a 3 week treatment programme can help problem drinkers improve their perception of physical self-worth. Adherence to exercise was a problem in this study with 26% having left the treatment programme (not just the exercise) at the end of 3 weeks and by the 2 month follow-up a further 30% had dropped out. Activity levels were sustained for the exercise groups for 8–12 weeks following the 3 week programme but had dropped to the level of the control group by 5 months (Donaghy & Mutrie, 1999).

Special challenges for this population include low starting levels of fitness and muscle weakness, relapse to drinking with consequent effects on exercise behaviour, social isolation and lack of support. There is clearly a need for help, such as telephone contact or monthly meetings, to sustain activity levels initiated in treatment programmes for this patient group. There is also a need to integrate the exercise to other treatments such as discussion groups, self-help groups or forms of cognitive behavioural therapy. Reinforcing the value of exercise and encouraging adherence could be topics for group leaders and therapists in these other forms of treatment.

Drug Rehabilitation

Evidence of the use of exercise in drug rehabilitation programmes is very hard to find. Indeed the only evidence of any research interest in this area comes from unpublished dissertations (Hyman, 1987; Murdoch, 1988; Adamson, 1991). There is anecdotal support for the use of sport and exercise in drug rehabilitation from a group in Glasgow called Carlton Athletic. This group is run by former drug users and involved sport participation as the primary vehicle used to support rehabilitation. Unfortunately, no evaluation has yet been carried out on this self-help process. The problems faced in drug rehabilitation are similar to those in alcohol rehabilitation; high levels of anxiety and depression are often reported, as are low self-esteem (Banks & Waller, 1988), and thus it might be assumed that exercise could have the same potentially therapeutic effect. One unique problem for drug rehabilitation is the variety of drugs and their effects during both addiction and withdrawal. In addition, drug misuse often involves the use of many drugs by the same person (Arif & Westermeyer, 1988). It may be that this variety of responses makes the standard 'clinical' trial experiment untenable, because there is likely to be a large variation in the dependent variables but only small subject numbers available because of the nature of the treatment programmes which are often residential. Qualitative methodology may therefore be the best way to gather information.

Murdoch (1988) carried out an experimental study on 14 people who were attempting to withdraw from tranquillisers (benzodiazepines) randomly assigning them to either an 8 week programme involving group therapy or an 8 week programme involving exercise and group therapy. The chaotic nature of the subjects' lives during withdrawal meant that very few actually completed the programme. The problems faced included agoraphobia brought on by the withdrawal, difficulty in keeping appointments for fitness testing and for supervised exercise, difficulty of contacting subjects to help adherence to appointments (some not on telephone, some changing abode frequently). Thus statistical tests were not viable due to small numbers. However, the four subjects who completed the exercise programme all reported that it had helped them cope with the withdrawal; two of the four felt that the exercise had made them feel 'very much better' while the other two reported more moderate benefits. The group therapy subjects proved to be equally difficult to deal with in terms of adherence with only three completing the 8 week programme. It is perhaps these difficulties which have prevented more experimental research in this area.

Adamson (1991) tried to deal directly with the adherence problem by evaluating the feasibility of exercise as part of treatment for drug misuse in four residential settings. Using extensive interviews with residents who were offered exercise programmes over an 8 week period, it was established that 10 of the 13 residents who participated in the exercise felt that the exercise had given them psychological benefits. The benefits ranged from improving mood, having a clearer mind, sleeping better and filling gaps created by withdrawal. All 13 subjects thought that exercise could help them continue to abstain from drugs. In explaining this one subject said, 'It (exercise) makes you feel as if you have achieved something . . . done something for yourself.' The residential staff were also interviewed and had very positive feedback about the exercise programmes. One of them said 'It (exercise) affected them where they were at physically and mentally and helped to build up and increase their self-esteem.' Adamson (1991) concluded that an exercise programme was feasible in a residential setting but that well-controlled research studies would be difficult to conduct because of the circumstances created by withdrawal from drugs.

The special challenges for exercise programming clearly include adverse withdrawal effects from drugs. Such patients are liable to forget appointments for exercise. The withdrawal effects may prevent exercise completely on some days or an inability to leave the house to go to an exercise facility. Keeping in regular contact with these patients is therefore very helpful to them. Perhaps home-based exercise, such as a video tape, could provide some support through difficult phases, but regular phone calls and visits may also be required.

Exercise Dependence

People can become dependent on exercise and will exhibit very high levels of activity on a very regular basis. Here we are faced with the opposite of most of the adherence discussion so far. There is often informal discussion amongst various professionals about the risk of creating people who are dependent on exercise when using exercise as part of treatment. This is particularly true in working with other dependencies such as alcohol or drug use. De Coverley Veale (1987) provided diagnostic criteria for exercise dependence, which were based on criteria established for the diagnosis of drug dependence, and these are shown in Table 4.2. However, there is no known prevalence for this problem.

Exercise dependence may well present at a mental health clinic, sports injury clinic or be associated with eating disorders. Given that only 20–30% of the population exercise three times per week (Sports Council and Health Education Authority, 1992) it is likely that only a very small percentage of the overall population could be diagnosed as exercise dependent. Furthermore, it is difficult to say how harmful exercise dependence really is

Table 4.2 Diagnostic criteria for exercise dependence (de Coverley Veale, 1987)

Criteria	
(A)	Narrowing of repertoire leading to a stereotyped pattern of exercise with a regular schedule once or more daily
(B)	Salience with the individual giving increasing priority over other activities to maintain the pattern of exercise
(C)	Increased tolerance to the amount of exercise performed over the years
(D)	Withdrawal symptoms related to a disorder of mood following the cessation of the exercise schedule
(E)	Relief or avoidance of withdrawal symptoms by further exercise
(F)	Subjective awareness of the compulsion to exercise
(G)	Rapid re-instatement of the previous pattern of exercise and withdrawal symptoms after a period of abstinence

Associated features	
(H)	Either the individual continues to exercise despite a serious physical disorder known to be caused, aggravated or prolonged by exercise and is advised as such by a health professional, or the individual has arguments or difficulties with his/her partner, family, friends, or occupation
(I)	Self-inflicted loss of weight by dieting as a means towards improving performance

to an individual. If the person continues to exercise against medical advice then the risk of chronic injury is clear. It may also be economically harmful to neglect work responsibilities in favour of exercise. Damage to personal and social relationships may be psychologically harmful. It is clear in these cases that the exercise-dependent individual needs to regain a balance in terms of their need to exercise and other important life issues. If exercise professionals notice someone who appears to be dependent then some information on seeking appropriate advice should be made available. However, someone who is exercise dependent (i.e. fulfils criteria A–G in Table 4.2) may manage to prevent physical, personal or financial harm, but may still acknowledge a compulsion to exercise. Is this harmful? Veale (1995), the author of the suggested diagnostic criteria, admits that he has interviewed (in his professional capacity as a psychiatrist) very few people who could be diagnosed as having primary exercise dependence. His conclusion is that many people who may have the characteristics of dependence are probably functioning quite well and have no need to seek help. Veale (1995) also pointed out that cases of secondary exercise dependence are more frequently encountered, that is a person who uses excessive exercise as part of another disorder such as an eating disorder. He recommended studies which attempt to determine whether or not primary exercise dependence exists independently of eating disorders.

One particularly difficult area in the definition of exercise dependence is whether or not competitive athletes in training would be defined as dependent. At first glance many athletes would fulfil the criteria in Table 4.2, but their 'dependence' is almost a requirement of the pursuit of their primary goal which is the enhancement of performance. Perhaps the major worry for athletes are the associated features H and I in Table 4.2 which can clearly lead to physical and mental harm over time. In addition, Morgan (1994) reminded us that overtraining can have detrimental mental health effects such as mood disturbances and depression. Coaches and sports scientists should therefore be aware of harmful effects of exercise dependence and be ready to counsel and assist athletes who appear to be displaying the associated features, or mood disturbances over prolonged periods of time.

It is not clear why exercise dependence occurs. It has been suggested that such extreme exercise behaviour is evidence of an obsessive compulsive personality trait, or that such a person has become addicted to the feelings associated with increased endorphin or adrenaline production as a result of exercise (Pierce, 1994) but these speculations remain difficult to demonstrate empirically. Other suggestions include the possibility that exercise is an analogue for anorexia nervosa although this has been heavily criticised and no supportive evidence has been produced (Biddle & Mutrie, 1991, p. 172).

Special concerns for health professionals dealing with exercise dependence include convincing exercise dependants that less exercise might be better. An exercise dependant finds the concept of a rest day abhorrent and is unlikely to agree to this harm-avoiding strategy. A counselling approach could be used to moderate exercise levels to less harmful levels. This would include a discussion of the benefits and barriers to reducing activity levels, a discussion of how these barriers might be overcome, and realistic goal-setting to help the person make gradual adjustments over a period of time.

CONCLUSIONS

The conclusions from this selected review of how exercise is promoted for those suffering from chronic conditions are consistent. There is little scientific evidence to guide strategies for initiation and maintenance of exercise for these clinical populations. The following points provide a set of conclusions from this chapter concerning what we know about adherence to exercise for clinical populations.

1. Good short-term adherence (4–12 weeks) can be achieved from supervised programmes of exercise. However, for some populations such as those in drug rehabilitation or those with HIV+ status, even short-term adherence may need special support systems.
2. Long-term adherence (12 months to 4 years) is poor and not well documented. The best information comes from follow up of those in cardiac rehabilitation, and suggests that 30–55% are still exercising after 4 years. This is the area which requires most research. The cardiac rehabilitation statistics can serve as a bench mark for other clinical populations. Home-based walking programmes seem to offer the best hope for long-term adherence but other modalities must be explored.
3. Very little is known about the level of exercise in clinical populations. For example only one third of Type 1 diabetics are regular exercisers despite the fact that exercise is well recognised as part of diabetic treatment.
4. Drop-out from exercise programmes is associated with factors to do with the programme and factors to do with the person and his/her circumstances.
5. Motivations for exercise are clearly to do with improved health.
6. Barriers to exercise are similar to non-clinical populations (e.g. lack of time) but also include issues to do with the particular disease state (e.g. fear of another MI or fear of worsening osteoporosis) which could be overcome by good patient education.

7. Cognitive behavioural strategies do seem to work and the use of a counselling approach which encourages decision balance, overcoming perceived barriers and setting individualised goals should be encouraged in all clinical settings.
8. It is worth reiterating the suggestions of Quaglietti and Froelicher (1994) for improving adherence in cardiac rehabilitation. It seems likely that these are principles which could apply to all clinical settings.

> . . . reduce the waiting time, provide expert supervision, tailor the exercise to avoid physical discomfort and frustration, use variable activities including games, incorporate social event, recall absent patients, involve the patient's family or spouse in the program, and involve the patient in monitoring his or her progress. (p. 599)

Unfortunately, there has been an underlying assumption that adherence is either not a problem (therefore no need to study) or that it can be ignored (results are only recorded for those who complete the programme). Oldridge (1992) pointed out that if we only record results (e.g. risk improvement) for those who complete an exercise programme then we introduce bias into our understanding of exercise as a treatment. Thus researchers must report the adherence level and analyse results on an intention to treat basis, that is include people even if they did not complete the exercise programme. There is enormous scope for exercise psychologists to be involved in this area, either as researchers establishing information or as practitioners providing programme advice. Coping with a chronic condition certainly presents a challenge and the role of exercise in providing a sense of confidence in a medically compromised body, a means to introduce an element of fun and a way to 'lift the spirits', a sense achievement in overcoming the difficulties of the condition and a sense of control in one's life certainly deserves further attention. Capturing some of these potential positive outcomes for patients is clearly associated with maintaining the exercise habit, but we need to know so much more about how to overcome barriers and provide support to assist such patients in maintaining an active lifestyle. The following section provides guidelines for this task.

THE WAY FORWARD FOR RESEARCH AND PRACTICE

Researchers and academics should try to form links with medical teams dealing with specific conditions. Once involved, the topics of psychological outcomes, initiation and maintenance of exercise are wide open for investigation and work in these areas will benefit both the specific population and the more general field of exercise psychology. Qualitative research may often provide a starting point because many of the situations do not lend themselves to standard clinical trials. For example, the small number of patients available at any one time makes experimental work on the role of exercise for some clinical groups very difficult. In addition, qualitative research may be the best way of investigating the value of exercise in enhancing quality of life since each person will have his or her own view of what quality of life means.

Future studies must also address the issue of long-term adherence to exercise programmes. The style of reporting adherence rates over the course of one year and the provision of detailed reasons for drop out adopted by Chow et al. (1987) for osteoporotic patients is to be commended and could act as a model for other researchers. Perri, Martin, Leermakers, Sears & Notelovitz (1997) also provided a template for the detail of adherence information which is required. In reporting the superiority of a home-based programme of exercise over a class-based programme for weight loss over 15 months they note that the home-based programme has better adherence. In order to report adherence these researchers described drop-out (attrition) as those attending less than half of the prescribed sessions and they provided reasons for drop-out. Then they described attendance at weight loss treatment sessions and finally they described participation rates for each of the 12 months of the study as a percentage of the number of prescribed sessions completed.

For those more interested in the practical aspects there is also plenty of scope for teaching patients and medical teams about the potential role of exercise and for conducting training in appropriate exercise prescription and counselling (Loughlan & Mutrie, 1995). The financial backing for such training will appear all the more quickly if the research community shows a cost–benefit advantage (Shephard, 1990) in favour of exercise as part of standard practice. Issues which deserve further attention from both researchers and practitioners include the use of functional exercise tests (e.g. ability to climb stairs without use of handrail) as well as diagnostic tests, the provision of home-based opportunities for exercise, the long term follow-up and support of patients, and the need for a 'team' approach in which the exercise behaviour is reinforced by all the medical staff involved in patient care.

Key Issues for Studying Exercise Adherence in Clinical Settings

- Both researchers and practitioners should operate with a model of adherence to guide them. At the very least, stage of exercise behaviour change should be recorded for the 6 months prior to exercise commencing and the processes of change recorded after exercise has commenced.

- Activity must be recorded before and after any exercise programme or intervention. The 7d recall (Lowther & Mutrie, 1996) is a suggested tool but other measurements might include monitoring movement via a motion sensing device such as a Caltrac.
- Report the uptake for any exercise programme from the potential client population
- Ideally investigate motivations and barriers to exercise in each patient group as a whole and also for those who have taken up the offer or completed an exercise programme.
- Record and report (via a register or via contact) adherence at regular intervals (e.g. weekly class register or monthly phone calls for home-based programmes). Report adherence to exercise prescription as a percentage of target in as many ways as possible, e.g. minutes of activity per week, number of sessions completed, full weeks of exercise. If this is self-report data provide corroboration via class registers, friends and relatives, pedometers etc. Once this is done various outcomes, including motivations, and barriers can be described for high and low adherers.
- Report drop-out rate. This will involve reporting those who dropped out before commencing and those who did not complete different stages. A definition of non-completion is required and completion of less than a half of the required programme is suggested as a working definition. Provide a between-groups analysis of drop-out rate so that potential causes for can be investigated. Make every effort to re-contact drop-outs to establish reasons for not continuing.
- Ideally include qualitative and quantitative analysis on motivations and barriers for high, low or no adherence.
- Describe the exercise programme and the amount of supervision and encouragement given.
- Aim to provide adherence information at 6 months but a longer follow-up is even better.
- Use standardised questionnaires which have known validity and reliability.
- If possible provide qualitative information from health professionals and medical staff of their view of the role of exercise for any given patient group.

REFERENCES

Adamson, M.J. (1991). The role of exercise as an adjunct to the treatment of substance abuse. Unpublished M.Ed. Thesis, University of Glasgow.

American College of Sports Medicine (1997a). *ACSM's exercise management for persons with chronic diseases and disabilities.* Champaign, IL: Human Kinetics.

American College of Sports Medicine. (1997b). American College of Sports Medicine and American Diabetes Association joint position statememt. Diabetes mellitus and exercise. *Medicine and Science in Sports and Exercise,* **29**(12), i-vi.

Anderson, B.L. (1992). Psychological interventions for cancer patients to enhance quality of life. *Journal of Consulting and Clinical Psychology,* **60**, 552–558.

Arif, A., & Westermeyer, J. (1988). *Manual of drug and alcohol abuse guidelines for teaching in medical and health institutions.* New York: Plenum.

Atkins, C.J., Kaplan, R.M., Timms, R.M., Reinsch, S., & Lofback, K. (1984). Behavioural exercise programmes in the management of chronic obstructive pulmonary disease. *Journal of Consulting and Clinical Psychology,* **52**, 591–603.

Banks, A., & Waller, T.A.N. (1988). *Drug misuse. A practical handbook for GPs.* London: Blackwell Scientific Publications.

Beck, A.T., Weissman, M., & Kovacs, M. (1976). Alcoholism, hopelessness and suicidal behaviour. *Journal of Studies on Alcohol,* **37**, 66–77.

Belman, M.J. (1989). Exercise in chronic obstructive pulmonary disease. In B.A. Franklin, G. Seymour, & G.C. Timmis (eds.), *Exercise in modern medicine* (pp. 175–191). Baltimore: Williams & Wilkins.

Berg, K. (1986). *Diabetic's guide to health and fitness.* USA: Life Enhancement Publishers.

Berk, T.J. (1996). HIV and exercise. *Exercise immunology review,* **2**, 84–95.

Biddle, S., & Mutrie, N. (1991). *Psychology of physical activity and exercise. A health related perspective* (1st edn). London: Springer-Verlag.

Bouchard, C., Shephard, R.J., & Stephens, T. (eds.). (1994). *Physical activity, fitness, and health.* Champaign, IL: Human Kinetics.

Calabrese, L.H. (1990). Exercise, immunity, cancer, and infection. In C. Bouchard, R.J. Shephard, T. Stephens, J.R. Sutton, & B.D. McPherson (eds.), *Exercise, fitness and health* (pp. 567–579). Champaign, IL: Human Kinetics.

Campbell, N., Grimshaw, J., Rawles, J., & Ritchie, L. (1994). Cardiac rehabilitation: the agenda set by post-myocardial-infarction patients. *Health Education Journal,* **53**, 409–420.

Chow, R., Harrison, J.E., & Notarius, C. (1987). Effect of two randomised exercise programmes on bone mass of healthy postmenopausal women. *British Medical Journal,* **295**, 1441–1444.

Cowles, E. (1898). Gymnastics in the treatment of inebriety. *American Physical Education Review,* **3**, 107–110.

'De Coverly Veale, D.M.W. (1987). Exercise dependence. *British Journal of Addiction*, **82**, 735–740.

Dishman, R.K. (1995). Physical activity and public health: Mental health. *Quest*, **47**, 362–385.

Donaghy, M., & Mutrie, N. (1997). Physical self-perceptions of problem drinkers on entry to an alcohol rehabilitation programme. *Physiotherapy*, **83**(7), 358.

Donaghy, M., & Mutrie, N. (1998). A randomised controlled study to investigate the effect of exercise on the physical self-perceptions of problem drinkers. *Physiotherapy*, **84**(4), 169.

Donaghy, M., & Mutrie, N. (1999). Adherence to class-based and home-based exercise as part of a rehabilitation programme for problem drinkers. *Journal of Sports Sciences*, **17**(1), 50–51.

Donaghy, M., Ralston, G., & Mutrie, N. (1991). Exercise as a therapeutic adjunct for problem drinkers. *Journal of Sport Sciences*, **9**(4), 440.

Dugmore, D. (1992). Exercise and heart disease. In K. Williams (Ed.), *The community prevention of coronary heart disease* (pp. 43–58). London: HMSO.

Dunn, A.L., Marcus, B.H., Kampert, J.B., Garcia, M.E., Kohl, H.W., & Blair, S.N. (1997). Reduction in cardiovascular disease risk factors: 6-month results from Project Active. *Preventive Medicine*, **26**, 883–892.

Dunn, S.W. (1993). Psychological aspects of diabetes in adults. In S. Maes, H. Leventhal, & M. Johnston (eds.), *International review of health psychology* (Vol. 2, pp. 175–197). London: Wiley.

Fox, K.R. (1997). *The physical self from motivation to well-being*. Champaign, IL: Human Kinetics.

Frankel, A., & Murphy, J. (1974). Physical fitness and personality in alcoholism: Canonical analysis of measures before and after treatment. *Quarterly Journal of Studies on Alcohol*, **35**, 1271–1278.

Fremont, J., & Craighead, L.W. (1987). Aerobic exercise and cognitive therapy in the treatment of dysphoric moods. *Cognitive Therapy and Research*, **11**, 241–251.

Friedenreich, C. M., & Courneya, K. S. (1996). Exercise as rehabilitation for cancer patients. *Clinical Journal of Sport Medicine*, **6**(4), 237–244.

Frost, H., Klaber Moffett, J.A., Moser, J.S., & Fairbank, J.C.T. (1995). Randomised controlled trial for evaluation of fitness programme for patients with chronic low back pain. *British Medical Journal*, **310**, 151–154.

Gannon, L. (1988). The potential role of exercise in the alleviation of menstrual disorders and menopausal symptoms: A theoretical synthesis of recent research. *Women and Health*, **14**(2), 105–127.

Gary, V., & Guthrie, D. (1972). The effects of jogging on physical fitness and self-concept in hospitalized alcoholics. *Quarterly Journal of Studies on Alcoholism*, **33**, 1073–1078.

Gloag, D. (1985). Rehabilitation of patients with cardiac conditions. *British Medical Journal*, **290**, 617–620.

Gordon, N.F. (1993a). *Arthritis. Your complete exercise guide*. Champaign, IL: Human Kinetics.

Gordon, N.F. (1993b). *Breathing disorders. Your complete exercise guide*. Champaign, IL: Human Kinetics.

Hasler, T., & Fisher, M. (1997). A counselling approach for increasing physical activity for patients attending a diabetic clinic. Presented at British Diabetic Association Meeting, October, Bournemouth, UK.

Heather, N., Robertson, I., & Davies, P. (1985). *The misuse of alcohol: Crucial issues in dependence treatment and prevention*. London: Croom Helm.

Higgins, M.W. (1989). Chronic airways disease in the United States: Trends and determinants. *Chest*, **96**, 328s–334s.

Holgate, S.T. (1993). Asthma: Past, present, and future. *European Respiratory Journal*, **6**, 1507–1520.

Holmes, D.S. (1993). Aerobic fitness and the response to psychosocial stress. In P. Seraganian (ed.), Exercise psychology. *The influence of physical exercise on psychological processes* (pp. 39–63). New York: Wiley.

Hyman, G.P. (1987). The role of exercise in the treatment of substance abuse. Unpublished MS Thesis, The Pennsylvania State University, State College PA.

Jette, A.M., Smith, K., Haley, S.M., & Davis, K.D. (1994). Physical therapy episodes of care for patients with low back pain. *Physical Therapy*, **74**, 101–110.

Kanis, J., Aaron, J., Thavarajah, M., McCluskey, E.V., O'Doherty, D., Hamdy, N.A.T., & Bickerstaff, D. (1990). Osteoporosis: Causes and therapeutic implications. In R. Smith (Ed.), *Osteoporosis* (pp. 45–56). London: Royal College of Physicians.

Klaber Moffett, J.A., Richardson, G., Sheldon, T.A., & Maynard, A. (1995). *Back pain: Its management and cost to society*. York: Centre for Health Economics, University of York.

Klein, M.J., Griest, J.H., Gurman, A.S., Neirneyer, R.A., Lesser, D.P., Bushnell, N.J., & Smith, R.E. (1985). A comparative outcome study of group psychotherapy vs.exercise treatments for depression. *International Journal of Mental Health*, **13**, 148–177.

Kriska, A.M., Bayles, C., Cauley, J.A., Laporte, R.E., Sandler, R.B., & Pambianco, G. (1986). A randomized exercise trial in older women: increased activity over two years and the factors associated with compliance. *Medicine and Science in Sports and Exercise*, **18**(5), 557–562.

Kugler, J., Seelbach, H., & Kruskemper, G.M. (1994). Effects of rehabilitation exercise programmes on anxiety and depression in coronary
patients: A meta-analysis. *British Journal of Clinical Psychology*, **33**,
401–410.

LaPerriere, A.R., Antoni, M.H., Schneiderman, N., Ironson, G., Klimas,
N., Caralis, P., & Fletcher, M. (1990). Exercise intervention attenuates
emotional distress and natural killer cell decrements following notifica-
tion of positive serological status for HIV-1. *Biofeedback and self regulation*, **15**(3), 229–242.

LaPerriere, A., Fletcher, M.A., Antoni, M.H., Klimas, N.G., Ironson, G., &
Schneiderman, N. (1991). Aerobic exercise training in an AIDS risk
group. *International Journal of Sports Medicine*, **12**(supp.1), s53-s57.

Lawless, D., Jackson, C., & Greenleaf, J. (1995). Exercise and human
imunodeficiency virus (HIV-1) infection. *Sports Medicine*, **19**(4), 235–
239.

Lindsay, R., Aitken, J.M., Anderson, J.B., Hart, D.M., MacDonald, E.B., &
Clarke, A. (1976). Long term prevention of postmenopausal osteoporosis by oestrogen. *Lancet*, **1**, 1038–1041.

Loughlan, C., & Mutrie, N. (1995). Conducting an exercise consulta-
tion:Guidelines for health professionals. *Journal of the Institute of Health
Education*, **33**(3), 78–82.

Loughlan, C., & Mutrie, N. (1997). A comparison of three interventions to
promote physical activity: fitness assessment, exercise counselling and
information provision. *Health Education Journal*.

Lowther, M., & Mutrie, N. (1996). Reliability and concurrent validity of the
Scottish physical activity questionnaire. *British Journal of Sports Medicine*, **30**, 368.

Lowther, M., & Mutrie, N. (1999). Attracting the general public to physical
activity interventions: A comparison of fitness assessments and exercise
consultations. *Journal of Sports Sciences*, **17**(1), 58–59.

Lox, C.L., McAuley, E., & Tucker, R.S. (1995). Exercise as an intervention
for enhancing subjective well-being in an HIV-1 population. *Journal of
Sport and Exercise Psychology*, **17**(4), 345–362.

McArthur, R.D., Levine, S.D., & Berk, T.J. (1993). Supervised exercise
training improves cardiopulmonary fitness in HIV infected persons.
Medicine and Science in Sports and Exercise, **25**(9), 648–688.

Marcus, B.H., Rossi, J.S., Selby, V.C., Niaura, R.S., & Abrams, D.B.
(1992). The stages and processes of exercise adoption and maintenance
in a worksite sample. *Health Psychology*, **11**, 386–395.

Marcus, R., Drinkwater, B., Dalsky, G., Dufek, J., Raab, D., Slemenda, C.,
& Snow-Harter, C. (1992). Osteoporosis and exercise in women. *Medicine and Science in Sports and Exercise*, **24**(6), s301-s307.

Marlatt, G.A., & Gordon, G.R. (1985). *Relapse prevention.* New York: Guilford Press.

Marsden, E. (1996). The role of exercise in the well-being of people with insulin dependent diabetes mellitus: perceptions of patients and health professionals. Unpublished Ph.D. Dissertation, University of Glasgow, Glasgow.

Martinsen, E.W., Hoffact, A., & Solberg, O. (1989). Comparing aerobic and non-aerobiv forms of exercise in the clinical treatment of depression: a randomized trial. *Comprehensive Psychiatry*, **30**, 324–331.

Milani, R.V., Lavie, C.J., & Cassidy, M.M. (1996). Effects of cardiac rehabilitation and exercise training programs on depression in patients after major coronary events. *American Heart Journal*, **132**(4), 726–732.

Mitchell, S., Grant, S., & Aitchison, T. (1998). Physiological effects of exercise on post-menopausal osteoporotic women. *Physiotherapy*, **84**(4), 157–163.

Moore, G.E. (1997). Introduction. In *ACSMs exercise management for persons with chronic diseases and disabilities* (pp. 3–5). Champaign, IL: Human Kinetics.

Morgan, W.P. (1994). Physical activity, fitness and depression. In C. Bouchard, R. J. Shephard, & T. Stephens (eds.), *Physical activity, fitness, and health* (pp. 851–867). Champaign: Human Kinetics.

Murdoch, F.A. (1988). Short term intervention for withdrawal from benzodiazepines: A comparitive study of group therapy plus exercise vs group therapy. Unpublished MBCHB Thesis, University of Glasgow, Glasgow.

Murphy, T.J., Pagano, R.R., & Marlatt, G.A. (1986). Lifestyle modification with heavy alcohol drinkers: Effects of aerobic exercise and meditation. *Addictive Behaviors*, **11**, 175–186.

Mutrie, N. (in press). A review of randomised controlled trials for the use of exercise in clinically defined depression. In S.J.H. Biddle & K. Fox (eds.), *A review of the relationships between mental health and exercise.* Somerset Health Authority.

Naughton, J. (1985). Role of physical activity as a secondary intervention for healed mycocardial infarction. *American Journal of Cardiology*, **55**, 210–260.

Neuberger, G.B., Kasal, S., Smith, K.V., & Hassanein, R. (1994). Determinants of exercise and aerobic fitness in outpatients with arthritis. *Nursing Research*, **43**(1), 11–17.

Norstrom, J. (1988). Get fit while you sit. Exercise and fitness options for diabetics. *Caring*, November, 52–58.

North, T.C., McCullagh, P., & Tran, Z.V. (1990). The effect of exercise on depression. *Exercise and Sports Science Reviews*, **19**, 379–415.

Oldridge, N.B. (1992). Compliance bias as a factor in longitudinal exercise research:osteoporosis. *Sports Medicine*, 13, 78–85.

Oldridge, N., Donner, A., & Buck, C. (1983). Predictors of dropout from cardiac exercise rehabilitation: Ontario exercise heart collaborative study. *American Journal of Cardiology*, **51**, 70–74.

Oldridge, N.B., Guyatt, G.H., Fischer, M.E., & Rimm, A.A. (1988). Cardiac rehabilitation after myocardial infarction. Combined experience of randomized clinical trials. *Journal of the American Medical Association*, **260**, 945–950.

Palmer, J., Vacc, N., & Epstein, J. (1988). Adult inpatient alcoholics: Physical exercise as a treatment intervention. *Journal of Studies on Alcohol*, **49**(5).

Pate, R.R., Pratt, M., Blair, S.N., Haskell, W.L., Macera, C.A., Bouchard, C., Buchner, D., Ettinger, W., Heath, G.W., King, A.C., Kriska, A., Leon, A.S., Marcus, B.H., Morris, J., Paffenbarger, R.S., Patrick, K., Pollock, M. L., Rippe, J.M., Sallis, J., & Wilmore, J.H. (1995). Physical activity and public health. *Journal of the American Medical Association*, **273**, 402–407.

Paton, L. (1993). Barriers and motivations to exercise in osteoporotic postmenopausal women. Unpublished M.App.Sci Thesis, University of Glasgow, Glasgow.

Pell, J., Pell, A., Morrison, C., Blatchford, O., Dargie, H. (1996). Retrospective study of influence of deprivation on uptake of cardiac rehabilitation. *British Medical Journal*, **313**, 267–268.

Perri, M.G., Martin, A.D., Leermakers, E.A., Sears, S.F., & Notelovitz, M. (1997). Effects of group-versus home-based exercise in the treatment of obesity. *Journal of Consulting and Clinical Psychology*, **65**, 278–285.

Pierce, E.F. (1994). Exercise dependence syndrome in runners. *Sports Medicine*, **18**(3), 149–155.

Proshaska, J.O., & DiClemente, C.C. (1983). Stages and processes of self-change in smoking: towards an integrative model of change. *Journal of Consulting and Clinical Psychology*, **51**, 390–395.

Quaglietti, S., & Froelicher, V.F. (1994). Physical activity and cardiac rehabilitation for patients with coronary heart disease. In C. Bouchard, R.J. Shephard, & T. Stephens (eds.), *Physical activity, fitness and health* (pp. 591–608). Champaign, IL: Human Kinetics.

Rickli, R.E., & McManus. (1990). The effect of exercise on bone mineral content in post menopausal women. *Research Quarterly*, **61**(3), 243–249.

Rigsby, L., Dishman, R.K., Jackson, W., McClean, G.S., & Rowen, P.B. (1992). Effects of exercise training on men seropositive for HIV-1. *Medicine and Science in Sports and Exercise*, **24**(1), 6–12.

Rovario, S., Holmes, D.S., & Holmsten, D. (1984). Influence of a cardiac rehabilitation program on the cardiovascular, psychological, and social functioning of cardiac patients. *Journal of Behavioral Medicine*, **7**, 61–81.

Sallis, J.F., & Hovell, M.F. (1990). Determinants of exercise behaviour. *Exercise and Sports Science Reviews*, **18**, 307–330.

Scott, J. (1996). Cognitive therapy of affective disorders: A review. *Journal of Affective Disorders*, **37**, 1–11.

Sharratt, M.T., & Sharratt, J.K. (1994). Potential health benefits of active living for persons with chronic conditions. In H.A. Quinney, L. Gauvin, & A.E.T. Wall (eds.), *Toward active living* (pp. 39–45). Champaign, IL: Human Kinetics.

Shephard, R.J. (1990). Costs and benefits of an exercising versus a non-exercising society. In C. Bouchard, R.J. Shephard, T. Stephens, J.R. Sutton, & B.D. McPherson (eds.), *Exercise, fitness and health* (pp. 49–60). Champaign, IL: Human Kinetics.

Simkin, A.J., Ayalon, J., & Leichter, I. (1987). Increased trabecular bone density due to bone-loading exercises on postmenopausal osteoporotic women. *Calcified Tissue International*, **40**, 59–63.

Simon, H.B. (1990). Discussion: Exercise, immunity, cancer, and infection. In C. Bouchard, R.J. Shephard, T. Stephens, J.R. Sutton, & B.D. McPherson (eds.), *Exercise, fitness and health* (pp. 581–588). Champaign, IL: Human Kinetics.

Sinyor, D., Brown, T., Rostant, L., & Seraganion, P. (1982). The role of physical exercise in the treatment of alcoholism. *Journal of Studies on Alcohol*, **43**, 380–386.

Smith, E.L. (1982). Exercise for the prevention of osteoporosis: a review. *The Physician and Sports Medicine*, **10**(3), 72–83.

Smith, E., Smith, K.A., & Gilligan, C. (1990). Exercise, fitness, osteoarthritis and osteoporosis. In C. Bouchard, R.J. Shephard, T. Stephens, J.R. Sutton, & B.D. McPherson (eds.), *Exercise, fitness and health* (p. 517–524). Champaign, IL: Human Kinetics.

Sports Council and Health Education Authority (1992). *Allied Dunbar National Fitness Survey*. London.

Stenstrom, C. H. (1994). Therapeutic exercise in rheumatoid arthritis. *Arthritis care and research*, **7**(4), 190–197.

Stringer, W.W., Berezovskaya, M., O'Brien, W., Beck, C.K., & Casaburi, R. (1998). The effect of exercise training on aerobic fitness, immune indices, and quality of life in HIV+ patients. *Medicine and Science in Sports and Exercise*, **30**, 11–16.

Swift, C.S., Armstrong, J.E., Beerman, K.A., Campbell, R.K., & Pond-Smith, D. (1995). Attitudes and beliefs about exercise among persons with non-insulin-dependent diabetes. *The Diabetes Educator*, **21**(6), 533–540.

Timm, K.E. (1991). Management of chronic low back patient pain: A retrospective analysis of different treatment approaches. *Isokinetics and exercise science*, **1**, 44–48.

Tsuang, M., Perkins, K., & Simpson, J.C. (1983). Physical diseases in schizophrenia and affective disorder. *Journal of Clinical Psychiatry*, **44**, 42–46.

Tsukue, I., & Shohoji, T. (1981). Movement therapy for alcoholic patients. *Journal of Studies on Alcohol*, **42**, 144–149.

Tunstall-Pedoe, H. and Smith, W.L.S. (1986). Level and trends of coronary heart disease mortality in Scotland compared to other countries. *Health Bulletin*, **44**, 153–161.

Vasterling, J. J., Sementilli, M. E., & Burish, T. G. (1988). The role of aerobic exercise in reducing stress in diabetic patients. *Diabetic Education*, **14**(3), 197–201.

Vaughn, C.C. (1976). Rehabilitation of post-menopausal osteoporosis. *Israeli Journal of Medical Sciences*, **12**, 652–659.

Veale, D. (1995). Does primary exercise dependence really exist? In J. Annett, B. Cripps, & H. Steinberg (eds.), *Exercise addiction. Motivations for participation in sport and exercise* (p. 71). Leicester: The British Psychological Society Sport and Exercise Psychology Section.

Waddell, G. (1992). Biopsychosocial analysis of low back pain. *Baillière's Clinical Rheumatology*, **6**, 523–557.

Weyerer, S. (1992). Physical inactivity and depression in the community: evidence from the Upper Bavarian Field Study. *International Journal of Sports Medicine*, **13**(6), 492–496.

Wing, R.R., Epstein, L.H., Nowalk, M.P., & Lamparski, D.M. (1986). Behavioral self-regulation in the treatment of patients with diabetes mellitus. *Psychological Bulletin*, **99**, 78.

Chapter 5

Adherence to Sport and Physical Activity in Children and Youth

Stuart Biddle

There is widespread recognition of the potential benefits to children and youth of participation in sport and other physical activities. Justification for young people's involvement is usually made on the grounds of health, sport performance, or education. The health rationale is well known. Young people are thought not to be active enough to gain significant health benefits and that sedentary habits are likely to continue into adulthood. However, there is a great deal of confusion concerning young people's health-related physical activity, often fuelled by inappropriate comments in the media.

A recent research consensus (Biddle, Sallis & Cavill, 1998) concluded that:

- Children and youth are the fittest and most active group in the population; they have similar aerobic fitness levels to children 40 years ago.
- There are no longitudinal data documenting a decline in physical activity despite anecdotal evidence to the contrary.

Adherence Issues in Sport and Exercise. Edited by Stephen J. Bull.
© 1999 John Wiley & Sons Ltd.

- The majority of young people take 30 minutes of moderate physical activity on most days of the week, but few take exercise of a more vigorous nature for prolonged periods.
- Data on tracking of physical activity from youth into adulthood are not strong.
- The nature of activity for children is sporadic.

However, it is also worth noting that many children have at least one elevated coronary heart disease risk factor and obesity levels are rising alarming in young people. For these reasons, the Health Education Authority in England are recommending that young people participate in an hour of moderate physical activity on most days of the week (Biddle et al., 1998). Therefore, despite the apparent spontaneity and prevalence of children's activity today, there is a need to study children's adherence to sport and other physical activities for health reasons.

A second rationale for studying adherence in this age group concerns sports performance. The social, economic, political and personal impact of successful sports performance can be highly significant and governments have often made the case that sporting success starts in childhood. For example, at the time of writing the English Sports Council is promoting the message 'more people, more places, more medals' in a bid to secure funding to improve sports performance and facilities. Some of this is targeted at young people. It is important, therefore, to know how young people are motivated to start and maintain sports training, including adherence to rigorous programmes.

Finally, a rationale to promote physical activity can be made in the context of education. In particular, physical education (PE) is unique in being able to offer physical activity to virtually all people aged 5–16 years. The potential impact of PE, therefore, is significant and any discussion on adherence must consider this.

An important consideration for adherence, however, is whether sport and physical activity programmes should be motivating for the 'here and now' or also consider motivation and adherence in the future. For example, should school PE programmes teach 'lifetime sports' in addition to sports rarely participated in after leaving school, such as gymnastics? Should coaches teach adherence skills, such as goal setting and lifestyle planning skills, so as to enhance adherence in the long term? These issues require some attention in any discussion on adherence.

In this chapter, adherence refers to what Maehr and Braskamp (1986) call 'continuing motivation'. This is persistence over time, usually months and years. This is different from motivation associated with the adoption of new behaviour. However, data are not always clear on this point and sometimes adoption and maintenance (adherence) becoming merged.

EVIDENCE ON ADHERENCE USING DESCRIPTIVE APPROACHES

Much of the research into sport and exercise adherence has been atheoretical and descriptive. Studies have often asked participants or non-participants why they have chosen to take part or not. In addition, many studies have sought reasons for ceasing participation. Much of the research on children's participation motivation tends to focus on competitive sport rather than more diverse aspects of exercise and physical activity.

Motives for Adherence

Research into young people's motivation for sport and physical activity now includes a number of quite large-scale studies from several countries. For example, research in Wales on over 4000 youth and young adults 16–24 years of age (Heartbeat Wales, 1987) asked non-participants what would act as incentives to become active in sport. The main responses were fitness/weight loss, having more free time, and sport that helped to maintain good health.

A study in Finland (Telama & Silvennoinen, 1979) of over 3000 11–19 year olds, showed clear changes in motivation for activity as a function of age and gender. Boys and younger children were more interested in achieving success in competition but by late adolescence very few showed an interest in this. This trend was reversed for motives associated with relaxation and recreation. Also of interest, given the current focus on children's exercise and fitness (Biddle et al., 1998), was that fitness motivation was strongest among those who often think about sport and take part in sports club activities. This fitness motive was unimportant for 18–19 year olds, or for those uninterested or inactive in sport.

In a study by Buonamano, Cei and Mussino (1995), with over 2500 Italian participants in youth sports, enjoyment was reported as the main reason for participation by just under half the sample. This was followed by physical (health/fitness) motives (32%), social reasons (8.9%), competition (4.2%), skill motives (2.9%), and social visibility or status (2.8%). A factor analysis of the questionnaire used by Buonamano et al. (1993) revealed factors of success/status, fitness/skill, extrinsic rewards, team factors, friendship/fun, and energy release.

Data from over 3000 children in Northern Ireland (Van Wersch, Trew & Turner, 1992) have shown that 'interest in physical education' remains relatively constant for boys from age 11 to 19 years, whereas during the same period interest declines sharply for girls. 'Interest' was assessed by questionnaire items pertaining to attitude, behaviour, motivation and perceptions of fun in the PE setting (see also Van Wersch, 1997).

Data from the English Sports Council's survey of young people and sport (Mason, 1995) shows that from a sample of over 4000 6–16 year olds, motives are diverse, ranging from general enjoyment to fitness and friendships. Similar results have been reported in North American research such as the Canada Fitness Survey (1983) which sampled over 4500 young people aged 10–19 years of age.

The results from Canada are consistent with reports from Europe that children are motivated for a variety of reasons. Reviews by Biddle (1992), and Gould and Petlichkoff (1988) concluded that children are motivated for diverse reasons, including fun and enjoyment, learning and improving skills, being with friends, success and winning, and physical fitness and health. The latter factor might also include weight control and body appearance for older youth. However, more research is needed to understand the differences in motives across activities, levels of participation, and developmental stages, although so far the research shows some similarity in motives across settings and groups.

Barriers and Reasons for Non-adherence

Various surveys are available on the reasons children and youth give for non-adherence in sport and exercise (Canada Fitness Survey, 1983; Heartbeat Wales, 1987; Mason, 1995). However, one of the problems is that many studies classify those who cease activity as 'dropouts', yet it is possible that they have switched their interest to another activity. Indeed, Gould and Petlichkoff (1988) make the important distinction between sport-specific dropout (ceasing participation in one sport) and domain-general dropout (ceasing sport participation altogether). This may need to be incorporated into future studies of adherence in sport.

As with motives for participation, there appear to be numerous reasons why children and youth cease their involvement. For example, Coakley and White (1992) conducted 60 in-depth interviews with 13–23 year olds in England, half of whom had decided to participate in one of five different sports initiatives in their local town. The others had either ceased involvement or had decided not to participate at all. The decision to participate or not appeared to be influenced by perceptions of competence, by external constraints, such as money and opposite sex friends, degree of support from significant others, and past experiences, including school PE. Negative memories of school PE included feelings of boredom and incompetence, lack of choice, and negative evaluation from peers. Mason's (1995) analysis of data on over 4000 youth in England provides support for this.

She found that some children reported feelings of embarrassment in sport settings, mainly due to perceived incompetence or concerns over self-presentation associated with their physique during puberty.

Heartbeat Wales (1987) found that youngsters aged 12–17 years lacked adherence to physical activity for the practical reasons of time, money and facilities, whereas Gould (1987) summarised the reasons for some children having poor adherence as conflicts of interest, lack of playing time, lack of fun, limited improvement in skills or no success, boredom, and injury. Competitive stress and dislike of the coach have also been cited in sport settings.

Children, therefore, appear to have multiple motives for their adherence and non-adherence in sport. However, less research is available on more diverse activity settings beyond sport and this should be a research priority in the future.

THEORETICAL APPROACHES TO UNDERSTANDING CHILDREN'S ADHERENCE

Descriptive approaches to adherence are useful, but they fail to advance our understanding of explanations of motivated or amotivated behaviours. For this reason, it is necessary to consider more theoretical perspectives on young people's adherence to physical activity. Three main areas will be discussed as they feature strongly in contemporary literature on motivation, sport and young people. These areas are attitudes, achievement goal orientations, and intrinsic motivation.

Attitudes, Adherence and Physical Activity

Attitudes are about thoughts and feelings: 'I think fitness training is good for me'; 'I like PE'. Typically attitude is used in an effort to predict intentions and behaviour. Attitude is only a conceptual or hypothetical construct and is not directly observable, although inferences can be made through observation. Attitudes, though, do not make sense unless they refer to an object, concept or behaviour. Likewise, the more specific the attitude, the more one might expect it to predict behaviour.

Attitudinal responses are also evaluative in nature. They reflect 'likes' and 'dislikes' concerning a specified object or action. For example, 'I like running, but not swimming'. This type of evaluation is developed through personal experience and interpersonal communication. Finally, attitudes involve knowledge and beliefs – the so-called 'cognitive' element of attitude, such as 'I like playing sport because I think it makes me healthy'.

Attitude–Behaviour Relationships

Several approaches have been used to explain how attitudes can predict future behaviour. However, attitudes are only part of a more complex decision-making process where other factors can also be of influence. Values, beliefs, perceptions of control and intentions are considered to moderate attitude–behaviour relationships. Specifically, attitudes cannot determine behaviour unless they lead to the development of intentions. In addition, contemporary theories, such as theory of reasoned action (TRA; Ajzen & Fishbein, 1980) and theory of planned behaviour (TPB; Ajzen, 1985), assert that 'subjective' (social) norms also influence intention. Social norms represent social influence by significant others, such as parents, teachers, peers, or others (e.g. 'my coach thinks I should play more sport at weekends'). Personal motivation to comply with such 'pressure' is important in determining whether social normative factors influence intentions (e.g. 'I want to do what my coach tells me'). The TRA predicts that attitude and social norms influence intention when one is able to control the behaviour in question. However, when control is not fully established, the TPB is a better model. This includes the variable of 'perceived behavioural control' (e.g. perceived barriers) and this directly influences intentions and sometimes behaviour. The TRA and TPB are illustrated in Figure 5.1.

In these theoretical approaches to behavioural choice and adherence, the attitudinal component of the model is a function of the beliefs held about the specific behaviour, as well as the evaluation (value) of the likely outcomes (see Ajzen, 1988). For example, two children may state 'I think that sport develops competitiveness' (belief), but one may say 'and I want to become more competitive' whereas the other says 'I do not think competitiveness is important' (value). The same belief accompanied by different values will lead to different attitudes and, one would predict, to different intentions and behaviours.

Measurement of attitudes, social norms and intentions should be highly specific to the behaviour in question in order to achieve correspondence, or compatibility, with the behaviour being predicted. For example, adherence to a swimming training programme is more likely to be predicted by attitudes concerning swimming training than generalised attitudes towards physical activity, or even swimming in general.

Results of research to date support the TRA and TPB, with intentions being explained quite well by attitude and social norm, and extra explanatory power is added by perceived behavioural control. However, relatively few studies have investigated children or youth and these will now be reviewed in brief (see Table 5.1 for a summary).

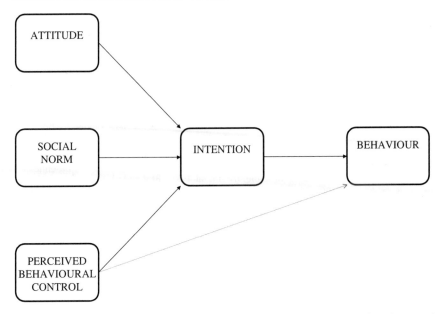

Figure 5.1 Theories of Reasoned Action and Planned Behaviour. The Theory of Planned Behaviour includes the variable of 'perceived behavioural control'

Results summarised in Table 5.1 suggest that the theories of reasoned action and planned behaviour provide some explanation of children's intentions and behaviour in sport and physical activity, but the explanatory power of the models is generally weak. As expected, intentions are better predicted than behaviours, with between 6% and 34% of the variance in intentions being explained by attitudes and social norms. When the TPB was used (Theodorakis, 1992), perceived behavioural control added significantly to the prediction of intention, suggesting that children's intention to be involved in sport might better be studied using the TPB than the TRA. Later, however, I will suggest some developments in the testing of the TRA/TPB using self-determination theory.

In summary, attitude research suggests that positive intentions are determinants of children's decision-making for physical activity and that such intentions are determined by attitudes, social norms and perceived behavioural control. 'Good' attitudes can be developed through positive beliefs and values concerning physical activity, and social norms are influential through the degree to which children wish to comply with the beliefs and actions of key people around them. Consequently, these significant others may be important agents in behaviour change and adherence.

Table 5.1 Summary of physical activity studies using the Theories of Reasoned Action (TRA) and Planned Behaviour (TPB) with children and youth.

Study	Design	Results
Godin & Shephard (1986)	12–14 year old Canadian children ($n = 698$) assessed on attitudes, social norms, and intentions. Theory tested: TRA	• Attitude and social norms predicted 34% of the variance in intentions to be physically active • Intentions, attitudes and social norms were 'higher' for boys than girls • Boys were more active than girls
Reynolds et al. (1990)	14–16 year old American youth ($n = 680$ at baseline; $n = 457$ at 4 month follow-up; $n = 374$ at 16 month follow-up). Theory tested: intention–behaviour relationships from TRA	• After controlling for baseline BMI and physical activity (PA), PA at 4 months was significantly predicted by intention (measured at baseline) for girls but not boys • After controlling for baseline BMI and PA, PA at 16 months was significantly predicted by intention (measured at baseline) for both girls and boys
Theodorakis et al. (1991)	10–11 year old Greek children ($n = 56$) assessed on TRA variables of attitude, social norm, and intention, as well as generalised physical activity attitudes. Theory tested: TRA	• Attitude and social norms predicted 19.4% of the variance in intentions to be physically active • 9% of the variance in PA predicted by intention • TRA variables intention and attitudes were 'higher' for sport participants than non-participants • Generalised PA attitudes did not discriminate between participants and non-participants
Theodorakis (1992)	10–13 year old Greek swimmers ($n = 98$) studied to test whether TPB variables could predict training frequency. Theory tested: TPB	• Attitude and social norms predicted 6% of the variance in swimming training intentions (mainly due to social norms, not attitudes) • An additional 18.25% of the variance in intention was explained by perceived behavioural control • 19% of the variance in training frequency was explained by intentions
Theodorakis et al. (1993)	9–12 year old Greek swimmers ($n = 105$) studied to test whether TRA variables could predict training frequency. Theory tested: TRA	• Attitude and social norms predicted 16% of the variance in swimming training intentions (due to both social norms and attitudes) • 9% of the variance in training frequency was explained by intentions

Achievement Goal Orientations and Motivational Climate

Sport and exercise psychologists have readily adopted the achievement goal orientations approach to the study of motivation, and quite often with children and youth (Duda, 1993; Roberts, 1992, 1993). This reflects the social cognitive *Zeitgeist* in psychology (Fiske & Taylor, 1991; Weiner, 1992). The achievement goals most often studied are 'task' and 'ego' goals. Nicholls (1989) has argued that different conceptions of ability in achievement contexts are embedded in these goals. Task-involved individuals view 'success' or 'ability' being demonstrated through mastery attempts. Those who are ego-involved, however, view ability as limiting the effects of effort on performance. This perspective is labelled 'ability as capacity'. Nicholls (1989), therefore, refers to task-involved individuals as holding a 'less differentiated' conception of ability (effort-based), whereas the ego-involved hold a 'more differentiated' view (ability and effort). Being task-involved means that perceptions of success and ability are made in terms of self-referenced criteria, such as task mastery, learning, and skill development. Ego-involved perceptions of success and ability are based on externally and normative-referenced criteria, such as outperforming others.

Nicholls (1989) has argued that task or ego goal involvement in specific situations may reflect more dispositional orientations. Consequently, sport and exercise psychologists have assessed task and ego goal orientations as potential antecedents of cognitions, emotions and behaviour, hence they are important constructs in the study of adherence to sport.

Correlates of Goal Orientations

The motivational properties of goal orientations for young people in sport can be studied from several different perspectives and these have implications for adherence. Goals have been shown to correlate with beliefs about the causes of success and ability, intrinsic motivation, and affect. In addition, limited evidence points to an association between goals and behaviour (Biddle, in press).

Goals and beliefs

The study of the links between goal orientations and beliefs about the causes of success is fundamental to the understanding of motivated achievement behaviour in youth. Research in classroom and PE/sport contexts has shown that task and ego goal orientations are differentially correlated with beliefs about the causes of success. For example, Duda, Fox,

Biddle & Armstrong (1992) found for 10–11 year old boys and girls that a task orientation was strongly correlated with the belief that success in sport is due to motivation/effort but unrelated to the belief that ability causes success in sport. Conversely, ego orientation was strongly correlated with ability beliefs but correlated with motivation/effort rather weakly. These findings have been replicated on many occasions (see Duda, 1993).

While ability and effort beliefs are important and highly salient in sport, research has suggested that beliefs concerning ability are multidimensional. For example, Dweck and colleagues have discussed conceptions of ability in terms of beliefs about the nature of intelligence (Dweck & Leggett, 1988; Elliott & Dweck, 1988). They distinguished between intelligence that is thought to be relatively fixed and intelligence that is thought to be changeable. Children believing in a more fixed notion of intelligence (an 'entity theory' of intelligence) were found to be more likely to adopt an ego-oriented achievement goal. Conversely, children believing that intelligence is changeable (an 'incremental theory' of intelligence) were more likely to adopt a task goal. There is also evidence showing that self-efficacy and perceptual–motor performance are more positively affected by conceptions of ability associated with acquirable skill than when ability is viewed as inherent aptitude (Jourden, Bandura, & Banfield, 1991; see also Bandura, 1997).

Using a short 'Sport Incremental Ability Scale' (SIAS), we tested whether beliefs concerning the fixed or incremental nature of sport ability were related to achievement goal orientations in 11–12 year old children (Sarrazin et al., 1996). We assessed goals using the Task and Ego Orientation in Sport Questionnaire (TEOSQ) as well as asking the children to choose their preferred goal in the same way as Dweck and Leggett (1988) had done; that is the children simply stated a preference for one of three goals offered. We found that children choosing a task goal were more likely to be represented in the incremental beliefs group (see Table 5.2). This provided support for the propositions of Dweck and Leggett and showed that such notions could be extended into the domain of sport.

Table 5.2 Percentage of children ($N = 194$) in the 'fixed' and 'incremental' sport ability belief groups choosing either a task, ego (easy), or ego (challenging) goal. (Data from Sarrazin et al., 1996)

Sport ability beliefs	Goal choice		
	TASK	EGO (easy)	EGO (challenging)
Fixed	42.0	26.0	32.0
Incremental	55.3	12.8	31.9

The conception of sport ability, however, is likely to be broader than that suggested by either Dweck or Nicholls. Consequently, we went back to the views of Fleishman (1964) in the motor behaviour literature. Fleishman distinguished between abilities and skills in his 'scientific' conception of motor performance factors. He distinguished abilities from skills in relation to their determinants (inheritance/learning), specificity (specific/general), and malleability (stable/changeable). He saw skills as evolving from learning and being specific to a task or group of tasks. Abilities were viewed as quite stable, sometimes genetically determined, rather general, and they limit the effect of learning on performance.

As well as Fleishman's scientific view, one can identify a 'lay view' of sport ability as expressed by parents, journalists or sport spectators. Such notions include beliefs that sport ability is a gift ('God-given') or is natural (see Bandura, 1997).

Using both scientific and lay conceptions, Sarrazin et al. (1996) developed a questionnaire to assess such beliefs and tested it with over 300 French adolescents. It was labelled the Conception of the Nature of Athletic Ability Questionnaire (CNAAQ) and it assessed beliefs in the following properties of sport ability:

- *learning*: sport ability is the product of learning;
- *incremental*: sport ability can change;
- *specific ability*: sport ability is specific to certain sports or types of sports;
- *general ability*: sport ability generalises across many sports;
- *stable ability*: sport ability is stable across time;
- *gift-induced*: sport ability is a 'gift', i.e. 'God-given'.

Correlations were in the predicted directions with task orientation being associated with beliefs that sport ability is incremental, the product of learning, and unstable. Beliefs that sport ability is a gift and general were associated with an ego goal orientation.

Nicholls (1989) has pointed out that task and ego goal orientations are largely orthogonal. This means that children may report high scores for both task and ego, or low scores on both factors, or some combination of this. To tackle task and ego goals separately, therefore, may not represent the true picture and therefore it is important to analyse goal profiles where possible (Fox, Goudas, Biddle, Duda & Armstrong, 1994). Most studies in this area have used a mean or median split to create the following four groups: high task and high ego (hi/hi), high task and low ego (hi-T/lo-E), high ego and low task (hi-E/lo-T), low task and low ego (lo/lo).

In terms of beliefs concerning sport success, we (Biddle, Akande, Vlachopoulos, & Fox, 1996) found no differences between the four goal groups concerning ability beliefs, but those in the hi-T/lo-E group were significantly stronger in their effort beliefs than those in the hi-E/lo-T and the lo/lo groups. Sarrazin et al. (1996) found that the highest scores on the incremental and learning scales were reported by those in the hi/hi and hi-T/lo-E groups, whereas the lowest score for gift beliefs were reported by those in the hi-T/lo-E group.

It is clear, therefore, that a task orientation is associated with the belief that effort is a main determinant of success in PE and sport for children. Effort is often believed to be controllable by the individual. Believing that trying hard will bring some success in terms of adherence, one might predict, since it reflects the 'I can!' feeling so often desired by teachers or coaches.

The approach we adopted in assessing the nature of sport ability beliefs (Sarrazin et al., 1996) leads to a more differentiated view of how pupils might think about sport ability and how these beliefs may impact on motivation. Consistent with the correlations between a task orientation and effort beliefs, we found that a task goal was associated with more controllable aspects of 'ability', such as sport ability being incremental and developed through learning. Central to adherence and motivational enhancement, therefore, is the controllable and self-determined nature of sport ability. Believing that sport ability can change is correlated with a task goal and seems more motivationally adaptive.

Data presented on the independent effects of these beliefs suggest that teachers and coaches of children and youth need to promote the belief that 'ability' is changeable through learning and trying. Using feedback based on personal rather than normative feedback is recommended.

Goals and intrinsic motivation

When goal orientations have been studied in respect of their relationships with motivational indices, one popular index has involved the assessment of intrinsic motivation using the Intrinsic Motivation Inventory (IMI; McAuley, Duncan & Tammen, 1989). The link between intrinsic motivation and goals has been made theoretically and empirically (see Deci & Ryan, 1985; Duda, 1993; Duda, Chi, Newton, Walling, & Catley, 1995; Thill & Brunel, 1995). For example, Duda et al. (1995) showed that a high task and low ego goal orientation was associated with the enjoyment subscale of the IMI for one sample, and a high task orientation was associated with the IMI effort subscale in another sample.

We studied achievement goals and 'intrinsic interest' of children in three PE classes, specifically boys in football (soccer), girls in netball, as well as both boys and girls in gymnastics (Goudas, Biddle & Fox, 1994a). Intrinsic interest was assessed by using the effort and enjoyment subscales from the IMI as well as a boredom scale. It was found that a task orientation was directly related to intrinsic interest for the football/netball lessons whereas the relationship between ego orientation and intrinsic interest was moderated by perceptions of competence. For gymnastics lessons, only a task orientation was related to intrinsic interest. These findings were supported by our study of Romanian children (Dorobantu & Biddle, 1997), confirming cross-cultural validity.

In addition to studying generalised perceptions of intrinsic motivation we (Goudas, Biddle and Fox, 1994b) assessed 255 adolescents performing an aerobic shuttle endurance run 'test' in normal PE lessons. Prior to the test the students completed the TEOSQ and immediately after the run they completed the IMI with reference to their current motivational state. Results were analysed according to the four goal groups specified earlier. In addition, the sample was split into two based on their objective running performance.

Results showed that for the less objectively successful runners, IMI enjoyment scores were higher for those in the hi-T/lo-E group in comparison to the lo/lo and hi-E/lo-T groups. Similarly, hi-T/lo-E children had higher IMI effort scores than those classified as hi-E/lo-T. These results suggest that a high task orientation, even for those performing below the group average, preserved some form of intrinsic motivation.

Goals and Behaviour

It is surprising that so few studies have investigated behavioural correlates of goals. We still know little about how goals may affect behaviours such as choice, persistence or adherence. One application of goal orientations we adopted was to study whether goals predicted voluntary participation in school PE (Spray & Biddle, 1997). Since PE classes are compulsory until the age of 16 years, we sampled students in the 16–18 year old age group. These students could choose to take PE as part of a wider programme of study options. The results are illustrated in Figure 5.2 and show clearly that participation is higher for those students with a high task orientation, either singly or in combination with a high ego orientation. However, we cannot conclude yet whether this reflects actual adherence over time or simply a short-term choice.

Similar participation differences were found in our study of 11–12 year old children (Fox et al., 1994). We assessed, through self-report, their frequency of voluntary participation in sport both in and out of school. Results revealed a graded relationship; sport involvement was higher for those high in task orientation both overall and for those high in perceived

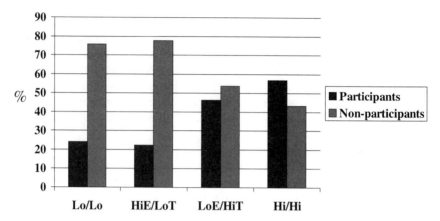

Figure 5.2   Rates of participation in voluntary PE programmes for 16–18 year olds in relation to their goal orientation profiles (data from Spray & Biddle, 1997)

competence. Low sport involvement was clear for those in the lo/lo group, especially when they reported low perceived competence. This group may be particularly vulnerable to amotivation and poor adherence.

Cury, Biddle, Sarrazin and Famose (1997) conducted two experiments with 12–15 year old French school pupils to see if goal orientations and perceived competence were predictive of adherence to learning a sport task. In their first study, Cury et al. selected 57 male students on the basis of their goal orientation and perceived competence profiles. Specifically, the following four groups were created: (a) high ego, low task, low perceived competence (PC); (b) high ego, low task, high PC; (c) low ego, high task, low PC; (d) low ego, high task, high PC. The study involved the boys taking part in a timed attempt at a basketball dribbling task around an obstacle course. The test was performed alone and was preceded by a period of training and practice. Since the main purpose of the experiment was to test for the amount of investment in practice shown by the boys, the PE teacher (experimenter) left the gymnasium for 5 minutes with a suitable excuse for his absence but leaving the instructions that the boys could practise if they wished. During this period the boys were observed unobtrusively and the time spent practising was recorded. After 5 minutes the experimenter returned and continued with the basketball test. The amount of time spent practising the task during the experimenter's absence was significantly less for those boys who were ego-oriented with low perceived competence compared to the other three groups.

In a second study, Cury et al. (1997) used similar methods to investigate the investment made in learning the same basketball task, but this time after failure. A different group of male French school students, aged 13–15 years of age, were selected on the basis of the same groupings as used in the first study. Again, the boys high in ego orientation with low perceived competence invested much less time in practice than others. Overall, therefore, the results of the two experiments confirm the difficulties ego-oriented pupils may have in adhering to practice when given the free choice to do so. However, it is important to note that it is not ego orientation *per se* that is the problem, but it is ego orientation *when accompanied by low perceived competence*. This is wholly consistent with theoretical predictions from goal orientations theory (Nicholls, 1989, 1992).

Task and Ego Goals: Good Guy–Bad Guy?

There is little doubt that a task goal orientation has many positive motivational correlates and hence important implications for adherence in sport and physical activity. However, does this make task orientation 'good' and, perhaps by default, ego 'bad'? Sometimes this has been the message in sport psychology, even if made unintentionally. Indeed, Hardy (1997) says that the often-proposed detrimental effect of outcome-oriented goals and an ego goal orientation is a 'myth' in applied sport psychology. For example, he argues that since task and ego goals are largely orthogonal, we should be investigating their interactive effects. Indeed, I have just summarised several studies using the interactive 'goal profiles' approach. The conclusion from such studies is that ego orientation is not 'bad' when it is accompanied by a high task orientation. However, ego orientation, coupled with low perceived competence, is generally detrimental to motivation (e.g. Cury et al., 1997). But I agree with Hardy when he questions whether much of the research can be applied to elite athletes since the knowledge base is largely drawn from studies on children in PE or recreational sport contexts. The issue of the use of process and outcome goals, as opposed to task and ego goal *orientations*, however, is beyond the scope of the present discussion (see also Duda, 1997).

Motivational Climate and Adherence

From the data presented, achievement goal orientations form an important and powerful influence on motivation and adherence. However, individual differences are sometimes difficult to influence directly and may not be a cost-effective approach for sport groups. As Treasure and Roberts (1995) have argued, 'a growing body of literature exists to suggest that the teacher plays an active role in the construction of children's perceptions of the motivational climate and, consequently, the quality of children's motivation' (p. 480). Some researchers, therefore, have emphasised the importance of the achievement environment, or climate.

Two main climates have been identified and follow the work of Ames in school classrooms (see Ames, 1992; Ames & Archer, 1988; Treasure & Roberts, 1995). A 'mastery' (task) climate is perceived by class or team members when they are directed towards self-improvement, the teacher/coach emphasises learning and personal progress, effort is rewarded, mistakes are seen as part of learning, and choice is allowed. On the other hand, a 'performance' (ego) climate is one that encourages interindividual comparison, where mistakes are punished, and high normative ability is rewarded (see Ames, 1992; Biddle et al., 1995; Papaioannou, 1995). Although the general dimensions of mastery and performance climate have been used satisfactorily in PE research (Biddle et al., 1995; Dorobantu & Biddle, 1997; Goudas & Biddle, 1994; Papaioannou, 1994), factors underlying these dimensions are less clear (Ntoumanis & Biddle, in press).

We have calculated effect sizes for a small number of physical activity climate studies to indicate the strength of relationships between motivational climate and selected cognitive and affective variables (Ntoumanis & Biddle, in press). Although the studies were not restricted to children, they indicate the strength of links between climate and associated psychological outcomes likely to influence adherence.

From a quantitative synthesis of 14 studies with a total sample size of almost 4484, the correlation, corrected for both sampling and measurement error, between mastery climate and positive motivational outcomes (e.g. satisfaction, positive attitudes towards lessons, intrinsic motivation) was 0.71, indicating a large effect. By contrast, performance climate correlated in a small-to-moderate way and in a negative direction with positive outcomes (ES = –0.30). Negative outcomes were also assessed and these comprised factors such as worry and the emphasis on normative ability. The effect for mastery climate on negative outcomes was small-to-moderate and negative (ES = –0.26), and for performance climate on these outcomes was moderate and positive (ES = 0.46). These results, overall, indicate the importance of a mastery climate in promoting positive psychological outcomes in physical activity.

Few studies have manipulated constructs associated with climate to test the efficacy of interventions in sport and physical activity. Therefore, we sought to investigate whether manipulating teaching styles in line with climate dimensions would result in differential motivational effects (Goudas, Biddle, Fox, & Underwood, 1995).

A small intact class of young adolescent girls was taught track and field for 10 weeks in their normal PE lessons. An experienced university lecturer, well versed in teaching styles, was the class teacher and alternated lessons according to two teaching styles:

- *Direct style.* Most of the decisions were made by the teacher; the type of task, duration of practice and degree of difficulty were determined by the teacher. This style was chosen to approximate the creation of a climate low in mastery orientation.
- *Differentiated style.* The teacher gave the children choices; varied activities were provided, degree of difficulty and pace of practice/learning were decided by the child. This style was chosen to approximate the creation of a climate high in mastery orientation.

At the end of each lesson, measures were taken of intrinsic motivation, task and work avoidance goal involvement (in the lesson), and intention to participate in future lessons. Results showed more positive effects for lessons taught by the differentiated style, suggesting an influence for mastery climate. Specifically, after the differentiated style lessons, the children reported higher intrinsic motivation and task involvement scores than after direct style lessons. Adherence to track and field, one might suggest, was enhanced through this teaching approach.

Of the few intervention studies that exist, it is clear that a mastery climate has positive cognitive and affective outcomes. However, most are short-term and limited in what they assess. Future research must address the issue of implementing more rigorous controlled trials for longer time periods in order to assess properly the effects on adherence.

Intrinsic Motivation and Self-Determination Approaches

Intrinsic and extrinsic motivation are well-known constructs in psychology and are thought to be central to any discussion on motivation and adherence. Those involved in promoting sport and exercise adherence believe that intrinsic motivation is key to sustaining involvement. Intrinsic motivation is motivation to do something for its own sake in the absence of external (extrinsic) rewards. Often this involves fun, enjoyment and satisfaction, such as in recreational activities and hobbies. The enjoyment is in the activity itself rather than any extrinsic reward such as money, prizes or prestige from others, and participation is free of constraints and pressure. Such intrinsically pursued activities are referred to as 'autotelic' (self-directing) by Csikszentmihalyi (1975). Such a notion is useful for the present discussion since it suggests that intrinsically motivated behaviour is linked to feelings of self-control or self-determination, or what I shall call 'autonomy' (Deci & Ryan, 1985).

Extrinsic motivation, on the other hand, refers to motivation directed by rewards, money, pressure or other external factors. This suggests that if these rewards or external pressures were removed, motivation would decline in the absence of any intrinsic interest.

The Development of Intrinsic Motivation Theories

Deci and Ryan (1985, 1991) suggest four main approaches to the study and measurement of intrinsic motivation: free choice, interest, challenge, and 'needs'. Studying intrinsic motivation through the assessment of free choice allows some behavioural measure to be estimated. In the absence of extrinsic rewards, those intrinsically motivated will be those who choose to participate in their own free time. Intrinsically motivated behaviour is also performed out of interest and curiosity, as well as challenge. Finally, Deci and Ryan (1985, 1991) outline the important role of psychological needs identified over time through constructs such as 'effectance' (White), 'personal causation' (deCharms), and 'competence' and 'self-determination' (Deci & Ryan, 1985).

Deci and Ryan (1985) propose that three key psychological needs are related to intrinsically motivated behaviour. These are the needs for competence, autonomy, and relatedness. Competence refers to strivings to control outcomes and to experience mastery and effectance. Humans seek to understand how to produce desired outcomes. Autonomy is related to self-determination. It is similar to deCharms' notion of being the 'origin' rather than the 'pawn', and to have feelings of perceived control and to feel actions emanate from the self. Finally, relatedness refers to strivings to relate to, and care for, others; to feel that others can relate to oneself; 'to feel a satisfying and coherent involvement with the social world more generally' (Deci & Ryan, 1991, p. 345).

Deci and Ryan (1991) state that 'these three psychological needs . . . help to explain a substantial amount of variance in human behavior and experience' (p. 345). People seek to satisfy these needs, but of more importance from the point of view of enhancing intrinsic motivation and adherence is that they predict the circumstances in which intrinsically motivated behaviour can be promoted.

Cognitive Evaluation Theory

The relationship between intrinsic and extrinsic motivation was, at one time, thought to be quite simple in that 'more' motivation would result from adding extrinsic to existing intrinsic motivation. This appeared logical given the evidence demonstrating that reinforcements (i.e. extrinsic rewards) will increase the probability of the rewarded behaviour reoccurring. However, a number of studies and observations, mainly with children, started to question whether intrinsic motivation was actually undermined by the use of extrinsic rewards. This was done through 'Cognitive Evaluation Theory' (CET), a 'mini-theory' within 'Self-Determination Theory' (Deci & Ryan, 1985).

CET states that rewards are likely to serve two main functions:

- *Information function.* If the reward provides information about the individual's competence then it is quite likely that intrinsic motivation can be enhanced with appropriate rewards.
- *Controlling function.* If the rewards are seen to be controlling behaviour (i.e. the goal is to obtain the reward rather than participate for intrinsic reasons), then withdrawal of the reward is likely to lead to subsequent deterioration in intrinsic motivation.

It is important to note that informational events are those events that are perceived to convey feedback about one's competence within the context of autonomy. Events where positive feedback occurs under pressure may be less powerful in influencing intrinsic motivation.

In summarising CET, Deci and Ryan (1985) present three propositions:

- *Proposition 1.* 'External events relevant to the initiation and regulation of behaviour will affect a person's intrinsic motivation to the extent that they influence the perceived locus of causality for that behaviour. Events that promote a more external locus of causality will undermine intrinsic motivation, whereas those that promote a more internal perceived locus of causality will enhance intrinsic motivation' (p. 62).

Deci and Ryan (1985) say that events that lead to an external locus of causality undermine intrinsic motivation because they deny people 'self-determination', that is they control peoples' behaviour. On the other hand, internal locus of causality may enhance intrinsic motivation by facilitating feelings of self-determination, thus creating greater autonomy.

- *Proposition 2.* 'External events will affect a person's intrinsic motivation for an optimally challenging activity to the extent that they influence the person's perceived competence, within the context of some self-determination. Events that promote greater perceived competence will enhance intrinsic motivation, whereas those that diminish perceived competence will decrease intrinsic motivation' (Deci & Ryan, 1985, p.63).

As Proposition 2 suggests, intrinsic motivation is not just about feelings of control but also about perceived competence.

- *Proposition 3.* 'Events relevant to the initiation and regulation of behaviour have three potential aspects, each with a functional significance. The informational aspect facilitates an internal perceived locus of causality and perceived competence, thus enhancing intrinsic motivation. The controlling aspect facilitates an external perceived locus of causality, thus undermining intrinsic motivation and promoting extrinsic compliance or defiance. The amotivating aspect facilitates perceived incompetence, thus undermining intrinsic motivation and promoting amotivation. The relative salience of these three aspects to a person determines the functional significance of the event.' (Deci & Ryan, 1985, p. 64).

Deci and Ryan (1985) conclude that, generally speaking, choice and positive feedback are perceived as informational, while rewards, deadlines and surveillance tend to be controlling. Negative feedback is seen to undermine motivation and is therefore referred to as 'amotivating'.

Since sport and exercise often require persistence, effort, time management, self-regulatory skills and many other things related to motivation, it is relevant to consider the role of intrinsic motivation and self-determination in this context. Whitehead and Corbin (1991), for example, tested Proposition 2 from CET in the context of fitness testing with children. Studying 12–13 year olds on an agility run test, they sought to test whether changes in perceived competence would vary with changes in intrinsic motivation. They assessed four dimensions of intrinsic motivation using the IMI: interest/enjoyment, competence, effort/importance, and pressure/tension.

After completing the agility run course, two groups of children were given bogus feedback, stating that they were either in the top or bottom 20% for their age. A third group was given no feedback. Clear support for CET was found with the low feedback group (low competence) showing less intrinsic motivation than those receiving the more positive feedback. Intrinsic motivation scores were influenced by perceptions of competence.

Towards Self-determination

CET involves the processing of the information concerning reward structures. Extending this perspective, and including the psychological needs for competence, autonomy and relatedness, Deci and Ryan (1985, 1991) have proposed their 'Self-determination Theory' (SDT) approach to intrinsic motivation. The nature of motivated behaviour, according to Deci and Ryan, is based on striving to satisfy these three basic needs. This, they say, leads to a process of 'internalisation'—'taking in' behaviours not initially intrinsically motivating.

Deci and Ryan (1985) have linked the internalisation concept to that of extrinsic and intrinsic motivation. In contrast to their earlier formulations in which these two motivational types were regarded as mutually exclusive, they proposed that they form a continuum where different types of extrinsically regulated behaviour can be located. Deci and Ryan (1991) refer to the continuum as one representing 'the degree to which the regulation of a nonintrinsically motivated behavior has been internalized' (p. 254).

The four main types of extrinsic motivation are external, introjected, identified, and integrated regulation, as shown in Figure 5.3. External regulation might be illustrated by a child saying 'OK, I'll go to the PE lesson if I really must.' This is an example of where behaviour is controlled by rewards and threats, such as in the case of coercion of children in school.

Introjected regulation might be when one says 'I feel guilty if I don't play for the school team.' This is more internal in the sense that the individual internalises the reasons for acting, but is not truly self-determined. The individual is acting out of avoidance of negative feelings, such as guilt, or to seek approval from others for their performance or behaviour. The term introjection has been used a great deal in different areas of psychology over the years and refers to someone 'taking in' a value but, at the same time, does not really identify with it; it is not accepted as one's own.

Identified regulation might be illustrated by the adolescent who says 'I must exercise to get fitter.' This is further towards the self-determined end of the motivation continuum where action is motivated by an appreciation of the outcomes of participation, such as disease prevention or fitness improvement. Although this is a more internalised perspective, and is moderately correlated with future intentions, it is still focused on a product or outcome. In physical activity it can be the most strongly endorsed reason for exercising (Chatzisarantis & Biddle, 1998) and has been identified by Whitehead (1993) as the 'threshold of autonomy'. It is behaviour acted out of choice where the behaviour is highly valued and important to the individual. It is illustrated by feelings of 'I want to . . .'. The values associated with the behaviour are now accepted.

Integrated regulation is illustrated by Whitehead (1993) through the phrase 'I exercise because it is important to me and it symbolises who and what I am'. Integrated regulation is the most self-determined form of behavioural regulation and the behaviour is volitional 'because of its utility or importance for one's personal goals' (Deci, Eghrari, Patrick & Leone, 1994, p. 121). However, it is important to note that even though the behaviour may be fully integrated, it can still be extrinsically motivated. This is because it may be an instrumental action, done to achieve personal goals rather than for the pure joy of the activity itself (Deci & Ryan, 1991). This is why the self-determination continuum can be construed as forms of extrinsic motivation without intrinsic motivation.

In contrast to these forms of extrinsic motivation, intrinsic motivation is shown when a child says 'I go swimming because I enjoy it.' The individual

132

AMOTIVATION	EXTRINSIC MOTIVATION				INTRINSIC MOTIVATION
	EXTERNAL REGULATION	INTROJECTED REGULATION	IDENTIFIED REGULATION	INTEGRATED REGULATION	
• Capacity-ability beyond beliefs • strategy beliefs • capacity-effort beliefs • helplessness beliefs					• to know • to accomplish • to experience stimulation
	− ←	SELF-DETERMINATION	→ +		

Figure 5.3 A continuum of self-determination represented by different types of motivation

participates for fun and for the activity itself. Clearly moving towards intrinsically, or integrated, motivated forms of behavioural regulation are advised for higher levels of intention and sustained adherence in sport and exercise since they are likely to involve stronger feelings of personal investment, autonomy and self-identity. Some have also proposed three types of intrinsic motivation: intrinsic motivation 'to know', 'to accomplish' and 'to experience stimulation' (Vallerand, 1997), as shown in Figure 5.3.

Ryan and Connell (1989) propose 'that the constructs described in internalisation theories can be related to several distinct classes of REASONS for acting that in turn have a lawful internal ordering. That is, these classes of reasons can be meaningfully placed along a continuum of autonomy, or of self-causality' (p. 750). They suggest that the continuum should be able to be demonstrated through a simplex-like or ordered correlation structure where variables are ordered 'such that those deemed more similar correlate more highly than those that are hypothetically more discrepant' (p. 750). We have shown this in the context of children's motivational orientations towards school physical education lessons (see Table 5.3) (Goudas et al., 1994a). Similarly, by weighting each subscale, an overall Relative Autonomy Index (RAI) can be computed, with higher scores indicating higher internality.

In addition, it has been suggested that the state of 'amotivation' exists where the individual has little or no motivation to attempt the behaviour. Whitehead (1993) describes the move from amotivation to external regulation as crossing the 'threshold of motivation'. Vallerand (1997) has likened amotivation to a feeling of learned helplessness although, as shown in Figure 5.3, there may be several types of amotivation involving not just beliefs of helplessness, but also feelings that one has inadequate ability, effort and strategies.

Surprisingly, the use of SDT for studying intrinsic motivation has not been extensive in physical activity. However, we have used the autonomy

Table 5.3 Correlations between self-determination theory variables in children's PE lessons, demonstrating the simplex-like pattern predicted by Ryan and Connell (1989) (data from Goudas et al., 1994a)

Motivational orientation	External		Introjected		Identification		Intrinsic	
	F & N	Gym	F & N	Gym	F & N	Gym	F & N	Gym
Amotivation	0.55	0.53	−0.14	−0.15	−0.62	−0.70	−0.72	−0.75
External			0.23	0.10	−0.25	−0.50	−0.38	−0.50
Introjection					0.42	0.35	0.33	0.25
Identification							0.87	0.78

Note: F & N: Football & Netball
Gym: Gymnastics

continuum, and the RAI, in analyses of children's motivation within the domain of physical activity. So far we have found that perceptions of autonomy, assessed with the RAI, are predictive of intrinsic interest in physical activity (Goudas et al., 1994a). For example, in a study of motivation towards team games lessons (football and netball), where intrinsic interest was already high, autonomy predicted intrinsic motivation but not intention to participate in the future. On the other hand, for the same group of children, but this time in gymnastics lessons, intrinsic motivation was lower and autonomy predicted both intrinsic motivation and intention.

In a study of 11–15 year olds in England, we assessed intentions to participate in leisure-time exercise in terms of both 'autonomous' and 'controlling' forms (Chatzisarantis, Biddle & Meek, 1997). Specifically, we asked the children to rate the degree to which they intended to exercise because they 'have to' (controlling) or because they 'want to' (autonomous). Results showed that intentions predict physical activity when they are autonomous rather than controlling, lending support to SDT.

Finally, we studied the relationship between participation motivation, self-determination and physical activity with 160 British and American students (mean age of 18 years) using a prospective design (Chatzisarantis, Biddle & Frederick, 1999). Specifically, motives for exercising, measures of self-determination, and both autonomous and controlling intentions were assessed, and physical activity was assessed both 4 and 8 weeks later.

The main results are illustrated in Figure 5.4. They show that exercise is predicted by autonomous, but not controlling, intentions, and that fitness and social motives act as more autonomous and self-determining forms of motivation than the motive for appearance. This is shown to be associated with external and introjected behavioural regulation. The construct of autonomy, therefore, appears to be important in the study of adherence and the prediction of physical activity behaviours.

EMOTION AS A DETERMINANT OF ADHERENCE

At the beginning of this chapter, I summarised research on participation motivation in sport for children and youth. One of the most common findings is for children to report that they play sport 'for fun'. Whether this reflects a true intrinsic state or simply an affective reaction from the satisfaction of other motives, we cannot tell. Nevertheless, it does suggest that adherence is related to the emotional experience children and youth have in sport and exercise. Put simply, and not withstanding the discussion on self-determination and different behavioural regulations, children are

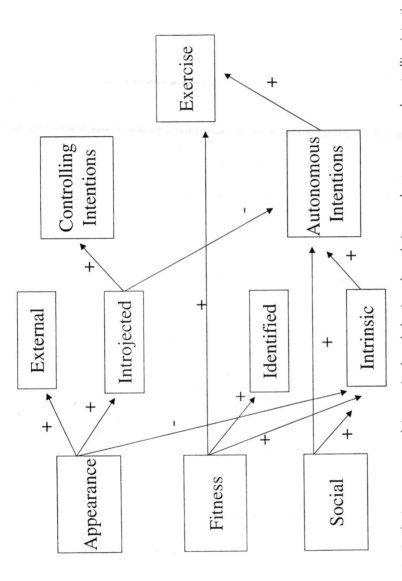

Figure 5.4 Predicting young people's exercise from behavioural regulations and autonomous and controlling intentions (Chatzisarantis et al., 1999)

unlikely to play sport, given the choice, if they don't like it! Consequently, it is necessary to consider the role of emotion in sport and exercise adherence.

Enjoyment as Motivation

Most adults recognise the important role of enjoyment in children's sports. A great deal of time is spent trying to find enjoyable ways of putting across concepts, actively engaging children, or simply creating an element of 'fun' so that the children want to come back. Enjoyment is not trivial, however. In an educational context enjoyment is an important element of motivation, particularly when physical effort might be required, as in sport and fitness/exercise contexts. Despite all of this, enjoyment has remained an illusive concept for many years. However, at least four approaches to enjoyment can be identified that have relevance to sport and exercise adherence:

- Csikzentmihalyi's 'flow' model;
- intrinsic motivation;
- Scanlan's study of sport enjoyment in children;
- exercise-induced feeling states.

Enjoyment and Flow

Csikszentmihalyi (1975) studied why people invested huge amounts of time and energy in tasks which appeared to yield limited external rewards. One of his conclusions was that motivation seemed highest when the challenge or difficulty of the task was matched by personal abilities and skills. This matching led to a state of 'flow', or supreme enjoyment and engagement in the task. A mismatch can lead to either boredom (low challenge/high skills) or anxiety (high challenge/low skills).

Enjoyment and Intrinsic Motivation

The development of intrinsic motivation is a key consideration for many physical educators and sports coaches working with children, and has already been discussed. High intrinsic motivation includes high effort, feelings of enjoyment, competence, and autonomy (self-determination), and low levels of pressure and anxiety.

Intrinsic motivation and flow are clearly interrelated. Csikszentmihalyi (1975) spoke of 'autotelic' (self-directed) activities being the ones where flow was most likely, and Deci and Ryan (1985) speak about the 'self-determination' of behaviour through intrinsic motivation.

Sport Enjoyment Model

A preliminary model of sport enjoyment for children was proposed by Scanlan and Lewthwaite (1986) after studying 9–14 year old American boys. They defined sport enjoyment as 'an individual's positive affective response to his or her competitive sport experience which reflects feelings and/or perceptions such as pleasure, liking, and experiencing fun' (p. 32). They also stated that sport enjoyment 'shares a common base with the construct of intrinsic motivation' (p. 32). Specifically, they proposed that sport enjoyment for children can be conceptualised as an interaction between achievement and intrinsic/extrinsic continua, as follows:

- *achievement-intrinsic*: predictors of enjoyment related to personal perceptions of competence and control;
- *achievement-extrinsic*: predictors of enjoyment related to perceptions of competence and control derived from other people (e.g. social recognition);
- *nonachievement-intrinsic*: predictors of enjoyment related to movement sensations;
- *nonachievement-extrinsic*: predictors of enjoyment related to non-performance aspects of sport, such as affiliation.

Exercise-induced Feeling States

Typically it is found that positive mood is improved after exercise. Many studies have used the Profile of Mood States (POMS), but this consists of five negative and only one positive mood. Abele and Brehm (1993), however, have produced the *Befindlichkeitsskalen* in Germany to better represent both the activation and evaluation dimensions of mood. Positive feelings, accompanied by high activation, could be associated with enjoyment during physical activity.

In our own research on goal orientations, we have found that positive mood after exercise for children in PE lessons is associated with perceived competence and a task oriented goal. First, we studied the affective reactions of 11–15 year olds to an 800 m run in a normal PE lesson (Vlachopoulos, Biddle & Fox, 1996). Using the Exercise-induced Feeling Inventory (EFI; Gauvin & Rejeski, 1993), we found that post-run feelings of positive engagement, revitalisation, and tranquillity were predicted by both task orientation and perceived competence ratings. In addition, a task orientation negatively predicted feelings of physical exhaustion. In a second study, we investigated generalised affective reactions to school PE in over 1000 11–16 year olds (Vlachopoulos & Biddle, 1997). Results showed that perceived success in PE influenced personally controllable attributions and positive affect but not negative affect. Perceived ability moderated the relationship between ego orientation and personally controllable attributions. Specifically, for low perceived ability children, an ego orientation was associated with personally uncontrollable attributions, but the opposite was the case for children high in perceived ability. We concluded that both a task orientation and high perceived ability are required for positive affective experiences in school PE.

SUMMARY AND FUTURE DIRECTIONS

The discussion so far has centred on adherence to physical activity in young people. Starting with descriptive approaches it was shown that youth are motivated to participate in or inclined to cease involvement with physical activity for a variety of reasons. However, descriptive approaches, it was claimed, are limited in their explanatory power and hence various theoretical perspectives were covered. These included attitude–behaviour models, achievement goal approaches, intrinsic motivation and self-determination, and emotion as a determinant of adherence. In all cases, evidence exists for the utility of such approaches for the study of physical activity adherence in children and youth.

In conclusion, two issues will be considered. These concern the use of social cognitive models for the investigation and explanation of young people's behaviour, and the role of adherence in aspects of physical activity other than sport and exercise.

Many of the theoretical approaches to physical activity behaviours, such as the TRA, TPB, self-efficacy theory, goal perspectives theory etc., are social cognitive in nature. In other words, they assume humans think through their actions, often rationally, in a social context. An example is the expectancy-value framework where people are thought to make decisions based on the expectancy of success and the value attached to the expected outcomes. Similarly, self-efficacy theory assumes cognitive activity in appraising the likelihood of one's actions and the beliefs that one can initiate the required behaviour. Often such information is gleaned through social interaction.

One could argue that such rational decision making is unlikely in children, although becomes more likely in older adolescents. This begs the question whether some of the social psychological models discussed here are wholly applicable to younger children. Certainly some researchers are clear about this issue. Nicholls (1989), for example, states that the differentiation of ability, effort and outcome is unlikely before the age of about 11 years, hence task and ego goal orientations are not fully formed before this.

Future research into adherence to physical activity in young people needs to consider these issues. This will require a wider developmental perspective than the one adopted currently. For example, if social cognitive approaches are less applicable to younger children, what is the role of parents, teachers and peers in adherence? What role might the environment play in encouraging or inhibiting adherence to play and physical activity of younger children? While some evidence exists supporting the influence of the family and environment on children's physical activity (Sallis, 1998), evidence is still patchy.

Adherence to physical activity has mainly centred on structured physical activity, usually sport or exercise. However, while most young people are likely to obtain the majority of their 'health-enhancing' activity this way, other forms of physical activity require investigation. For example, little is known about 'free play' activity in younger children. Prepubescent children adopt sporadic activity patterns and therefore we should not expect them to be active in an adult-like manner, such as sustaining periods of activity at high heart rates. The study of physical activity adherence in this context, therefore, remains a challenge for the future, and in particular in the measurement of children's physical activity itself. This is much easier if taken in structured and vigorous bouts, but it is precisely this form of physical activity that is unlikely to occur in children.

The other area requiring further investigation is that of physical activity as personal transport. We know little about adherence to cycling or walking as modes of transport. These activities are used by adolescents but we need more information on the determinants of such participation. For example, cycling to school may be for reasons of enjoyment, necessity (no other form of transport available), or for some other reason, such as going to school immediately after delivery of morning newspapers. Understanding why young people adopt, and then adhere, to such behaviours is important.

REFERENCES

Abele, A. & Brehm, W. (1993). Mood effects of exercise versus sports games: Findings and implications for well-being and health. *International Review of Health Psychology*, **2**, 53–80.

Ajzen I. (1985). From intentions to actions: A theory of planned behavior. In J. Kuhl & J. Beckmann (eds.), *Action control: From cognition to behavior* (pp. 11–39). Heidelberg: Springer-Verlag.

Ajzen I. (1988). *Attitudes, personality and behaviour.* Buckingham: Open University Press.

Ajzen I. & Fishbein, M. (1980). *Understanding attitudes and predicting social behavior.* Englewood Cliffs, NJ: Prentice-Hall.

Ames, C. (1992). Achievement goals, motivational climate, and motivational processes. In G.C. Roberts (ed.). *Motivation in sport and exercise* (pp. 161–176). Champaign, IL: Human Kinetics.

Ames, C. & Archer, J. (1988). Achievement goals in the classroom: Students' learning strategies and motivation processes. *Journal of Educational Psychology*, **80**, 260–267.

Bandura, A. (1997). *Self-efficacy: The exercise of control.* New York: W.H. Freeman.

Biddle, S.J.H. (1992). Sport and exercise motivation: A short review of antecedent factors and psychological outcomes of participation. *Physical Education Review*, **15**, 98–110.

Biddle, S.J.H. (in press). Enhancing motivation in physical education. In G.C. Roberts (ed.), *Advances in sport and exercise motivation.* Champaign, IL: Human Kinetics.

Biddle, S.J.H., Akande, A., Vlachopoulos, S., & Fox, K.R. (1996). Towards an understanding of children's motivation for physical activity: Achievement goal orientations, beliefs about sport success, and sport emotion in Zimbabwean children. *Psychology and Health*, **12**, 49–55.

Biddle, S., Cury, F., Goudas, M., Sarrazin, P., Famose, J-P., & Durand, M. (1995). Development of scales to measure perceived physical education class climate: A cross-national project. *British Journal of Educational Psychology*, **65**, 341–358.

Chatzisarantis, N.L.D., Biddle, S.J.H., & Frederick, C. (1999). *The concepts of autonomous and controlling intentions: Formation and the prediction of exercise behaviour.* Manuscript under review.

Biddle, S.J.H., Sallis, J.F., & Cavill, N. (eds.) (1998). *Young and Active? Young people and health-enhancing physical activity: Evidence and implications.* London: Health Education Authority.

Buonamano, R., Cei, A., & Mussino, A. (1995). Participation motivation in Italian youth sport. *The Sport Psychologist*, **9**, 265–281.

Canada Fitness Survey (1983). *Canadian youth and physical activity.* Ottawa, Canada: Author.

Chatzisarantis, N.L.D. & Biddle, S.J.H. (1998). Functional significance of psychological variables that are included in the Theory of Planned Behaviour: A Self-Determination Theory approach to the study of attitudes, subjective norms, perceptions of control and intentions. *European Journal of Social Psychology*, **28**, 303–322.

Chatzisarantis, N.L.D., Biddle, S.J.H., & Meek, G.A. (1997). A self-determination theory approach to the study of intentions and the intention-behaviour relationship in children's physical activity. *British Journal of Health Psychology*, **2**, 343–360.

Coakley, J.J. & White, A. (1992). Making decisions: Gender and sport participation among British adolescents. *Sociology of Sport Journal*, **9**, 20–35.

Csikszentmihalyi, M. (1975). *Beyond boredom and anxiety*. San Francisco: Jossey-Bass.

Cury, F., Biddle, S., Sarrazin, P., & Famose, J-P. (1997). Achievement goals and perceived ability predict investment in learning a sport task. *British Journal of Educational Psychology*, **67**, 293–309.

Deci, E.L., Eghrari, H., Patrick, B.C., & Leone,D.R. (1994). Facilitating internalization: The Self-Determination Theory perspective. *Journal of Personality*, 62, 119–142.

Deci, E.L. & Ryan, R.M. (1985). *Intrinsic motivation and self-determination in human behavior*. New York: Plenum.

Deci, E.L. & Ryan, R.M. (1991). A motivational approach to self: Integration in personality. In R.A. Dienstbier (ed.), *1991 Nebraska symposium on motivation: Perspectives on motivation*, Vol. 38 (pp. 237–288). Lincoln, NE: University of Nebraska Press.

Dorobantu, M. & Biddle, S.J.H. (1997). The influence of situational and individual goals on the intrinsic motivation of Romanian adolescents towards physical education. *European Yearbook of Sport Psychology*, **1**, 148–165.

Duda, J.L. (1993). Goals: A social-cognitive approach to the study of achievement motivation in sport. In R.N. Singer, M. Murphey, & L.K. Tennant (eds.). *Handbook of research on sport psychology* (pp. 421–436). New York: Macmillan.

Duda, J.L. (1997). Perpetuating myths: A response to Hardy's 1996 Coleman Griffith Address. *Journal of Applied Sport Psychology*, **9**, 303–309.

Duda, J.L., Chi, L., Newton, M.L., Walling, M.D., & Catley, D. (1995). Task and ego orientation and intrinsic motivation in sport. *International Journal of Sport Psychology*, **26**, 40–63.

Duda, J.L., Fox, K.R., Biddle, S.J.H., & Armstrong, N. (1992). Children's achievement goals and beliefs about success in sport. *British Journal of Educational Psychology*, **62**, 313–323.

Dweck, C.S. & Leggett, E.L. (1988). A social-cognitive approach to motivation and personality. *Psychological Review*, **95**, 256–273.

Elliott, E.S. & Dweck, C.S. (1988). Goals: An approach to motivation and achievement. *Journal of Personality and Social Psychology*, **54**, 5–12.

Fiske, S.T. & Taylor, S.E. (1991). *Social cognition*. New York: McGraw-Hill.

Fleishman, E.A. (1964). *Structure and measurement of physical fitness.* Englewood Cliffs, NJ: Prentice-Hall.

Fox, K., Goudas, M., Biddle, S., Duda, J., & Armstrong, N. (1994). Children's task and ego goal profiles in sport. *British Journal of Educational Psychology*, **64**, 253–261.

Gauvin, L. & Rejeski, W.J. (1993). The Exercise-Induced Feeling Inventory: Development and initial validation. *Journal of Sport and Exercise Psychology*, **15**, 403–423.

Godin, G. & Shephard, R.J. (1986). Psychosocial factors influencing intentions to exercise of young students from grades 7 to 9. *Research Quarterly for Exercise and Sport*, **57**, 41–52.

Goudas, M. & Biddle, S.J.H. (1994). Perceived motivational climate and intrinsic motivation in school physical education classes. *European Journal of Psychology of Education*, **9**, 241–250.

Goudas, M., Biddle, S.J.H. & Fox, K.R. (1994a). Perceived locus of causality, goal orientations, and perceived competence in school physical education classes. *British Journal of Educational Psychology*, **64**, 453–463.

Goudas, M., Biddle, S.J.H. & Fox, K.R. (1994b). Achievement goal orientations and intrinsic motivation in physical fitness testing with children. *Pediatric Exercise Science*, **6**, 159–167.

Goudas, M., Biddle, S.J.H., Fox, K.R., & Underwood, M. (1995). It ain't what you do, it's the way that you do it! Teaching style affects children's motivation in track and field lessons. *The Sport Psychologist*, **9**, 254–264.

Gould, D. (1987). Understanding attrition in children's sport. In D. Gould & M. Weiss (eds.), *Advances in pediatric sport sciences*: Vol II. *Behavioral issues* (pp. 61–85). Champaign, IL: Human Kinetics.

Gould, D. & Petlichkoff, L. (1988). Participation motivation and attrition in young athletes. In F.L. Smoll, R.A. Magill, & M.J. Ash (eds.), *Children in sport* (3rd edn, pp. 161–178). Champaign, IL: Human Kinetics.

Hardy, L. (1997). The Coleman Roberts Griffith Address: Three myths about applied consultancy work. *Journal of Applied Sport Psychology*, **9**, 277–294.

Heartbeat Wales (1987). *Exercise for health: Health-related fitness in Wales.* Cardiff: The Sports Council for Wales.

Jourden, F., Bandura, A., & Banfield, J.T. (1991). The impact of conceptions of ability on self-regulatory factors and motor skill acquisition. *Journal of Sport and Exercise Psychology*, **13**, 213–226.

McAuley, E., Duncan, T., & Tammen, V. (1989). Psychometric properties of the Intrinsic Motivation Inventory in a competitive sport setting: A confirmatory factor analysis. *Research Quarterly for Exercise and Sport*, **60**, 48–58.

Maehr, M.L. & Braskamp, L.A. (1986). *The motivation factor: A theory of personal investment.* Lexington, MA: Lexington Books.

Mason, V. (1995). *Young people and sport in England, 1994*. London: The Sports Council

Nicholls, J.G. (1989). *The competitive ethos and democratic education*. Cambridge, MA: Harvard University Press.

Nicholls, J.G. (1992). The general and the specific in the development and expression of achievement motivation. In G.C. Roberts (ed.). *Motivation in sport and exercise* (pp. 31–56). Champaign, IL: Human Kinetics.

Ntoumanis, N. & Biddle, S.J.H. (in press). A review of motivational climate in physical activity. *Journal of Sports Sciences*.

Papaioannou, A. (1994). Development of a questionnaire to measure achievement orientations in physical education. *Research Quarterly for Exercise and Sport*, **65**, 11–20.

Papaioannou, A. (1995). Motivation and goal perspectives in children's physical education. In S.J.H. Biddle (ed.), *European perspectives on exercise and sport psychology* (pp. 245–269). Champaign, IL: Human Kinetics.

Reynolds, K.D, Killen, J.D., Bryson, S.W., Maron, D.J., Taylor, C.B., Maccoby, N., & Farquhar, J.W. (1990). Psychosocial predictors of physical activity in adolescents. *Preventive Medicine*, **19**, 541–551.

Roberts, G.C. (1992). Motivation in sport and exercise: Conceptual constraints and convergence. In G.C. Roberts (ed.). *Motivation in sport and exercise* (pp. 3–29). Champaign, IL: Human Kinetics.

Roberts, G.C. (1993). Motivation in sport: Understanding and enhancing the motivation and achievement of children. In R.N. Singer, M. Murphey & L.K. Tennant (eds.), *Handbook of research on sport psychology* (pp. 405–420). New York: Macmillan.

Ryan, R.M. & Connell, J.P. (1989). Perceived locus of causality and internalization: Examining reasons for acting in two domains. *Journal of Personality and Social Psychology*, **57**, 749–761.

Sallis, J.F. (1998). Family and community interventions to promote physical activity in young people. In S.J.H. Biddle, J.F. Sallis, & N. Cavill (eds.), *Young and active? Young people and health-enhancing physical activity: Evidence and implications* (pp. 150–161). London: Health Education Authority.

Sarrazin, P., Biddle, S., Famose, J-P., Cury, F., Fox, K., & Durand, M. (1996). Goal orientations and conceptions of the nature of sport ability in children: A social cognitive approach. *British Journal of Social Psychology*, **35**, 399–414.

Scanlan, T.K. & Lewthwaite, R. (1986). Social psychological aspects of competition for male youth sport participants: IV. Predictors of enjoyment. *Journal of Sport Psychology*, **8**, 25–35.

Spray, C.M. & Biddle, S.J.H. (1997). Achievement goal orientations and participation in physical education among male and female sixth form students. *European Physical Education Review*, **3**, 83–90.

Telama, R. & Silvennoinen, M. (1979). Structure and development of 11 to 19 year olds' motivation for physical activity. *Scandinavian Journal of Sports Sciences*, **1**, 23–31.

Theodorakis, Y. (1992). Prediction of athletic participation: A test of planed behavior theory. *Perceptual and Motor Skills*, **74**, 371–379.

Theodorakis, Y., Doganis, G., Bagiatis, K., & Goudas, M. (1991). Preliminary study of the ability of reasoned action model in predicting exercise behavior of young children. *Perceptual and Motor Skills*, **72**, 51–58.

Theodorakis, Y., Goudas, M., Bagiatis, K., & Doganis, G. (1993). Reasoned action theory and the prediction of training participation in young swimmers. *British Journal of Physical Education Research Supplement*, **13**, 10–12.

Thill, E.E. & Brunel, P. (1995). Cognitive theories of motivation in sport. In S.J.H. Biddle (ed.). *European perspectives on exercise and sport psychology* (pp. 195–217). Champaign, IL: Human Kinetics.

Treasure, D.C. & Roberts, G.C. (1995). Applications of achievement goal theory to physical education: Implications for enhancing motivation. *Quest*, **47**, 475–489.

Vallerand, R.J. (1997). Toward a hierarchical model of intrinsic and extrinsic motivation. In M.P. Zanna (ed.), *Advances in experimental social psychology*: Vol 29 (pp. 271–360). New York: Academic Press.

Van Wersch, A. (1997). Individual differences and intrinsic motivations for sport participation. In J. Kremer, K. Trew, & S. Ogle (eds.), *Young people's involvement in sport* (pp. 57–77). London: Routledge.

Van Wersch, A., Trew, K., & Turner, I. (1992). Post-primary school young people's interest in physical education: Age and gender differences. *British Journal of Educational Psychology*, **62**, 56–72.

Vlachopoulos, S. & Biddle, S. (1997). Modeling the relation of goal orientations to achievement-related affect in physical education: Does perceived ability matter? *Journal of Sport and Exercise Psychology*, **19**, 169–187.

Vlachopoulos, S., Biddle, S., & Fox, K. (1996). A social-cognitive investigation into the mechanisms of affect generation in children's physical activity. *Journal of Sport and Exercise Psychology*, **18**, 174–193.

Weiner, B. (1992). *Human motivation: Metaphors, theories and research*. Newbury Park, CA: Sage.

Whitehead, J.R. (1993). Physical activity and intrinsic motivation. *President's Council on Physical Fitness and Sports Physical Activity and Fitness Research Digest*, **1**(2), 1–8.

Whitehead, J.R. & Corbin, C.B. (1991). Youth fitness testing: The effect of percentile-based evaluative feedback on intrinsic motivation. *Research Quarterly for Exercise and Sport*, **62**, 225–231.

Chapter 6

Adherence to Sport Injury Rehabilitation Regimens

Britton W. Brewer

Unfortunately, physical injury is a common occurrence in association with participation in sport and exercise. Indeed, as regular involvement in physical activity has increased in the general population, sport injury has emerged as an important public health issue (Caine, Caine, & Lindner, 1996). In the United Kingdom, for example, sport/exercise was identified by respondents to a recent population survey as the leading cause of physical injury, accounting for roughly one-third of all injuries experienced (Uitenbroek, 1996). Similarly, it has been estimated that 3–17 million sport- and recreation-related injuries occur each year in the United States (Booth, 1987; Kraus & Conroy, 1984).

People whose sport injuries are serious enough to warrant medical attention may, as part of their treatment, receive a prescribed rehabilitation regimen from their medical practitioners. Such regimens, which are typically administered by sport physiotherapists, athletic trainers, and other sport rehabilitation professionals, entail activities and procedures designed to enhance the physical recovery process. It is widely assumed that the success of sport injury rehabilitation programs is contingent on following the prescribed protocol (Fisher, Domm, & Wuest, 1988; Taylor & Taylor,

Adherence Issues in Sport and Exercise. Edited by Stephen J. Bull.
© 1999 John Wiley & Sons Ltd.

1997). Accordingly, adherence to sport injury rehabilitation regimens has emerged as an area of inquiry in sports medicine and sport psychology.

The purpose of this chapter is to review the current state of knowledge on adherence to sport injury rehabilitation regimens. After addressing definitional and measurement issues, theory and research on adherence to sport injury rehabilitation are examined and recommendations for future research and practice are provided.

DEFINING SPORT INJURY REHABILITATION ADHERENCE

Before discussing in depth empirical and applied issues associated with sport injury rehabilitation adherence, it is useful to define the term. Given the vast array of injuries (e.g., major, minor, chronic, acute, hard tissue, soft tissue) experienced by athletes, it is not surprising that sport injury rehabilitation regimens encompass a wide range of activities. Consequently, the specific behaviors involved in adhering to sport injury rehabilitation vary across different injuries and rehabilitation protocols. Some of the more common behaviors involved in following sport injury rehabilitation regimens are complying with instructions to engage in appropriate restriction of physical activity (e.g., rest, workout limitations), completing home rehabilitation exercises, completing home cryotherapy (icing), complying with medication prescriptions, and participating in clinic-based rehabilitation exercises and therapy. It is clear that sport injury rehabilitation adherence is a broad construct that involves a variety of behaviors performed in several settings (e.g., clinic, home).

Although the extensive variability in activities across different injuries and rehabilitation programs prohibits a uniform definition of sport injury rehabilitation adherence, there is consensus among sport rehabilitation practitioners that adherence to sport injury rehabilitation is less than full. Indeed, athletic trainers (Larson, Starkey, & Zaichkowsky, 1996), sport physiotherapists (Gordon, Milios, & Grove, 1991), and sports medicine physicians (Brewer, Van Raalte, & Linder, 1991) have identified nonadherence as occurring with moderate frequency among their patients. Case histories have documented poor adherence among athletes undergoing rehabilitation (Meani, Migliorini, & Tinti, 1986; Satterfield, Dowden, & Yasamura, 1990) and, depending on the particular measure of sport injury rehabilitation used, adherence rates ranging from 40 to 91% have been obtained (Almekinders & Almekinders, 1994; Daly, Brewer, Van Raalte, Petitpas, & Sklar, 1995; Laubach, Brewer, Van Raalte, & Petitpas, 1996; Taylor & May, 1996). Thus, sport injury rehabilitation appears to be a concept that is both meaningful and multifaceted (i.e., operationalizable in multiple ways).

MEASURING SPORT INJURY REHABILITATION ADHERENCE

Taking into consideration the wide variety of activities potentially involved in adherence to sport injury rehabilitation regimens, researchers have developed and implemented nearly a dozen different measures of sport injury rehabilitation adherence (see Table 6.1). Clearly, an adequate assessment of the wide range of behavioral demands constituting sport injury rehabilitation adherence requires multiple indices. Unfortunately, little psychometric information is available for most of the adherence measures that have been devised and deployed. Complicating matters, there is uncertainty as to whether sport injury rehabilitation adherence is best conceptualized as a unitary or multidimensional construct (Fisher, 1990; Johnson, 1993). Supporting a unitary conceptualization, Duda, Smart, and Tappe (1989) found that several measures of sport injury rehabilitation adherence loaded on a single factor and were highly intercorrelated. Other investigators, however, have found low to moderate intercorrelations among various adherence measures (Brewer, Cornelius, et al., 1998; Brewer, Daly, Van Raalte, Petitpas, & Sklar, 1994; Brewer, Van Raalte, et al., 1998; Brewer, Van Raalte, Petitpas, Sklar, & Ditmar, 1995; Culpepper, Masters, & Wittig, 1996; Daly et al., 1995; Lampton, Lambert, & Yost, 1993; Laubach et al., 1996; May & Taylor, 1994; Taylor & May, 1996). Only through further factor analytic research in which multiple measures of adherence are taken will the issue of dimensionality of the sport injury rehabilitation adherence construct be resolved.

In selecting an appropriate index of adherence to sport injury rehabilitation regimens, researchers and practitioners must take into account the nature of the rehabilitation protocol. Some measures of adherence will be more appropriate for rehabilitation protocols with large clinic-based components than for protocols with an emphasis on primarily home-based activities and vice versa. For example, if treatment requires only two or three clinic visits, then attendance at rehabilitation sessions would be an inappropriate index of sport injury rehabilitation adherence. Regardless of the particular rehabilitation protocol, however, healing rate should not be used as an adherence measure. The assumption that athletes who recover rapidly from their injuries do so because they adhere better than those who recover more slowly is not necessarily valid. Using healing rate as a measure of sport injury rehabilitation adherence, as has been done in several

Table 6.1   Indices of sport injury rehabilitation adherence

Index	Studies using the index
Patient self-reports of medication use	Almekinders & Almekinders, 1994
Patient self-reports of home exercise completion	Almekinders & Almekinders, 1994; Brewer et al., 1994; Brewer, Van Raalte et al., 1998; May & Taylor, 1994; Noyes et al., 1983; Quinn, 1996; Taylor & May, 1995a, 1996, 1997
Patient self-reports of compliance with activity restrictions	May & Taylor, 1994; Taylor & May, 1995a, 1996, 1997
Patient use of an electromyographic biofeedback for home exercises	Levitt et al., 1996
Practitioner estimates of patient home exercise completion	May & Taylor, 1994; Taylor & May, 1995a, 1996, 1997
Practitioner estimates of patient compliance with activity restrictions	May & Taylor, 1994; Taylor & May, 1995a, 1996, 1997
Patient attendance at physical therapy	Brewer, Cornelius et al., 1998; Brewer et al., 1994; Brewer, Van Raalte et al., 1998; Brickner, 1997; Byerly et al., 1994; Culpepper et al., 1996; Daly et al., 1995; Derscheid & Feiring, 1987; Duda et al., 1989; Fields et al., 1995; Fisher et al., 1988; Lampton et al., 1993; Laubach et al., 1996; Udry, 1997
Practitioner ratings of patient adherence during physical therapy	Brewer, Cornelius et al., 1998; Brewer et al., 1994; Brewer, Van Raalte et al., 1998; Brewer et al., 1995; Byerly et al., 1994; Culpepper et al., 1996; Daly et al., 1995; Duda et al., 1989; Eichenofer et al., 1986; Fields et al., 1995; Lampton et al., 1993; Laubach et al., 1996; Wittig & Schurr, 1994
Patient self-ratings of adherence behaviour during physical therapy	Brewer et al., 1994; Shank, 1988
Patient knowledge of the rehabilitation protocol	May & Taylor, 1994; Taylor & May, 1995a, 1996, 1997; Webborn et al., 1997
Practitioner judgements of patient recovery progress	Fisher et al., 1988; Lampton et al., 1993

studies (Fisher et al., 1988; Lampton et al., 1993), confounds adherence with rehabilitation outcome and reveals nothing about how well athletes are actually adhering to the rehabilitation regimen (Johnson, 1993; Meichenbaum & Turk, 1987). In the following sections, other considerations in selecting a measure of adherence to sport injury rehabilitation regimens are outlined for the three most commonly used indices of sport injury rehabilitation adherence (as indicated in Table 6.1).

Attendance at Rehabilitation Sessions

For rehabilitation protocols with significant clinic-based components, examination of athletes' attendance at rehabilitation sessions can yield vital information about their adherence. By calculating a ratio or percentage of clinic-based rehabilitation sessions attended to rehabilitation sessions scheduled, it is possible to determine the extent to which athletes are present for rehabilitation activities. Despite the simplicity and convenience of attendance indices, they do not provide any information on what athletes actually do during rehabilitation sessions. Further, because athletes tend to show up for the vast majority of their scheduled appointments, attendance distributions are often constricted and negatively skewed. Consequently, attendance at rehabilitation sessions should not be the sole index of adherence, but should instead be used in conjunction with other adherence measures.

Practitioner Behavioral Observations/Judgments

A detailed account of athletes' adherence to clinic-based activities in sport injury rehabilitation regimens requires information not only on their attendance at rehabilitation sessions but also on their behavior during rehabilitation sessions. Given the nature and frequency of their contact with athletes in sport injury rehabilitation settings, rehabilitation practitioners are often well situated to observe and make judgments about athletes' adherence to prescribed clinic-based activities. Recording observations of athletes' behavior during rehabilitation sessions is a cumbersome and laborious process, but one that can provide a highly detailed account of how well athletes adhere to the rehabilitation protocol. To facilitate collection of behavioral data in sport rehabilitation settings, Crossman and Roch (1991) developed the Sports Medicine Observation Code (SMOC). The SMOC has 13 categories of behavior (e.g., active rehabilitation, waiting, non-activity) that observers can use to code athlete behaviors at regular time intervals over the course of rehabilitation sessions. Although preliminary support for the validity of the SMOC has been obtained (Crossman & Roch, 1991), it has not been used in sport injury rehabilitation adherence studies.

Instead of using the more rigorous recording of behavioral observations during rehabilitation sessions, researchers have opted to assess adherence to clinic-based activities by means of rating scales on which rehabilitation practitioners indicate their judgments of athlete adherence (based presumably on their observations of athlete behavior). The only such measure with documented psychometric properties is the Sport Injury Rehabilitation Adherence Scale (SIRAS) (Brewer et al., 1995). The SIRAS is a brief instrument consisting of three items that assess rehabilitation practitioners' perceptions of the extent to which athletes engage in several key adherence behaviors during rehabilitation sessions. Specifically, the three items are: (a) 'Circle the number that best indicated the intensity with which this patient completed the rehabilitation exercise during today's appointment'; (b) 'How frequently did this patient follow your instructions and advice?'; and (c) 'How receptive was this patient to changes in the rehabilitation program?' Scale anchors for the three items are minimum effort/maximum effort, never/always, and very unreceptive/very receptive, respectively. Depending on whether it is worded in the present tense or the past tense, the SIRAS can be used on a single occasion to measure adherence tendencies or on repeated occasions to measure adherence in specific rehabilitation sessions. In preliminary research, the SIRAS has been shown to possess acceptable internal consistency, test–retest reliability, interrater reliability, factorial validity, and construct validity (Brewer et al., 1994; Brewer et al., 1995; Brewer, Van Raalte, Petitpas, Sklar, & Ditmar, 1996; Brewer, Weinstock, Van Raalte, Petitpas, & Sklar, 1996; Daly et al., 1995; Laubach et al., 1996).

A primary consideration in implementing measures of practitioner behavioral observations or judgments is that the observations or judgments are recorded as close in time to the actual occurrence of the pertinent rehabilitation behaviors as possible. By applying such a practice, accuracy can be enhanced and the influence of retrospective recall biases can be reduced.

Home Exercise Completion

In addition to clinic-based activities, sport injury rehabilitation regimens may also have a home-based component. Indeed, in some sport injury rehabilitation systems, home-based activities may constitute the primary mode of treatment. Common aspects of home-based rehabilitation protocols include completing exercises, icing (cryotherapy), taking medications, and restricting physical activity. Completion of home exercises is the component of home-based rehabilitation programs that has been examined most frequently in adherence research (Almekinders & Almekinders, 1994; Brewer et al., 1994; Brewer, Van Raalte, et al., 1998; May & Taylor, 1994; Noyes, Matthews, Mooar, & Grood, 1983; Quinn, 1996; Taylor & May, 1995a, 1996, 1997) and is, therefore, the primary focus of this measurement discussion.

In the majority of studies examining adherence to home rehabilitation exercise protocols, adherence has been assessed with a single retrospective self-report of adherence over the entire rehabilitation period. This approach to measuring adherence, although convenient, is subject to biased, distorted, and inaccurate recall, problems inherent in retrospective self-report (Dunbar-Jacob, Dunning, & Dwyer, 1993; Meichenbaum & Turk, 1987). The utility of retrospective self-reports is further hampered by the fact that athletes may have only a limited understanding of their home rehabilitation programs (Webborn et al., 1997).

Several promising alternatives to retrospective self-report of adherence to home rehabilitation exercises are available. To reduce the memory-based limitations of self-report, a daily log or diary of home exercises completed can be used. Of course, the daily diary approach raises the issue of adherence to filling out the diary. Nevertheless, rates of diary completion in excess of 99% can be obtained if the format is user-friendly and adequate support is given for full participation (Stone, Kessler, & Haythornthwaite, 1991; Tennen & Affleck, 1996; Tennen, Affleck, Urrows, Higgins, & Mendola, 1992). It should be noted that daily monitoring of home rehabilitation exercises may function as an intervention and enhance adherence, thereby leading to overinflation of adherence estimates (Meichenbaum & Turk, 1987; Taylor & May, 1996).

Because even daily self-reports of adherence to home exercises can be problematic, other less transparent, more unobtrusive approaches to measuring home rehabilitation adherence are needed. For some types of home rehabilitation exercises, objective assessment of adherence is possible. For example, Levitt, Deisinger, Wall, Ford, and Cassisi (1995) recorded patients' home use of an electromyographic biofeedback unit following minor arthroscopic knee surgery with a portable computer connected to the biofeedback unit. For home rehabilitation protocols that involve performing exercises to audio or video tapes, it is possible to measure surreptitiously the number of times the tapes have been played (Hoelscher, Lichstein, & Rosenthal, 1984, 1986; Martin, Collins, Hillenberg, Zabin, & Katell, 1981; Taylor, Agras, Schneider, & Allen, 1983). Because they are less susceptible to response distortion than self-report indices, objective measures may provide the most accurate account of adherence to home rehabilitation exercises.

THEORY AND RESEARCH ON SPORT INJURY REHABILITATION ADHERENCE

For the most part, research on adherence to sport injury rehabilitation regimens has been atheoretical, using primarily retrospective or concurrent research designs to explore factors associated with sport injury rehabilitation adherence. Only three theoretical approaches have received direct, intentional empirical tests: (a) personal investment theory (Maehr & Braskamp, 1989); (b) protection motivation theory (Maddux & Rogers, 1983; Rogers, 1975, 1983); and (c) cognitive appraisal models (Brewer, 1994; Wiese-Bjornstal & Smith, 1993; Wiese-Bjornstal, Smith, & LaMott, 1995; Wiese-Bjornstal, Smith, Shaffer, & Morrey, 1998). In the following sections, research findings (including those from investigations not explicitly designed to examine a particular theory) on predictors of sport injury rehabilitation adherence are discussed in the context of these theoretical perspectives.

Personal Investment Theory

In applying personal investment theory (Maehr & Braskamp, 1986) to the study of adherence to sport injury rehabilitation, Duda et al. (1989) examined the extent to which factors reflecting the interaction between personal characteristics and aspects of the rehabilitation situation were predictive of adherence. Specifically, indices of subjective meaning of the rehabilitation context to the individual (i.e., personal incentives, sense-of-self beliefs, and perceived options) were used to predict adherence (assessed in terms of attendance at rehabilitation sessions, completion of clinic-based rehabilitation exercises, and intensity of clinic-based rehabilitation exercise completion) in a prospective research design. Duda et al. found that one personal incentive (task involvement), five sense-of-self beliefs (perceived social support, trait sport confidence, self-motivation, internal locus of control for rehabilitation, and perceived physical ability), and four perceived option variables (belief in efficacy of treatment, knowledge of treatment, plans for future sport activity, and perceived team role since injury) were associated with one or more of the adherence measures.

Although Duda et al. (1989) are the only researchers to expressly test hypotheses generated from personal investment theory in the context of sport injury rehabilitation, other investigators have obtained support for components of the theory. With respect to personal incentives, Lampton et al. (1993) found that ego involvement was inversely related to sport injury rehabilitation adherence. Sense-of-self beliefs associated with adherence in studies other than that conducted by Duda et al. (1989) are self-motivation (Brewer et al., 1994; Brewer, Van Raalte et al., 1998; Culpepper et al., 1996; Fields et al., 1995; Fisher et al., 1988; Noyes et al., 1983) and social support for rehabilitation (Byerly et al., 1994; Fisher et al., 1988). Belief in the efficacy of treatment (Noyes et al., 1983; Taylor & May, 1996) and plans for future sport activity (Shank, 1988) are perceived option variables that have received support in studies not explicitly testing personal investment theory.

Protection Motivation Theory

Taylor and May (1996) examined the utility of protection motivation theory (Maddux & Rogers, 1983; Rogers, 1975, 1983) for explaining sport injury rehabilitation adherence. According to this theoretical perspective, factors influencing adherence to a given health behavior include the perceived severity of threat to one's health, one's susceptibility to the health threat, one's belief that the health behavior will enable one to avert the threat, and one's belief in his or her ability to perform the health behavior (Maddux & Rogers, 1983). In support of protection motivation theory, Taylor and May found that perceived injury severity, perceived susceptibility to further complications without rehabilitation, belief in the efficacy of treatment, and rehabilitation self-efficacy were associated with athletes' adherence to sport injury rehabilitation. Support for the treatment efficacy component of protection motivation theory has also been obtained by Duda et al. (1989) and Noyes et al. (1983). These results are bolstered by those of Rendall and Mohtadi (1997), who found that 'felt the treatment was not successful' (p. 109) was the leading reason given by competitive distance runners for nonadherence to treatment for injury management.

Cognitive Appraisal Models

With their foundations in the stress and coping literature, cognitive appraisal models are the broadest of the theoretical approaches that have been used to guide research on sport injury rehabilitation adherence. Cognitive appraisal models are a group of related theoretical frameworks that consider postinjury behaviour (e.g., rehabilitation adherence) to be influenced by cognitive and emotional responses to sport injury, which themselves are thought occur as a function of the interaction between personal and situational factors. Udry (1997) and Wiese-Bjornstal and her colleagues (Wiese-Bjornstal & Smith, 1993; Wiese-Bjornstal et al., 1995; Wiese-Bjornstal et al., 1998) are responsible for the most recent theoretical developments in this area.

Although only two published studies in the sport injury rehabilitation adherence domain (Daly et al., 1995; Udry, 1997) have had the stated intention of testing hypotheses generated from cognitive appraisal models, findings from many investigations are applicable to the cognitive appraisal framework. In the sections that follow, empirical support for various components of cognitive appraisal models is identified.

Personal factors associated with adherence

Personal factors are fairly stable, dispositional characteristics of people. Self-motivation, the 'behavioral tendency to persevere independent of situational reinforcements' (Dishman & Ickes, 1981, p. 421), is the personal factor most consistently correlated (positively) with adherence to sport injury rehabilitation (Brewer et al., 1994; Brewer, Van Raalte, et al., 1998; Culpepper et al., 1996; Duda et al., 1989; Fields et al., 1995; Fisher et al., 1988; Noyes et al., 1983). Other personal factors that have been positively associated with rehabilitation adherence are pain tolerance (Byerly et al., 1994; Fields et al., 1995; Fisher et al., 1988), task involvement (Duda et al., 1989), and tough-mindedness (i.e., a trait reflecting assertiveness, independence, and self-assurance) (Wittig & Schurr, 1994). Ego involvement (Lampton et al., 1993) and trait anxiety (Eichenhofer et al., 1986) are personal factors that have been inversely related to sport injury rehabilitation adherence.

Situational factors associated with adherence

Situational factors, which reflect the interface of people with the social and physical environment, are thought to interact with personal factors to influence cognitive, emotional, and behavioral responses to sport injury (Brewer, 1994). In sport injury rehabilitation adherence research, situational variables have dealt primarily with perceptions of the rehabilitation context and unstable, nondispositional aspects of the individual (i.e., states) that may influence or be influenced by the rehabilitation situation.

Situational factors associated with greater adherence in multiple investigations are academic class status (Culpepper et al., 1996; Shank, 1988), belief in the efficacy of the treatment (Duda et al., 1989; Noyes et al., 1983; Taylor & May, 1996), comfort of the clinical environment (Brewer et al., 1994; Fields et al., 1995; Fisher et al., 1988), convenience of rehabilitation scheduling (Fields et al., 1995; Fisher et al., 1988), perceived exertion during rehabilitation activities (Brewer et al., 1994; Fisher et al., 1988), and social support for rehabilitation (Byerly et al., 1994; Duda et al., 1989; Fisher et al., 1988). Situational factors related to greater adherence in single studies are academic performance level (Shank, 1988), degree of career goal definition

(Shank, 1988), importance or value of rehabilitation to the athlete (Taylor & May, 1996), injury duration (Culpepper et al., 1996), perceived academic load (Shank, 1988), perceived amount of sport participation time (Shank, 1988), perceived availability of time for rehabilitation (Shank, 1988), perceived injury severity (Taylor & May, 1996), perceived susceptibility to further complications without rehabilitation (Taylor & May, 1996), plans for postcollegiate sport participation (Shank, 1988), rehabilitation practitioner expectancy of patient adherence (Taylor & May, 1995a).

Cognitive responses associated with adherence

In cognitive appraisal models, cognitive responses to sport injury are thought to play a central role in mediating emotional and behavioral responses to sport injury (Brewer, 1994). Cognitive responses associated with greater adherence to sport injury rehabilitation programs are attribution of recovery to personally controllable factors (Laubach et al., 1996), attribution of recovery to stable factors (Laubach et al., 1996), cognitive appraisal of the ability to cope with injury (Daly et al., 1995), rehabilitation self-efficacy (Taylor & May, 1996), and self-esteem certainty (i.e., absence of a perceived threat to self-esteem) (Lampton et al., 1993).

Emotional responses associated with adherence. Behavioral responses such as adherence to rehabilitation are thought to be directly related to emotional reactions to sport injury (Brewer, 1994). In support of this argument, negative correlations between mood disturbance and sport injury rehabilitation adherence have been found in two studies (Brickner, 1997; Daly et al., 1995).

Behavioral responses associated with adherence

In the cognitive appraisal model proposed by Udry (1997), coping responses (which may involve implementation of cognitive and/or behavioral strategies) are posited to influence sport injury rehabilitation adherence. Consistent with her hypothesis, Udry found that instrumental coping was positively correlated with adherence to rehabilitation following knee surgery. Instrumental coping consists of behaviors such as athlete requests for additional information about the injury or rehabilitation protocol (Udry, 1997).

DIRECTIONS FOR FUTURE RESEARCH AND PRACTICE

As a domain of scientific inquiry, research on adherence to sport injury rehabilitation regimens is still at an exploratory stage and without a well-defined agenda for further study. Similarly, because sport injury rehabilitation adherence is a relatively recent focus of practical endeavor, there is not a set of empirically validated guidelines for applied work in this area. To facilitate optimal advancement of knowledge on sport injury rehabilitation adherence, it will be essential to attend to important theoretical, methodological, and measurement issues in future research. Likewise, there are vital pragmatic considerations that need to be addressed to enable productive practice with respect to adherence in the sport injury rehabilitation realm. Recommendations for research and practice are provided in the following sections.

Recommendations for Research

Theoretical considerations

As noted previously, only a few studies on sport injury rehabilitation adherence have been developed to test the validity of an established theoretical framework (Daly et al., 1995; Duda et al., 1989; Taylor & May, 1996; Udry, 1997). To facilitate interpretation of research findings, it is important for scholars to couch their investigations in a relevant theoretical perspective. In addition to personal investment theory, protection motivation theory, and cognitive appraisal models, other perspectives drawn from the exercise adherence literature (Godin, 1994; Prochaska & Marcus, 1994) may be useful in understanding adherence to sport injury rehabilitation programs. Although the time-limited nature of sport injury rehabilitation may limit their utility, approaches such as those posited in self-efficacy theory (Bandura, 1977, 1982), the theory of reasoned action (Fishbein & Ajzen, 1975), the theory of interpersonal behavior (Triandis, 1977), the theory of planned behavior (Ajzen, 1991), and the transtheoretical model (Prochaska, 1979; Prochaska & DiClemente, 1984) offer researchers a number of alternatives to the perspectives discussed above.

Regardless of the theoretical perspective adopted, it is essential for investigators to strive for conceptual clarity in their research. For example, it is critical for researchers conducting studies based on cognitive appraisal models to provide precise operational definitions of personal factors, situational factors, cognitive responses, emotional responses, and behavioral responses. Although personal and situational factors are not completely independent (Meichenbaum & Turk, 1987), it is important to minimize the overlap between these and other key constructs as much as possible. By operationalizing theoretical constructs in a clear and consistent manner across investigations, it will be possible to compare competing theoretical explanations for sport injury rehabilitation adherence. Such comparisons may be made by aggregating the results of multiple studies and evaluating the proportion of variance in adherence accounted for by different theoretical perspectives (as in meta-analyses) or, preferably, by administering simultaneously measures of constructs from competing theoretical perspectives and examining the extent to which they differentially predict adherence within a single study.

Methodological considerations

From the empirical investigations that have been conducted on adherence to sport injury rehabilitation regimens, it is possible to identify several methodological issues that should be addressed in future research. Of primary concern is selection of an appropriate research design. Despite the convenience of retrospective designs, in which potential 'predictors' of adherence are assessed after measurement of adherence, they are severely limited in terms of the conclusions that can be drawn about the findings. Cross-sectional designs, in which predictor variables and adherence are measured at the same point in time, are similarly limited. Consequently, prospective designs (in which purported antecedents of adherence are measured prior to adherence) are recommended when feasible. Although it is desirable to assess potential predictors of adherence (e.g., demographic and personality characteristics) prior to surgery or to the beginning of rehabilitation, variables involving knowledge of or experience with the rehabilitation regimen (e.g., comfort of the rehabilitation environment, rehabilitation self-efficacy) should, of course, be measured after the onset of rehabilitation (but before the corresponding episode of adherence).

Another key research design issue involves the decision to use a correlational design or an experimental design. Without exception, the designs used in extant research have been correlational. This is understandable given the preliminary nature of the studies. Correlational designs allow for the simultaneous examination of many possible predictors of adherence. Nevertheless, because causal inferences cannot be drawn from the findings of correlational studies (even those with prospective designs), investigations with experimental designs can provide the strongest possible support for hypothesized explanations for sport injury rehabilitation adherence.

Study sample composition is a third important methodological consideration for research on adherence to sport injury rehabilitation regimens. At issue is the degree to which study samples should be homogeneous with respect to level of athletic involvement and type of injury. In terms of athletic involvement, some investigations have had homogenous samples (Byerly et al., 1994; Culpepper et al., 1996; Duda et al., 1989; Fields et al., 1995; Fisher et al., 1988; Quinn, 1996; Shank, 1988; Wittig & Schurr, 1994),

featuring participants from a single level of athletic involvement (e.g., intercollegiate athletes, elite athletes, recreational athletes). Other investigations, however, have had heterogeneous samples, with participants ranging
from recreational athletes to elite competitors (Brewer, Cornelius, et al.,
1998; Brewer, Van Raalte, et al., 1998; Brickner, 1997; Daly et al., 1995;
Lampton et al., 1993; Laubach et al., 1996; Taylor & May, 1995a, 1996,
1997). Until it is demonstrated that the process of adhering to sport injury
rehabilitation programs differs as a function of level of athletic involvement, researchers can legitimately include participants of varying levels of
athletic involvement as long as they describe the composition of their
samples on this variable.

With regard to type of injury, although a few sport injury rehabilitation
adherence studies have had homogeneous samples, focusing exclusively on
participants with knee injuries (Brewer, Cornelius, et al., 1998; Brewer,
Van Raalte, et al., 1998; Daly et al., 1995; Laubach et al., 1996; Noyes et al.,
1983; Udry, 1997), the majority of studies have included participants with a
cross-section of various sport injuries (Brickner, 1997; Byerly et al., 1994;
Culpepper et al., 1996; Duda et al., 1989; Eichenhofer et al., 1986; Fields et
al., 1995; Fisher et al., 1988; Lampton et al., 1993; Quinn, 1996; Shank, 1988;
Taylor & May, 1995a, 1996, 1997; Wittig & Schurr, 1994). The critical factor
in determining whether individuals with different sport injuries (e.g., anterior cruciate ligament tears, stress fractures) should be included as participants in the same study is the extent to which the behavioral demands for
the rehabilitation programs associated with the different injuries are similar. If the rehabilitation activities for particular injuries are too dissimilar, it
is unwise to include people with those injuries in the same study unless
separate data analyses are conducted for each injury in addition to the data
analyses aggregated across various injuries. Such an analytic approach bal-
ances issues of internal and external validity.

Measurement issues

It is critical for researchers to use psychometrically sound measures, not
only of adherence to sport injury rehabilitation regimens but also of variables intended to predict adherence. Considerations in selecting appropriate indices of sport injury rehabilitation adherence were discussed
extensively earlier in this chapter. With regard to predictors of adherence,
standardized instruments are available to assess a number of variables that
are hypothesized to relate to sport injury rehabilitation adherence (e.g.,
self-motivation, social support, mood disturbance). Care should be taken
to ensure that measures developed for the general population are sufficiently reliable for people with sport injuries. Several measures have been

devised for use in the context of sport injury rehabilitation, including the Rehabilitation Adherence Questionnaire (RAQ) (Fisher et al., 1988), the Sports Injury Clinic Athlete Satisfaction Scale (SICASS) (Taylor & May, 1995b), and the Sports Injury Rehabilitation Beliefs Survey (SIRBS) (Taylor & May, 1993, 1996). Although the RAQ has been used with some frequency (Brewer et al., 1994; Byerly et al., 1994; Fields et al., 1995; Fisher et al., 1988), it has been criticized on psychometric grounds (Brewer et al., 1994). Preliminary psychometric data (Taylor & May, 1993, 1995b, 1996) suggest that the theoretically based SICASS and SIRBS are reliable and valid measures of the constructs they are intended to assess.

Recommendations for practice

As knowledge on factors affecting adherence to sport injury rehabilitation regimen accrues through scientific inquiry, opportunities for application of research findings in sport injury rehabilitation settings are likely to emerge. Current recommendations for enhancement of sport injury rehabilitation adherence have been based primarily on reports of athletes undergoing rehabilitation, suggestions from sport injury rehabilitation professionals, and writings in the general adherence literature (Brewer, 1998; Fisher, 1990; Fisher & Bitting, 1996; Fisher & Hoisington, 1993; Fisher, Mullins, & Frye, 1993; Fisher, Scriber, Matheny, Alderman, & Bitting, 1993; Worrell, 1992). Suggested adherence enhancement interventions tend to focus on what rehabilitation practitioners can do to educate athletes about the rehabilitation process, communicate effectively with athletes during the rehabilitation period, and set appropriate rehabilitation goals with the athlete (Brewer, 1998).

Although the recommended adherence enhancement interventions have an intuitive appeal, there are no experimental data supporting their use in the context of sport injury rehabilitation. Moreover, the critical question of whether better adherence to sport injury rehabilitation programs actually produces better therapeutic outcomes has not been resolved. Before investing too much in attempting to develop, implement, and evaluate the effectiveness of procedures designed to improve sport injury rehabilitation adherence, it should be demonstrated adherence is positively associated with outcomes of interest. This sounds simple enough to do, but positive relationships between adherence and outcome have not been found on a consistent basis in the health psychology literature (Dunbar-Jacob & Schlenk, 1996; Hays et al., 1994).

Although research findings suggest a positive adherence outcome association for orthopedic conditions not directly related to sport participation (DiFabio, Mackey, & Holte, 1995; Ettinger et al., 1997; Friedrich, Cermak,

& Maderbacher, 1996; Hawkins & Switlyk, 1993; Rejeski, Brawley, Ettinger, Morgan, & Thompson, 1997; Rives, Gelberman, Smith, & Carney, 1992), the data for sport injuries are equivocal. Although the adverse effects of poor adherence on sport injury rehabilitation outcomes have been documented in several studies (Brewer, Van Raalte, et al., 1998; Derscheid & Feiring, 1987; Hawkins, 1989; Meani et al., 1986; Satterfield et al., 1990), nonsignificant (Noyes et al., 1983) and inverse (Shelbourne & Wilckens, 1990) adherence outcome relationships have been obtained in other clinical investigations. Indeed, Quinn (1996) found inverse, nonsignificant, and positive adherence–outcome relationships depending on the particular phase of rehabilitation and adherence index under consideration within a single study! Resolution of the adherence–outcome issue is essential before applying adherence enhancement interventions in sport injury rehabilitation. Given the possibility that there are different relationships between adherence and outcome across injuries and rehabilitation protocols (Johnson, 1993), the recommendation for homogenous research samples with respect to injury type and rehabilitation protocol is underscored.

Once positive adherence–outcome relationships are demonstrated for particular injuries and rehabilitation protocols, levels of adherence needed to bring about optimal outcomes for those injuries and rehabilitation protocols should be ascertained. For some injuries and rehabilitation protocols, it may be that less than 100% adherence is sufficient to produce rapid, complete rehabilitation and that further adherence beyond a certain level may yield diminishing returns (Meichenbaum & Turk, 1987; Rejeski et al., 1997). Knowledge of the level of adherence needed to effect optimal recovery can help sport injury rehabilitation practitioners design adherence enhancement interventions and can assist athletes with injuries in achieving a realistic and beneficial level of rehabilitation activity. Identifying adherence–outcome parameters for various sport injury rehabilitation regimens should be a focus of scientific inquiry.

CONCLUSIONS

Sport injury is a significant public health concern. As in other domains of health care service delivery (Meichenbaum & Turk, 1987), adherence has been identified as an important issue in sport injury rehabilitation. Although theory and research on adherence to sport injury rehabilitation regimens are still in their infancy, guiding theoretical frameworks and consistent empirical findings are beginning to emerge. By confronting a number of methodological challenges (e.g., research design selection, study sample composition, measure selection), researchers can advance knowledge on sport injury rehabilitation adherence and provide information of potential utility to practitioners. However, before research findings are put into practice in an attempt to enhance adherence, it is essential to determine the likely impact of improved adherence on sport injury rehabilitation outcomes. Such an assessment will enable sport injury rehabilitation professionals to gauge the relative worth of investing in adherence enhancement interventions. By carefully considering theoretical, empirical, and practical issues in sport injury rehabilitation adherence, researchers and practitioners can, ultimately, contribute to the physical and psychological well-being of athletes with injuries.

AUTHOR NOTE

This chapter was supported in part by grant number R15 AR42087–01 from the National Institute of Arthritis and Musculoskeletal and Skin Diseases. Its contents are solely the responsibility of the author and do not represent the official views of the National Institute of Arthritis and Musculoskeletal and Skin Diseases. I thank Trent Petrie, Brickett Ranunculus, and Judy Van Raalte for their helpful comments on earlier drafts. Portions of this chapter, which is an expanded and updated version of an article that appeared in the *Journal of Applied Sport Psychology* (1998, **10**, 70–82), were presented at the annual meeting of the American Psychological Association in Toronto, Ontario, Canada in August 1996.

REFERENCES

Ajzen, I. (1991). The theory of planned behavior. *Organizational Behavior and Human Decision Processes*, **50**, 179–211.

Almekinders, L.C., & Almekinders, S.V. (1994). Outcome in the treatment of chronic overuse sports injuries: A retrospective study. *Journal of Orthopaedic and Sports Physical Therapy*, **19**, 157–161.

Bandura, A. (1977). Self-efficacy: Toward a unifying theory of behavior change. *Psychological Review*, **84**, 191–215.

Bandura, A. (1982). Self-efficacy mechanism in human agency. *American Psychologist*, **37**, 122–147.

Booth, W. (1987). Arthritis Institute tackles sports. *Science*, **237**, 846–847.

Brewer, B.W. (1994). Review and critique of models of psychological adjustment to athletic injury. *Journal of Applied Sport Psychology*, **6**, 87–100.

Brewer, B.W. (1998). Fostering treatment adherence in athletic therapy. *Athletic Therapy Today*, **3**(1), 30–32.

Brewer, B.W., Cornelius, A.E., Van Raalte, J.L., Petitpas, A.J., Sklar, J.H., Pohlman, M.H., Krushell, R.J., & Ditmar, T.D. (1998). Attributions for recovery and adherence to rehabilitation following anterior cruciate ligament reconstruction: A prospective analysis. Manuscript submitted for publication.

Brewer, B.W., Daly, J.M., Van Raalte, J.L., Petitpas, A.J., & Sklar, J.H. (1994). A psychometric evaluation of the Rehabilitation Adherence Questionnaire [Abstract]. *Journal of Sport & Exercise Psychology*, **16**(Suppl.), S34.

Brewer, B.W., Van Raalte, J.L., Cornelius, A.E., Petitpas, A.J., Sklar, J.H., Pohlman, M.H., Krushell, R.J., & Ditmar, T.D. (1998). Psychological factors, rehabilitation adherence, and rehabilitation outcome following anterior cruciate ligament reconstruction. Manuscript submitted for publication.

Brewer, B.W., Van Raalte, J.L., & Linder, D.E. (1991). Role of the sport psychologist in treating injured athletes: A survey of sports medicine providers. *Journal of Applied Sport Psychology*, **3**, 183–190.

Brewer, B.W., Van Raalte, J.L., Petitpas, A.J., Sklar, J.H., & Ditmar, T.D. (1995). A brief measure of adherence during sport injury rehabilitation sessions [Abstract]. *Journal of Applied Sport Psychology*, **7**(Suppl.), S44.

Brewer, B.W., Van Raalte, J.L., Petitpas, A.J., Sklar, J.H., & Ditmar, T.D. (1996). Internal consistency of multisession assessments of sport injury rehabilitation adherence [Abstract]. *Journal of Applied Sport Psychology*, **8**(Suppl.), S161.

Brewer, B.W., Weinstock, J., Van Raalte, J.L., Petitpas, A.J., & Sklar, J.H. (1996, August). Interrater reliability of the Sport Injury Rehabilitation Adherence Scale. Paper presented at the annual meeting of the American Psychological Association, Toronto.

Brickner, J.C. (1997). Mood states and compliance of patients with orthopedic rehabilitation. Unpublished master's thesis, Springfield College, MA.

Byerly, P.N., Worrell, T., Gahimer, J., & Domholdt, E. (1994). Rehabilitation compliance in an athletic training environment. *Journal of Athletic Training*, **29**, 352–355.

Caine, D.J., Caine, C.G., & Lindner, K.J. (Eds.). (1996). *Epidemiology of sports injuries*. Champaign, IL: Human Kinetics.

Crossman, J., & Roch, J. (1991). An observation instrument for use in sports medicine clinics. *The Journal of the Canadian Athletic Therapists Association*, April, 10–13.

Culpepper, W.L., Masters, K.S., & Wittig, A.F. (1996, August). Factors influencing injured athletes' adherence to rehabilitation. Paper presented at the annual meeting of the American Psychological Association, Toronto.

Daly, J.M., Brewer, B.W., Van Raalte, J.L., Petitpas, A.J., & Sklar, J.H. (1995). Cognitive appraisal, emotional adjustment, and adherence to rehabilitation following knee surgery. *Journal of Sport Rehabilitation*, **4**, 23–30.

Derscheid, G.L., & Feiring, D.C. (1987). A statistical analysis to characterize treatment adherence of the 18 most common diagnoses seen at a sports medicine clinic. *Journal of Orthopaedic and Sports Physical Therapy*, **9**, 40–46.

DiFabio, R.P., Mackey, G., & Holte, J.B. (1995). Disability and functional status in patients with low back pain receiving workers' compensation: A descriptive study with implications for the efficacy of physical therapy. *Physical Therapy*, **75**, 180–193.

Dishman, R.K., & Ickes, W. (1981). Self-motivation and adherence to therapeutic exercise. *Journal of Behavioral Medicine*, **4**, 421–438.

Duda, J.L., Smart, A.E., & Tappe, M.K. (1989). Predictors of adherence in rehabilitation of athletic injuries: An application of personal investment theory. *Journal of Sport & Exercise Psychology*, **11**, 367–381.

Dunbar-Jacob, J., Dunning, E.J., & Dwyer, K. (1993). Compliance research in pediatric and adolescent populations: Two decades of research. In N. A. Krasnegor, L. Epstein, S. B. Johnson, & S. J. Yaffe (eds.), *Developmental aspects of health compliance behavior* (pp. 29–51). Hillsdale, NJ: Erlbaum.

Dunbar-Jacob, J., & Schlenk, E. (1996). Treatment adherence and clinical outcome: Can we make a difference? In R. J. Resnick & R. H. Rozensky (eds.), *Health psychology through the life span: Practice and research opportunities* (pp. 323–343). Washington, DC: American Psychological Association.

Eichenhofer, R.B., Wittig, A.F., Balogh, D.W., & Pisano, M.D. (1986, May). Personality indicants of adherence to rehabilitation treatment by injured athletes. Paper presented at the annual meeting of the Midwestern Psychological Association, Chicago.

Ettinger, W.H., Jr., Burns, R., Messier, S.P., Applegate, W., Rejeski, W.J., Morgan, T., Shumaker, S., Berry, M.J., O'Toole, M., Monu, J., & Craven, T. (1997). A randomized trial comparing aerobic exercise and resistance exercise with a health education program in older adults with knee osteoarthritis: The Fitness Arthritis and Seniors Trial (FAST). *Journal of the American Medical Association*, **277**, 25–31.

Fields, J., Murphey, M., Horodyski, M., & Stopka, C. (1995). Factors associated with adherence to sport injury rehabilitation in college-age recreational athletes. *Journal of Sport Rehabilitation*, **4**, 172–180.

Fishbein, M., & Ajzen, I. (1975). *Belief, attitude, intention, and behavior.* Reading, MA: Addison-Wesley.

Fisher, A.C. (1990). Adherence to sports injury rehabilitation programmes. *Sports Medicine*, **9**, 151–158.

Fisher, C.A., & Bitting, L.A. (1996). Rehabilitation adherence: Do's and don'ts for both parties. *Athletic Therapy Today*, **1**(3), 42–44.

Fisher, A.C., Domm, M.A., & Wuest, D.A. (1988). Adherence to sports-injury rehabilitation programs. *The Physician and Sportsmedicine*, **16**(7), 47–52.

Fisher, A.C., & Hoisington, L.L. (1993). Injured athletes' attitudes and judgments toward rehabilitation adherence. *Journal of Athletic Training*, **28**, 48–54.

Fisher, A.C., Mullins, S.A., & Frye, P.A. (1993). Athletic trainers' attitudes and judgments of injured athletes' rehabilitation adherence. *Journal of Athletic Training*, **28**, 4347.

Fisher, A.C., Scriber, K.C., Matheny, M.L., Alderman, M.H., & Bitting, L.A. (1993). Enhancing rehabilitation adherence. *Journal of Athletic Training*, **28**, 312–318.

Friedrich, M., Cermak, T., & Maderbacher, P. (1996). The effect of brochure use versus therapist teaching on patients performing therapeutic exercise and on changes in impairment status. *Physical Therapy*, **76**, 1082–1088.

Godin, G. (1994). Social-cognitive models. In R. K. Dishman (ed.), *Advances in exercise adherence* (pp. 113–136). Champaign, IL: Human Kinetics.

Gordon, S., Milios, D., & Grove, J. R. (1991). Psychological aspects of the recovery process from sport injury: The perspective of sport physiotherapists. *Australian Journal of Science and Medicine in Sport*, **23**, 53–60.

Hawkins, R.B. (1989). Arthroscopic stapling repair for shoulder instability: A retrospective study of 50 cases. *Arthroscopy: The Journal of Arthroscopic and Related Surgery*, **2**, 122–128.

Hawkins, R.J., & Switlyk, P. (1993). Acute prosthetic replacement for stress fractures of the proximal humerus. *Clinical Orthopaedics and Related Research*, **289**, 156–160.

Hays, R.D., Kravitz, R.L., Mazel, R.M., Sherbourne, C.D., DiMatteo, M.R., Rogers, W.H., & Greenfield, S. (1994). The impact of patient adherence on health outcomes for patients with chronic disease in the medical outcomes study. *Journal of Behavioral Medicine*, 17, 347–360.

Hoelscher, T.J., Lichstein, K.L., & Rosenthal, T.L. (1984). Objective vs. subjective assessment of relaxation compliance among anxious individuals. *Behaviour Research and Therapy*, **22**, 187–193.

Hoelscher, T.J., Lichstein, K.L., & Rosenthal, T.L. (1986). Home relaxation practice in hypertension treatment: Objective assessment and compliance induction. *Journal of Consulting and Clinical Psychology*, **54**, 217–221.

Johnson, S.B. (1993). Chronic diseases of childhood: Assessing compliance with complex medical regimens. In N.A. Krasnegor, L. Epstein, S.B. Johnson, & S.J. Yaffe (eds.), *Developmental aspects of health compliance behavior* (pp. 157–184). Hillsdale, NJ: Erlbaum.

Kraus, J.F., & Conroy, C. (1984). Mortality and morbidity from injury in sports and recreation. *Annual Review of Public Health*, 5, 163–192.

Lampton, C.C., Lambert, M.E., & Yost, R. (1993). The effects of psychological factors in sports medicine rehabilitation adherence. *Journal of Sports Medicine and Physical Fitness*, **33**, 292–299.

Larson, G.A., Starkey, C.A., & Zaichkowsky, L.D. (1996). Psychological aspects of athletic injuries as perceived by athletic trainers. *The Sport Psychologist*, **10**, 37–47.

Laubach, W.J., Brewer, B.W., Van Raalte, J.L., & Petitpas, A.J. (1996). Attributions for recovery and adherence to sport injury rehabilitation. *Australian Journal of Science and Medicine in Sport*, **28**, 30–34.

Levitt, R., Deisinger, J.A., Wall, J.R., Ford, L., & Cassisi, J.E. (1995). EMG feedback-assisted postoperative rehabilitation of minor arthroscopic knee surgeries. *Journal of Sports Medicine and Physical Fitness*, **35**, 218–223.

Maddux, J.E., & Rogers, R.W. (1983). Protection motivation and self-efficacy: A revised theory of fear appeals and attitude change. *Journal of Experimental Social Psychology*, **19**, 469–479.

Maehr, M., & Braskamp, L. (1986). The motivation factor: A theory of personal investment. Lexington, MA: Lexington Books. Martin, J.E., Collins, F.L., Hillenberg, J.B., Zabin, M.A., & Katell, A.D. (1981). Assessing compliance to home practice: A simple technology of a critical problem. *Journal of Behavioral Assessment*, **3**, 193–198.

Martin, J.E., Collins, F.L., Hillenberg, J.B., Zabin, M.A., & Katell, A.D. (1981). Assessing compliance to home practice: A simple technology of a critical problem. *Journal of Behavioural Assessment*, **3** 193–198.

May, S., & Taylor, A.H. (1994). The development and examination of various measures of patient compliance, for specific use with injured athletes. *Journal of Sports Sciences*, **12**, 180–181.

Meani, E., Migliorini, S., & Tinti, G. (1986). La patologia de sovraccarico sportivo dei nuclei di accrescimento apofisari [The pathology of apophyseal growth centres caused by overstrain during sports]. *Italian Journal of Sports Traumatology*, **8**, 29–38.

Meichenbaum, D., & Turk, D.C. (1987). *Facilitating treatment adherence: A practitioner's guidebook*. New York: Plenum.

Noyes, F.R., Matthews, D.S., Mooar, P.A., & Grood, E.S. (1983). The symptomatic anterior cruciate-deficient knee. Part II: The results of rehabilitation, activity modification, and counseling on functional disability. *Journal of Bone and Joint Surgery*, **65-A**, 163–174.

Prochaska, J.O. (1979). *Systems of psychotherapy: A transtheoretical analysis.* Homewood, IL: Dorsey Press.

Prochaska, J.O., & DiClemente, C.C. (1984). *The transtheoretical approach: Crossing traditional boundaries of therapy.* Pacific Grove, CA: Brooks/Cole.

Prochaska, J.O., & Marcus, B.H. (1994). The transtheoretical model: Applications to exercise. In R. K. Dishman (Ed.), *Advances in exercise adherence* (pp. 161–180). Champaign, IL: Human Kinetics.

Quinn, A.M. (1996). The psychological factors involved in the recovery of elite athletes from long term injuries. Unpublished doctoral dissertation, University of Melbourne, Australia.

Rejeski, W.J., Brawley, L.R., Ettinger, W., Morgan, T., & Thompson, C. (1997). Compliance to exercise therapy in older participants with knee osteoarthritis: Implications for treating disability. *Medicine and Science in Sports and Exercise, 29,* 977–985.

Rendall, E.O., & Mohtadi, N.G.H. (1997). Survey of competitive distance runners in Alberta: Satisfaction with health care services with respect to running injuries. *Clinical Journal of Sport Medicine, 7,* 104–112.

Rives, K., Gelberman, R., Smith, B., & Carney, K. (1992). Severe contractures of the proximal interphalangeal joint in Depuytren's disease: Results of a prospective trial of operative correction and dynamic extension splinting. *Journal of Hand Surgery,* **17A,** 1153–1159.

Rogers, R.W. (1975). A protection motivation theory of fear appeals and attitude change. *Journal of Psychology,* **91,** 93–114.

Rogers, R.W. (1983). Cognitive and physiological processes in attitude change: A revised theory of protection motivation. In J. Cacioppo & R. Petty (eds.), *Social psychophysiology* (pp. 153–176). New York: Guilford Press.

Satterfield, M.J., Dowden, D., & Yasamura, K. (1990). Patient compliance for successful stress fracture rehabilitation. *Journal of Orthopaedic and Sports Physical Therapy,* **11,** 321–324.

Shank, R.H. (1988). Academic and athletic factors related to predicting compliance by athletes to treatments. Unpublished doctoral dissertation, University of Virginia, Charlottesville.

Shelbourne, K.D., & Wilckens, J.H. (1990). Current concepts in anterior cruciate ligament rehabilitation. *Orthopaedic Review,* **19,** 957–964.

Stone, A., Kessler, R., & Haythornthwaite, J. (1991). Measuring daily experiences: Decisions for the researcher. *Journal of Personality,* **59,** 575–608.

Taylor, A., & May, S. (1993, September). Development of a survey to assess athletes' sports injury rehabilitation beliefs. Paper presented at the annual meeting of the European Health Psychology Society, Brussels.

Taylor, A.H., & May, S. (1995a). Physiotherapist's expectations and their influence on compliance to sports injury rehabilitation. In R. Vanfraechem-Raway & Y. Vanden Auweele (eds.), *IXth European Congress on Sport Psychology proceedings*: Part II (pp. 619–625). Brussels: European Federation of Sports Psychology.

Taylor, A.H., & May, S. (1995b). Development of a Sports Injury Clinic Athlete Satisfaction Scale for auditing patient perceptions. *Physiotherapy Theory and Practice*, **11**, 231–238.

Taylor, A.H., & May, S. (1996). Threat and coping appraisal as determinants of compliance to sports injury rehabilitation: An application of protection motivation theory. *Journal of Sports Sciences*, **14**, 471–482.

Taylor, A.H., & May, S. (1997). A prospective study of the relationship between patient satisfaction and sports injury rehabilitation compliance. In R. Lidor & M. Bar-Eli (eds.), *IX World Congress of Sport Psychology: Proceedings* (Part II, pp. 685–687). Netanya, Israel: International Society of Sport Psychology.

Taylor, C.B., Agras, W.S., Schneider, J.A., & Allen, R.A. (1983). Adherence to instructions to practice relaxation exercises. *Journal of Consulting and Clinical Psychology*, **51**, 952–953.

Taylor, J., & Taylor, S. (1997). *Psychological approaches to sports injury rehabilitation*. Gaithersburg, MD: Aspen.

Tennen, H., & Affleck, G. (1996). Daily processes in coping with chronic pain: Methods and analytic strategies. In M. Zeidner & N. Endler (eds.), *Handbook of coping* (pp. 151–180). New York: Wiley.

Tennen, H., Affleck, G., Urrows, S., Higgins, P., & Mendola, R. (1992). Perceiving control, construing benefits, and daily processes in rheumatoid arthritis. *Canadian Journal of Behavioural Science*, **24**, 186–203.

Triandis, H. C. (1977). *Interpersonal behavior*. Monterey, CA: Brooks/ Cole.

Udry, E. (1997). Coping and social support among injured athletes following surgery. *Journal of Sport & Exercise Psychology*, **19**, 71–90.

Uitenbroek, D. (1996). Sports, exercise, and other causes of injuries: Results of a population survey. *Research Quarterly for Exercise and Sport*, **67**, 380–385.

Webborn, A.D.J., Carbon, R.J., & Miller, B.P. (1997). Injury rehabilitation programs: 'What are we talking about?' *Journal of Sport Rehabilitation*, **6**, 54–61.

Wiese-Bjornstal, D.M., & Smith, A.M. (1993). Counseling strategies for enhanced recovery of injured athletes within a team approach. In D. Pargman (ed.), *Psychological bases of sports injuries* (pp. 149–182). Morgantown, WV: Fitness Information Technology.

Wiese-Bjornstal, D.M., Smith, A.M., & LaMott, E.E. (1995). A model of psychologic response to athletic injury and rehabilitation. *Athletic Training: Sports Health Care Perspectives*, **1**, 17–30.

Wiese-Bjornstal, D.M., Smith, A.M., Shaffer, S.M., & Morrey, M.A. (1998). An integrated model of response to sport injury: Psychological and sociological dynamics. *Journal of Applied Sport Psychology*, **10**, 46–69.

Wittig, A.F., & Schurr, K.T. (1994). Psychological characteristics of women volleyball players: Relationships with injuries, rehabilitation, and team success. *Personality and Social Psychology Bulletin*, **20**, 322–330.

Worrell, T.W. (1992). The use of behavioral and cognitive techniques to facilitate achievement of rehabilitation goals. *Journal of Sport Rehabilitation*, **1**, 69–75.

Chapter 7

Adherence to Psychological Preparation in Sport

Christopher J. Shambrook and Stephen J. Bull

Sport psychology is now well into its age of accountability (Smith, 1989). In line with the increasing levels of expectation being placed upon sport psychologists it is essential that academic developments within the field contribute to the sport psychologist's scientific and professional credibility. The role of adherence research in relation to the delivery of sport psychology services certainly has the potential to contribute to the development of the field.

Gould et al. (1990) noted that 'too often sport psychologists have blindly assumed that the educational or clinical services offered are successful.' (p. 250), and a similar line of critical thinking provides the basis for adherence research applied to sport psychology services. In the health care setting, Meichenbaum and Turk (1987) identified that factors which can be deemed to affect adherence to a treatment can be grouped into the areas of: (a) characteristics of the patient, (b) characteristics of the treatment regimen, (c) features of the disease, (d) the relationship between the health care provider and the patient, and (e) the clinical setting (p. 41).

Adherence Issues in Sport and Exercise. Edited by Stephen J. Bull.
© 1999 John Wiley & Sons Ltd.

In relation to the work of the sport psychologist, these categories can be adapted to highlight potential problem areas, and perhaps begin to account for lack of success with services offered. Amongst the many potential factors for the lack of effectiveness of services it could be suggested that the following are viable, common sense applications of Meichenbaum and Turk's (1987) categories:

- *Client characteristics*: Lack of interest of the target group in the service offered—e.g., perhaps target group is *required* to receive sport psychology input, and does not *choose* to receive the service.
- *Relationship between the sport psychologist and the client group/ characteristics of the problem*: Ineffective delivery of the service to the target audience by the sport psychologist, e.g., not making the input relevant and specific to the sport, or perceptions of the individual.
- *Clinical setting/characteristics of the treatment regimen*: Mode of service delivery to the performer (e.g., seminar, workshop, team delivery, individual consultancy).

If accountability issues are to be addressed, sport psychologists must be able to demonstrate that they are working towards ensuring that problem areas such as those mentioned above are being addressed and overcome. Within research and applied work, sport psychologists need to be able to demonstrate that effectiveness is being maximised through (i) the successful implementation of programmes by coaches and athletes, (ii) the provision of appropriate delivery to maximise the likelihood of successful implementation, and (iii) the demonstration of the ability to assist those recipients who have problems implementing the service on offer. At this point in time there is a paucity of research which has addressed topics such as these.

In support of points (i) and (ii) above, it has been noted that 'receptivity alone is not enough to guarantee implementation' (Blinde & Tierney, 1990, p. 142), when considering sport psychology services. The possible lack of successful implementation by athletes suggests that a problem exists in getting athletes to employ newly introduced sport psychology strategies. The recognition of this problem suggests that it is dangerous to assign performance change directly to the introduction of a psychological intervention. In this age of accountability it is no longer acceptable to 'blindly assume' that athletes have adhered to a recommended programme of intervention, *or* that any performance change can be directly assigned to the intervention of the sport psychologist. Therefore, sport psychologists should be looking to assess their effectiveness by examining performance change and adherence to interventions concomitantly.

A decade ago, Bull (1989) identified the need for systematic research in the area of adherence to mental skills training. In addition, Orlick (1989) called for sport psychologists to begin examining adherence to psychological training programmes. Similarly, Crocker (1989) stated that programme adherence is critical in the evaluation of any psychological intervention, and Hardy, Jones and Gould (1996) have suggested that good sport psychology consultants should be aware of the potential adherence problem and respond accordingly in the delivery of psychological interventions. More recently still, Grove, Norton and Eklund (1997) suggest that sport psychology needs to focus more research upon factors associated with mental skills training. However, despite this repeated recognition of the potential importance of adherence to psychological preparation, there has not been an accompanying increase in adherence research.

In order to go some way towards responding to these calls for adherence-related research in relation to psychological preparation for performance, this chapter will firstly consider research which supports the value of addressing the adherence issue. Second, the existing literature which has directly addressed adherence to psychological preparation for sport will be reviewed. In connection with the direct literature, an initial model of adherence to psychological preparation will be proposed. Finally, issues of importance to research and practice in this area will be highlighted and used as a basis for recommendations for future research.

ESTABLISHING THE PROBLEM

An important initial requirement of this chapter is to establish that there are potential adherence problems inherent within psychological preparation work of sport psychologists. This can be achieved in several ways. First, by assessing the recommended mechanisms by which sport psychology interventions are delivered, it is possible to determine where adherence problems may occur. Second, intervention evaluation, and professional practice literature can be examined for indirect evidence of adherence problems within the field. A final, indirect approach to establishing the potential relevance of adherence issues for psychological intervention is to examine where such problems may have been identified in areas of psychological intervention other than sport.

Within the other varied chapters of this book it is evident that adherence is a problem within many different areas of sport and exercise. The behavioural changes required of athletes to ensure the successful implementation of a programme of psychological intervention are not dissimilar from the changes required of an athlete implementing an injury rehabilitation programme, or a person attempting to adhere to an exercise regime. Therefore, it would be naïve to believe that psychological preparation was immune from adherence problems. Many sport psychologists have stated that systematic training is a prerequisite for the success of psychological interventions (e.g., Daw & Burton, 1994). Similarly, various models of sport psychology delivery highlight the importance of a training phase. For example, Martens (1987) suggests that athletes need to go through an *education phase*, then an *acquisition phase*, and finally the *practice phase* before skills will be successfully acquired. The acquisition phase highlights the need for systematic training of psychological skills away from the sport environment, and the practice phase highlights the need for systematic training within the sport environment in order to integrate newly acquired skills into performance. Therefore, it can be suggested that if athletes do not manage to accomplish the systematic training then skills will not be developed, and the potential for a performance enhancing effect minimised. Vealey (1988) has also proposed a three-phase approach to psychological skills training. Vealey includes an *attainment phase*, a *sustainment phase*, and finally a *coping phase*. The attainment and sustainment phases both suggest the need for behavioural changes and the systematic practising of psychological skills, if the skills are to be developed. In a more extensive model, Thomas (1990) outlines a cyclical, seven-phase performance enhancement process for psychological intervention. Phase six in this model is the *implementation phase* in which athletes would start to utilise the previously developed psychological skills from phase five (*psychological skills training*). The final phase of the model is the *evaluation phase* and Thomas (1990) recommends that compliance and adherence to the performance enhancement process should be assessed within this phase.

All of the models outlined above, either directly or indirectly, recognise that adherence to psychological skills training is required if athletes are to develop skills to the extent whereby a performance enhancing effect may be achieved. Ravizza (1990) has recognised this in his applied work, claiming that 'players need to be constantly reminded if they are going to integrate these into their daily performance.' (p. 337). Therefore, without adherence it is unlikely that intervention efficacy will be maximised. Furthermore, without convincing demonstrations of intervention efficacy, it is unlikely that athletes would be compelled to adhere to psychological training due to the lack of evidence to suggest that the training has produced a worthwhile impact. This potential cyclical effect suggests that it would be beneficial for sport psychologists to begin to address adherence issues within intervention research, firstly to improve the adherence of athletes to the programmes, and secondly to maximise the likelihood that efficacy perceptions (and therefore adherence) will be positive.

An examination of the sport psychology intervention evaluation literature can also provide insight into the possible importance of assessing adherence to programmes. In a very thorough evaluation of the impact of a psychological skills workshop programme for wrestlers, Gould et al. (1990) provide two key pieces of information which link with adherence to psychological skills training. First, when carrying out a post-education evaluation of the skills delivered within a workshop, results showed that perceived use of all of the skills dissipated over a three-month period. Although the self-rated usage levels were still high, the perceived dissipation suggests that post-workshop the athletes had difficulty in implementing the skills successfully. The drop-off in usage prompted Gould et al. (1990) to recommend the use of support networks to assist with post-workshop implementation of psychological skills training. Within the same study, Gould et al. (1990) reported that there were attrition rates of 25% and 21% in their two samples within the study, suggesting that not all those who begin a programme of psychological preparation are able to stick with it. These attrition rates are obviously lower than those reported elsewhere in this book, but still signify that there may be a problem in keeping athletes involved in programmes of psychological preparation. The results also suggest that there may be adherence issues in the *education phase* and the *acquisition phase*. Brewer and Shillinglaw (1992) showed similar attrition rates when working with a varsity lacrosse team. However, the programme of psychological skills training was delivered with much more social support for the performers (due to the daily contact common in a varsity sports team), and a potential benefit of this environment was that participants did not perceive a drop-off in usage of psychological skills.

In accordance with Gould et al.'s findings, Le Scanff (1995) reported that, from an initial group of 25 table tennis players, five players did not choose to be involved in the programme, and a further six dropped out during the course of the season. Athletes cited reasons for drop-out as: lack of motivation, lack of programme success, low prioritisation of psychological skills training and lack of support from the coach. These variables can easily be paralleled with those cited in many other chapters of this book as negative influences upon adherence. Therefore, these athletes provide further support for the notion that there may be an adherence problem for psychological preparation programmes.

Another recent study evaluating a season long intervention within gymnastics, reported subject ratings of perceived usefulness of different aspects of the intervention (Cogan and Petrie, 1995). It is interesting to note that of the eleven elements of the intervention, the two areas perceived to be the least helpful were those which required independent utilisation of the psychological skills training by the athletes. These areas were identified as *Practising relaxation on own*, and *Cue-controlled relaxation applied in gym*. The other areas of the intervention all appear to be group sessions with direct input from consultants, with the subjects being involved by their presence at the session. The two low-scoring areas would have required the athletes to plan and implement training independently without group support, or direct input from the sport psychologist. Therefore, this difference suggests that the mode of training associated with psychological preparation may have an influence upon successful adherence.

In the evaluation of a cognitive–behavioural intervention in golf, Cohn, Rotella, and Lloyd (1990) measured adherence to both behavioural and mental components of a pre-shot routine. Although post-intervention means were very high for adherence to both the mental and physical aspects of the pre-shot routine, it is noticeable that in all three of the subjects the adherence to the mental elements of the routine was consistently lower than that to the physical elements of the routine. Ravizza (1990) has noted that 'a sincere commitment to incorporate mental skills into performance is a difficult task for most athletes because they have been conditioned to perform.' (p. 331). Regardless of the reasons for the differences in the adherence level, developing an understanding of the reasons for any differences would obviously be of great assistance to the sport psychologist.

In addition to the aforementioned research, which suggests that adherence may be a problem for athletes, a recent area of enquiry highlights another potential barrier to adherence within psychological preparation. Anecdotal and research evidence suggests that working with sport psychologists can be perceived negatively by athletes and coaches (Ravizza, 1988; Van Raalte et al., 1990). Misconceptions regarding the role of the sport psychologist are thought to possibly lead to a 'negative-halo' effect for those athletes who consult sport psychology professionals (Linder et al., 1991). This stigmatisation of those athletes consulting a sport psychologist could obviously be a strong deterrent from entering into, or continuing with, consultancy and associated interventions. The identification of such problems highlights that there may well be adherence issues prior to the sport psychologist even beginning work with athletes and coaches.

In line with Meichenbaum and Turk's (1987) recognition that the relationship between the health care practitioner and the client is an important influence upon adherence, the perception of the sport psychologist has also been recognised as important to the success of sport psychology consultancy. Orlick and Partington (1987) identified characteristics of 'highly effective' and 'least effective' sport psychologists with the help of Canadian Olympic athletes. It seems fair to assume that athletes are more likely to take advice, and adhere to that advice, from consultants who are perceived to possess favourable qualities. In contrast, it could be assumed that those consultants perceived unfavourably by athletes will have greater problems in encouraging athletes to implement and adhere to recommended strategies. As Ravizza (1988) noted, 'Like it or not, the average athlete views a sport psychologist with a degree of apprehension due to the perception that psychology is associated with problems.' (p. 244). Such apprehension about the nature of the sport psychology consultant could certainly have implications for initiating and adhering to a programme of psychological preparation. Therefore, the perception of, and professional behaviour of, the sport psychology consultant, can be seen as a potential influence upon the use of sport psychology techniques (Shambrook and Bull, 1997), and recognition of this key factor should be built into the education and training of aspiring professionals in the field.

Adherence to Psychological Preparation Research

Although the research highlighted within the previous section has not directly evaluated adherence to psychological preparation for sport, the evidence suggests that a direct examination of the area is required in order to increase knowledge and provide sport psychologists with methods to minimise the adherence problem. Although there is a scant amount of research directly assessing adherence to psychological preparation, there is a critical amount of specific adherence research which warrants reviewing within this chapter.

The majority of psychological preparation adherence research has been carried out in the UK over the past decade. This research programme has produced a conceptual framework to aid in the understanding of the specific adherence process under examination. This framework will be presented and discussed later in the chapter.

Prior to examining the conceptual framework some key literature must be briefly reviewed. Although not addressing adherence directly, and an additional source of information to the UK-based research, Greaser (1994) examined influences upon an athlete's intention to utilise sport psychology. Using the theory of reasoned action, and focusing upon the athlete's perceived value and expectations of psychological preparation, Greaser (1994) proposed seven approaches which sport psychologists could use in order to help increase the intention of athletes to utilise sport psychology techniques. Such recommendations obviously have implications for adherence to programmes in both the short and long term. The recommendations made were:

1. Create an environment which reinforces the use of sport psychology techniques.
   (a) Ensure that participants understand what skills are required to enhance performance;
   (b) Ensure that participants believe they can operationalise the skills.

2. Strengthen the belief that practising and mastering sport psychology skills will enhance an individual's ability to achieve personal goals and perform well in sport activities.
3. Reinforce athletes' appreciation and/or feelings of enjoyment gained from using sport psychology strategies.
4. Facilitate the attainment of personal values, such as achievement needs, through the use of sport psychology techniques.
5. Reduce perceived costs (not enough time) that are associated with employing self-motivational skills.
6. Structure the practice environment to incorporate routine use of motivational enhancement techniques.
7. Teach skills so they have transfer value to the competitive sport setting as well as achievement settings.

(Greaser, 1994, p. 88–89)

It is evident that if the above recommendations could be achieved, an athlete would be more likely to enter into, and adhere to, a programme of psychological preparation, due to an increased perceived value of beginning, and continuing, to utilise the strategies. The introduction that athletes have to psychological preparation will have important implications for future adherence patterns. Ravizza (1988, 1990) has outlined many pertinent issues for the sport psychologist in his reflections upon key issues for gaining entry to teams and working as a sport psychologist in professional sport. Ravizza's (1988, 1990) reflections, and Greaser's (1994) recommendations suggest that sport psychologists should recognise the importance of this early phase of the implementation process and its potential influence upon long-term acceptance and adherence to sport psychology techniques.

Since Bull's (1989) call for systematic study of adherence to psychological preparation, only one such study has been published in one of the major sport psychology journals. Bull (1991) examined personal and situational influences upon adherence to psychological preparation over an 8 week training period. Bull (1991) reported very poor levels of adherence over the course of the 8 week period (a mean of 17 minutes per week, at a frequency of just over one session per week). This low level of adherence followed an 8 week introduction to key areas of mental skills training, after which participants could then implement the training of their choice. For the university athlete sample used within this study, key issues of lack of time and lack of programme individualisation emerged as having a negative impact upon adherence. Self-motivation (measured using the Self-Motivation Inventory, Dishman and Ickes, 1981) and sport goal progress (the extent to which the athlete had fulfilled his or her sporting ambitions) were significantly related to the adherence of the subjects. Those participants with higher self-motivation scores, and further from achieving their sporting goals, demonstrated higher levels of adherence. However, Bull (1991) noted that even those participants in this study who were the 'high' adherers, were still managing only modest amounts of psychological training during the 8 week period.

As an addition to examining adherence to workshop-initiated psychological preparation, Bull (1995) examined adherence to psychological preparation in elite junior tennis players. Players within this sample were receiving regular consultancy from a sport psychologist, and were therefore a very different sample from that studied by Bull (1991). All players rated their desired, and perceived, amounts of time devoted to psychological preparation in a typical week. Additional data were collected from one group within the sample where access to the sport psychologist was acquired. In this case, the consultant was asked to carry out ratings of desired and perceived adherence for each of the players. Although the data for this study were collected retrospectively, several findings of note emerged. First, the sport psychologist's ratings of perceived athlete adherence demonstrated a general belief by the consultant that actual adherence to personalised programmes was low. Second, perceived intervention efficacy demonstrated a significant relationship with both the frequency, and duration, of training carried out by the players. Although generally quite high in adherence terms, great individual variation was apparent in the degree of self-reported programme adherence of the players. The findings of the study also partially supported Bull (1991) in terms of self-motivation. A significant relationship between self-motivation and adherence was demonstrated in one of the groups. Unsurprisingly, players in the sample who had more regular contact with their consultant appeared to adhere more than those receiving less regular input from their sport psychologist.

In the process of developing this line of research, Bull (1994) proposed a preliminary conceptual framework of adherence to psychological preparation. This framework summarised the findings of Bull's (1991, 1995) initial work, and also provided a foundation for the development of research in the area. Therefore, further examination of the area was undertaken with four key aims in mind: (a) to examine the extent to which adherence to psychological preparation may be a problem, (b) to examine the relationships identified by Bull (1994) in order to develop confidence in the preliminary adherence to psychological preparation conceptual framework, (c) to develop a greater working knowledge of variables influencing adherence to psychological preparation for sport, and (d) to examine the extent to which intervention strategies may be able to maximise programme adherence.

As a first step in this process, Shambrook and Bull (1995) carried out two single-case research designs to evaluate (a) the impact of the sport psychology consultant upon adherence, (b) the impact of individualising, and (c) the impact of structuring psychological preparation programmes during times of non-contact with the consultant. From the non-concurrent multiple baseline design across subjects it was apparent that adherence was influenced as a result of cessation of meetings with the consultant (four subjects in design), but overall, the programme individualisation appears to have fostered good levels of adherence when compared to the previous group-based studies. The structuring (achieved via goal-setting) during times of non-contact between consultant and athlete appeared to lessen the degree of drop-off in adherence (three subjects in design). Furthermore, qualitative data collected within the study reinforced the effectiveness of the individualisation process with all subjects providing positive feedback about the initial needs analysis procedure. The qualitative data also revealed a perception of the subjects that programme adherence increased as competition approached. Evidence of increased usage of imagery-based skills in the lead-up to competition has been reported elsewhere (Rodgers, Hall & Bucholz 1991). Therefore, as well as subject-oriented influences upon adherence, it appears that external influences may be important determinants of adherence to psychological preparation.

Utilising the information gained in the single-case studies, and building upon the work of Bull (1991), Shambrook and Bull (1999a) carried out two studies which examined adherence levels to imagery training. Subjects were university athletes who received a workshop format for practical and theoretical imagery education. Subjects undertook a 6 week period of imagery training after the workshop and recorded adherence in imagery diaries. Semi-structured interviews were conducted post-data collection in order to examine individual adherence issues. In the second study, the subjects received performance profiling education (Butler & Hardy, 1992) which was used to help with individualisation of imagery training content. The subjects also agreed upon personal weekly training targets for the imagery programme. The adherence levels (frequency and duration) for the two studies are shown in Figures 7.1–7.4. A significant decrease in adherence (frequency and duration) was evident in study one, with the same analysis revealing no such significant decrease in the second study. The level of adherence for both frequency and duration of training was improved between study one and study two with mean adherence levels of $20.13 \pm 23.17\%$ (duration) and 12.57 ± 11.37 (frequency) for study one, and $50.77 \pm 24.86\%$ (duration) and $35.14 \pm 14.4\%$ (frequency) for study two. These results suggest that the addition of the individualisation of the imagery training and outlining of personal targets may have a positive impact upon short-term adherence, although it is evident that adherence is still not high.

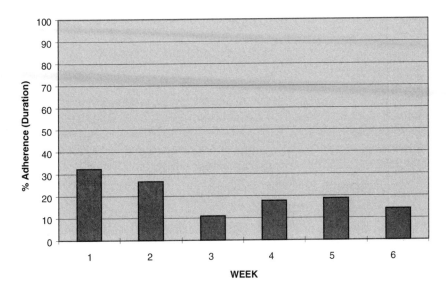

Figure 7.1 Bar chart to show successive group duration scores (percentage) over a six-week period of imagery training (*n* = 18)

A sport commitment measure was used in the second study and this correlated significantly with both frequency and duration of imagery training. The commitment measure employed built upon the sport goal progress measure developed by Bull (1991), asking the subjects to rate how committed they were to achieving their ultimate sport goal. Therefore, those subjects with self-rated higher commitment to fulfilling their potential were more likely to adhere more effectively to the imagery training.

The interview data revealed diverse influences upon adherence to the imagery training. Lack of participation (either through injury, or moving into close season) caused athletes to stop using the imagery training, suggesting that athletes may utilise psychological preparation in a cyclical

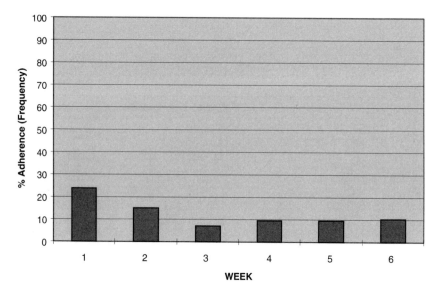

Figure 7.2   Bar chart to show successive group frequency scores (percentage) over a six-week period for imagery training (*n* = 18)

fashion, as they would with other forms of physical and technical training. In support of Blinde and Tierney (1990) all of the athletes in the studies reported positive perceptions of imagery training, but this high perceived efficacy failed to lead to successful implementation.

In the most recent study, Shambrook & Bull (1999b) gathered data from 46 international athletes (mean age = 24.6 ± 4.8) who had been working with a sport psychologist for a minimum of one complete year. Each athlete was asked to rank ten potentially adherence-influencing variables in relation to three key questions. The key questions related to short-term adherence to psychological preparation, long-term adherence to psychological preparation (maintenance), and not dropping out from using

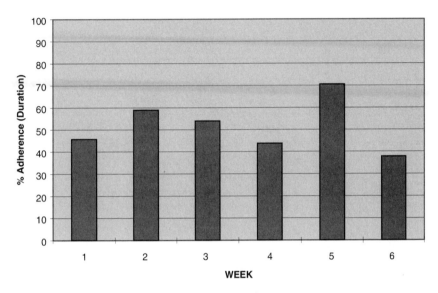

Figure 7.3 Bar chart to show successive group duration scores (percentage) over a six-week period for imagery training ($N = 15$)

psychological preparation programmes. The three rankings from each subject were subjected to Cultural Consensus Analysis (Romney, Weller & Batchelder, 1986) to ascertain: (a) degree of consensus between the athletes as to the 'correct' ranking, and (b) an estimated correct ranking for the ten variables for each of the three questions.

The analyses revealed no strong consensus between the athletes as to the 'correct' ordering of the items for each of the three questions. However, 'having a strong desire to succeed in your sport', and 'perceiving psychological training to be of benefit to you' emerged as highly ranked items across the three questions. The lack of consensus further highlights the importance of individualisation already evident throughout the other studies, and

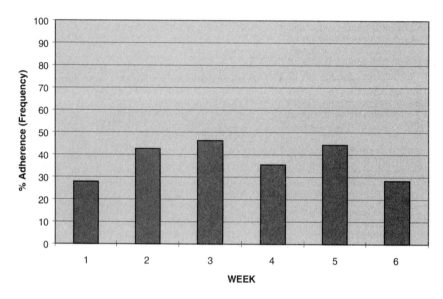

Figure 7.4 Bar chart to show successive group frequency scores (percentage) over a six-week period for imagery training (*N* = 15)

suggests that this issue is as important with elite athletes as has been shown to be the case with the other samples studied previously. These findings support those of Zinsser (1992) who discovered that the high adhering athletes in his imagery adherence study were more committed to their sport, and had higher levels of perceived imagery efficacy. Greaser (1994) also identified efficacy as an important influence upon the intention to use psychological preparation. Therefore, it is evident that similar variables may be working at different stages of the development of psychological preparation programmes.

In summary of the programme of work focusing on adherence to psychological preparation, the main recommendations from the studies are:

- Perceived value of psychological preparation should be promoted as much as possible prior to an athlete beginning work with a sport psychologist.
- Athlete adherence to psychological preparation may not be as high as anticipated by sport psychologists.
- Due to the many potential influencing variables, programmes of psychological preparation should be individualised in terms of content and adherence-related strategies.
- The consultant (perception of, behaviour of, and degree of involvement), is a potential influence upon the adherence process and efforts should be made to ensure that the consultant impacts as positively as possible upon adherence.
- As well as traditional sport psychology education, athletes should be directed *how* to implement newly introduced programmes. Time-management, and programme structuring and scheduling advice should be provided.
- Efforts should be made to integrate psychological preparation strategies into existing routines in order to reduce the likelihood of programme cessation.
- Perceived intervention efficacy should be maximised in order to facilitate adherence.
- Athlete commitment to fulfilling sporting potential is a key influence upon adherence.

A Conceptual Framework of Adherence to Psychological Preparation

As a result of the programme of adherence-focused research to date, Bull's (1994) initial conceptual framework of psychological preparation adherence was updated and an extended framework of adherence was developed (Shambrook and Bull, 1995). The origins of this framework came from the health care setting (Kristeller and Rodin, 1984), and the exercise adherence literature (Sallis and Hovell, 1990). Kristeller and Rodin's (1984) work provides the core structure with the *entry* phase (entering into a programme of psychological preparation), the *adherence* phase (initial programme adherence—the first few months of a programme), and the *maintenance* phase (long-term adherence to psychological preparation strategies—up to and beyond a season). The work of Sallis and Hovel (1990) adds the concept of cyclical use of psychological preparation strategies by athletes evident in the findings of the research. The possibility of a cyclical usage pattern is allowed for by adding a *non-use* phase (prior to beginning a programme, or after discontinuing use), the *drop-out* phase (the point at which the athlete decides to discontinue use), and the *resumption* phase (the point at which the athlete decides to re-employ the psychological preparation strategy). The conceptual framework is dynamic in nature, recognising that an athlete may move backwards and forwards through the stages identified. The conceptual framework also recognises the long-term goal of the sport psychologist as moving the athlete successfully into the maintenance stage, at which point the psychological preparation has become a fully integrated and fundamental part of performance preparation.

Interestingly, the development of this sequential conceptual framework of adherence can be closely paralleled with Prochaska and DiClemente's (1983) Transtheoretical Model as described by Gabe Reed in Chapter 2. As an athlete passes through the different stages of non-use to maintenance, with drop-out and resumption along the way, the process of change can be closely allied to the changes evident within the dynamic evolution from pre-contemplation stage to maintenance stage (Shambrook, 1995). There have, indeed, already been some initial attempts to utilise the Transtheoretical Model to examine concepts related to adherence to psychological preparation in sport (Leffingwell & Smith, 1998; Rider, Leffingwell & Williams, 1996).

As well as providing a conceptual framework of the core processes underlying adherence to psychological preparation, key *situational, programme,* and *athlete* characteristics are identified which will be important influences upon successful transition through the various stages proposed. Many of these characteristics have received empirical support in the various studies highlighted previously. However, some of the other characteristics have been included in the conceptual framework as a result of initial research, or preliminary information in the sport psychology literature reviewed.

The characteristics presented are not exhaustive, but represent those areas deemed to be key to developing understanding at this point in the research programme. Therefore, both an applied sport psychologist and research sport psychologist can make use of the framework. The framework is designed to be applicable to the 'real world' of sport psychology, and therefore, lends itself to applied research, and should be tested out as thoroughly as possible in realistic consultancy settings.

Research Issues

Terminology

If research is to work towards the validation of a model of adherence to psychological preparation, then there are some key research issues which

185

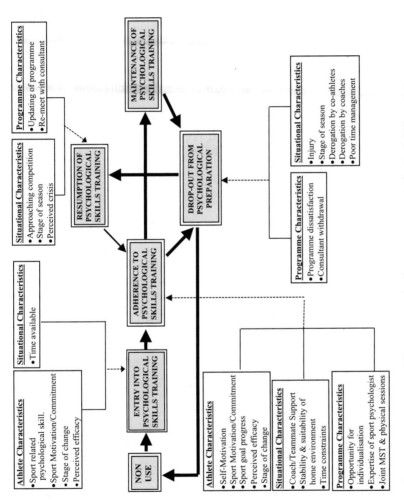

Figure 7.5 Conceptual framework of adherence to psychological skills training

need to be highlighted and addressed. These important issues will now be highlighted within this next section. Perhaps the most important influence upon the conformity between future research in the area is the terminology employed by researchers. As a result of the problems of conflicting terminology in many other areas of sport and exercise psychology (Gould & Krane, 1992; Jones & Hardy, 1991; Leith & Taylor, 1992; Perkins & Epstein, 1988) it is evident that there is a need for a standardised terminology to be employed in future investigations within this area. Within sport psychology many different techniques are employed to help produce improved psychological performance for an athlete or group. *Psychological preparation* has been used throughout this chapter as an umbrella term to encompass all of the possible areas of work covered by an applied sport psychologist. However, it is evident from the studies carried out that the nature of the intervention can vary, and along with this variation there will be differing adherence challenges for the athlete and sport psychologist. To help with the development of research in this area, it is important for researchers to identify the exact type of *psychological preparation* being employed. In line with the previously highlighted models of psychological skills development (e.g., Vealey, 1988), it can be suggested that the majority of the techniques included within *psychological preparation* require systematic, structured training sessions to be carried out by the athlete. The areas covered by this systematic training would typically be concentration training, confidence building, anxiety/arousal management, and imagery training (e.g., imagery to help improve confidence). These four areas combine to make the category of *psychological skill training* (PST). Imagery training sessions (along with other forms of covert rehearsal) may also be used to help an athlete refine or change a physical skill, e.g., learning a new manoeuvre in gymnastics, or re-modelling a golf swing. In line with definitions provided by Suinn (1983), such physical skill development is a different use of imagery, and should be termed *mental practice* (MP), along with other mental practice techniques.

In addition to the very structured 'armchair', or home based training sessions often required by *PST* or *MP*, there are many other areas of *psychological preparation* to which adherence may be a problem. These can be categorised as: *training adherence* and *strategy adherence*. The *Strategy Adherence* refers to many of the structures that a sport psychologist will put in place with an athlete in order to develop the way in which a performer prepares for performance. An obvious example of *strategy adherence* is that of meetings with the sport psychologist. The sport psychologist will make recommendations for the frequency of meetings with an athlete. The role of the athlete is then to simply attend the sessions. Attendance at therapy sessions for clinical patients has been shown to be a problem for clinical populations which would benefit from attendance (e.g.,

Waller, 1997). Similarly, it can be suggested that athletes would be in a position to benefit from regular consultancy with a sport psychologist. Other examples of *strategy adherence* are adherence to goal-setting strategies, record keeping of *PST* or *MP* sessions, completion of performance or training reviews, recording of confidence reminders, and completion of homework readings.

Training adherence refers to techniques and strategies agreed by the sport psychologist and athlete which require adherence within actual training for performance. During training an athlete may be required to practise a pre-shot routine, stress management technique, or error parking strategy. This type of adherence requires an athlete to be using psychological techniques during activity. The obvious extension of this type of adherence, and perhaps the most important evaluation of adherence within *psychological preparation*, would determine how successfully an athlete had been able to employ techniques under the pressure of competition. The specific, and successful application of the learned techniques to the performance environment should therefore be referred to as *competition adherence*.

It should also be recognised at this stage that in many instances applied sport psychologists will be working with teams and squads. The team, or squad, scenario will bring with it unique adherence issues. Just as with the individual there will be *strategy*, *training*, and *PST/MP* related adherence. The *strategy adherence* relates to evaluating the degree to which all members engage in team meetings, team building exercises, communication improvement sessions, or team performance review. *Training adherence* relates to the execution of agreed team interventions during training and competition, e.g., team re-focusing strategies, or involvement in pre-match rituals. The notion of team adherence to psychological preparation could represent a future direction for psychological preparation research, as to date this area of service delivery has not been studied. Therefore, it is appropriate to use the same terminology when examining teams or groups.

Essentially, when studying adherence to psychological preparation, researchers should ensure that the category of adherence is identified and reported in order that studies examining similar areas can be assimilated more readily.

Measurement

As well as terminological issues, there are obvious potential problems related to the measurement of adherence to psychological techniques. The problems relate primarily to the nature of the techniques. First, unlike medication or attendance at exercise classes, psychological preparation cannot be readily observed. Depending upon the nature of the

Table 7.1 Adherence categories within psychological preparation

	Type of adherence			
	Strategy	Psychological skills training/ mental practice	Training	Competition
Athlete	e.g., Goal-setting, attendance at meetings, homework, diary keeping, performance/ training reviews, confidence reminders	e.g., Concentration training, confidence building, arousal management, imagery training (varied uses)	e.g., Pre-shot routines, re-focusing strategies, error parking	e.g., Pre-shot routines, Re-focusing strategies, error parking
Team	e.g., participation in team meetings, involvement in team evaluations/ performance reviews, involvement in team building exercises	e.g., Team confidence building, team imagery sessions	e.g., Team re-focusing strategies, improving team communication	e.g., Team re-focusing strategies, involvement in pre-match rituals

psychological preparation technique being evaluated there will be specific measurement difficulties. Obviously with completion of homework tasks and other *strategy* techniques it will be possible to assess usage and adherence. However, as the athlete moves more towards *PST/MP* and into *training* and *competition adherence*, and usage becomes more and more integrated into performance of skills, the ability to assess adherence decreases greatly.

It could be argued that by measuring performance, and assessing changes in performance, it could be inferred that adherence had been present. However, without consistently demonstrating that there is a linear relationship between degree of adherence and level of performance enhancement, such a deterministic assumption cannot provide sport psychologists with a high level of confidence in the efficacy of interventions, or a delineation of the role of adherence in the performance enhancement process. Furthermore, with the existence of factors such as the Hawthorne and placebo effects, and demand characteristics, sport psychologists would be treading a dangerous path to suggest that a given intervention had produced a performance enhancing effect. The relationship between degree of adherence to psychological preparation and degree of performance impact has yet to be established, and this would be seen as a key challenge for sport psychology researchers to address.

As it is very difficult to assess PST/MP usage directly, indirect and more subjective evaluation of athlete usage of psychological preparation routines must be employed. Perhaps the most practicable vehicle for evaluating usage patterns is that of a self-report diary. The self-report approach allows athletes to keep records in their home and training environment, and does not require the intrusion of the sport psychologist. Information about usage patterns and influences upon adherence can be then fed back to the sport psychologist by the athlete through examination of the diary. Although the use of a training diary was not supported by athletes as an important influence upon adherence (Shambrook and Bull, 1999b), the diary would appear to be a very practical solution for measurement. There are obvious limitations with this approach. Social desirability and potential positive or negative adherence influences from the diary should be recognised when interpreting the information collected via this self-report measure. Few alternatives to collecting the required information appear to exist. Therefore, until such time as a more satisfactory alternative exists, researchers should look to interpret information from diaries with potential limitations in mind, and look to make use of social validation techniques (e.g., Kazdin, 1982) to provide support for data collected. Although the limitations potentially confound the efficacy of the diary, the actual data available from a diary lends itself to examining another important measurement areas within adherence, that of frequency and duration of psychological preparation engaged in.

During the development of a programme of psychological skills training a sport psychologist will normally provide an athlete with a recommended amount of training to be engaged in. This may take the form of recommended frequency of sessions, and/or duration of sessions. When assessing how effectively an athlete has adhered to a programme, it is therefore possible to determine success of implementation for both the frequency and/or duration elements. The initial research in the area suggests that athletes may have more of a problem adhering to the frequency demands of a programme (Shambrook and Bull, 1999a) and the potential differences in adherence patterns is an important distinction to retain for the development of knowledge in the area.

In addition to the delineation between frequency and duration of training, being able to compare adherence levels of different athletes is also important. In a consultancy situation, simply using absolute adherence measures (i.e., number of minutes, number of sessions) in an intra-individual fashion is an obvious way to assess the degree of adherence. However, this approach does not facilitate comparison of data from different subjects, as programme demands may naturally differ due to a variety of factors (e.g., level or performer, nature of sport). If comparisons across, and within, sports are to be made there is a need to use adherence values which are comparable. The most obvious way to achieve this is to use percentage adherence levels. With targets for both frequency and duration of training it is very simple to calculate the percentage of the target achieved on a weekly basis. Again, if researchers can all categorise and report adherence levels in the same manner, the pooling of data from different studies becomes more readily achieved.

A final measurement variable which requires consideration relates to the quality of psychological preparation achieved by an athlete. For example, an athlete might be achieving 100% adherence for frequency and duration aspects of training, but not be achieving a satisfactory level of quality in the work. The potentially low-quality sessions may hinder the development of the psychological preparation programme, and lead the athlete to dispense with the training altogether in the belief that it is ineffective. Therefore, assessing the quality of sessions is an equally important adherence issue. Athletes should be encouraged to report quality of sessions (via visual analogue scales, or percentage ratings) as well as the simple frequency and duration components of the sessions. By implementing this approach, the sport psychologist has a more rounded view of the athlete and the programme together, and this can only be of benefit in relation to providing a quality service in the practical setting, and fully assessing effectiveness of an intervention in the research setting.

Future Challenges

It is evident from the contents of this chapter that adherence to psychological preparation research is still in its infancy. If development takes place the growth of the adherence area would hold equal interest to both the research sport psychologist and the applied consultant.

A key challenge of future research in the area would be to establish the predictive validity of the conceptual framework presented. Validation using traditional methods such as structural equation modelling will always be a problem due to the difficulties in recruiting large samples of elite athletes. It is therefore recommended that validation is sought through the utilisation of qualitative, as well as quantitative, research methods in a complementary manner. Marlow & Bull (1998) recommended complementary approaches to adherence research in sport. Such an approach would allow the synthesis of data collected from performers experienced in the long-term employment of psychological preparation strategies.

From the studies reported within this chapter there is an obvious lack of research which has employed world-class athletes. Due to the truism of elite performers being a small population, and the percentage of those who have employed the services of a sport psychologist being even smaller, it is unrealistic to expect studies with large sample sizes. Therefore, researchers should look to employ methodologies which promote the use of small sample sizes such as single-case research designs (e.g., Kazdin, 1982). However, alternative approaches are considered elsewhere in this text (such as those described in Chapter 11) and a consideration of other options is strongly recommended.

In addition to examining the conceptual framework in a more rigorous manner, another pressing concern for the area is to address the relationship between adherence to psychological preparation and degree of performance enhancement. As has been pointed out earlier, sport psychology has repeatedly failed to provide evidence to further understanding of this important relationship.

The research in this area was initiated in order to provide information which could be translated readily into practical recommendations for the applied sport psychologist. In keeping with this initial aim, future research should continue to develop research projects with the applied consultant in mind. This line of inquiry also highlights the need for greater amounts of quality assurance research (e.g., cost–benefit analysis, models of best practice) in order that sport psychology is able to keep developing professional standards and maintain a strong standing within the world of sport.

Practical Recommendations

As well as the research based issues derived from the work carried out to date, there are some key practical recommendations which should be recognised. Bull, Albinson & Shambrook (1996) have suggested that in order to maximise adherence (and therefore effectiveness) of psychological preparation programmes, the following steps should be taken:

1. In order to maximise motivation towards psychological preparation, techniques to ensure that programmes are individualised should be employed (e.g., performance profiling).
2. Psychological and physical training programmes should be integrated as soon as possible in order that perceptions of time constraints are minimised, and that techniques can be developed in the most appropriate manner for use during performance.
3. In order to minimise perceptions of time constraints, a little and often approach to implementing psychological preparation strategies should

be used. Short, frequent sessions is a useful starting point for many athletes.

4. Psychological preparation sessions should be structured in advance so that a priority time is set aside to carry out the training. The content of these sessions should be planned and the session should be reviewed to allow progress to be evaluated. Goals should be set for psychological preparation as with other elements of training.

5. Variety should be built into the psychological preparation sessions, and the programme should be updated every 6–8 weeks in order to avoid boredom.

6. The help of significant others should be recruited to assist adherence to the programme. The creation of support networks to facilitate the habit of utilising psychological preparation techniques is recommended.

CONCLUSION

Despite efforts to promote the importance of the area of psychological preparation over the past decade, it is evident that sport psychology has been slow to take up the challenge of addressing this area. A key reason for this may be the difficulty in measurement associated with the area. As has become obvious, there is not a completely satisfactory measure of adherence for psychological preparation strategies. However, recommendations made within this chapter may go some way towards raising awareness of the key issues for this area of research, and provide a foundation from which future research can be built.

REFERENCES

Blinde, E.M., & Tierney, J.E., (1990). Diffusion of Sport Psychology into Elite U.S. Swimming Programs. *The Sport Psychologist*, **4**, 130–144.

Brewer, B.W., & Shillinglaw, R. (1992). Evaluation of a psychological skills training workshop for male intercollegiate lacrosse players. *The Sport Psychologist*, **6**, 139–147.

Bull, S.J. (1989). Adherence to mental skills training: The need for systematic research. In C.K. Giam, K.K. Chook & K.C. The (eds.), *Proceedings of VII World Congress of Sport Psychology* (p. 164–165). ISSP and Singapore Sports Council.

Bull, S.J. (1991). Personal and situational influences on adherence to mental skills training. *Journal of Sport and Exercise Psychology*, **13**, 121–132.

Bull, S.J. (1994). Towards a model for understanding adherence to mental skills training. In J.R. Nitsch & R. Seiler (eds.), *Movement and Sport-psychological Foundations and Effects: Psychological Training*. Sankt Augustin: Academia Verlag.

Bull, S.J. (1995). Mental training adherence in elite junior tennis players. In R.Vanfraechem, & Y. Vanden Auweele (eds.), *Proceedings of the IXth European Congress on Sport Psychology*, Part III. Brussels, Belgium: Belgian Federation of Sport Psychology, Société Francophone de Psychologie du Sport, Vlaamse Vereniging Voor Sport Psychologie.

Bull, S.J., Albinson, J.G. & Shambrook, C.J. (1996). *The Mental Game Plan: Getting psyched for sport*. Eastbourne, Sports Dynamics.

Butler, R.J., & Hardy, L. (1992). The performance profile: theory and application. *The Sport Psychologist*, **6**, 253–264.

Cogan, K.D., & Petrie, T.A. (1995). Sport Consultation: An evaluation of a season-long intervention with female collegiate gymnasts. *The Sport Psychologist*, **9**, 282–296.

Cohn, P.J., Rotella, R.J., & Lloyd, J.W. (1990). Effects of a cognitive–behavioral intervention on the preshot routine and performance in golf. *The Sport Psychologist*, **4**, 33–47.

Crocker, P.R.E. (1989). A follow-up of cognitive-affective stress management training. *Journal of Sport and Exercise Psychology*, **11**, 236–242.

Daw, J., & Burton, D. (1994). Evaluation of a comprehensive psychological skills training program for collegiate tennis players. *The Sport Psychologist*, **8**, 37–57.

Dishman, R.K., & Ickes, W.D. (1981). Self-Motivation in adherence to therapeutic exercise. *Journal of Behavioral Medicine*, **4**, 421–438.

Gould, D., & Krane, V. (1992). The arousal–athletic performance relationship: current status and future directions. In T.S. Horn (ed.), *Advances in Sport Psychology*. Champaign, IL: Human Kinetics.

Gould, D., Petlichkoff, L., Hodge, K., & Simons, J. (1990). Evaluating the Effectiveness of a Psychological Skills Educational Workshop. *The Sport Psychologist*, **4**, 249–260.

Greaser, J.R. (1994). Examining the effects of perceived desirability of a task on an athlete's intention to practice sport psychology skills. *Applied Research in Coaching and Athletics*, March, 79–95.

Grove, J.R., Norton, P. & Ecklund, R.C. (1997). Mental skills training for baseball: personality correlates of adherence and a multidimensional evaluation of program impact. *Journal of Applied Sport Psychology*, **9** (supplement), S100.

Hardy, L., Jones, J.G. & Gould, D. (1996). *Understanding Psychological Preparation for Sport: Theory and Practice of Elite Performance*. Chichester: Wiley.

Jones, J.G. & Hardy, L. (1991). *Stress and Performance in Sport.* Chichester: Wiley.

Kazdin, A.E. (1982). *Single-case Research Designs: Methods for Clinical and Applied Settings.* Oxford: Oxford University Press.

Kristeller, J.L., & Rodin, J. (1984). A three-stage model of treatment continuity: Compliance, adherence, and maintenance. In A. Baum, S.E. Taylor & J.E. Singer (eds.), *Handbook of Psychology and Health*, Volume IV: *Social Psychological Aspects of Health.* Hillsdale, NJ: Lawrence Erlbaum Associates.

Leffingwell, T.R., & Smith, R.E. (1998, August). Stages of change and psychological skills training in professional baseball. Paper presented at the 106th meeting of the American Psychological Association, San Francisco.

Leith, L.M., & Taylor, A.H. (1992). Behavior modification and exercise adherence: a literature review. *Journal of Sport Behavior*, **15**, 60–74.

Le Scanff, C. (1995). Mental training for table tennis players at national level. In R.Vanfraechem, & Y. Vanden Auweele (eds.), *Proceedings of the IXth European Congress on Sport Psychology*, Part III. Brussels, Belgium: Belgian Federation of Sport Psychology, Société Francophone de Psychologie du Sport, Vlaamse Vereniging Voor Sport Psychologie.

Linder, D.E., Brewer, B.W., Van Raalte, J.L., & De Lange, N. (1991). A negative halo for athletes who consult sport psychologists: replication and extension. *Journal of Sport and Exercise Psychology*, **13**, 133–148.

Marlow, C. & Bull, S.J. (1998). Exploring alternative paradigms in the investigation of training adherence. *Journal of Sport Sciences*, **16**, 78.

Martens, R. (1987) *Coaches Guide to Sport Psychology.* Champaign, IL: Human Kinetics.

Meichenbaum, D. & Turk, D.C. (1987). Facilitating treatment adherence; a practitioner's guidebook. New York: Plenum Press.

Orlick, T. (1989). Reflections on SportPsych consulting with individual and team sport athletes at summer and winter olympic games. *The Sport Psychologist*, **3**, 358–365.

Orlick T., & Partington, J. (1987). The sport psychology consultant: Analysis of critical components as viewed by Canadian athletes. *The Sport Psychologist*, **1**, 4–17.

Perkins, K.A., & Epstein, L.H. (1988). Methodology in exercise adherence research. In R.K. Dishman (ed.), *Exercise Adherence: Its Impact on Public Health.* Champaign, IL: Human Kinetics.

Prochaska, J., & DiClemente, C. (1983). Stages and processes of self-change in smoking: Towards an integrative model of change. *Journal of Consulting and Clinical Psychology*, **51**, 390–395.

Ravizza, K. (1988). Gaining entry with athletic personnel for season-long consulting. *The Sport Psychologist*, **2**, 243–254.

Ravizza, K. (1990). SportPsych consultation issues in professional baseball. *The Sport Psychologist*, **4**, 330–340.

Rider, S, Leffingwell, T.R. & Williams, J.M. (1996). The transtheoretical model and sport psychology consultation – rationale and preliminary findings. *Journal of Applied Sport Psychology*, **8** (Supplement), S97.

Rodgers, W., Hall, C., & Buckolz, E. (1991). The effect of an imagery training program on imagery ability, imagery use, and figure skating performance. *Journal of Applied Sport Psychology*, **3**, 109–125.

Romney, A.K., Weller, S.C., & Batchelder, W.H. (1986). Culture as consensus: A theory of culture and informant accuracy. *American Anthropologist*, **88**, 313–338.

Sallis, J.F., & Hovell, M.F. (1990). Determinants of exercise behavior. *Sport and Exercise Science Reviews*, **19**, 307–330.

Shambrook, C.J. (1995). Adherence to mental skills training for sports performance. Unpublished doctoral disseration. University of Brighton.

Shambrook C.J., & Bull, S.J. (1995). Towards a further understanding of adherence to psychological skills training. In Vanfraechem-Raway, R., & Vanden Auweele, Y. (eds.), *Proceedings of IXth European Congress on Sport Psychology: Integrating Laboratory and Fields Studies*, Part II. (p. 966–973). Brussels, Belgium: Belgian Federation of Sport Psychology.

Shambrook, C.J. & Bull, S.J. (1997). Perceptions of the sport psychologist: A consideration of influences upon adherence to psychological skills training programmes. In R. Lidor & M. Bar-Eli (eds.), *Innovations in sport psychology: Linking theory and practice—Proceedings of the IXth World Congress of Sport Psychology*, Part Two (p. 620–622). International Society of Sport Psychology.

Shambrook, C.J., & Bull, S.J. (1999a). Considerations in the delivery of imagery training: Influences upon adherence to systematic training. Submitted for publication.

Shambrook, C.J., & Bull, S.J. (1999b). Examining the changing role of personal and situational variables upon adherence, drop-out, and maintenance of psychological skills training. Submitted for publication.

Smith, R.E. (1989). Applied sport psychology in an age of accountability. *Journal of Applied Sport Psychology*, **1**, 166–180.

Suinn, R.M. (1983). Imagery and Sports. In A.A. Sheikh (ed.), *Imagery: Current Theory Research and Application* (p. 507–534). New York: John Wiley & Sons.

Thomas, P. (1990). *An Overview of the Performance Enhancement Process in Applied Psychology*. United States Olympic Center, Colorado Springs, CO.

Van Raalte, J.L., Brewer, B.W., Linder, E.L., & De Lange, N. (1990). Perceptions of sport-oriented professionals: a multidimensional scaling analysis. *The Sport Psychologist*, **4**, 228–234.

Vealey, R.S. (1988). Future directions in psychological skills training. *The Sport Psychologist*, **2**, 318–336.

Waller, G. (1997). Drop-out and failure to engage in individual outpatient cognitive behaviour therapy for bulimic disorders. *International Journal of Eating Disorders*, **22**, 35–41.

Zinsser, N.W. (1992). The effects of a cognitive intervention and perceived value on adherence to imagery practice. Unpublished doctoral dissertation, University of Virginia.

Chapter 8

Environmental Determinants of Adherence in Applied Sport Psychology

Derek Milne

If there is a greater challenge for psychologists than facilitating initial behaviour change then it is surely that of arranging for such change to generalise. As Machiavelli put it many centuries ago:

> there is nothing more difficult to carry out nor more doubtful of success, nor more dangerous to handle than to initiate a new order of things. (c. 1513)

While there has been considerable progress latterly in elucidating how behaviour can be changed in the short term (Milne, 1996), the analysis of generalisation remains relatively meagre. In particular, empirical study of the process and determinants of generalisation in natural settings (i.e., not artificially engineered for research purposes) with 'real' participants (e.g.

Adherence Issues in Sport and Exercise. Edited by Stephen J. Bull.
© 1999 John Wiley & Sons Ltd.

athletes, not students) is called for, if we are to develop theory and practice (Biddle, 1989; Strean & Roberts, 1992).

The broad purpose of the present chapter is to overview the relevant generalisation literature, to integrate it with the adherence literature and to indicate how this new model of adherence can be implemented, in terms of the important environmental determinants. Illustrations of two examples of such influences on adherence (coaches and parents) are provided, to indicate how we can foster the generalisation of techniques across time (i.e. 'maintenance'), settings, behaviours and persons. Some new instruments with which to measure this generalisation are also presented. Emphasis is given to the need to employ such instruments to assess whether or not adherence-promoting interventions are conducted correctly (the 'manipulation check'), tied to a collaborative team effort based on a constructive attitude to the sharing of psychological skills.

As already indicated by the above terminology, the present chapter draws from several literatures in applied psychology, in order to provide an integrative account of adherence. This 'pan-disciplinary' emphasis is necessary if we are to successfully tackle the major challenge of generalisation. For example, occupational psychology teaches us about the importance of the physical and social environment, while clinical psychology stresses the need to empower individuals with the kind of personal coping skills that will allow them to transact effectively with that environment. These two applied disciplines can therefore be regarded as addressing the context or environment for the sport and exercise programmes, particularly those programmes that develop intrapersonal competencies (e.g. attentional control training or emotional self-regulation). It is argued that this kind of systemic or ecological perspective will enrich and develop our understanding of adherence. In order for this integrative and ecological perspective to be helpful, it is next necessary to clarify the key terms and concepts.

WHAT IS GENERALISATION?

Generalisation is the transfer of a behaviour change from the learning environment to other settings, persons, responses and times without comprehensive programming (Stokes & Baer, 1977; Stokes & Osnes, 1988). In sport psychology this would include the occurrence of skills taught in the classroom or in training to a competition taking place in another city at another time (i.e. setting and temporal generalisation—also known as maintenance). If such a sport psychology intervention were very successful it might also transfer to other responses and to other athletes. For example, someone taught to concentrate on a pre-shot routine may recognise that this is also helpful as a self-pacing technique during the period of pre-competition attuning (response generalisation). Lastly, other athletes, noticing the improved consistency of their colleague, may initiate the technique in their own performance (person generalisation).

PROMOTING GENERALISATION

In their seminal paper, Stokes and Baer (1977) reviewed 270 studies of these forms of generalisation, identifying nine different ways that researchers promoted it. These forms are summarised in Table 8.1, together with their definitions.

Table 8.1   Increasingly more systematic ways to promote generalization (Stokes & Baer, 1977)

Approach to generalization	Definition
1. 'Train and hope':	following behaviour change, generalisation is noted but not actively programmed
2. 'Sequential modification':	if generalization fails to occur or is deficient, then procedures are introduced to accomplish change
3. 'Introduction to natural maintaining contingencies':	transferring behavioural control from the trainer or researcher to the naturally occurring contingencies ('trapping' or 'entrapment')
4. 'Train sufficient examplars':	training a series of responses until the purpose of generalization is achieved
5. 'Train loosely':	teaching with relatively little control over the material covered or attention to the learner reactions that are desired
6. 'Use indescriminable contingencies':	using unpredictable reinforcement for the trained response
7. 'Programme common stimuli':	ensuring that sufficient features of the training and generalization environments are similar
8. 'Mediate generalization':	establishing a response (e.g. problem-solving skills) as part of new learning that can be used in the solution of generalization problems
9. 'Train to generalise':	placing a contingency on the occurrence of generalization (e.g. extended use of problem-solving skills is reinforced)

The least systemic of these was the so-called 'train and hope' approach, in which the psychologist provided appropriate initial training to the client, but paid no real attention to the factors that influenced generalisation (such as ensuring that the client has the opportunity to use the training in the 'back-home' environment and to receive positive reinforcement for so doing). Half of the studies that they reviewed fell into the 'train and hope' category. Far more systemic were those approaches that ensured that the training environment paralleled the 'back-home' one in some critical respects ('programming common stimuli'), or which taught clients to develop self-regulation skills, such as activation or calming (termed 'mediated generalisation'). They concluded that generalisation probably does not occur without such programming, and subsequent research has consolidated this finding.

There are exceptions to the need for programmed generalisation, but these depend on the fortuitous 'trapping' of the newly learned behaviours by unprogrammed environmental contingencies. For instance, athletes may attend a workshop on mental training (e.g. goal setting) techniques without the prior support or involvement of their coach, but on return the coach may notice and praise a technique that the athlete has generalised from the workshop to the training ground. A behavioural trap is therefore any stimulus that encourages or reinforces exercise or sporting activity and which occurs 'naturally', i.e. without the programming of generalisation by a researcher.

In careful consideration of the environmental 'traps' for behaviour change, Kohler & Greenwood (1986) noted the need to identify how an individual's behaviour alters and becomes entrapped by their environment; and the importance of developing approaches that re-programme those naturally occurring traps that either support problematic behaviour (e.g. non-adherence to an exercise regime) or which fail to maintain desirable behaviours. They outlined five types of evidence that defined how behaviour becomes entrapped by the environment, using the example of entrapment by peer reinforcement. But they emphasised that this reasoning also applied to social contingencies from parents, spouses, teachers, etc., as well as to non-social environmental factors (e.g. equipment). For example, in one study a child's use of outdoor play equipment was reinforced by the researchers during a training phase, and this was then entrapped by reinforcing social interactions with peers. The longer such entrapment occurs, can be shown to covary with the identified natural contingencies (e.g., prompts to exercise; attention or approval for exercising), and can be replicated across people and settings, then the greater the evidence that the entrapment process has taken place.

By way of illustration, Table 8.2 indicates the values of a range of trapping factors, as perceived by a small sample of tennis players, their parents

Table 8.2 A summary of the mean rating of adherence factors as provided by athletes ($N = 4$), their parents ($N = 4$) and the associated sport scientists ($N = 4$)

'Trapping' factors (things that may influence how much an athlete sticks to advice)	Rating of influence (how important was each factor 0 = not important or influential at all; 10 = very important/ influential)
	Mean rating
1. **Player's own motivation:** how much each individual tennis player was keen to follow advice and to develop his game	8.9
2. **Individual advice:** receiving advice that was personally relevant	8.8
3. **Expert advice:** the advice provided by the sport scientists	8.7
4. **Progress:** the player feeling that he is advancing towards better play: the advice is helpful or successful	8.4
5. **Confidence in the academy:** the player believing that the programme (advice and coaching) is valuable	8.3
6. **Parental support:** the way that parents reacted positively to the advice	8.2
7. **Self-confidence:** the extent to which the tennis player feels sure of himself and committed to things	7.9
8. **Coach support:** the coaches' positive reaction to the advice (interested and tying it into his coaching)	7.4
9. **Time limits:** The time available to follow the advice	6.9
10. **Facilities:** the rooms, equipment and indoor court	6.8
11. **Peer support:** positive reactions of the peer group; how much the others in the Academy adhered to advice	6.6
12. **Positive past experiences:** athlete having had useful sport science advice in the past	5.1
13. **'Side-effects':** any drawbacks or worries about the advice (e.g. embarrassment at receiving help)	4.6

and the participating sport scientists (including the author). These people were involved in a local tennis 'academy', designed to foster generalisation of the advice provided by the sport scientists (from the specialisms of nutrition, fitness, sport medicine and psychology). It can be seen that all 13 listed factors were thought to have had a bearing on the athlete's adherence, some of them being personal, some interpersonal and others being concerned with the physical environment. This reflects the theoretical points made by Kohler & Greenwood (1986) and suggests that the environmental determinants for these four tennis players were socially complex, numerous, and generally reinforcing.

WHAT IS THE DIFFERENCE BETWEEN GENERALISATION AND 'ADHERENCE'?

Within some branches of applied psychology, such as Health Psychology and Sport and Exercise Psychology, following advice is usually referred to as adherence or compliance. According to Bull (1994), whereas compliance concerns the client's agreement to enter into treatment, adherence refers to 'the extent to which the patient continues a negotiated treatment under limited supervision' (p. 52). This therefore contrasts with a narrower definition of generalisation in terms of maintenance (generalisation of behaviour across time without supervision) and setting generalisation. Thus, 'adherence' refers to a mid phase in skill acquisition, one that is not normally considered under the term generalisation but which is nonetheless essential.

This comparison between the terms adherence and generalisation illustrates the symbiotic potential of an integrative approach in applied psychology. In the present instance, the blending of sport psychology with clinical psychology yields a fresh conceptual model of 'adherence', as set out in Figure 8.1.

The attentive reader will notice that step two in Table 8.1 is unannounced. The notion of 'intervention adherence' is introduced to highlight the necessity on the one hand for an athlete to, for example, adhere to a psychological skills training programme (PSTP) as a prior condition for 'adherence' as defined by Bull (1994), at least where the athlete is learning a mental skill (e.g. goal setting). A failure to comply with a sport psychologist's advice during a PSTP (e.g. by non-attendance at sessions or by misunderstanding techniques) would surely interfere with adherence. This represents one kind of 'manipulation check', i.e. ensuring that a treatment as delivered does indeed correspond to the espoused intervention. On the other hand, it is important to know how well a psychologist provides the

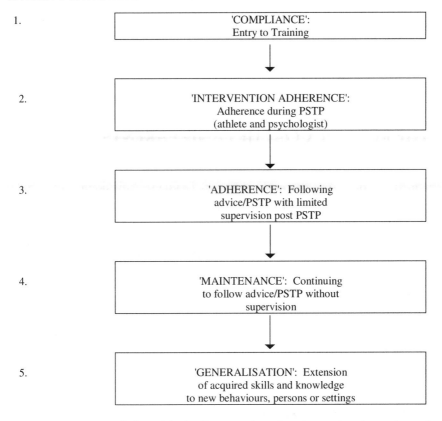

Figure 8.1 An extended model of adherence, based on integrating the notions of the manipulation check (Phase 2) and generalisation (Phases 4 and 5)

advice or instruction that is to be adhered to (i.e. competence), and whether this is consistent with best practice (i.e. intervention adherence). To illustrate, if athletes are given confusing or complex advice then they may adhere very well to what they erroneously understand to be required. However, the psychologist concerned would not regard this as constituting adherence. Secondly, the advice may be inappropriate, as in departing in some important respect from what other psychologists or theory would deem to be best practice. In this instance an athlete may again follow the advice religiously, but, because the psychologist did not adhere to good practice, there remains an error and hence a generalisation problem. This is elaborated below, in the section labelled 'manipulation checks'.

Thus, adherence can usefully be taken to cover the interface between initial behaviour change and generalisation, involving both psychologist and athlete. In summary, Figure 8.1 depicts two necessary conditions for adherence, firstly that the sport psychologist conforms to good practice (i.e. phase 2: intervention adherence) and secondly that this is done skilfully (Waltz et al., 1993). Once these have occurred the athlete can acquire the given psychological techniques (phase 2), a precondition for adherence (phase 3), maintenance (phase 4), and generalisation (phase 5).

THE ROLE OF COACHES AND PARENTS

According to the model depicted in Figure 8.1, only the sport psychologist influences the athletes adherence. This is highly improbable in applied sport psychology (i.e. which is based in natural environments with real athletes). In practice a vast array of factors are likely to influence the extent to which an athlete adheres to the psychologist's advice, as referred to by such terms as situational and personal variables (Bull, 1991), as illustrated earlier in Table 8.2.

In order to cope with this complexity, the sport psychologist needs to identify those factor clusters that can be manipulated and measured in a fairly systematic fashion. Cases in point are an athlete's coach and parents. Either may have a highly significant bearing on adherence, although again it should be recognised that there are many other potential influences on athletes (e.g. their peer group: Bull, 1994). For present purposes, it is convenient to think of the coach as a 'mediator' of the sport psychologist's advice, collaborating with the psychologist so as to maximise the athlete's adherence and the generalisation effect. In turn, the role of parents may be assumed to be to provide support and encouragement to the athlete, a 'moderator' role. Figure 8.2 illustrates this more systemic and ecological account of the critical variables to adherence, set out as an 'educational pyramid'.

THE ROLE OF THE SPORT PSYCHOLOGIST

Therefore, Figure 8.2 recognises that coaches and parents mediate and moderate the athlete's adherence, all of which is guided by the sport psychologist. It also underscores the role of the sport psychologist as a collaborator with other support individuals, as opposed to working solely with performers, a necessary focus for research (Hardy & Jones, 1994).

In what important respects does this differ from Figure 8.1? There are at least three rather significant differences, which amount to a strong argument for sport psychologists working as per Figure 8.2. Firstly, if we wish to help athletes optimally we need to establish ways that enable our interventions to have maximum impact. By involving the coach and the parents as

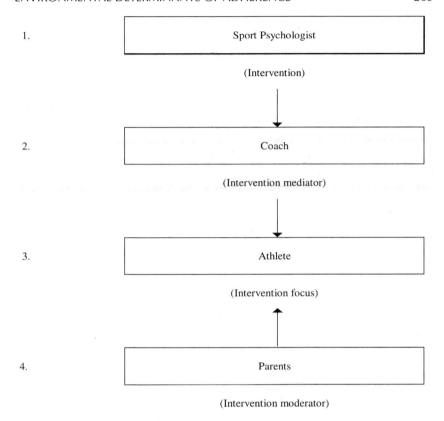

Figure 8.2 The educational pyramid: A more ecological or systemic representation of the relationship between adherence and generalisation, showing the mediating and moderating role of coach and parents

necessary collaborators (and ideally others too) in the consultation we create one of the aforementioned conditions for generalisation, the programming of common stimuli. It also adds a second condition, introducing the athlete to the natural reinforcers for change. In practice this means that the coach's greater contact with the athlete (i.e. more hours over more months than the psychologist can manage) will tend to foster adherence and generalisation. Secondly, this arrangement differs in that it offers psychologists a more efficient way to disseminate psychological skills to athletes. This is because the coach, as mediator of these skills, acquires the capacity to pass them on to other athletes (e.g. to teams other than the one with which the psychologist was involved). Or when the psychologist next works with that coach, there is less input required to implement the programme with an athlete. Finally, we should perhaps recognise a professional responsibility to acknowledge and empower coaches and parents.

Some psychologists decry the 'giving away' of psychological skills to such mediators. However, this is a practically and ethically flawed position, since the practice of psychology cannot practically be restricted to psychologists. How could a coach or parent—even the most anti-psychologist versions—possibly help an athlete to develop without the use of psychology? There are surely no examples of athletes learning skills without attention, memory, encouragement, rehearsal, feedback and so on. More logically and constructively, we should invest our effort in sharing psychological skills. This recognises what is inevitably occurring psychologically between coach, parent and athlete and the stakes that they have in adherence, and encourages this to develop appropriately. On this 'stakeholder collaborative' approach (Ayers, 1987) we can realistically expect generalisation to take place (Porras & Hoffer, 1986), and we can avoid an immoral position in which the professional security needs of psychologists take precedence over the needs of our clients, namely athletes, coaches and parents (Humphreys, 1996). The discussion of skill-sharing is resumed below.

The following sections elaborate the major adherence issues (identified in Figure 8.2). The work of the sport psychologist is put under the microscope first, since (as argued above) it is necessary to demonstrate 'intervention adherence' prior to claiming adherence by a mediating coach or an athlete. This includes a review of the principles and findings of such manipulation checks, concluded with an outline of an instrument that can measure intervention adherence. The role of the coach as 'intervention mediator' is also analysed with equal care. Instruments for measuring the psychologist and coach interventions are detailed, and illustrative data are provided from the local 'academy' evaluation. Finally, the role of coaches and parents as collaborators in the pursuit of adherence (the 'intervention mediators and moderators' in Figure 8.2) will be considered, focusing on the issue of team working.

MANIPULATION CHECKS

As already touched upon above, intervention adherence includes both athlete and psychologist (see Figure 8.1). As regards the athlete, it is recognised that there are problems as regards determining whether or not the athlete is actually following advice. Consider the example of mental imagery, designed to facilitate athlete performance. One may often observe athletes in pre-performance phases in an eyes closed situation in which their body is moving in keeping with the upcoming sport performance (for example Sottomeyer in the high jump). As noted by Murphy and Jowdy

(1992) scenes of this kind have been reported as evidence of somebody's mental concentration, without there being accompanying evidence that this was indeed the case. Studies of imagery rarely provide more than a couple of lines by way of description of what the participants were actually instructed to imagine, or how well they managed to carry out the imagery instructions. Variables identified by Murphy and Jowdy (1992) include the athlete's imagery ability, the imagery perspective, the presence of covert verbalisations, the length of time spent on imagery, and the athlete's prior experience and competence in the use of imagery. They concluded that imagery instructions should be classified as an independent variable in research, so that the database concerning the effects of such interventions are clarified. Possible ways of addressing this challenge include the use of psychophysiological measurement during imagery and careful debriefing of participants following the use of such techniques as imagery. There is evidence that when such checks are conducted, the athletes report different experiences from those designed by the researchers (Murphy and Jowdy, 1992).

Turning to the sport psychologist, the need to clearly measure the content of any advice or intervention alongside information on the competence of the intervention is at least as important as information concerning the athlete. This need has been referred to by a number of terms, including 'manipulation check', 'intervention fidelity', 'technique specification' and assessing the 'integrity of the independent variable' (Peterson et al., 1982). In keeping with the applied psychology emphasis in this chapter, the next step is to show how this analysis of the independent variable might be conducted, drawing first on the clinical psychology literature before returning to a clear example from sport and exercise.

The primary goal of research on adherence is to demonstrate a functional relationship between changes in adherence as related to some independent variable, such as advice from a sport scientist. Precise demonstrated control over the independent variable and measurement of the dependent variables is therefore necessary for the demonstration of a functional relationship (Peterson et al., 1982). To cite from a classic text, Johnstone and Pennybacker (1980) noted that

> The independent variable must be represented by some environmental event, the physical parameters of which are known, specified, and controlled to the extent required. Such a clear description of the independent variable is essential if any factually accurate statement is to issue from the experimental effort. (p. 39).

It follows that inadequate assessment of an intervention can render conclusions about the functional relationship between some dependent variables (such as adherence) and some independent variable (such as an expert's advice) highly suspect. In the clinical psychology literature a curious double standard has developed over the past couple of decades, one in which the sophistication and effort devoted to the dependent variable (for example, changes in mood or activity) is given much greater emphasis than the treatment that supposedly results in changes to these variables (for example, cognitive therapy). This double standard may in part by driven by a logical fallacy, the fallacy of 'affirming the consequent'. According to this logic, predictable changes in the dependent variable are seen to provide sufficient demonstration of its functional relationship to an intervention. This is fallacious because, amongst other things, the researcher never has complete control over the important variables that might impinge on the dependent variable. Interventions should be operationally defined and there should be a reliability check to demonstrate that the intervention did indeed correspond to the supposed treatment. In one survey of published research (Peterson et al., 1982) the proportion of studies adhering to these two requirements was calculated and it was found that although a slight majority of articles did report an operational definition of the intervention, only in 16% of studies was some check on the accuracy of the implementation of the independent variable carried out. These authors concluded that there was insufficient assessment of the independent variable. They argued that researchers must not only define their intervention in replicable terms, but they should also use some instrument to measure the accuracy (fidelity) with which the treatment is implemented and this measurement should be checked for reliability, in exactly the same way as one would do in relation to the dependent variable.

To illustrate, Biddle et al. (1995) set out to compare the motivational effects of two different teaching styles in physical education. However, direct observation of the teaching indicated that there was in fact no difference in the teacher's behaviour across the two conditions. As they noted, this precluded an analysis of the role of the teaching style on the students' motivation.

It has been suggested that, in addition to showing that an intervention does indeed correspond reliably to some clear operationalisation (for example, as set out in an intervention manual) it is desirable to show that any such intervention is properly differentiated from other interventions from which it should be clearly distinguished (Kazdin, 1986). To illustrate, Startup and Shapiro (1993) analysed the use of two psychotherapy manuals for 'prescriptive' (i.e. cognitive behavioural interventions) and 'exploratory' (i.e. interpersonal/psychodynamic) therapy. By means of a therapist response mode coding instrument, these authors analysed 220 therapy sessions provided by five therapists varying in their degree of experience. In this way, they found that the two treatments could be reliably differentiated from one another with great accuracy. The reliability between raters making this coding was also very acceptable. This study illustrates how careful attention to the intervention can be carried out, to provide much richer information concerning what is meant by broad intervention categories such as 'cognitive behavioural therapy', in addition to providing the basis for a causal analysis.

The comments above refer to one dimension of adherence within a manipulation check. Namely to whether or not the researcher follows a particular style with fidelity. In addition, one should ask about whether they do it with competence or proficiency (Waltz et al, 1993). A good example from the clinical literature again is the 'red line' concept, a quality assurance judgement that defines whether or not a therapist is functioning sufficiently competently to be included within an outcome evaluation study. As before, a critical ingredient is a properly validated instrument with which to operationalise and measure competence in a given intervention approach. One popular example is the cognitive therapy scale (Young and Beck 1988), which measures 11 aspects of this therapy (including focusing on key cognitions, collaboration, and setting homework for the client). Shaw (1984) has shown how the cognitive therapy scale can be used to define competence by the use of the red line concept, borrowed from motorcar racing to indicate a dangerous situation. This is one in which the intervention is not provided at or above an agreed standard of proficiency, defined as a point one standard deviation below the mean of cognitive therapy scale scores for certified cognitive therapists. If a therapist falls below this red line on two consecutive treatment sessions within a clinical outcome trial, then the research team will contact the therapist to express concern and arrange for additional training until the performance improves. Failure to improve, or an excessive number of sessions below the red line, would result in a therapist's outcomes being excluded from the treatment evaluation.

Finally, in addition to assessing whether or not an intervention is in keeping with a particular style and is delivered competently, one should also enquire as to whether the treatment is applied by an interpersonally effective manager (Schaffer, 1982). A key concept in framing interpersonal effectiveness is the 'therapeutic alliance'. This consists of at least two components, namely an emotional bond between therapist and client and secondly collaborative engagement in problem solving. One popular way to measure this learning alliance is to encourage the client to provide satisfaction ratings on the nature and extent of collaboration. For example, in analysing my own therapy I found that although there was a relatively low level of fidelity, there were high levels of client satisfaction with the interpersonal aspects of the intervention (Milne, 1989). Similarly in sport and exercise one might use instruments such as the Consultant Evaluation Form (Partington and Orlick, 1987).

Illustration of a Manipulation Check

The following illustrations of adherence by the coach and the sports psychologist are drawn from the same local analysis of an Academy as touched on above in relation to Table 8.2. In chronological order, the first task is to demonstrate that sport scientists adhere to the manipulation of relevance, in this case providing teaching to the coach and the athletes that is in keeping with the stated manipulation. This should correspond to a workshop format, characterised by high levels of experiential learning (for example engagement in learning exercises during the workshop and homework tasks in between workshop sessions). In a format very similar to the earlier discussion of assessing therapy fidelity (Startup and Shapiro, 1993) the MASTER instrument (Ashworth and Milne, 1996) was used to code the different forms of speech used by four sport scientists contributing to this local academy. The profile of their teaching was created from randomly selected, direct observations of 1 hour long presentations made by each of the four contributing sport scientists. The most frequent utterances by the sport scientists fell in the didactic areas of information giving and listening, with correspondingly low levels of the experiential style of teaching that would more properly correspond to a workshop format (i.e., very low levels of process advisement or general advisement). This particular manipulation check, therefore, indicated that there was a lack of integrity or fidelity in the manipulation of the teaching intervention, as it corresponded more closely to a didactic lecture format than to the intended and more appropriate appropriate experiential workshop format.

In terms of the coach's adherence to the advice provided through these lectures from the sport scientists, the local academy offered an illustration based on the use of the short Coach Observation System (Rushall, 1977). Observation of the coach following these teaching sessions indicated that the range of adherence to advice extended from 20% to 65%, a relatively high level of adherence in the context of the literature. This indicates that direct observation of adherence can be practicable, contrary to the view expressed by Bull (1989).

In terms of the sport psychologists' adherence to an experiential style of practical consultancy, observations were also carried out on the sport psychologists' activity immediately following the teaching sessions mentioned above. That is, an hour of each academy meeting was dedicated to teaching, followed by an hour of on-court practice, during which the psychologist worked closely with the tennis coach. The behaviour of the psychologist towards both the coach and the tennis players was coded using a new observation instrument called Consulting Psychologist; Advisory Categories Tool (COMPACT: Milne & Briggs, 1997). COMPACT is described in Table 8.3.

Table 8.3 An operationalisation of sport psychology consultancy, from the Consulting Psychologist: Advisory Categories Tool (COMPACT)

Consultant/supervisor interventions

1. Supporting, reassuring and nurturing

2. Reframing, conceptualising and refocusing

3. Probing, questioning and inquiring

4. Drawing coach/trainee out, enhancing and evoking

5. Directing, advising and teaching

6. Restating, summarising and clarifying

7. Challenging, confronting and disagreeing

8. Silence (no SP intervention; speech by coach/supervisor or pupil/client)

9. Other/miscellaneous (any additional interventions) specify here:

As this table indicates, COMPACT consists of nine categories of consultancy, drawn from the supervision literature (especially from Rabinowitz et al., 1986). A momentary time sampling procedure is used to code the activity of the coach at 10 second intervals. At each such moment, defined by watching a second hand of a watch, the given behaviour of the psychologist is coded. Such observations need to be conducted reliably and in the case of this illustration two raters achieved high inter-rater reliably in the use of COMPACT (85% exact agreement: Milne & Briggs, 1997).

The data from this analysis of the psychologist's adherence to a particular style of consultancy indicated that for over half of the observed time the psychologist was listening and attending to the coach and athletes, followed by teaching (13% of occasions), questioning (9%), summarising (9%), supporting (8%) and finally other/miscellaneous (8%). These data indicate that the psychologist adopted more of an exploratory than prescriptive style of consultancy, since the prescriptive item (teaching) represented only 13% of utterances during the sampled period.

Therefore, these illustrative manipulation checks of the behaviour of the coach and the psychologist show how one can operationalise the relevant interventions and measure them reliably. Most significantly, however, they show that even well-intentioned interventions may not correspond to the proposed approach; the teaching provided by the sport scientist (including the sports psychologist) was more characteristic of didactic lecturing than of the intended workshop format; similarly the consultancy provided by the psychologist was not as prescriptive as was intended within a broadly cognitive behavioural approach. These findings bear out the need to study our manipulations carefully.

SHARING PSYCHOLOGICAL SKILLS

While the above section addresses the intervention provided by the psychologist and the coach (the intervention mediator) as depicted in Figure 8.2, it says little about the way that these two parties interact with both the athlete and other interested groups such as the athlete's parents (level 4 in Figure 8.2, the intervention focus and moderator, respectively). Team work in sport and exercise is most often construed in terms of building team spirit. To illustrate, Syer (1991) described the creative energy or 'synergy' that can be released when a group of individuals combine their strength and ability. Another product of successful team building is a sense of belonging to the team, which is experienced by each member of the team ('confluence'). In order to create these two desirable conditions Syer (1991) emphasises the need to clarify needs, establish effective working relationships, improve communication and to develop a positive attitude.

The importance of synergy and confluence is also true of teams of sports scientists working collaboratively with each other and with coaches and athletes. The quality of such collaboration is surely one of the major environmental determinants of adherence. According to an influential paper by Carron (1982), team working was construed in terms of group cohesion, a multidimensional phenomenon consisting of four antecedents and two consequences. The antecedents were defined as leadership qualities of the coach, situational factors, personal factors and team factors. These were thought to lead to individual and group outcomes. This formulation was incorporated into the group environment questionnaire (Carron et al. 1985), which has been used to measure such aspects of team functioning as group resistance and adherence to physical activity. Effective leadership from a coach or indeed a sports scientist is thought to be a major determinant of cohesive teams. A popular measure for this variable is the Leadership Scale for Sports (Chelladurai and Saleh, 1980). The Leadership Scale consists of one instructional behaviour (training and instruction), two decision making styles (autocratic and democratic) and two motivational tendencies (social support and positive feedback).

To illustrate the link between leadership and team working, consider the study by Gardner et al. (1996), who analysed high school and junior college baseball and softball teams. They found from a correlational analysis that coaches who were perceived as high in training and instruction, democratic behaviour, social sport and positive feedback; and who were viewed as low in autocratic behaviour had the more cohesive teams. A study by Dale and Wrisberg (1996) further suggested how such crucial determinants of exercise and athletic performance as an open atmosphere and effective communication can be developed. They worked with a women's volleyball team and its coach, by means of constructing performance profiles. These profiles provided a basis for a constructive team meeting in which the athletes set personal and group goals for the upcoming training season. The consulting psychologist explained the concept of performance profiling of the group and facilitated their completion. As a result of this exercise, athletes and coaches become aligned in terms of what is regarded as important components of individual and team performance. In creating a team profile, the group are initially asked to consider the characteristics of a successful volleyball team, leading to a discussion of what they thought successful meant, in terms of describing a volleyball team. After much discussion, the athletes unanimously agreed that 'successful' applied to a team that consistently finished at the top of the final standings in their league table. The characteristics of such a team were then brainstormed and recorded on a flip chart, with the consultants facilitating specificity and combining related characteristics. For example, the notion of dedication to hard work and the capacity to work hard were combined into 'dedicated to giving maximum effort each practice'. Finally, each athlete was then asked to record on a sheet of paper a value from 1 to 10 in relation to each of the brainstormed characteristics. This allowed a mean profile for all team members' perceptions of a successful team to be generated. As regards the profile of the coach, the team meeting also involved a session in which the characteristics of the ideal coach were brainstormed, defined and rated as per the team characteristics. This profile indicated that the most important characteristic of the coach was being knowledgeable about the game, followed by being dedicated, confident about the training programme, then in less salient order treating all players equally, having realistic expectations, being calm under pressure, being encouraging and a good communicator. Similar meetings were held in the middle and at the end of the season, and Dale and Wrisberg (1996) reported significant improvements in these ratings on one or more characteristic by each athlete, the team and the coach. Also, athletes and coach agreed that there was a more open atmosphere for communication resulting from this exercise.

Once more it may be helpful to combine the sports psychology approach to team working with that from clinical and occupational psychology. A case in point is the work that has been done on multidisciplinary team working in clinical psychology and on organisational team working in occupational psychology. An illustration from the latter sphere is the Team Climate Inventory (Anderson and West, 1994), which measures somewhat similar variables to the above study by Dale and Wrisberg (1996). The four variables are participative safety (i.e. comfort in sharing information openly), supporting innovation (in terms of both talk and action), having a vision that is shared, and an orientation to the task (particularly to excellence). The Team Climate Inventory was administered in the local academy evaluation, as touched on above. The perceptions of the coach and the four sports scientists were recorded for two successive academies with efforts being made the second time round to improve communication and team working in general. As Table 8.4 illustrates, there was some progress in three of the four Team Climate Inventory areas. Improvements in such things as having a shared vision surely contributes to the environment that surrounds the athlete and coach, improving adherence to advice.

Some further comments about team working are offered in the final discussion section.

Table 8.4 Recommendations for effective team working, drawn from the clinical psychology literature

Recommendation	Tips
1. Become 'team wise' (Marshall, 1989)	Understand the nature of relationships that may exist and be prepared for personal attacks; Draw on professional skills and self-belief.
2. Develop Cohesiveness (Craft & Brown, 1985)	Negotiate who is going to do what for whom and record this as part of a 'partnership' approach; Ensure that clear lines of accountability exist and that team members have influence over decisions. Encourage awareness of expertise and ways of working (get beyond stereotypes).
3. Contribute to effective leadership ('champions': Corrigan & McCracken, 1997)	'Champions' are needed to lead the team through the minefields of interdisciplinary working. Such people foster problem identification and resolutions by realistic brainstorming with team members; they 'chase' actions to ensure progress and they feedback to the team. Champions and others ensure effective 'engagement' and support for the work of the team (e.g. in host organisation).

CONCLUSIONS AND RECOMMENDATIONS

This chapter puts forward two main proposals. The first is conceptual and involves an elaborated model of adherence, as set out in Figure 8.1. This suggests an integration of the sport and exercise psychology literature with that from applied psychology, with its emphasis on generalisation. This blend of literatures suggested five steps in adherence, commencing with the athlete's compliance to an intervention and then leading onto intervention adherence. This was detailed at some length under the heading of the 'manipulation check'. Several detailed examples were provided of how such a check could be carried out, based on a local 'academy' to which the author contributed. Following correct intervention adherence, one can reasonably expect the athlete to adhere to advice with limited supervision and if this happens then there can be maintenance and in turn generalisation. This integrative model of adherence provides a richer formulation of the phenomenon and so may be useful to future researchers.

The second major contribution in this chapter is to provide a pragmatic way of responding to this integrative formulation of adherence in the form of instruments that can be used to tap each of the levels in the educational pyramid, as set out in Figure 8.2. This pyramid builds the integrative formulation of adherence into a service delivery paradigm, one in which the psychologist (or other consultant) works with coaches to produce adherence in athletes. This has also been termed the 'organisational empowerment' approach (Hardy & Jones, 1994). The educational pyramid approach recognises the moderating role of people like parents and peer groups. Again, the local academy provided some practical examples of how this can be measured and manipulated, indicating ways of ameliorating the kind of conflicts and power struggles that often occur (Hellstedt, 1987).

Aside from the above main proposals, two subsidiary points are stressed in this concluding discussion, namely team working and the related issue of skill sharing with non-professionals. Starting with the issue of skill sharing (since this is a precondition for truly collaborative team working), one touches on an issue of profound importance throughout the history of professional psychology. On the one hand are those who oppose skill sharing, referring to it as 'giving psychology away'. Advocates of this cautious position stress how the relatively unskilled mediators and moderators, such as coaches and parents, may abuse or dilute psychological methods in a way which is ultimately harmful to athletes. In opposition to this lobby are those who believe that it is vital for psychologists to share their skills with non-psychologists if they are to be effective in disseminating helpful methods to as large a sample of the community as possible: only in this way can psychologists expect to have any impact on large samples of the population. In addition, this impact is likely to involve better adherence and generalisation, because in sharing skills psychologists are usually teaming up with people like coaches and parents who can entrap adherence by means of the naturally occurring reinforcers in the athlete's environment. This skill sharing model is based on the educational pyramid as set out in Figure 8.2. The pyramid dates back to the work of Sigmund Freud in the early 20th Century when he acted as the consultant to the father of little Hans. Freud indicated that the father was entirely respons-ible for the implementation of the psychodynamic treatment, and that the father's natural relationship with his son was a crucial ingredient in the successful treatment. More recently, the educational pyramid has received increasing support in that a number of psychological skills have been suc-cessfully disseminated through mediators such as parents, nurses, teachers, spouses and peer groups (Milne, 1986).

Not only is skill sharing an effective approach if conducted skilfully, it is also morally more appropriate than the alternative model of not giving psychology away. This is true in the sense that professionals need to be wary of creating a situation in which their own professional security needs take precedence over the needs of their clients (Humphreys, 1996). The constructive and ethical dissemination of psychological skills to such im-portant environmental agents as coaches and parents is therefore a priority for sports scientists. The issue nowadays revolves more around the most appropriate methods for providing such skill sharing, and as indicated above (see for example Table 8.2) it is clear that appropriate skill sharing is not a straightforward matter. A number of key tasks need to be handled skilfully if the transmission of psychological methods to key environmental figures is to be executed successfully (Milne and Noone, 1996).

Turning to the final issue in this discussion, successful skill-sharing ex-ercises depend on a collaborative style of working. This has been charac-terised in terms of such variables as cohesion and leadership in the sport and exercise literature. However, one of the main facets of this chapter is to integrate the sport and exercise literature with that of the other applied sciences, particularly clinical and occupational psychology. These buttress and extend the sport and exercise research by indicating in more detail how, for example, parents and coaches can be engaged in a collaborative working relationship that promotes their involvement and the longer-term adherence to any intervention (Ayers, 1987). According to Ayers (1987), within 'a stakeholder collaborative' model of working with such groups as parents and coaches, the sports scientists will engage them in the deter-mination of the goals and methods of a programme, in keeping with the profiling example provided by Dale and Wrisberg (1996). There will then be regular opportunities to discuss and review a programme, as well as collaboration over practical aspects of the venture (for example the com-pletion of evaluation forms). As a consequence of such a stakeholder col-laborative approach, the sports scientist is likely to reap greater rewards, particularly in terms of adherence and generalisation that depends on trap-ping by coaches or parents (Papineau and Kiely, 1996). Improving collab-oration in this way should develop communication and team functioning as illustrated by the measurement of team climate (see Figure 8.4). Such successful effort should not be taken for granted, since it is clear from the clinical field that when multidisciplinary teams are asked to work together the results can be counter-productive. For example, Marshall (1989) referred to the dissatisfaction and conflicts that can exist in such teams in terms of 'blood and gore', before providing a psychodynamic perspective of how team members may often cope with the anxieties of working collaboratively by such strategies as depersonalisation, denial and splitting. Similarly, Paxton (1995) bemoaned the unfocussed, inefficient and low-quality services provided by teams and expressed relief at the move away from this ineffectual attempt to combine incompatible approaches.

What guidelines or recommendations does this literature offer to sports scientists? Firstly that the interventions that are used to influence adherence pay due reference to the environmental factors, such as coaches and parents, that play a large part in influencing generalisation. Secondly, it is clear from this chapter that the interventions themselves should be carefully described in a manual with sufficient detail for them to be replicated by others subsequently. Thirdly, once such interventions are manualised they should be measured reliably in research studies so that one can indeed infer that changes in the dependent variable (for example an athlete's adherence) are indeed attributable to a specified intervention. Only in this way can the field be expected to move forward on a secure footing. Fourthly, to have the necessary impact on the number of people who can benefit from advice on exercise and sport, psychologists and other sports scientists need to disseminate their work through key figures in the environment, be they parents, peer groups, teachers or other key figures. Similarly, they need to pay attention to physical aspects of the environment that may also play a significant part (for example attractive changing rooms and good-quality sporting facilities). Finally, it has been emphasised that to be effective either in individual consultation or through skill-sharing endeavours, sports scientists need to work very collaboratively with key figures in the athlete's environment. Particular emphasis was given to team-working based on the occupational and clinical psychology literature. Table 8.4 summarises some recommendations for working effectively with groups made up of people like coaches, teachers and parents. A special issue of the *Journal of Applied Sport Psychology* has detailed other considerations (e.g., goal setting and social support: 1997, **9**, 1–154).

While there may be 'nothing more difficult to carry out nor more doubtful of success' than to attempt to shift the environmental determinants of adherence, this is surely a major challenge to be accepted by those who would promote exercise and sport adherence. In order to succeed in this challenge, it is necessary to not only tackle skilfully a number of complex variables arising in the natural environment of the athlete, but also to draw on the relevant literature from the range of applied psychology. This chapter is a gesture in that innovative and integrative direction.

REFERENCES

Anderson, M.A. and West, M. (1994). *Team Climate Inventory*. Windsor: NFER-Nelson.

Ashworth, P. and Milne, D. (1996). Learning from the MASTER. *Journal of Clinical Psychology & Psychotherapy* **3**, 103–108.

Ayers, T.D. (1987). Stakeholders as partners in evaluation: A stakeholder-collaborative approach. *Evaluation & Program Planning*, **10**, 263–271.

Biddle, S. (1989). Research trends in British sports psychology: What is our applied research base? *Journal of Sport Sciences*, **7**, 78–79.

Biddle, S., Goudas, M., Underwood, A.M., & Fox, K.R. (1995). Teaching styles, intrinsic motivation and goal-involvement in physical education. *Journal of Sports Sciences*, **13**, 49.

Bull, S.J. (1989). Adherence to mental skills training: The need for systematic research. In: C.K. Giam, K.K. Chook & K.C.Teh (eds), *Proceedings, 7th World Congress in Sport Psychology*, Singapore, 7–12th August.

Bull, S.J. (1991). Personal & situational influences on adherence to mental skills training. *Journal of Sport & Exercise Psychology*, **13**, 121–132.

Bull, S.J. (1994). Towards a model for understanding adherence to mental skills training. In: J.R. Nitsch & R. Seiler (eds), *Movement & Sport Psychological Foundations & Effects: Psychological Training*. Sankt Augustin: Academia Verlag.

Carron, A.V. (1982). Cohesiveness in sport groups: Interpretations and considerations. *Journal of Sport Psychology*, **14**, 123–128.

Carron, A.V., Widmeyer, N. & Brawley, L. (1985). The development of an instrument to assess cohesion in sport teams: The Group Environment Questionnaire. *Journal of Sport and Exercise Psychology*, **10**, 244–266.

Chelladurai, P. and Saleh, S.D. (1980). Dimensions of leader behaviour in sports: Development of a leadership scale. *Journal of Sport Psychology*, **2**, 34–35.

Corrigan, P.W. and McCracken, S.G. (1997). *Interactive Staff Training: Rehabilitation Teams that Work*. NY: Plenum Press.

Craft, A. and Brown, H. (1985). Getting a team to pull together. *Health & Social Services Journal*, September 19, 1168.

Dale, G.A. & Wrisberg, C.A. (1996).The use of a performance profiling technique in a team setting: Getting the athletes and coach on the 'same page'. *The Sport Psychologist*, 10, 261–277.

Gardner, D.E., Shields, D.L.L., Bredemeier, B.J.L. & Bostrom, A, (1996). The relationship between perceived coaching behaviours and team cohesion among baseball and softball players. *The Sport Psychologist*, **10**, 367–381.

Hardy, L. and Jones, J.G. (1994). Current issues and future directions for performance related research in sports psychology. *Journal of Sports Sciences*, **12**, 61–92.

Hellstedt, J.C. (1987). The coach/parent/athlete relationship. *The Sport Psychologist*, **1**, 151–160.

Humphreys, K. (1996). Clinical psychologists as psychotherapists: History, future & alternatives. *American Psychologist*, 51, 190–197.

Johnston, J. & Pennypacker, H.S. (1980). *Strategies and Tactics of Human Behavioural Research*. Hillsdale, NJ: Erlbaum.

Kazdin, A.E. (1986). Comparative outcome studies of psychotherapy: Methodological issues and strategies. *Journal of Consulting and Clinical Psychology*, **54**, 95–105.

Kohler, F.W & Greenwood, C.R. (1986). Toward a technology of generalization: The identification of natural contingencies of reinforcement. *The Behaviour Analyst*, **9**, 19–26.

Marshall, R.J. (1989). Blood and gore. *The Psychologist*, March, 115–117.

Milne, D.L. (1986). *Training Behaviour Therapists: Methods, Evaluation and Implementation With Parents, Nurses and Teachers*. London: Croom-Helm.

Milne, D. (1989). Multi dimensional evaluation of therapist behaviour. *Behavioural Psychotherapy*, **17**, 253–266.

Milne, D. (1996). Critical reviews of the literature: Using a rigorous approach to bridge the qualitative-quantitative divide. In: C. Robson, B. Cripps & H. Steinberg (eds), *Quality & Quantity: Research Methods in Sport & Exercise Psychology*. Leicester: BPS Books.

Milne, D. and Briggs, R. (1997). The sport psychologist as practical consultant: A rare 'manipulation check'. *Journal of Sports Sciences*, **15**, 97.

Milne, D.L. and Noone, S. (1996). *Teaching & Training for Non-Teachers*. Leicester: BPS Books.

Murphy, S.M. & Jowdy, D.P. (1992). Imagery and mental practice. In: T.S. Horn (ed.): *Advances in Sport Psychology*, Champaign, IL: Human Kinetics.

Papineau, D. and Kiely, M.C. (1996). Participatory evaluation in a community organisation: Fostering stakeholder empowerment and utilization. *Evaluation and Programme Planning*, **19**, 79–93.

Partington, J. and Orlick, T. (1987). The sport psychology consultant evaluation form. *The Sport Psychologist*, **1**, 309–317.

Paxton, R. (1995). Goodbye community mental health teams—at last. *Journal of Mental Health*, **34**, 331–334.

Peterson, L., Homer, A.L. & Wonderlich, S.A. (1982). The integrity of independent variables in behaviour analysis. *Journal of Applied Behaviour Analysis*, **15**, 477–492.

Porras, J.I and Hoffer, S.J. (1986). Common behavioural changes in successful organization development efforts. *Journal of Applied Behavioural Sciences*, **22**, 477–494.

Rabinowitz, F.E., Heppner, P.P. and Roehlke, H.J. (1986). Descriptive study of process & outcome variables of supervision over time, *Journal of Counselling Psychology*, **3**, 292–300.

Rushall, B.S. (1977). Two observational schedules of sporting & physical education environments. *Canadian Journal of Applied Sport Sciences*, **2**, 15–21.

Schaffer, N.D. (1982). Multi dimensional measures of therapist behaviour as predictors of outcome. *Psychological Bulletin*, **92**, 670–681.

Shaw, B.F. (1984). Specification of the training and evaluation of cognitive therapists for outcome studies. In: J.B.W. Williams and R.L. Spitzer (eds): *Psychotherapy Research: Where Are We and Where Should We Go?* New York: Guilford Press.

Startup, M. & Shapiro, D.A. (1993). Therapist treatment fidelity in prescriptive vs exploratory psychotherapy. *British Journal of Clinical Psychology*, **32**, 443–456.

Stokes, T. and Baer, J. (1977). An implicit technology of generalization. *Journal of Applied Behaviour Analysis*, **10**, 349–367.

Stokes, T. and Osnes, P. (1988). The developing applied technology of generalization and maintenance. In: R.H. Horner, G. Dunlop, & R.L. Keogel (eds). *Generalization and Maintenance: Life Style Changes in Applied Settings*. Baltimore: Brookes.

Strean, W.B. and Roberts, G.C. (1992). Future directions in applied sport psychology research. *The Sport Psychologist*, **6**, 55–65.

Syer, J. (1991). Team building: The development of team spirit. In: S.J. Bull (ed.), *Sport Psychology: A Self-Help Guide*. Marlborough, Wilts: Crowood Press.

Waltz, J., Addis, M.E., Koerner, K. and Jacobson, N.S. (1993). Testing the integrity of a psychotherapy protocol: assessment of adherence and competence. *Journal of Consulting and Clinical Psychology*, **61**, 620–630.

Young, J.E. & Beck, A.T. (1988). *Cognitive Therapy Scale. Centre for Cognitive Therapy*, University of Pennsylvania, Room C02, 133 South 36th Street, PA 19104, USA.

Chapter 9

The Client–Practitioner Interaction and its Relationship to Adherence and Treatment Outcomes

Al Petitpas

Although interest in the field of exercise and sport psychology has grown dramatically over the last two decades, there still exists considerable debate over what services sport psychologists provide (e.g., Murphy, 1995; Silva, 1989). Several authors (e.g., Danish, Petitpas, & Hale, 1993; Singer, 1996) have suggested that sport and exercise psychologists should not only be involved in helping individuals improve athletic performance but they should also be concerned with the overall well-being of the athlete or exercise participant. Unfortunately, many within the field have misinterpreted this suggestion to mean that sport and exercise psychologists should also be expected to address clinical problems. Clearly, there will be a small number of athletes and exercise participants who will experience some form of psychopathology that will require a referral to an appropriately trained mental health professional, but, as Corlett (1996) has pointed

Adherence Issues in Sport and Exercise. Edited by Stephen J. Bull.
© 1999 John Wiley & Sons Ltd.

out, not all forms of emotional reactions to athletic experiences are rooted in pathology. Many athletes and exercise participants will have difficulty managing emotions, making decisions, or coping with life transitions that do not require traditional clinical services, but may require something beyond mental skills training. For the purpose of this chapter, these types of non-clinical interventions will be called counseling interactions.

Singer (1996) suggested that of all the groups of professionals who are engaged to assist athletes in maximizing their performance, sport and exercise psychologists may be the only ones who focus on more than just winning. Sport and exercise psychologists by virtue of their unique relationship with athletes are often in a position to be confronted with issues that extend beyond athletic performance enhancement and require more that just mental skills training (Danish et al. 1993; Orlick, 1990). Therefore, it is not surprising that training in basic counseling skills is a standard competency included in the credentialing criteria necessary to become a sport and exercise psychologist in many countries (Zaichkowsky & Perna, 1996).

Although the field of counseling psychology has long recognized the centrality of the client–practitioner interaction in facilitating treatment adherence, little has been written about this interaction in the sport and exercise psychology literature. The purpose of this chapter is to examine the role of sport and exercise psychologists in the delivery of counseling interventions. In particular, the following questions will be discussed: (a) What is known about the impact of the client–practitioner interaction in relationship to adherence to intervention plans and treatment outcomes?; (b) How might this knowledge affect future research directions in exercise and sport psychology; and (c) What are the implications of this knowledge for training and supervision of individuals interested in entering the field?

THE COUNSELING RELATIONSHIP

Sport and exercise psychology is at a point in its evolution where it needs to validate the efficacy of its interventions (Singer, 1996). Although considerable research exists to show how the use of mental skills, such as goal setting (e.g., Weinberg, 1994) and imagery (e.g., Murphy, 1994), impacts performance goals, little if any research has examined those factors in the process of service delivery that might enhance treatment adherence and contribute to successful outcomes.

However, an extensive body of research from the field of counseling psychology provides a helpful framework for examining service delivery in

the context of exercise and sport psychology interventions. This work assumes that counseling interactions consist of two basic elements. The first of these is the techniques used by the helper. The second element is the relationship between the parties involved. Although these factors are often examined independently, Gelso and Fretz (1992) concluded that they are also highly interdependent. Therefore, elements of the relationship are likely to impact how the techniques are employed and vice versa.

For over forty years, researchers from counseling, psychology, and psychiatry have examined the counseling process in hopes of identifying the specific factors that influence adherence and therapeutic outcomes. Based on the results of this body of work, it is safe to state that counseling interventions have the potential to be effective with most clients. However, research attempts to isolate the factors responsible for successful counseling outcomes have been inconclusive. Of all the techniques, personality characteristics, and other factors that have been examined, only one, the client–practitioner relationship, has been proven to consistently relate to treatment adherence and positive outcomes (Sexton & Whiston, 1994). It appears that the success of most helping relationships is based on the development of a working alliance that is characterized by trust, openness, and collaboration (Ivey, Ivey, & Simek-Morgan, 1993).

Most of the research on the counseling relationship can be divided into three main frameworks: transference relationships, facilitative conditions, and the working alliance. Because the work on transference relationships addresses clinical interactions primarily, it will not be discussed here. However, both the facilitative conditions and working alliance models have clear implications for sport and exercise psychology interventions.

Facilitative Conditions

Forty years ago, Rogers (1957) postulated that there are six facilitative conditions that are both necessary and sufficient for change to occur in clients. Since that time, these conditions have been the subject of considerable research. The conclusion seems to be that even though these conditions may not be sufficient to account for the achievement of counseling goals, they do in most cases facilitate treatment adherence and are important to achieving successful outcomes (Gelso & Fretz, 1992). In particular, three of these conditions, congruence, empathetic understanding, and unconditional positive regard, have received the most research attention.

The first of these conditions is the counselor must be congruent in the relationship. Over the years, several terms have been used to describe this condition, including genuineness, authenticity, and congruence. The primary feature of this condition is that counselors should be real and consistent in their interactions with their clients. Self-presentation and self-disclosure are two of the variables most frequently examined in order to evaluate the relationship between congruence and counseling outcomes (Sexton & Whiston, 1994). Although these variables have not been examined in relationship to sport and exercise psychology interventions, Orlick and Partington (1987) determined that elite athletes are more likely to adhere to intervention strategies if they 'accept and like their consultants as human beings' (p. 7).

The second facilitative condition is the counselor's ability to develop empathetic understanding of the client's experience. Rogers (1957) suggested that if clients believe that their counselors understand what they are going through, then they are apt to have more faith in the counselor and devote more energy to the treatment objectives. Several studies have supported the notion that empathetic understanding is a shared characteristic of successful counselors independent of their theoretical orientation (Fiedler, 1950; Sloane & Staples, 1984).

The third facilitative condition is the counselor's ability to accept the client as a person of worth unconditionally. That is, the counselor should strive to be non-judgmental in accepting all of the client's behaviors, not just some of them. Although this is a key characteristic of a Rogerian approach to helping, it is a difficult concept to measure and, as a result, it has received less attention in the literature. Researchers (e.g., Barrett-Lennard, 1981; Sexton & Whiston, 1994) have concluded that unconditional positive regard is a multidimensional concept and they have focused their attention on the counselor's ability to communicate a warm, positive, and accepting attitude toward the client. These attitudes are often referred to in regards to treating clients with respect and dignity. Counselors demonstrating these qualities will be attentive to clients' communications, display interest in their clients' experiences, and try to identify clients' positive aspects and resources (Ivey et al., 1993). These same qualities were identified by Orlick and Partington (1987) as characteristic of effective sport psychology consultants.

Although studies of the quality of the therapeutic relationship, as measured by various facilitative conditions, have been marked by inconsistent findings, most researchers concur that empathetic understanding is clearly related to treatment adherence and positive counseling outcomes (Ivey et al., 1993). For example, Patterson's (1984) review of related studies indicated considerable support for a strong relationship between counselor genuineness, warmth, and empathy and therapeutic effectiveness. This belief has clear implications for both research and practice in sport and exercise psychology interventions, and these implications will be outlined later in this chapter.

THE WORKING ALLIANCE

Although the literature suggests several definitions of the working alliance, they all contain the notion of some type of collaborative relationship where both parties are working together to address whatever is bothering or impeding the growth of the client (Osachuk & Cairns, 1995). The working relationship reflects not only a shared commitment to work on issues, but it also accounts for the client's willingness to work through plateaus or setbacks during the course of treatment (Gelso & Fretz, 1992). Therefore, the ability to establish a good working alliance is likely to have clear implications for adherence to treatment plans and ultimately to the attainment of counseling goals and outcomes (Horvath & Symonds, 1991).

Bordin (1979) suggested that the working alliance is composed of three main components: agreement on goals, agreement on tasks, and the development of an emotional bond between the client and the practitioner. Clearly, agreement on goals and tasks would appear to be a critical component in the work of most sport and exercise psychologists. If clients do not agree with the treatment goals or believe in the efficacy of the strategies suggested to reach them, it is doubtful that they would put forth the effort necessary to achieve the desired results (Danish et al., 1993). However, the working alliance is an interactive process between the client and the practitioner. If the counselor is able to communicate the facilitative conditions of congruence, empathetic understanding, and unconditional positive regard, it is more likely that agreement on goals and tasks is apt to occur because a relationship of trust has been established (Bordin, 1979).

Although reviews of the research on the working alliance would clearly support its relationship to successful counseling outcomes (Horvath & Greenberg, 1989), this relationship is quite complex, may change during different time phases of the interaction, and may be viewed quite differently by the client and the practitioner (Sexton & Whiston, 1994). Therefore, any attempts to study this interaction must take into consideration individual differences (e.g., ethnicity and gender), the length and quality of the working alliance, and check the perceptions of both client and practitioner.

In addition, there is also support for the importance of building a working alliance within the first three sessions of the counseling relationship (Horvath & Symonds, 1991). This would seem to be particularly important for sport and exercise psychology interventions that tend to be short term and solution focused (Meyers, Whelan, & Murphy, 1996). However, a working alliance cannot be forced. It develops over time based on the abilities of the participants to listen to and understand each other. Although practitioners can be taught a series of attending behaviors to facilitate rapport building between the participants, it is critical to go at the client's pace and to be sensitive to issues of diversity (Ivey et al., 1993).

In order to be effective in building a working alliance, sport and exercise psychologists should consider their role within the context and process of the client–practitioner interaction. For example, initial contacts with clients are likely to be marked by interpersonal complementarity. That is, the role that each of the participants assumes is apt to be one of unequal status, with the sport and exercise psychologist being in the superior or one-up position (Kiesler & Watkins, 1989). If this is the case, the athlete or exercise participant will probably wait for the sport psychologist to set the tone and structure for the interaction. It is important to note that how one establishes the structure and ground rules for the interaction goes a long way toward the creation of a collaborative relationship. For example, Kivlighan and Schmitz (1992) found that counselors who attempt to explore clients' feelings or offer encouragement before the working alliance is established often place their clients in a passive role that negatively impacts client–practitioner collaboration. Instead, it may be more productive for sport and exercise psychologists to initially try to develop empathetic understanding of clients' situations and to provide them with a sense of what they can expect from their counseling involvement (Petitpas & Danish, 1995).

From a working alliance perspective, client–practitioner agreement on goals and tasks is most likely to occur within a climate of trust. Therefore, even though counselors may be in a one-up position, they need to spend sufficient time to understand clients' situations from their perspectives and to make sure that the clients have understood accurately any information or directives that have been provided to them. To accomplish these objectives, counselors can demonstrate their understanding of clients' situations through the use of basic attending skills such as paraphrasing and summarization, and then request that their clients summarize what they have heard and outline the action steps that are to follow (Ivey et al., 1993).

Although many sport and exercise psychologists are likely to view their role as that of teacher or educator exclusively, it is not unusual for emotional bonds to develop between clients and practitioners over the course of helping relationships. In fact, Izzo (1994) found that athletic counselors and sport psychologists were identified second only to parents as sources of emotional support to a group of athletes who were recovering from athletic injuries. It appears that counselors who build empathetic understanding and treat their clients with respect are more apt to be perceived as competent and trustworthy. For example, Bachelor (1991) found that counselors who were supportive and who developed collaborative involvement accounted for about 50% of the outcome variance from the clients' perspective. This finding supports Danish's (1986) notion of the importance of treating the individual and not just his or her symptoms.

It appears that sport and exercise psychologists who are able to demonstrate an empathetic understanding of clients and their concerns are apt to create an emotional bond between themselves and their clients. The relative strength of this bond may vary according to the intensity of the problems presented, the orientation and personality characteristics of the counselor, and the time phase of the interaction (Gelso & Fretz, 1992). However, the quality of this bond is likely to have clear implications for treatment adherence, particularly in situations where clients are facing major obstacles or roadblocks to goal attainment (Danish et al., 1993).

In summary, there is strong evidence that the quality of client–practitioner relationship is a major factor in treatment adherence and in the success of most counseling interventions. If this is true of counseling relationships, there is a strong possibility that the quality of the client–practitioner relationship is also a significant factor in facilitating successful outcomes in sport and exercise psychology interventions. In the next two sections, the implications of our knowledge of the counseling relationship will be examined in light of research and training in sport and exercise psychology.

IMPLICATIONS FOR RESEARCH

Based on the findings suggesting the importance of the client–practitioner relationship in counseling interactions, one would think that there would be a similar line of research in applied sport and exercise psychology. However, this does not seem to be the case. To date, there are only a handful of studies that have looked at some aspect of the client–practitioner relationship and these tend to focus on what athletes perceive as helpful characteristics of sport psychology consultants (e.g., Gould, Murphy, Tammen, & May, 1991; Martin, Wrisberg, Beitel, & Lounsbury, 1997). Although this research is limited, successful sport psychology consultants are described as individuals who can establish rapport with athletes, who are sensitive to individual needs, and who care about the athletes they work with (Orlick & Partington, 1987). This finding would lend support to the notion that the client–practitioner interaction is an important factor in facilitating successful sport and exercise intervention outcomes.

Sport and exercise psychology may be at a point in its evolution that mirrors that of the field of counseling psychology in the United States in the 1970s. At that time, federal agencies, insurance companies, and various consumer protection groups began to question the efficacy of counseling interventions on a variety of mental health issues (Gladdings, 1992). Counselors were challenged to prove the cost-effectiveness of their services in order to justify reimbursement from third party carriers. Ironically, the leaders of several sport and exercise psychology organizations have identified a similar challenge for their memberships. For example, Robert Singer (1996), President of the Exercise and Sport Psychology Division of the American Psychological Association, wrote, 'What is important is that the research advance the body of knowledge and provide a suitable and defensible basis for the services rendered' (p. 46). If there is such a clear mandate for this line of research, why is there so little work in this area? The answers to this question are probably quite varied, but one clear obstacle is the complexity of the client–practitioner interaction.

Gelso (1979) used the term 'bubble hypothesis' to describe the difficulties one encounters in trying to connect counseling psychology research to practice. He believed that the counseling relationship is so complex that as researchers control for one variable another one will pop up. Therefore, research in this area is likely to require a series of trade-offs. For example, experience-near research has the most relevance for practice, but it is also often viewed as less rigorous and less well-controlled (Gelso & Fretz, 1992). In the end, our knowledge of the implications of the client–practitioner relationship on interventions outcomes, as imperfect as it may be, is most likely to be advanced by using a variety of methods.

Reviews of the counseling psychology research can be broken down into four contrasting emphases: (a) laboratory versus field, (b) basic versus applied, (c) process versus outcome, and (d) quantitative versus qualitative (Gladdings, 1992). Based on Singer's (1996) observations, the field of sport and exercise psychology has made significant strides over the last decade in generating more field-based, applied, and qualitative studies. These research efforts have clearly tried to connect theory to the practice of sport and exercise psychology. However, few studies in the sport and exercise psychology literature have tackled the challenges of process research.

Unlike outcome research that focuses on the results of interventions, process research examines the factors that produce the results. For example, how important is the quality of the client–practitioner relationship in predicting treatment adherence or successful outcomes using various types of psychological skills training for athletic performance enhancement? If the client–practitioner relationship is important, does the quality of the relationship change at different stages of the intervention process? Is the establishment of a working alliance important in psychological skills training? Does the working alliance change as a factor of race, gender, or the ages of the participants? These are just four of the process-oriented research questions that come to mind and each of these could be broken down into a large number of specific components.

Recently, several researchers (Hankes, Harmison, Petrie, & Murphy, 1996) have begun to explore the connection between social influence theory and the effectiveness of sport psychology interventions. Their work is based on Strong's (1968) conceptualization of counseling as a process of social influence wherein the counselor seeks to influence the client toward attitude and behavior change. Strong believed that successful counseling outcomes would be a factor of the extent that clients' perceived their counselors as possessing qualities of expertness, attractiveness, and trustworthiness. Hankes (1996) tested Strong's hypothesis by having a group of high-level female college athletes from the United States rate sport psychology consultants' effectiveness in working with athletes. Hankes found that consultants with positive interpersonal skills were rated more favorably on a series of dependent measures regardless of academic training or past athletic experience. Although this study has a number of limitations, it appears to be one of the first to examine the client–practitioner relationship in sport and exercise psychology interventions and, if the findings are accurate, it raises several questions about outcome research and the training of sport and exercise psychology students.

The fields of counseling psychology and exercise and sport psychology have borrowed extensively from social psychology research. For example, Strong (1997) and Strong, Welsh, Corcoran, and Hoyt (1992) concluded that many of the ideas generated by social psychologists have been used to understand the process of counseling interventions. Brawley (1993) echoed this same conclusion in examining the application of several social psychological models to sport and exercise psychology. Maybe it is time to examine the efficacy of an interface between counseling and exercise and sport psychology research, particularly in relationship to the impact of the client–practitioner interaction on adherence and intervention outcomes.

For four decades, counseling psychologists have examined process concerns, such as social influence, facilitative conditions, and interpersonal complementarity (Sexton & Whiston, 1994). From this body of work, practitioners have learned the importance of gaining self-knowledge and an understanding of how their personal characteristics and presentation style influences the therapeutic relationship. However, during the last decade, there has been a significant shift in interest to brief counseling and therapy models (Steenbarger, 1997). Although this trend may be driven by the realities of current managed health care and insurance reimbursement policies, surveys have found that most clients are typically seen for less than ten sessions (Garfield, 1989). This trend toward brief therapies has also spawned a parallel line of research exploring the same set of process concerns that have been examined in traditional therapies. As might be expected, the formation of a positive working alliance is also predictive of treatment adherence and favorable outcomes in various types of brief therapy, including cognitive behavioral and coping skills models (Steenbarger, 1997). This finding is of particular interest because cognitive strategies dominate sport psychology research and practice (Williams & Leffingwell, 1996) and a meta-analysis on these types of interventions for athletic performance enhancement yielded similar findings to those of clinical outcome studies (Meyers, et al. 1996).

If brief counseling is a process of interpersonal influence, could the same be true of many sport and exercise psychology interventions? If this is the case, the integration of counseling psychology research paradigms into sport and exercise psychology research has the potential to advance our knowledge base and to provide information that would assist practitioners in identifying factors that are likely to promote adherence and lead to successful intervention outcomes. This knowledge would also have clear implications for training.

IMPLICATIONS FOR TRAINING

For the most part, sport and exercise psychology is generally regarded as a multidisciplinary profession that requires cross training in psychology and the sport sciences (Zaichkowsky & Perna, 1996). Although many countries throughout the world have identified specific knowledge bases and experiences necessary to meet credentialing standards, most have not done a good job of defining specific training requirements. This is particularly true in regards to counseling skills. For example, the certification criteria for the Association for the Advancement of Applied Sport Psychology (AAASP) includes graduate level 'Training designed to foster basic skills in counseling; (e.g., course work on basic intervention techniques in counseling; supervised practicum in counseling, clinical, or industrial–organizational psychology) (Zaichkowsky & Perna, 1996, p.400).' However, as Gelso and Fretz (1992) point out,

> Graduate study in counseling psychology is qualitatively different from that in, for example, history, physics, or music. Becoming an effective counselor happens only by learning a great deal about yourself. It is not simply a matter of applying a set of techniques. You are the major tool—one that must be highly adaptable to be effective with a wide range of clients and interventions. To become adaptable, many of your values, assumptions, and personal styles will have to be examined. (p.557)

An examination of the AAASP certification criteria failed to uncover any reference to self-knowledge and it is likely that the emphasis on self-knowledge distinguishes counseling preparation from training in other fields, including sport and exercise psychology.

Even though research has been unable to prove that one helping strategy is more effective than another, there is considerable support for the belief that treatment adherence and successful outcomes are as much a factor of the quality of the client–practitioner relationship as they are of the techniques or strategies used (Sexton & Whiston, 1994). If this belief were extended to sport and exercise psychology interventions, then it follows logically that training should include experiences designed to enable students to learn about their values, needs, interests, and personal styles. It is through this kind of knowledge that one gains the level of self-understanding required to build an effective working alliance (Okun, 1987; Sexton & Whiston, 1994). In addition to self-knowledge, the development of an effective working relationship is greatly enhanced by having an understanding of the processes that occur during client–practitioner interactions (Steenbarger, 1997). Awareness of processes such as complementarity, control battles, stages of treatment, and working alliances provides practitioners with a road map for what is done, when, and why, and has been proven to improve counselor effectiveness (Burlingame, Fuhriman, Paul, & Ogles, 1989).

Gaining self-knowledge and a better understanding of the processes involved in the delivery of sport and exercise psychology interventions is likely to be an on-going learning experience, and one that separates expert practitioners from novices. However, if sport and exercise psychology graduate students are to truly acquire basic counseling skills, then they need to begin to examine not only what they do with their clients, but also how they do it. The logical starting place for this to occur is for the individual to become more aware of his or her values, needs, interests, and personal style.

It has long been believed that the journey to self-awareness begins with a willingness to look at yourself and to allow yourself to be open to feedback from others. The more a person is willing to self-disclose, the more likely that others will get to trust them and care about them enough to give them feedback. Although most people develop images of themselves that they project to the world, it is not unusual to discover that one's self-perceptions may not all be consistent with how one person comes across to others. For example, Mary may view herself as outgoing and enthusiastic, but if she is perceived as intrusive by others, she is likely to have difficulty establishing relationships with some people. The same could be true of a client–practitioner interaction in sport and exercise psychology. Therefore, training programs should contain opportunities for students to get feedback about their personal style to help eliminate any 'blind spots' they may have concerning their self-presentation. Structured values clarification and needs identification activities are just two of the numerous methods used to gain self-knowledge.

Many of the strategies that are frequently used in counselor education to promote self-understanding and awareness of process concerns can be applied to training in sport and exercise psychology. Six of the most frequently used are:

1. *Being a client.* Graduate students in counseling programs are encouraged to become clients, both in actual therapy and in role play situations. This not only helps them learn about the process of counseling, but it also assists them in identifying their own concerns and issues. The same is apt to be true for students in sport and exercise psychology. At the very least, students should try psychological skills such as goal setting and imagery on themselves before they use them on their clients.
2. *Video taping and live supervision.* One of the best ways to learn about yourself and the process of psychological skills training is to review video tapes of your own intervention work with clients and to observe the work of others. Programs that have interview labs are also able to use live supervision models where a student and client working in one room can be viewed through one-way mirrors and critiqued by a supervisor and other students. The live supervision model has the advantage of offering students instant feedback on their performance and of providing suggestions for different strategies or adjustments during the actual session. In each case, it is helpful to examine your self-presentation and then go back over the video to analyze the interactions and processes that occur.
3. *The verbatim.* A verbatim is a type of feedback method that allows students to analyze the impact of their specific statements in relationship to the responses that are elicited from their clients. Students would transcribe from a video or audio tape everything that is said during a session. This process allows the session to be broken down into a series of specific exchanges that enable students and supervisors to evaluate these interactions in terms of content, affect, types of attending and influencing skills used, effectiveness, and other process-related information.
4. *The training log.* The training log is a type of diary in which students record their individual reactions to their counseling experiences. The goal of recording this information is to allow each student to examine how their values, needs, beliefs, and emotions play out during their interactions with various clients. Training logs can take the form of open-ended self-disclosures or they can be structured around a series of specific questions, such as (a) Did I feel uncomfortable during any of the sessions? (b) What was happening when I felt best about myself during a session? and (c) Did any thoughts or feelings get in the way of my effectiveness in working with my clients today?

5. *The supervisory relationship.*   Probably the most frequently used and most effective method of gaining self-knowledge and an understanding of the processes involved in the counseling interaction is the student–supervisor relationship. Students can learn a lot about the process of their interactions with clients by paying attention to their own relationship with their supervisors. It is quite common for the supervisory relationship to evolve from a student–teacher relationship toward a more collegial and consultative one (Berger & Graff, 1995). Understanding how the power differential and other interactive processes change over time is likely to provide self-knowledge and process awareness that parallels what happens in some client–practitioner relationships.

6. *Process versus content supervision.*   Supervision can focus on the content of the sessions or the patterns of interaction that take place between client and practitioner. The latter focus is called process-oriented supervision. Consider the following scenario. A female athlete comes to a sport psychologist because of a fear of failure (content). During their initial interactions, she discloses her doubts about her abilities, but does so in a very tentative manner in hope of getting some reassurance from her sport psychologist (process). The sport psychologist does not attend to her subtle requests for reassurance (process). She then shifts her focus to her problems communicating with her coach (content). From a process-oriented perspective, the communication problem was just played out with her sport psychologist (process). It is interesting to note that this same scenario could just as easily play out in a student–supervisor relationship by substituting the student for the athlete and the supervisor for the sport psychologist. In any event, having both content and process-oriented supervision is apt to provide the best learning opportunities.

CONCLUSIONS

The field of sport and exercise psychology is at a point in its evolution that closely parallels that of counseling psychology in the 1970s. At that time, counseling psychologists began a comprehensive examination of the factors that impact adherence to treatment and successful intervention outcomes. The results of this work suggest that of all the various factors and treatment approaches that have been studied, it is only the counseling relationship that has been found to consistently correlate with treatment adherence and positive outcomes.

The purpose of this chapter was to examine the client–practitioner relationship in sport and exercise psychology interventions in light of what is know about this relationship in the delivery of counseling psychology interventions. Clearly, counseling psychologists believe in the importance of establishing a working alliance and paying close attention to the processes that take place during counseling interactions. It would seem logical that these same factors are likely to be critical to treatment adherence and successful outcomes in sport and exercise psychology interventions as well. However, this belief needs to be verified through research.

This chapter was designed to open discussion about the implications of the counseling relationship for both future research and training in sport and exercise psychology.

REFERENCES

Bachelor, A. (1991). Comparison and relationship to outcome of diverse dimensions of the helping alliance as seen by client and therapist. *Psychotherapy*, **28**, 534–549.

Barrett-Lennard, G.T. (1981). The empathy cycle: The refinement of a nuclear concept. *Journal of Counseling Psychology*, **28**, 91–100.

Berger, N., & Graff, L. (1995). Making good use of supervision. In D.G. Martin & A.D. Moore (eds.), *First steps in the art of intervention: A guidebook for trainees in the helping professions* (pp. 408–432). Pacific Grove, CA: Brooks/Cole.

Bordin, E.S. (1979). The generalizability of the psychoanalytic concept of the working alliance. *Psychotherapy: Theory, Research, and Practice*, **16**, 252–260.

Brawley, L.R. (1993). Introduction to the special issue: Application of social psychological theories to health and exercise behavior. *Journal of Applied Sport Psychology*, **5**, 95–98.

Burlingame, G.M., Fuhriman, A., Paul, S., & Ogles, B.M. (1989). Implementing a time-limited therapy program: Differential effects of training and experience. *Psychotherapy*, **26**, 303–313.

Corlett, J. (1996). Sophistry, Socrates, and sport psychology. *The Sport Psychologist*, **10**, 84–94.

Danish, S.J. (1986). Psychological aspects in the care and treatment of athletic injuries. In P.E. Vinger & E.F. Hoerner (eds.), *Sports injuries: The unthwarted epidemic* (2nd edn., pp. 345–353). Boston, MA: Wright.

Danish, S.J., Petitpas, A.J., & Hale, B.D. (1993). Life developmental interventions for athletes: Life skills through sports. *The Counseling Psychologist*, **21**, 352–385.

Fiedler, F. (1950). The concept of an ideal therapeutic relationship. *Journal of Consulting Psychology*, **14**, 339–345.

Garfield, S.L. (1989). *The practice of brief psychotherapy*. New York: Pergamon.

Gelso, C.J. (1979). Research in counseling: Clarifications, elaborations, defenses, and admissions. *The Counseling Psychologist*, **8**, 61–67.

Gelso, C.J., & Fretz, B.R. (1992). *Counseling Psychology*. Fort Worth, TX: Harcourt Brace Jovanovich.

Gladdings, S.T. (1992). *Counseling: A comprehensive profession* (2nd edn.). New York: Macmillan Publishing.

Gould, D., Murphy, S., Tammen, V., & May, J. (1991). An evaluation of the U.S. Olympic sport psychology consultant effectiveness. *The Sport Psychologist*, **5**, 111–127.

Hankes, D.M. (1996, October). The influence of sport psychology consultant education, sport experience, and interpersonal skills on athletes' perceptions of sport consultant effectiveness. Paper presented at the annual meeting of the Association for the Advancement of Applied Sport Psychology, Williamsburg, VA.

Hankes, D.M., Harmison, R.J., Petrie, T.A., & Murphy, S. (1996, October). The examination of sport psychology consultant effectiveness: An application of social influence theory. Paper presented at the annual meeting of the Association for the Advancement of Applied Sport Psychology, Williamsburg, VA.

Horvath, A.O., & Greenberg, L.S. (1989). Development and validation of the Working Alliance Inventory. *Journal of Counseling Psychology*, **36**, 223–233.

Horvath, A.O., & Symonds, B.D. (1991). Relation between working alliance and outcome in psychotherapy: A meta-analysis. *Journal of Counseling Psychology*, **38**, 139–149.

Ivey, A.E., Ivey, M.B., & Simek-Morgan, L. (1993). *Counseling and psychotherapy: A multicultural perspective* (3rd edn.). Needham Heights, MA: Allyn and Bacon.

Izzo, C.M. (1994). The relationship between social support and adherence to sport injury rehabilitation. Unpublished master's thesis, Springfield College, Springfield, MA.

Kiesler, D.J., & Watkins, L.M. (1989). Interpersonal complementarity and the therapeutic alliance: A study of relationship in psychotherapy. *Psychotherapy*, **26**, 183–194.

Kivlighan, D.M., & Schmitz, P.J. (1992). Counselor technical activity in cases with improving working alliances and continuing-poor working alliance. *Journal of Counseling Psychology*, **39**, 32–38.

Martin, S.B., Wrisberg, C.A., Beitel, P.A., & Lounsbury, J. (1997). NCAA Division I athletes' attitudes toward seeking sport psychology consultant: The development of an objective instrument. *The Sport Psychologist*, **11**, 201–218.

Meyers, A.W., Whelan, J.P., & Murphy, S.M. (1996). Cognitive behavioral strategies in athletic performance enhancement. In M. Hersen, R.M.

Eisler, & P.M. Miller (eds.), *Progress in behavior modification* (Vol. 30) (pp. 137–164). Pacific Grove, CA: Brooks/Cole.

Murphy, S.M. (1994). Imagery interventions in sport. *Medicine and Science in Sports and Exercise*, **26**, 486–494.

Murphy, S.M. (1995). Introduction to sport psychology interventions. In S. M. Murphy (ed.), *Sport psychology interventions* (pp. 1–15). Champaign, IL: Human Kinetics.

Meyers, A.W., Whelan, J.P., & Murphy, S.M. (1996). Cognitive behavioral strategies in athletic performance enhancement. In M. Hersen, R.M. Eisler, & P.M. Miller (eds.), *Progress in behavior modification* (Vol. 30) (pp. 137–164). Pacific Grove, CA: Brooks/Cole.

Okun, B.F. (1987). *Effective helping: Interviewing and counseling techniques* (3rd edn.). Monterey, CA: Brooks/Cole.

Orlick, T. (1990). *In pursuit of excellence* (2nd edn.). Champaign, IL: Human Kinetics.

Orlick, T., & Partington, J. (1987). The sport psychology consultant: Analysis of critical components as viewed by Canadian Olympic athletes. *The Sport Psychologist*, **1**, 4–17.

Osachuk, T.A.G., & Cairns, S.L. (1995). Relationship issues. In D.G. Martin & A.D. Moore (eds.), *First steps in the art of interventions: A guidebook for trainees in the helping professions* (pp. 19–43). Pacific Grove, CA: Brooks/Cole.

Patterson, C.H. (1984). Empathy, warmth, and genuineness in psychotherapy: A review of reviews. *Psychotherapy*, **21**, 431–438.

Petitpas, A., & Danish, S.J. (1995). Caring for injured athletes. In S.M. Murphy (ed.), *Sport psychology interventions* (pp. 255–282). Champaign, IL: Human Kinetics.

Rogers, C. (1957). The necessary and sufficient conditions of therapeutic personality change. *Journal of Consulting Psychology*, **21**, 95–103.

Sexton, T.L., & Whiston, S.C. (1994). The status of the counseling relationship: An empirical review, theoretical implications, and research directions. *The Counseling Psychologist*, **22**, 6–78.

Silva, J.M. III. (1989). Toward the professionalization of sport psychology. *The Sport Psychologist*, **3**, 265–273.

Singer, R.N. (1996). Future of sport and exercise psychology. In J. L. Van Raalte & B. W. Brewer (eds.), *Exploring sport and exercise psychology* (pp. 451–468). Washington, DC: American Psychological Association.

Sloane, R. & Staples, F. (1984). Psychotherapy versus behavior change: Implications for future psychotherapy research. In J. Williams & R. Spitzer (eds.), *Psychotherapy research: Where are we and where should we go?* (pp. 203–215). New York: Guilford.

Steenbarger, B.N. (1997). Toward science–practice integration in brief counseling and therapy. *The Counseling Psychologist*, **20**, 403–450.

Strong, S.R. (1968). Counseling: An interpersonal influence process. *Journal of Counseling Psychology*, **15**, 215–224.

Strong, S.R. (1997). Enhancing the social-counseling interface. *The Counseling Psychologist*, **25**, 274–279.

Strong, S.R., Welsh, J.A., Corcoran, J.L., & Hoyt, W.T. (1992). Social psychology and counseling psychology: The history, products, and promise of an interface. *Journal of Counseling Psychology, **39**, 139–157.

Weinberg, R.S. (1994). Goal setting and performance in sport and exercise settings: A synthesis and critique. *Medicine and Science in Sports and Exercise*, **26**, 469–477.

Williams, J.M, & Leffingwell, T.R. (1996). Cognitive strategies in sport and exercise psychology. In J. L. Van Raalte & B. W. Brewer (eds.), *Exploring sport and exercise psychology* (pp. 51–73). Washington, DC: American Psychological Association.

Zaichkowsky, L., & Perna, F. (1996). Certification in sport and exercise psychology. In J.L. Van Raalte & B.W. Brewer (eds.), *Exploring sport and exercise psychology* (pp. 395–412). Washington, DC: American Psychological Association.

Chapter 10

Collaboration and Reflection: Adopting Action Research Themes and Processes to Promote Adherence to Changing Practice

David Gilbourne

This chapter explores the topics of collaboration and reflection and considers how these processes can enhance adherence to change in professional practice. Collaboration is presented as a process through which practitioners (insiders) are encouraged to review and alter aspects of practice by an 'outsider'. In this case, outsiders are depicted as individuals who 'visit' other practitioners and provide professional support. Examples from within sport could include a sport psychologist working with a team or

Adherence Issues in Sport and Exercise. Edited by Stephen J. Bull.
© 1999 John Wiley & Sons Ltd.

squad, an advisory teacher supporting a cohort of teachers or a regional coach delivering a coach education programme.

Reflection is associated with practitioners thinking about their own practice, for example, a coach might 'reflect on' the efficacy of a particular training session or a teacher may consider whether a particular teaching approach had been successful. Some texts also refer to reflexive thinking (Hart & Bond, 1995). This is a more practical process and is associated with reflection and 'action'. In this sense, the term action is associated with changes in professional practice. This chapter suggests that action research, a paradigm commonly affiliated with the disciplines of education and health care, is applicable to sport. It is also proposed that action research can facilitate adherence to the processes that generate change and to change itself.

Both involvement and improvement feature as core components of action research (Hart & Bond, 1996). Although action research is not commonplace in sport-based research, Jackson (1995) has suggested that it may appeal to those sport psychologists who see themselves as agents of change. This chapter supports these sentiments and suggests that the time is right to consider adopting alternative research approaches.

A sports focus is examined primarily through the discipline of sport psychology. The early phase of the chapter reviews trends in sport psychology research and explores the intellectual challenges that accompany recent suggestions for paradigmatic expansion (Gould, 1997). Action research typologies are also presented and implications for researcher competency are discussed. Finally, links between the theme of adherence and the processes of collaboration and reflection are illustrated by referring to the author's sport-based research.

PROPOSING AN ALTERNATIVE APPROACH TO RESEARCH AND CONSULTANCY

Although action research may include the administration of quantitative and qualitative research techniques, the longitudinal nature of collaboration and the need to explore issues like reflexive thinking encourages the deployment of qualitative techniques.

Within the discipline of sport psychology some commentators suggest that qualitative research is gaining credibility (Dale, 1996). There is certainly some evidence that qualitative approaches are gaining acceptance, for example, qualitative research papers have reported on a range of topics including, investigations into the psychosocial processes of sport injury (Rose and Jevne, 1993), the sources of enjoyment in elite figure skaters

(Scanlan, Stein, & Ravizza, 1989) and sources of stress in golf (Cohn 1990). However, these papers do not necessarily signify that qualitative research is in the ascendancy, a point reinforced by a recent review of current trends in sport psychology which suggests 'relatively' few studies are adopting qualitative methods (Biddle, 1997).

Although there may be doubts over the number of qualitative projects being undertaken, it is clear that there is an emerging interest in qualitative research itself. This has encouraged researchers to suggest increasingly refined approaches to data collection (Gould, Jackson, & Finch, 1993) and data analysis (Cote, Salmela, Baria, & Russell, 1993).

Although many researchers within sport psychology welcome these developments, it seems that qualitative research has been rather dominated by a limited number of techniques. For example, sport psychology research papers have reported overwhelmingly on projects that have deployed the procedures of interview, transcription, and content analysis (Scanlan, Stein, & Ravizza, 1989; Gould, Jackson, & Finch, 1993; Gould, Eklund, & Jackson, 1992). Gould (1997) has attempted to widen the methodological debate by focusing on the opportunities offered by alternative methods of data collection and analysis. He encouraged sport psychologists to expand their methodological horizons and stressed the importance of exploring other approaches to research. In fact, a small number of researchers have already undertaken 'new-paradigm' work. For example, Cote, Salmela, Trudel, Baria, and Russell (1995) used a grounded theory approach to examine expert coach knowledge, Dean and Choi (1996) adopted the same paradigm to understand attitudes to exercise and health, and Krane, Eklund, and McDermott (1991) have reported on a coaching case-study that utilised a collaborative action-research design. Although such papers question Gould's concerns over methodological paralysis, they remain isolated examples of paradigmatic exploration.

Any move towards 'new paradigms' is likely to introduce sport psychology to different research cultures and for many of these (education in particular) the topic of research methodology is an intellectual debate in its own right (i.e. Carr & Kemmis, 1986; McFee, 1993). Although methodological debates are uncommon in sport psychology, occasional papers have discussed qualitative issues from a philosophical perspective. Philosophical thinking encourages the researcher to appreciate 'what they might come to know' and embodies a distinctive nomenclature. For example, Bain (1989; 1995) examined the difference between interpretive and critical research approaches, Dale (1996) commented on conducting research based on existential phenomenology and Ziegler (1995) discussed the notion of competency in critical thinking.

These papers offer more than a critique of research technique, they focus upon the intellectual factors that underpin the research process itself.

Whilst they all discuss the research experience from a philosophical perspective, they also introduce the topic of epistemology; this is concerned with understanding the 'nature of the knowledge'. For example, within action research the epistemology of the researcher's own reflection often features prominently in the thesis or in subsequent publications.

There are increasing calls for researchers in sport psychology to engage with methodologically oriented literature, to reflect on their own research from a philosophical and epistemological standpoint and to gain a more in-depth understanding of the intellectual foundations that support qualitative research (Jackson, 1995; Biddle, 1997).

Some researchers within the discipline of social science have questioned the benefits of greater philosophical and epistemological awareness. For example, Melia (1997) argued that as 'methods' debates have focused increasingly on philosophical and epistemological issues, they have become less useful for the 'doing' of research. He appears to advocate an approach that (largely) ignores philosophy and epistemology, perceiving such factors to be unnecessary complications that can 'trap' the researcher or 'catch' them out, and suggests that researchers 'get out there', 'get data' and 'tell a story'.

Furthermore, undertaking an examination of research philosophy can be problematical as methodological definitions can vary within sport psychology texts. For instance, in the sport-based literature, Jackson (1995) differentiates between positivist and interpretive *philosophy*, Hardy, Jones, and Gould (1996) refer to positivist and *naturalist paradigms* and Tenenbaum and Bari-Eli (1995) discuss *interpretive* or *critical paradigms*.

These definitional problems are compounded when mainstream literature is reviewed. Terms such as, naturalist, constructivist, pluralist, interpretist, or criticalist are referred to in some texts and ignored in others. These examples of semantic inconsistency highlight the problems faced by qualitative researchers who attempt to engage with philosophical and epistemological issues whilst the available literature can appear inconsistent and, at times, contradictory.

One way to overview the intellectual and practical components of the research process is suggested in Figure 10.1. For purposes of illustration, three dominant 'intellectual positions' are highlighted, positivist, interpretist and criticalist. Positivism is associated with 'traditional' science, is theory driven, predictive in orientation and associated with the hypothetico-deductive approach to research (Bryman, 1988). Interpretist research, in contrast, is concerned with subjective meaning and examines how social rules and environmental factors can influence thinking (Carr & Kemmis, 1986). Finally, critical research is associated with the terms like 'enlightenment' and 'emancipation'. Through these 'critical' experiences practitioners are thought to become more self-aware and break *free* from the dictates of tradition or from institutional constraints (Kemmis, 1991).

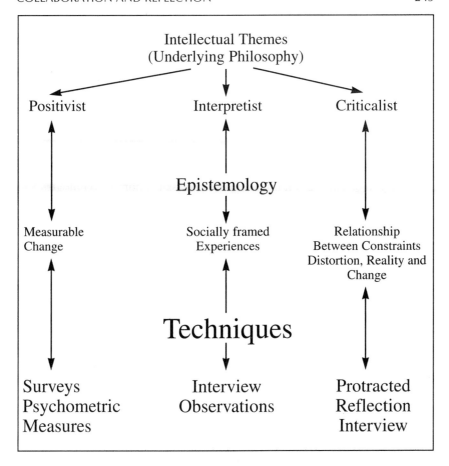

Figure 10.1   Relationship between components of research methodology

The integrated nature of Figure 10.1 suggests that these intellectual positions form an underlying research philosophy which can be associated with a particular form of knowledge (epistemology). Whilst some put forward the case for epistemology 'in place of' philosophy (e.g. Schwandt, 1997), Figure 10.1 proposes a different perspective and places philosophical considerations at the top of the methodological hierarchy. This is intended to depict philosophy as a core intellectual phenomenon, something that reflects the methodological essence of the inquiry. This foundation point informs the epistemological nature of research and clarifies the type of knowledge that the researcher can expect to collect and present. This facet of the model aligns with the earlier work of Bryman (1988) who referred to the 'interlocking' of philosophy and epistemology and defined philosophy as something that sustains epistemology through the provision of an intellectual undercurrent. Finally, epistemological clarity is linked to the technical aspects of the research process. This suggests that understanding the epistemological location of a forthcoming project directs how data could most appropriately be collected and analysed.

Summary

The rationale for introducing these methodological issues is that action research can be carried out under different classifications or typologies and these often accommodate separate philosophical or epistemological assumptions. Furthermore, the intellectual foundations and the epistemology of action research are frequently focal points for discussion. For example, within the field of education Hart (1995) has examined how systematic reflection by teachers can generate 'new' knowledge that challenges the epistemology of positivist science, whilst Tinning, MacDonald, Tregenza, and Boustead (1996) reflect on why 'critical' research is difficult to conduct within educational settings. Within action research literature these discussions are commonplace and indicate how methodological exploration (that takes researchers beyond the status quo) may necessitate the understanding of a different vocabulary and culture. The following section introduces the nomenclature of action research, outlines the processes within it and considers the different classifications proposed by researchers in education and health care.

ACTION RESEARCH: DEFINITIONS AND APPROACHES

Action research is associated with addressing practical problems in the workplace and encourages individuals to promote change and improve working procedures through their own enquiry (Castle, 1994). Waters-Adams (1994) stressed how action research encouraged practitioners to understand their own practice and Elliott (1978) defined action research as a process that leads to an improvement in the 'quality of action' within a social situation. Similarly, Carr and Kemmis (1986) described action research as:

> a form of self-reflective enquiry undertaken by participants in social situations in order to improve the rationality and justice of their own practice. (p.162)

The conceptual foundations of action-research can be traced to the earlier work of Lewin (1946, 1952). Action research was viewed as a pioneering approach to social science research which placed emphasis on practitioners influencing their own practice. It was also associated with a systematic procedure that featured 'cycles' of fact-gathering, planning, and action (Lewin, 1946). More recently, this cyclical process has been described as 'action' and 'evaluation' proceeding separately but simultaneously (Banister, Burman, Parker, Taylor, & Tindall, 1994). For example, a sports coach may stand back and take note of how his or her club or team operates and consider how established practice could change. Once a 'change strategy' is identified and the *planning* stage has clarified how the strategy would be employed, the practitioner would *monitor* the process and *reflect* upon the efficacy of the change strategy. Finally, the procedure would be *reviewed* and further adjustments to the strategy may be made. A new cycle of implementation and monitoring could then begin (see Figure 10.2).

These procedures generate data that is often presented in a form of words which captures the *experience* of action (McFee, 1993). In this sense,

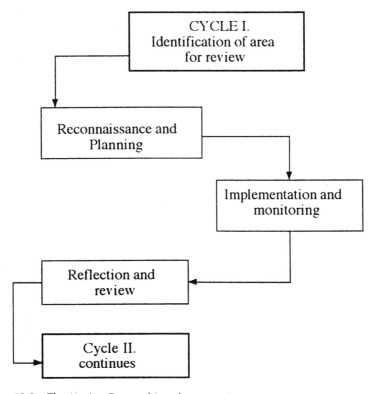

Figure 10.2   The 'Action Research' cycle

action research is essentially a social process which endeavours to add to practical knowledge through practitioner *reflection*. This reflective process can be either facilitated by an outside researcher or undertaken by practitioners themselves.

Despite assurances from the fields of education (McFee, 1993), health (Street & Robinson, 1995) and sport (Krane, Eklund, & McDermott, 1991) that action research is a valuable research paradigm, there are likely to be those who have difficulties in accepting that action research is 'real research'. In this sense, the nature of action research has been identified as a weakness by those who have sought to discredit the process, for example, 'action' and 'research' are terms that are acknowledged to have differing agendas and procedures (Castle, 1994). In a similar way, other contributors point out that many aspects of action research could be seen to conflict with the ethos of orthodox science and accept that (in some quarters) there will be a reluctance to associate the central themes of *action* and *reflection* with research (Banister, Burman, Parker, Taylor, & Tindall, 1994). In contrast, McFee (1993) provides a more upbeat assessment of action research, arguing it to be 'research like any other' in that it seeks to answer 'why' questions and involves the gathering and collating of original knowledge.

Action research has many forms and establishing the methodological location of action research is challenging as the literature can appear inconsistent in a definitional sense. Some of these issues are considered further in the following pages; however, it is fair to conclude that different action research themes and processes exist, and that both across and within professions, definitions can vary.

Typologies with Action Research

Within some health-based literature 'experimentally' oriented approaches to action research have been highlighted (Hart & Bond, 1996). These associate certain types of action research with quantitative research techniques. Most commentators do, however, differentiate between action research and more traditional or orthodox approaches to research. For example, Smith (1996) located action research within the context of critical science, a position consistently reinforced with the education literature (Aspland, MacPhearson, Proudford, & Whitmore, 1996; Waters-Adams, 1994; Toomy, 1997; Haggerty & Postlethwaite, 1995). Critical research is, however, not always attained and, in general, the end 'epistemological' product within action research is often associated with an interpretist perspective (Tinning, MacDonald, Tregenza, & Boustead, 1996).

Carr and Kemmis (1986) proposed a typology (based on the thinking of Habermas, 1974) that classifies different levels of human interest, the knowledge with which this interest is associated, and the form of 'science' that is used to acquire knowledge. In this model, technical, practical or emancipatory interest are associated with empiricist, interpretive and critical sciences respectively (Carr & Kemmis, 1986). O'Hanlon (1994) also refers to the work of Habermas (1972, 1974) and describes the three 'interest' pathways as processes through which we come to know and understand things about the world. The practical and emancipatory themes described by Carr and Kemmis (1986) often provides a template for those who undertake action research.

Hart and Bond (1995, 1996) proposed a typology which differentiates action research into four categories, experimental, organisational, professionalizing and empowering. In this framework, experimental action research is associated with the use of orthodox protocols (I have already suggested some contributors may find this problematical, e.g. Smith, 1996). In contrast, organisational and professionalising research is considered more 'humanistic' in orientation and associated with value-free 'interpretive' terms like 'consensual definitions of success' and 'improvements in practice as defined by professionals'. Professionalising also highlights empowerment as an *outcome*. This is differentiated from the philosophy behind the 'empowering' *category* which emphasises the empowerment of the oppressed.

Holter and Schwartz-Barcott (1993) also classify action research by appearing to draw on the work of Carr and Kemmis (1986). For example, they refer to 'technical action research' and argue that this (like the experimental framework suggested by Hart and Bond, 1996) has an underlying goal to 'test' a particular intervention. Within technical action research the problem is defined in advance, the researcher acts as a facilitator of change and it is possible for subsequent analysis of that change to be associated with established theory. Technical and experimentally oriented action research are thought, therefore, to validate or refine existing understanding.

Holter and Schwartz-Barcott (1993) also propose a 'mutual' modality which has similarities with what Hart and Bond (1995) describe as organisational research. According to Holter and Schwartz-Barcott, a mutual project is more of a shared, emergent, experience with researcher and practitioner working together as a team. It is less likely to involve the introduction of pre-arranged, theoretically grounded interventions and decisions about how changes evolve are heavily influenced by the practitioner. As the researcher and practitioner reflect upon on-going practice 'new' theory is allowed to emerge (Holter & Schwartz-Barcott, 1993). Finally, the mutual model is portrayed as being 'evenly' collaborative in nature and is based upon partnership between researcher and practitioner.

Although these models provide many points of divergence, the thinking of Carr and Kemmis (1986), Holter and Schwartz-Barcott (1993) and Hart and Bond (1995) converge in their reference to 'emancipatory', 'enhance-ment' or 'empowering' models of action research. Although Hart and Bond (1995) question what Holter and Schwartz-Barcott (1993) mean by enhancement research (they feel Holter and Schwartz-Barcott use the term enhancement to describe what they call professionalising), it is not unrea-sonable to consider these terms as being thematically similar as they focus, to varying degrees, upon critical ideals.

As noted earlier, a 'critical' approach to research encourages practi-tioners to reflect upon the underlying values that underpin their work and to consider the way that the structure of the workplace influences their view of practice. This process may include focusing upon social, economic or political constraints and becoming aware of opportunities for change. In this sense, it is possible to associate a critical approach to research with the notion of emancipation.

Deciding what exactly constitutes emancipatory research is not a straightforward process. Emancipation is an 'elusive' concept and can be viewed from an institutional or intrapersonal perspective (Tinning, Mac-Donald, Tregenza, & Boustead, 1996). For example, action research which raised consciousness could claim to have evoked a state of 'intrapersonal emancipation'. This implies that a practitioner has experienced change or undergone a process of self-realisation.

By striving to create and understand any desire for (or obstruction to) change, a researcher may sense that intrapersonal emancipation is medi-ated by certain 'intrinsic' attitudes or beliefs. In contrast, antecedents of emancipation may be located at an institutional or organisational level. In the former, emancipation might be aligned with notions of self-actualization (Rogers, 1991) and 'Socratic' approaches to practice (Corlett, 1996). In turn, organisational emancipation might be more to do with questioning and changing institutional structures (Aspland, MacPhearson, Proudford & Whitmore, 1996).

Carr and Kemmis (1986) associate emancipatory research with the exam-ination of global or 'macro' forces, and suggested that researchers should seek to understand how prevailing economic climates influence perceptions and language. In this sense, emancipation is associated with global issues, the process of awareness raising and the liberation of the individual.

The view that social science should not be content to reflect and illus-trate, but should rather seek to create conditions for real change, links emancipatory action research with a desire to be critical of, and overcome, 'restrictive' conditions and to liberate humanity from oppression (Carr & Kemmis, 1986).

> What we have to accomplish at this time is all the more clear: relentless
> criticism of all existing conditions, relentless in the sense that the criticism is

not afraid of its findings and just as little afraid of conflict with the powers that be. (Marx, K. (1967). Writings of the young Marx on philosophy and society. (p.212). In Carr and Kemmis (1986), p. 138.)

In a practical sense, if emancipation is to be recognised and reported upon, then somehow changes in awareness and cognition need to be identified. This suggests that research which hopes to monitor emancipation should not *start* at the point of practice but should first of all focus upon the practitioner. For example, observation of the practitioner in their work environment and formal interviews that encouraged reflective thinking, would confirm what they presently do, why they do it, and most importantly establish how they feel about things. This baseline assessment should contextualise their sense of work and embed this into an account of their view of the world. Processes like these establish a foundation point from which change can be evaluated. Although these steps are likely to enhance the chances of detecting emancipatory experiences, it is clear that emancipation is a difficult concept for the researcher to capture particularly as it is is fundamentally linked to reflection of, which O'Hanlon (1994) comments as follows:

> . . . reflection is such a personal activity, no one else can 'see' it, except when it is consciously or deliberately shared. (O'Hanlon, 1994. Reflection and action research. *Educational action Research Journal*, **2**, 283.)

Competency and Facilitating Critical Forms of Collaboration

Research with an emancipatory agenda can be associated with critical science, a process that deliberately sets out to challenge constraints or assumptions (Carr & Kemmis, 1986), to free participants from the dictates of tradition (Southwell & Welsch, 1995) or to engage in a process of intellectual reconstruction (Kemmis, 1991).

These 'critical criteria' have conceptual similarities with aspects of counselling literature. For example, the action research of Waterman, Webb and Williams (1995) draws from the writing of Carr and Kemmis (1986) and Winter (1989). They describe critical research as something that uncovers distortions between experience and reality. The parallels between these principles and the aims of a number of counselling approaches is quite striking. For example, within psychodynamic counselling, distortion is associated with denial, a process that prevents true meanings from being acknowledged. Similarly, critical criteria can be associated with person-centred therapy which places great emphasis on people understanding the relationship between their experiences and the inner self (Hough, 1994).

These issues reinforce the importance of understanding the philosophy and epistemology of qualitative approaches and move the debate forward to a consideration of the ethical and competency issues that surround particular forms of research. It is possible to question whether practitioners are necessarily emotionally balanced enough to participate in a critically oriented project. Whilst some practitioners may be 'ready' (in a psychological sense) for critical reflection, it seems reasonable to suggest that others may not.

In a similar manner, it would seem that particular researcher skills would need to be in place before critical research is initiated. The core competencies of any 'critical' skill base could be drawn from the discipline of counselling and associated with skills such being an empathic listener (Rogers, 1991), having the ability to identify recurrent themes and possessing the capacity to summarise (Hough, 1994).

Another prerequisite for counselling, which could also relate to critical researcher competency is the understanding of self. If researchers are encouraging others to uncover distortions in their lives, it seems reasonable to expect the researcher to have faced up to any distortions they may harbour themselves. This line of thinking is again associated with the development of counselling competencies.

> Self-development and self-awareness are important elements in counselling training because these processes, which are often difficult and painful, enable students to understand themselves more fully. Unless students can get in touch with their own personal feelings they will be unable to understand the wide range of emotions experienced by clients and may even confuse their own feelings with that of the client. (Hough, 1996, p.12).

In summary, according to Carr and Kemmis (1986) critical action research was something *deliberate* that aimed to emancipate practitioners from *unseen* constraints or assumptions. If critical research is indeed a premeditated, manageable process then there appears to be a case for researchers acquiring the necessary skills before such an exercise is initiated.

This section has focused attention on critical or emancipatory approaches to action research and linked the issues of philosophy, epistemology and researcher competency. This may have portrayed collaborative research to be a rather daunting process. Although it is important to recognise the challenges of critical research, it is also important to stress that there are other approaches to collaboration which focus on the development of working practice without necessarily seeking to invoke emancipation.

The Sport Psychologist as Collaborator

Collaboration is defined as a process in which people 'co-labour' or 'labour together' to meet or accomplish particular goals (Aspland, MacPhearson,

Proudford, & Whitmore, 1996). Collaborative involvement may be classified further, for example, as technical, mutual or empowering. This could result to a project having an 'expert'-led 'technical' orientation. In contrast, if specialists such as sport psychologists collaborate with the intention of sharing ideas and integrating their knowledge with the knowledge of other sports practitioners, then a more mutual or empowering process may emerge.

The Role of the External Collaborator

The relationship between researcher and practitioner is an important feature of collaborative action research (Titchen & Binnie, 1993). For example, a 'university-based' sport psychologist might help to initiate and then monitor a project that is being conducted by a group of coaches. Within action research terminology the sport psychologist may be classified as an 'outsider', whilst the coaching cohort would be referred to as 'insiders'.

Within action research the issue of 'ownership' reflects to what extent 'outsider' involvement has influenced decision making (Castle, 1994). Titchen and Binnie (1993) also refer to the cohesiveness of action research and note that 'tensions' between researcher and practitioner are not uncommon. Furthermore, they suggest that outsiders who are engaged in a project, as a part of an academic award, may often be the catalyst for unease. Titchen and Binnie (1993) justify this observation by explaining that a reliance upon 'an outside, institutionally-driven' research design may 'lock' the researcher into an inflexible mind-set. This is likely to have negative consequences, for example, a researcher may fail to ascertain whether the practitioner cohort share their commitment to a project.

Concerns over ownership and the outsider's capacity to forge sound relationships with practitioners can be intuitively associated with the underlying motive that drives the research. If one imagines a project in which only the researcher can benefit from the data, it is not difficult to visualise the dark side of the ownership equation.

On a more positive note, Carr and Kemmis (1986) refer to the idea of *outside* researchers becoming the critical friend of the practitioner or *insider*. They depict the outsider as someone who assists insiders to act wisely as they alter their working practices. Finally, they argue that the litmus test of this relationship is the outsider's capacity to facilitate the 'holistic' growth of the insider.

The outsider can also act as an organiser of meetings and so help to sustain the tempo of any collaborative venture. It is at this point that the relationship between action research and the theme of adherence becomes clear. Haggerty and Postlethwaite (1995) comment on this issue and illus-

trate how teachers felt about the researchers' facilitative contribution to a
school-based project:

> ... the group would have stopped had it not been for the fact that relentlessly
> you turn up to the meetings ... so we have to do something ... without you
> two we wouldn't still be going ... but we have to carry on ... we have to
> solve this. (Haggerty and Postlethwaite. 1995, p.179)

In the above example, the outsider has helped to sustain a desire for
change and encouraged a group of teachers to adhere to the necessary
processes of discussion and review. Similar responses have been noted
within the author's own sport-based research. Practitioners have referred
to the 'outsider' creating a sense of momentum, asking the 'right questions'
and 'making' them sit down and think about how they work.

> The time to do this (reflect on practice) does not get time-tabled in ... it is
> easy for things to plod on ... (without the collaborative research) we
> wouldn't have the opportunity to sit down and talk about these things ... we
> need someone to come in and ask the right questions ... we don't routinely
> ask these questions ... you need the reflective meetings to really deal with
> the specific issues. (Transcribed interview material from a collaborative re-
> search project undertaken by the author: Citation extract illustrates a sports
> physiotherapist's thoughts on the value of 'outsider'-led meetings.)

In conclusion, issues of external involvement and ownership within collaborative action research appear to centre upon the *nature* of any external
involvement rather than external involvement itself. Defining the 'ideal'
involvement state is always likely to be problematic and insider–outsider
difficulties may arise in any project. However, it seems fair to suggest that
outside researchers should facilitate rather than dictate and ensure that
practitioners are not *coerced* to engage in 'change strategies' for which they
have little or no enthusiasm.

Finally, the action research literature and the author's own research
experiences indicate that outsider involvement can help to facilitate *adherence* to the processes that lead to change. The rationale here is that
change requires commitment and effort, both of which can be systematically managed within the action research themes of reflection,
change, monitoring and review. Outsiders are often charged with 'organising' and 'overseeing' this cyclical process and this involvement can help to
sustain momentum and ensure adherence.

An Example of Collaboration within a Sports Injury Setting

The following section provides an example of collaborative research undertaken by the author (referred to throughout as the sport psychologist).

Before the collaborative phases are outlined the research is introduced by referring to the core topics that have been highlighted in this chapter.

The research was undertaken at a specialist sports injury centre in the UK. The sport psychologist acted as an outside facilitator and collaborated with the physiotherapists who worked at the centre $(n = 2)$. The project aimed to examine how practice at the centre could be improved, and focused on the idea of introducing mental skills training into day-to-day physiotherapy practice. The sport psychologist worked as an outsider and facilitated collaboration by initiating reconnaissance procedures, organising reflection meetings and directing workshops on mental training approaches.

From a methodological perspective the project could be classified as interpretist in orientation. This is justified on the grounds that the sport psychologist explored the subjective meaning of sports injury by spending time with, and interviewing, the injured athletes who attended the centre. Similar interviews were held with the physiotherapists as they reflected on how the project had influenced their own practice.

The epistemology was eclectic in nature and qualitative in form and included the thoughts and feelings of injured athletes, the reflections of the physiotherapists and the sport psychologist and the reflexive activities of the physiotherapists and sport psychologist. These different sources of knowledge were gained through the sport psychologist undertaking participant observation and conducting taped interviews with athletes and physiotherapists. In addition, data was also collected from the goal-setting diaries of injured athletes who participated in the intervention programme. Finally, the sport psychologist maintained field note records throughout the research process. These records collated his own subjective interpretations of the research process.

Classification of this project (using the lexicon of action research) would encourage the use of the term 'mutual' collaboration (Holter & Schwartz-Barcott, 1993). Mutuality should, however, be viewed in a flexible manner as the research dynamic alternated as the project unfolded. At times the research was led by the sport psychologist. On other occasions the physiotherapists had control of affairs. This notion of flexibility is outlined in the action research literature (Hart and Bond, 1995). They proposed that a collaborative project may begin as a mutual exercise, develop into a phase of researcher or practitioner dominance, and revert again towards a mutual status. The following section outlines the research process by referring to the phase- by-phase framework outlined in Figure 10.2.

Reconnaissance Phase

Initially participant observation techniques were used to familiarise the sport psychologist with the way the sport injury practitioners conducted their own practice and also to monitor the injured athletes as they worked through their rehabilitation programme, interviews with injured athletes were also conducted. This exercise provided qualitative material that was discussed at a series of reflection meetings. These meetings were organised by the sport psychologist so that practitioners could formally reflect on the reconnaissance findings.

Planning Phase

The research group identified goal-setting as an appropriate change strategy to improve practice within the sports injury centre . A 'rehabilitation-specific' goal-setting programme was developed as a collaborative venture between the sport psychologist and practitioner group. Planning for the introduction and monitoring of the goal-setting programme took place and following a review of contemporary motivation literature the sport psychologist suggested a task-oriented framework for the goal-programme (see Gilbourne & Taylor, 1998). A series of workshops ensued in which the practitioners and sport psychologist discussed the practical implications of introducing a goal-setting strategy within the centre. These workshops were organised by the sport psychologist and illustrate how the outsider plays a central role in maintaining a sense of 'tempo', facilitating dialogue, and sustaining adherence to the procedures that allow changes in practice to occur.

Implementation and Monitoring Phase

Finally, an administration procedure was designed and the goal-setting programme was introduced to a cohort of six athletes. The athletes' and practitioners' perceptions of the goal-setting programme were monitored by the sport psychologist conducting semi-structured interviews. The injured athletes also maintained a goal-setting diary. Interview and diary-based feedback from the goal-setting group suggested that goal-setting could assist injured athletes deal with the demands of injury rehabilitation (see Gilbourne, Taylor, Downie, & Newton, 1996).

Reflection and Review Phase

At the end of the project the practitioners' perceptions of the collaborative project were reviewed. Their comments were supportive and revealed how sharing knowledge, reflecting on practice and introducing new procedures had helped them gain a greater understanding of their own working profession. The following citations (taken from transcribed interview material) illustrate how the practitioners viewed the experience of collaboration and reflection and how they now felt about the change strategy of goal-setting. First, their thoughts on collaboration:

> I felt for the first time that I'd been summoned to give (my) work direction. It certainly motivated me . . . it gave me a structure for the first time. (Physiotherapist A)

> I could start offering them (the patients) something else . . . which I could understand, rather than confused jumble It gave a focus of direction to what we would already do. (Physiotherapist A)

> I think it has kind of validated the rehabilitation process. It (the collaboration) has supported our 'gut' feeling that what we do is valuable. (Physiotherapist B)

> You feel more confident in (your own practice). (Physiotherapist B)

Secondly examples of their thoughts on the reflective component of collaboration.

> It's about getting people to look at themselves really. (Physiotherapist B)

> It comes back to reflection again . . . I think the whole process has been reflective. . . it's taking stock of what we actually do here and not necessarily improve but optimise what we do. (Physiotherapist B)

Finally, the physiotherapists' thoughts on the change strategy:

> In the past I knew what I was trying to achieve but sometimes I was thinking how does this fit into that . . . this (the goal-setting) gave me a kind of structure to try and achieve something, sometimes physical goals, sometimes mental goals. (Physiotherapist A)

> If you have these terms in your mind (associated with goal-setting) it orders your thoughts. If he (an injured player) had asked me before about gaining 'control' of the situation, I don't know what I would have done . . . I may have gone over his case again and given him a motivating talk. But now I can say . . . I see what your problem is . . . let's break down your rehab . . . your simplifying it, give a few labels a few terms process and long-term goals . . . that's useful. (Physiotherapist B)

> To have labels and structures to focus on something which may be subconsciously a bit nebulous, it has got to be helpful, it's got to be. (Physiotherapist B)

Outsider Reflections on the Project

Experiences in this project suggest that the collaborative approaches to research can help professionals, from different disciplines, to share knowledge and reflect on working practice and introduce change. The *process* of regular meetings, on-going reflection, and discussions between sport psychologist and practitioner helped to cement a degree of personal commitment and encouraged both parties to 'stay with' the project. In this sense, adherence and action research can be linked to the notion of a systematic procedure sustaining involvement. The process of collaboration and reflection produced change that was overt and observable (i.e. handing out goal-setting booklets and calling meetings to establish a goal-programme) and change that was more covert and personal in nature (i.e. changes in the narrative used by the practitioner). In this particular study, the more subtle, narrative-based, alterations in practice appear the most resilient or permanent features of change. They represent a fundamental shift in the way the practitioners 'get across' their ideas to the injured athletes and therefore influence the way they organise and deliver the rehabilitation regimen. This can also be presented as evidence of action research processes facilitating adherence to change. In this case, aspects of the goal-setting process became ingrained into daily practice.

These changes in practitioner narrative have a theoretical foundation and are associated with the sport psychologist (as outsider) helping to integrate psychological theory into established practice (Gilbourne and Taylor, 1998). This occurred by reflection, monitoring, and review encouraging practitioners to 'blend' changes in practice (theoretically grounded in sport psychology) into their daily routine.

Although this exercise has been discussed primarily from a research perspective it is also possible to apply the rationale that underpins action research to applied consultancy. In this case, mental skills techniques could introduced by working *alongside* practitioners such as coaches, teachers, and physiotherapists. This elevation in practitioner involvement might encourage the integration of mental skills into established practice and, in doing so, realign the underlying rationale behind the consultancy process.

This emphasis on working practice can be facilitated by adopting the cyclical structure of reflection and monitoring common to all action research design. Furthermore, the action research themes of involvement and improvement can be sustained within this consultation model. The notion of empowerment, a feature in some action research projects and also a feature of 'Life Development' approaches to applied practice, can also be stressed (Danish, Petitpas, & Hale, 1992).

SUMMARY AND CONCLUSIONS

This chapter has emphasised the themes of collaboration and reflection which stress a sense of cooperation, listening and sharing. Change and *adherence* to change is associated with practitioners being *involved* in the systematic improvement of their own working practices. Improvement is linked to involvement and within any collaborative project the practitioners should be present at all the phases of planning, action, and reflection.

Collaborative research is demanding and outside facilitators require a number of competencies. As suggested earlier, a researcher's capacity to reflect, empathise, and understand would increase the possibility of facilitating critically oriented research and identifying any form of cognitive emancipation. This view has competency implications and it is suggested that any desire to engage in 'critical science' should be matched with a commitment to acquire the appropriate researcher skills. For example, pre-research interview training could draw from counselling perspectives and longer-term counselling training could further enhance listening skills and encourage greater self-awareness. Collaborative research which is more interpretive in orientation also demands sound interviewing skills and an awareness of appropriate qualitative analysis procedures.

In this chapter the notion of collaborative research has drawn upon the themes and processes contained within action research. This research approach constitutes a radical departure from the dominant paradigm of positivist or natural science and researchers should be aware that action research has been criticised for being more about change in the workplace than the process of research (Castle 1994). It is clear that collaborative research has limitations. For example, data is context specific and is closely associated with the dynamics of any one workplace. As a result, it may be difficult to extrapolate conclusions to other settings; however, research that documents *process* rather than *outcome* could be interpreted on a wider scale.

On a more positive note, collaboration, reflection, and changes in working practice can all be monitored through the administration of qualitative techniques. As these techniques are gaining acceptance within sport-based research, then action research procedures seem to provide an ideal framework from which researchers can facilitate reflection and encourage adherence to change.

Finally, the primary aim of this chapter was to link the theme of adherence to action research and the processes of collaboration and reflection. The author's own research experience, and the wider reports of collaboration in the literature, indicate that the formalised nature of systematic reflection can enhance awareness of practice. Similarly, the tendency for such methodic collaboration to be longitudinal in nature encourages adherence to change.

REFERENCES

Aspland, T., MacPhearson, I., Proudford, C., & Whitmore, L. (1996). Critical collaborative action research as a means of curriculum inquiry and empowerment. *Educational Action Research*, **4**(1), 93–104.

Bain, L.L. (1989). Interpretive and critical research in sport and physical education. *Research Quarterly For Exercise and Sport*, **60**(1), 21–24.

Bain, L.L. (1995). Mindfulness and subjective knowledge. *QUEST*, **47**(2), 238–253.

Banister, P., Burman, E., Parker, I., Taylor, M., & Tindall, C. (1994). *Qualitative methods in psychology*. Open University Press: Buckingham.

Biddle, S.J.H. (1997). Current trends in sport and exercise psychology research. *The Psychologist*, 63–69.

Bryman, A. (1988). *Quantity and quality in social research*. London: Unwin Hyman.

Carr, W., & Kemmis, S. (1986). *Becoming critical: education, knowledge and action research*. Falmer: London.

Castle, A. (1994). Action research for developing professional practice. *British Journal of Therapy and Rehabilitation*, **3**, 155–157.

Cohn, P.J. (1990). An exploratory study for the sources of stress and athletic burnout in youth golf. *The Sport Psychologist*, **4**, 95–106.

Corlett, J. (1996). Sophistry, socrates and sport psychology. *The Sport Psychologist*, **10**, 84–94.

Cote, J., Salmela, J.H., Baria, A., & Russell, S. (1993). Organising and interpreting unstructured qualitative data. *The Sport Psychologist*, **7**, 127–137.

Cote, J., Salmela, J., Trudel, P., Baria, A., & Russell, S. (1995). The coaching model: A grounded theory assessment of expert gymnastic coaches' knowledge. *Journal of Sport and Exercise Psychology*, **17**, 1–17.

Dale, G.A. (1996). Existential phenomenology: Emphasizing the experience of the athlete in sport psychology research. *The Sport Psychologist*, **10**, 307–321.

Danish, S.J., Petitpas, A.J., & Hale, B.D. (1992). A developmental–educational intervention model of sport psychology. *The Sport Psychologist*, **6**, 403–415.

Dean, P., & Choi, P. (1996). The meaning of exercise and health: A qualitative approach. In C. Robson, B. Cripps, & Steinberg, H. (eds.), *Quality and quantity: Research methods in sport and exercise psychology*. The British Psychological Society: Leicester.

Elliott. J. (1978). What is action research in schools? *Journal of Curriculum Studies*, **10**(4), 335–337.

Gilbourne, D., & Taylor, A.H. (1998). From theory to practice: The integration of goal-perspective theory and life development approaches within an injury specific goal-setting programme. *Journal of Applied Sport Psychology*, **10**(1), 124–139.

Gilbourne, D., Taylor, A., Downie, G., & Newton, P. (1996). Goal-setting during sports injury rehabilitation: a presentation of underlying theory, administration procedure, and an athlete case study. *Sports Exercise and Injury*, **2**, 1–10.

Gould, D. (1997). In praise of varied qualitative methods approaches in stress and performance research. Paper presented at the ISSP IX World Congress of Sport Psychology. Israel.

Gould, D., Eklund, R.C., & Jackson, S.A. (1992). 1988 U.S. Olympic wrestling excellence: I. Mental preparation, precompetitive cognition, and affect. *The Sport Psychologist*, **6**, 358–362.

Gould, D., Jackson, S., & Finch, L. (1993). Sources of stress in national champion figure skaters. *Journal of Sport and Exercise Psychology*, **15**, 134–159.

Habermas, J. (1972). *Knowledge and human interests*. (Trans. J. Shapiro). Heinemann: London.

Habermas, J. (1974). *Theory and practice*. (Trans. J. Viental). Heinemann: London.

Haggerty, L., & Postlethwaite, K. (1995). Working as consultants on school-based teacher-identified problems. *Educational Action research*, **3**(3), 169–181.

Hardy, L., Jones, G., & Gould, D. (1996). *Understanding psychological preparation for sport: Theory and practice of elite performers*. Wiley: Chichester.

Hart, E., & Bond, M. (1995). *Action research for health and social care: A guide to practice*. Open University Press: Buckingham.

Hart, E., & Bond, M. (1996). Making sense of action research through the use of typology. *Journal of Advanced Nursing*, **23**, 152–159.

Hart, S. (1995). Action-in-reflection. *Educational Action Research*, **3**,(2), 211–232.

Holter, I.M., & Schwartz-Barcott, D. (1993). Action research: What is it? how as it been used? and how can it be used in nursing? *Journal of Advanced Nursing*, **18**, 298–304.

Hough, M. (1996). *Counselling skills*. Longman: Harlow.

Hough, M. (1994). *A practical approach to counselling*. Longman, Singapore.

Jackson, S.A. (1995). The growth of qualitative research in sport psychology. In T. Morris & J. Summers (eds.), *Sport Psychology: Theory, applications and issues*. Wiley: Milton Qld.

Kemmis, S. (1991). Emancipatory action research and postmoderdisms. *Curriculum Perspectives*, **11**(4), 59–65.

Krane, V., Eklund, R., & McDermott, M. (1991). Collaborative action research and behavioural coaching intervention: A case study. *Applied Research in Coaching and Athletics Annual*, **1**, 119–147.

Lewin, K. (1946). Action research and minority problems. *Journal of Social Issues*, **2**, 34–36.

Lewin, K. (1952). Group discussion and social change. In G.E.Swanson., T.M. Newcomb., & F.E. Hartley. (eds.) *Readings in social psychology*, Holt: New York.

McFee. G. (1993). Reflections on the nature of action-research. *Cambridge Journal of Education*, **23**, 173–183.

Mason, J. (1996). *Qualitative researching*. Sage: London.

Melia, K.M. (1997). Producing 'plausible stories': Interviewing student nurses. In G. Miller & R. Dingwell (eds.), *Context and method in qualitative research*. Sage: London.

O'Hanlon, C. (1994). Reflection and action research: Is there a moral responsibility to act? *Educational action research*, **2**(2), 281–289.

Rogers, C. (1991). *On becoming a person*. Constable: London.

Rose, J., & Jevne, R.F.J. (1993). Psychological processes associated with athletic injuries. *The Sport Psychologist*, **7**, 309–328.

Scanlan, T.K., Stein, G.L., & Ravizza, K. (1989). An in-depth study of former elite figure skaters: II. Sources of enjoyment. *Journal of Sport and Exercise Psychology*, **11**, 65-82.

Schwandt, TA. (1997). *Qualitative Inquiry: A dictionary of terms*. Sage: USA.

Smith, B. (1996). Addressing the delusion of relevance: Struggles in connecting educational research and social justice. *Educational Action Research*, **4**(1), 73–91.

Southwell, M., & Welsch, J. (1995). Reflections on professional cynicism in education and the managment of education organisations: An exploratory action research approach. *Educational Action Research*, **3**(3), 337–345.

Street, A., & Robinson, A. (1995). Advanced clinical roles: Investigating dilemmas and changing practice through action research. *Journal of Clinical Nursing*, **4**, 349–357.

Tenenbaum, G., & Bari-Eli, M. (1995). Contemporary issues in exercise and sport psychology research. In S.J.H. Biddle (ed.), *European perspectives on exercise and sport psychology*. Human Kinetics: Champaign IL.

Tinning, R., MacDonald, D., Tregenza, K., & Boustead, J. (1996). Action research and the professional development of teachers in the health and physical education field: The Australian NPDP experience. *Educational Action research*, **4**(3), 389–405.

Titchen, A., & Binnie, A. (1993). Research partnerships: Collaborative action research in nursing. *Journal of Advanced Nursing*, **18**, 858–865.

Toomy, R. (1997). Transformative action research. *Educational Action research*, **5**(1), 105–123.

Waterman, H., Webb, C., & Williams, A. (1995). Changing nursing and nursing change: A dialectical analysis of an action research project. *Education Action Research*, **3**(1), 55–70.

Waters-Adams, S. (1994). Collaboration and action research: A cautionary tale. *Educational Action Research*, **2**(2), 195–209.

Winter, R. (1989). *Learning from experience: Principles and practice of action research*. Falmer Press: London.

Ziegler, E.F. (1995). *Competency in critical thinking: A requirement for the 'allied professional'*. *QUEST*, **47**, 196–211.

Chapter 11

Multi-method Approaches to the Investigation of Adherence Issues within Sport and Exercise: Qualitative and Quantitative Techniques

Lynne H. Johnston, Rod M. Corban, & Patricia Clarke

Theory-based interventions aimed at increasing adherence have had limited success as outlined in some of the previous chapters. These interventions are typically one dimensional in their approach, with a small number of participants, homogenous in gender, race, ethnicity, health status, and economic and educational status. Moreover, methodological flaws in application of theories, such as measuring attitude and behaviour at different levels of specificity, or undermining psychometric principles of

Adherence Issues in Sport and Exercise. Edited by Stephen J. Bull.
© 1999 John Wiley & Sons Ltd.

behaviour measurement by using only single assessment methods, have all contributed to low prediction rates in such things as adherence to exercise (e.g. Godin, 1993). On a parallel plane, the potential for true qualitative research to inform the debate on adherence in sport and exercise is becoming recognised (Marlow & Bull, 1998) and David Gilbourne's preceding chapter contributes to this recognition. The inherent complexity and richness of qualitative research does not lend itself easily to the accepted traditional methods of succinct publication. In addition, validity and generalisability of such research is questioned in terms of small sample sizes and illustrative quotations. The major concern with qualitative methods is that their applicability cannot be quantified.

This chapter discusses two exploratory approaches that have been used to study adherence in sport and exercise settings, and suggests a confirmatory procedure, which may be applied in future adherence research. The first exploratory approach (Grounded Theory) is regarded as a traditional qualitative approach. The second (Multidimensional Scalogram Analysis, MDS) may be viewed by some readers as a qualitative approach, given the inherent subjectivity involved in its application. However, it shall be referred to as an exploratory quantitative procedure for the purposes of this chapter in view of the distinct positivistic epistemological origins.

Qualitative and quantitative approaches to research stem from opposing epistemological stances. The qualitative paradigm is concerned with the search for meaning (*verstehen*) not universal laws. A constructivist epistemology acknowledges that knowledge is socially created. Information that is amassed and analysed is usually non-numerical. These forms of data allow qualitative researchers to explore, interpret and construct meaning within a time specific social context. The quantitative paradigm is based on a natural science approach where knowledge is viewed as objective. Numerical data is preferred as this allows the researcher to measure observable data and to statistically test a specific pre-defined hypothesis. In this chapter we argue that both methodologies can be used to produce a holistic (multi-method) approach to the study of adherence in sport and exercise settings.

A QUALITATIVE APPROACH TO THE STUDY OF ADHERENCE: ADHERENCE TO SPORT INJURY REHABILITATION PROGRAMMES

In 1988, Perkins and Epstein highlighted the lack of agreement concerning the definition of adherence. Ten years on, we have still not resolved this issue for adherence in general, let alone adherence to sport injury rehabilitation programmes. Thus, even if researchers are convinced of the merits of a quantitative approach, one must question the legitimacy of comparisons between studies at this stage:

> Qualitative studies are concerned with answering questions such as 'What is X and how does X vary in different circumstances, and why?' rather than 'How many X's are there?—Answering the 'what is X' question, though, is the foundation of quantification: until something is classified it cannot be measured (Pope & Mays, 1995, p. 43).

Furthermore as Brewer pointed out in Chapter 6 of this book, researchers have been somewhat premature in their study of adherence to sport injury rehabilitation, as the effect of adherence on physical recovery has still not been empirically tested.

The question of how one should measure adherence to sport injury rehabilitation programmes has been discussed in detail by Brewer (in Chapter 6) and elsewhere (see Brewer, 1998). However, even if researchers successfully develop a psychometrically acceptable measure of rehabilitation adherence there are a multitude of personal and situational variables which must be statistically controlled for, together with the often overlooked temporal phase of rehabilitation. It is often problematic for quantitative researchers to gain access to large enough samples to legitimately compute the type of statistical tests which are required to control for the range of mediating and moderating variables (see Baron & Kenny, 1986 for a discussion of the distinction between mediating and moderating variables) identified (see Brewer 1994, 1998 for review). Thus, even with a psychometrically 'efficient' measure, one must question the extent to which such an instrument can *truly* assist in the discovery of situationally and temporally specific predictors of rehabilitation adherence.

A further methodological limitation with existing quantitative studies, which are largely exploratory in nature (a distinction between exploratory and confirmatory quantitative studies is discussed in a later section: 'Exploratory Verses Confirmatory Analysis: Testing Exercise Adherence Models') is that participants included in the analysis are those who adhere to the study (e.g. Duda, Smart, & Tappe, 1989; Fields, Murphey, Horodyski, & Stopka, 1995; Fisher, Domm, & Wuest, 1988). Yet it is highly likely that those who adhere to studies examining adherence are also likely to adhere to their physical rehabilitation programme. Qualitative research, which purposefully samples those who do not adhere to physical formal rehabilitation, is likely to add significantly to our understanding.

On a theoretical note Brewer correctly states that 'to facilitate interpretation of research findings, it is important for scholars to couch their investigations in a relevant theoretical perspective' (Chapter 6, p. 156). The key issue here is how does one determine theoretical relevance? It is not acceptable for scholars to simply borrow and subsequently impose pre-existing theory without an empirical basis (Rose & Jevne, 1993).

GROUNDED THEORY: A SUGGESTED APPROACH

Grounded theory (Glaser & Strauss, 1967; Strauss & Corbin, 1990) is suggested as an ideal methodology for the study of adherence to sport injury rehabilitation programmes for three main reasons. First, it is appropriate in research spheres that are difficult to examine with quantitative methods. Second, grounded theory is suitable when there is some research in an area but no comprehensive theoretical models. Finally, grounded theory is particularly suited to the discovery of processes. The temporal context is clearly central to sport injury rehabilitation adherence research, yet existing quantitative research has paid the temporal dimension little heed (e.g. Duda, Smart, & Tappe, 1989; Fields, Murphey, Horodyski, & Stopka, 1995; Fisher, Domm, & Wuest, 1988).

Several articles published in sport psychology in the last 10 years have discussed various forms of qualitative analysis based upon the principles of grounded theory. Unfortunately differences in terminology have resulted in some confusion. Côté, Salmela, Baria, and Russell (1993) have termed it 'interpretational qualitative analysis'. Gould, Jackson and Finch (1993) called it 'hierarchical inductive analysis', while Scanlan, Stein, and Ravizza (1989) simply describe it as 'inductive content analysis'.

Four qualitative papers that have examined athletes' psychological responses to injury and which are based on the principles of grounded theory have recently been published within the psychology of sport injury literature. All four papers appear to be based on the same sample of 21 injured skiers (Gould, Udry, Bridges & Beck, 1997a, b; Udry, Gould, Bridges & Beck, 1997; Udry, Gould, Bridges & Tuffey, 1997). Unfortunately, these studies suffer from a number of methodological inconsistencies that are not compatible with the traditional grounded theory method. This may cause some confusion to those who base their reading on the mainstream grounded theory literature (e.g. Strauss & Corbin, 1990). It is worth highlighting some aspects which may cause confusion.

All four studies describe the use of 'in-depth' interviews yet go on to describe a semi-structured format to 'facilitate comparisons across participants' (Udry, Gould, Bridges & Tuffey, 1997, p. 372) and to 'standardise all interviews and to minimise bias' (Gould, Udry, Bridges, & Beck, 1997b, p. 382). However, in grounded theory data analysis drives further data collection and the interview format should be open and flexible for change over the course of the study. The groundedness of grounded theory results from researchers pledging to analyse what they actually discover in the data. The emergent themes need to be further investigated and should be permitted to direct the research in unexpected ways (Charmaz, 1990). Additionally, it seems that rather than employing purposeful sampling, the number of interviewees was defined in advance of data collection. This was explained by the authors as being consistent with other studies that 'have used similar methodologies and that have reached saturation' (Udry, Gould, Bridges and Beck, 1997, p. 232). Theoretical saturation is the point in data analysis when no new themes emerge from the data. It cannot therefore be pre-defined prior to data collection.

In view of the apparent confusion concerning the grounded theory method the following section shall introduce a useful schematic framework (Figure 1) to assist in the description of the grounded theory method. A more detailed account of the grounded theory method described in this chapter can be found elsewhere (Charmaz, 1990; Henwood & Pigeon, 1992, 1995; Strauss & Corbin, 1990, 1998).

THE GROUNDED THEORY METHOD

Yardley and Savage (1998) developed Figure 11.1 to encapsulate a social constructionist perspective of the grounded theory method. The constructionist view assumes and acknowledges an interaction between the researcher and the data that shapes and directs the analytical process and the emergent theory (Charmaz, 1990). The systematic set of procedures outlined by Strauss and Corbin (1990) has been influential in both the development of and the language used in Figure 11.1.

Figure 11.1 shows three core strands that co-occur throughout the grounded theory process: reflexive; resonant; and generative. Yardley and Savage (1998) argue that resonance, defined as interest, engagement and commitment generated by the initial broad focus of the inquiry, is the core concept of their model. They argue that if the research foci and methods do not facilitate a commitment to co-generational learning and a self reflexive research process and product, then the potential to develop deep, rich, vibrant applied research within sport psychology is severely constrained (Yardley & Savage, 1998). The reflexive concept refers to the researchers' own self reflection on decisions made and questions asked throughout the research process. Generativity refers to the potential of grounded theory to generate meaningful insights with applied implications.

As Figure 11.1 shows, the initial focus of a grounded theory project is fairly broad. This provides flexibility and freedom to explore the research area in depth. Sampling is purposeful or deliberate. This encourages the identification of cases with the greatest generative potential. The data

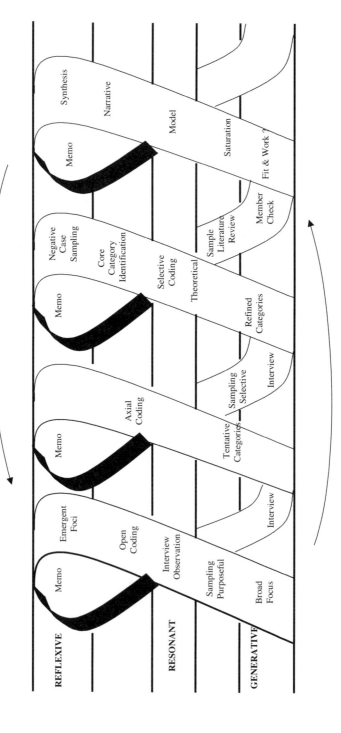

Figure 11.1 A schematic summary of the grounded theory process

collected may comprise field observations, interviews, letters, diaries, historical accounts, autobiographies, biographies, newspaper and other media materials. The first analytical step within the research spiral is termed open coding. Open coding involves the initial conceptualisation of the data whereby data are broken down into different meaning units (meaningful pieces of information). Theoretical memos and logic diagrams are recorded to reflect the emergent theoretical ideas. Strauss and Corbin (1990) stress that memos and diagrams are extremely important elements of analytic process and should not be omitted. Memos and logic diagrams can help the researcher to gain analytical distance from the data (if systematically recorded, they may also help to provide an audit trail of theoretical ideas over the course of a research project). This permits abstract conceptualisation before returning to the data for verification. Meaning units are compared and contrasted so that similar phenomena are grouped together and preliminary or tentative categories are developed via this initial 'constant comparison' of cases.

The next stage in the research spiral is called axial coding. Axial coding is concerned with linking subcategories to form higher-order categories. Like open coding, axial coding involves deductive and inductive thinking whereby the researcher proposes a relationship, then searches for verification in the data by making comparisons and asking questions. However, axial coding is more focused and arguably more systematic than open coding. This systematisation is facilitated through the use of the 'Paradigm Model', which adds density and precision to the theoretical analysis (see Strauss & Corbin, 1990 for a review and an applied example).

Selective coding involves the selection of a central or core category, systematically relating it to other categories, and developing and refining additional categories where necessary. Thus, selective coding is concerned with integrating and making sense of the coding that has been done to date. As Strauss and Corbin (1990) point out 'the question is: How do you take that which is in a rough form, and hopefully in your memos, and systematically develop it into a picture of reality that is conceptual, comprehensible, and above all grounded?' (p. 117). Negative case sampling directs further sample selection. This facilitates the search for incongruencies and allows the researchers to explore the reasons for such contradictions.

Reviewing the research literature is delayed in grounded theory projects to ensure that the emergent constructions result from the data rather than pre-existing borrowed theory. If pre-existing theoretical constructs are integrated into a project, they must be verified by the data. Member checks are performed, whereby the researcher consults with participants regarding the theoretical ideas or constructions. This is an essential component and reflects the 'active hermeneutic dialogue between researcher and participants' (Yardley & Savage, 1998) [The word hermeneutics may be defined as the process of interpretation. 'The word is thought to derive from Hermes, the Greek messenger god and trickster, who carried messages from the gods to the people. His role was to interpret these messages from the gods and to make them understandable to humans' (Addison, 1992, p. 110)]. The grounded theorist terminates data collection at the point of theoretical saturation. This is said to occur when: 'no new or relevant data seem to emerge regarding a category; the category development is dense in so far as all of the paradigm elements are accounted [and] the relationships between categories are well established' (Strauss & Corbin, 1990, p. 188). The results of a grounded theory project are presented in terms of a theoretical model or in narrative form. A model may be preferable when a temporal process is being communicated. This may be facilitated by the use of computer software programmes such as Decision Explorer[1].

The arrows at the top and bottom of Figure 11.1 highlight the inherent reciprocity within the research spiral. Thus, although Figure 11.1 has been described in a linear fashion it should be emphasised that each type of coding can take place simultaneously and researchers will often cycle back and forth between types of coding. However, open and axial coding would be expected to take place at an earlier stage in the analytic process.

It is worth noting at this stage that the increasing popularity of qualitative approaches within psychology has been paralleled by an increased acceptance and use of computer software programmes such as QSR NUD*IST[2]. Thus, increased popularity may reflect the perceived legitimisation of qualitative research through such software packages. The use of computer software packages such as QSR NUD*IST 4 does undoubtedly accelerate the mechanical search and retrieval procedures involved in the analytical process. They are also extremely helpful in terms of organisation and management of the data, memos, logic diagrams etc. However, computer packages such as QSR NUD*IST 4 are not a substitute for the rigorous analytical process itself (such as that outlined in Figure 11.1). The same criticism can be made with statistical packages such as SPSS which are open to misuse in quantitative research projects. Richards and Richards (1998) provide an excellent overview of the use of computers in qualitative research and point out the dangers involved in allowing the software to dictate the direction of the project. A number of useful

---

1 Full details and a free demonstration copy of decision explorer are available from Banxia Software: *http://www.banxia.co.uk* or *http://www.banxia.com*

2 Full details of QSR NUD*IST 4, including a free demonstration copy, are available from the following web sites: *http://www.sagepub.co.uk; http://www.sagepub.com; http://www.qsr.com.au*

examples of previous qualitative research projects using QSR NUD*IST can be accessed via the internet (e.g., *http://www.qsr.com.au*).

The next section offers an example of one study that adopted a grounded theory approach to explore the issues surrounding athletes' psychological responses to injury and rehabilitation. Due to space limitations the description and discussion of Figure 11.2 will be restricted to features which are pertinent to rehabilitation adherence. A full account of this work is discussed elsewhere (Johnston, 1997; Johnston & Carroll, 1998).

A Grounded Theory Model of Athletes' Emotional, Cognitive, and Behavioural Responses Following Injury

Figure 2 provides a summary of the prominent events and behaviours, and appraisals associated with athletes' emotional responses following injury (Johnston & Carroll, 1998). The development of Figure 11.2 resulted from a grounded theory analysis of interviews with 16 seriously injured athletes. Criteria for inclusion restricted recruitment to individuals who had sustained a severe injury within the preceding 12 months or were currently injured. The athlete had to be prevented, or be expected to be prevented if currently injured, from participating in sport or exercise for a minimum of 21 days. Severity classification was based on a National Athletic Injury/ Illness Reporting System (Levy, 1988). Injuries did not have to be incurred within a sporting context, although all but one were.

The initial interview format was broad and open ended. Participants were asked to describe the sequence of events from injury onset until full return to participation, or until the time of interview if still injured. All interviews began with the question 'Please talk me through your experience of the injury and how you felt throughout.' In line with the principles of theoretical saturation (Glaser & Strauss, 1967), data collection was terminated after the sixteenth interview when no new themes emerged from the data. In accordance with the principles of grounded theory, a detailed review of the literature was delayed until after the coding procedures took place when the key elements from existing cognitive appraisal models: cognitions, emotions, behaviours (see Brewer, 1994) were verified in the data.

As can be seen from Figure 11.2, rehabilitation adherence is centrally located within the conceptual framework. The central theme associated with the main period of rehabilitation was preoccupation with rehabilitation progress. Assessment of rehabilitation progress involved the following cues: pain, mobility, visibility, and social support. Informational and emotional support (as defined by Ford, Gordon, & Horsley, 1993), was usually provided by physiotherapists, other injured athletes, and previously injured

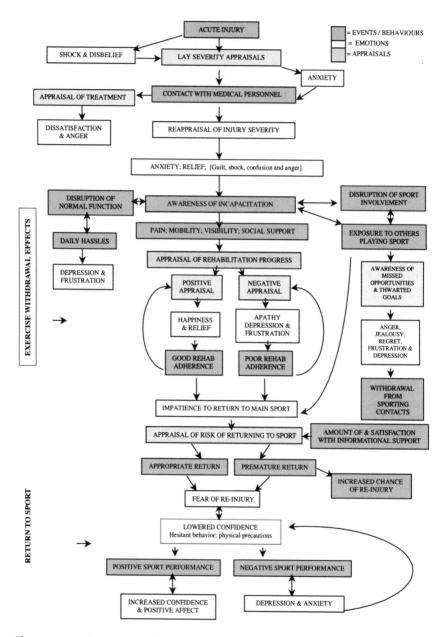

Figure 11.2   The situational and temporal context of injury rehabilitation

sporting friends. Those who perceived their rehabilitation as successful felt happy and relieved. This reinforced a belief in an ultimately successful outcome. This sense of optimism appeared to encourage adherence to the rehabilitation regime. Several of the athletes appraised their rehabilitation progress negatively. For these individuals, frustration, depression, and apathy resulted. This, in turn, had a negative effect on their adherence to rehabilitation. Reappraisal of rehabilitation progress continued throughout the main rehabilitation period in a cyclic fashion.

Throughout the main period of rehabilitation exercise withdrawal effects exerted a confounding effect. The main provocation appeared to be direct exposure to others playing sport, although the main stated cause of withdrawal symptoms was lack of physical activity *per se*. Reactions were greater in the more incapacitated participants, and those who had the largest time investment in sport prior to injury. This led, over time, to an increasing impatience to return to sport participation that resulted in an appraisal of whether or not to risk returning to sport participation prematurely.

Clear differences were noted between those who did return and those who chose to wait. Participants who did return: tended initially to have under-estimated the severity of their injury; displayed the most extreme symptoms of exercise addiction; focused on short-term sporting goals; ignored long-term consequences of their injury; did not receive adequate informational support; and set unrealistic rehabilitation goals, such as doing too much too soon. Those who did not risk returning to sport prematurely had often undergone surgery, followed by a long formalised rehabilitation programme. They were more likely: to have incurred a similar injury in the past; to make accurate appraisals of injury severity and rehabilitation progress; and to have received physiotherapy treatment, informational and emotional support. The applied implication here is that athletes may have a tendency to *over* not *under*-adhere to treatment and the physiotherapist has a key role in monitoring adherence and warning against over-adherence and premature return to sport.

Two basic psychological processes, described by Rose and Jevne (1993), 'running the risks' and 'opening to the messages' receive support in Figure 11.2. Athletes' appraisal of whether to risk returning prematurely to sport during late rehabilitation corresponds to the third phase of the risks model. Although this emerges as an important dilemma, previous quantitative research pays little attention to the risk of premature return to sport following injury. 'Opening to messages' (Rose & Jevne, 1993) refers to messages from the body, such as pain and muscle stiffness, or messages from health professionals, such as information regarding injury severity and progress. This corresponds to the severity appraisal and rehabilitation cues in Figure 11.2.

Although the Wiese-Bjornstal and Smith (1993) model has been influential in recent years (Smith, 1996; Wiese-Bjornstal & Smith, 1993; Wiese-Bjornstal, Smith, LaMott, 1995), many of its components lack empirical support and others have been examined only from the perspective of health care providers (Gordon, Milios, & Grove, 1991; Wiese, Weiss, & Yukelson, 1991). Smith (1996) suggests that the Wiese-Bjornstal and Smith (1993) model may provide a 'blueprint' for empirical testing. However, the model fails to highlight the dynamic nature of the recovery process and is not firmly grounded in the data. It is interesting to note that the results of the Johnston and Carroll (1998) study appear to have more in common with the only other study based in grounded theory in this area compared to the suggested blueprint.

Further research employing the grounded theory method as shown in Figure 11.1 offers a great deal of potential for rehabilitation adherence research. Such a method may afford the examination of particular components of Figure 11.2, such as the risk of premature return to sport and/or the role of social support in connection with rehabilitation adherence. The latter may be particularly appropriate given the inherent difficulties in questionnaire measures of social support (e.g. O'Reilly, 1988).

It is hoped that the discussion thus far has highlighted the potential of grounded theory as one approach to the study of adherence, and has offered a social constructivist example of how one actually *does* a grounded theory project. However, grounded theory is only one of a range of qualitative approaches (see Chapters 10 and 11). Those who wish to explore additional qualitative approaches are referred to Denzin and Lincoln (1998a,b,c) for a useful starting point. As mentioned earlier, the purpose of this chapter is not to advocate a qualitative versus a quantitative approach but rather to explore a range of methods which may be of use to those interested in exploring adherence issues within sport and exercise settings. The next section will focus on the collection and interpretation of exploratory quantitative data. As an example, the use of card sort techniques and Multidimensional Scalogram Analysis (MDS) in exercise adherence research is presented.

EXPLORATORY QUANTITATIVE TECHNIQUES IN SPORT AND EXERCISE RESEARCH

Within the last decade or so there has been an endemic increase in the use of complex multivariate techniques in exercise adherence research, potentially as a direct result of a concomitant increase in the accessibility of relevant computer packages. A major problem in any data analysis is how to find the underlying structure in a set of multivariate observations. One solution is the use of multidimensional scaling techniques (MDS). That is, mathematical tools that enable researchers to obtain some kind of spatial representation of complex data sets.

Multidimensional scaling techniques encompasses increasingly varied and powerful techniques. However, the unifying purpose of all these diverse techniques is to uncover whatever pattern or structure may otherwise lie hidden in the empirical data and to represent that structure in a form that is much more accessible to the human eye, namely as a geometric model or picture. Multidimensional scaling techniques use proximities among variables as input. These proximities are the primary means for recovering the underlying structure of relationships among a group of stimuli. The identification of underlying dimensions or attributes can take place from the structures obtained by scaling and clustering. Detailed discussions of particular MDS techniques such as Smallest Space Analysis, Multi-dimensional Scalogram Analysis and Partial Order Scalogram Analysis can be found elsewhere (e.g., Kruskal & Wish, 1978).

Methods of Data Collection

As with any research, the first step towards a better understanding of exercise adherence is the collection of good quality data. Traditionally, the data collection procedure has been limited by the availability of computing procedures for analysis. However, the development of techniques such as MDS removes constraints on the nature of data. It is possible to use systematic data collection techniques such as rating scales, sorting, triadic comparisons, rank order methods, while using MDS techniques for analysis (see Weller & Romney, 1990).

Sorting stimuli has traditionally been used as a qualitative data-gathering method in a number of substantive areas such as word meaning, lay conceptions of personality, and perceived similarities among nations and ethnic groups (Rosenberg & Kim, 1975). Typically the participant is presented with the total stimuli set and asked to sort them into groups of like stimuli. Normally the participant determines the number of groups, but the experimenter can specify a number of groups, if desired. The stimuli can be actual articles but it is obviously more convenient to use photographs or cards with the stimulus names. One of the main advantages of sorting as a data-gathering method is its economy, particularly in dealing with a large number of objects. In addition the task can be easily performed in the field, with participants of different age groups (i.e., children versus adults) and different ethnic groups (minority group versus English speaking individuals).

MDS as a Method for Quantifying Qualitative Material

The primary purpose of an MDS representation is to gain a better understanding of the underlying pattern of inter-relations in the data. The aim of interpretation, then, is to identify physical or other correlates of these psychological dimensions, or to specify their psychological meaning in some way. The simplest way to do this is by visual inspection. However, visual inspection may not be sufficient and other systematic statistical procedures may be desirable. Property vector fitting models afford one statistical method of interpretation. These models attempt to ascertain which properties of the stimuli were important to the participants while making their similarity judgements.

In many cases quite different aspects of the spatial configuration, such as the way the points cluster into several homogeneous groups, constitutes the most interpretable aspect of that configuration. Often, neighbourhoods or regions of the space may have meaning associated with other shared characteristics. One way to interpret neighbourhoods involves the application of clustering techniques. Clustering techniques are systematic methods for finding clusters based directly on the proximity matrix. The clusters can be drawn in the multidimensional spaces as loops around the relevant stimulus points. Subsequently, characteristics common to the objects in a cluster can be constructed. Usually, this is done subjectively as an act of interpretation. Any labelling then gives meaning to the neighbourhood where the cluster is located. An important reason why a neighbourhood interpretation can reveal other patterns in the data is that its focus is primarily on the small distances (large similarities), while a dimensional approach attends mostly to the large distances. Thus, in a neighbourhood approach the closer two points are in Euclidean space the closer they are thought to be conceptually. Guttman (1965) has argued that a neighbourhood or pattern approach is preferable to the traditional dimensional approach. Often one may not know in advance which of these possible structural features of the configuration will be the most susceptible to meaningful interpretation and it is wise to use additional approaches such as neighbourhood interpretation to supplement and clarify the dimensions. The following example outlines how qualitative analyses of health and exercise beliefs impeding on adherence behaviour can be explored via MDS, card-sorting techniques and cluster analysis.

Use of MDS in Exercise Adherence Research: An Example

Clarke (1996a,b) utilised a sorting procedure and MDS techniques to examine beliefs about health and exercise in a sample of beginner exercisers. Ninety-five exercisers sorted a 52-item pack of cards into groups of similar items in a single-sort design. Each card depicted a concept related to health or exercise. The adjective descriptors represented on each cards were determined by conducting a thorough search of the literature pertaining to health and exercise (e.g. Health Education Authority and Sports Council, 1992; Cox, 1987; Naea DeValle & Norman, 1992; Norman, 1991; Wallston, Wallston & DeVellis, 1978; Lalljee, Lamb & Carnibella, 1993). A data matrix was constructed to represent perceived differences between each pair of cards. These proximity distances were subjected to a series of iterations using the INSDCAL procedure (Carroll & Chang 1970).

Gender has been consistently reported as an influencing factor in exercise adherence and although the level of physical activity in the previous seven days did not vary by gender, underlying differences may exist in the cognitive beliefs pertaining to health and exercise. Averaged over male and female matrices a three-dimensional spatial representation was the most appropriate solution. This solution explained 63 percent of the variance and had an overall stress value of 0.23. However, looking at the male and female matrices separately over the dimensions, a two-dimensional solution is more appropriate for males (explaining variance of 71.1 percent and overall stress value of 0.25) while a five-dimensional solution is more appropriate for females (explaining variance of 76.2 percent and overall stress value of 0.16). The interpretation of the dimensions was based on axis orientation and neighbourhood approach using hierarchical clustering analysis. For males the dimensions were interpreted as 'positive aspects of healthy/ sporty lifestyle', and 'negative aspects of an unhealthy lifestyle'. For females the dimensions were interpreted as 'coronary heart disease (CHD) risk factors', 'exercise', ' negative aspects/ unpleasantness of taking part in exercise/ sport', ' sport', and ' positive aspects of taking part in exercise/ sport'.

Multidimensional scaling techniques combined with the card-sorting procedure provided an informative, alternative approach to exercise and health research. Gender differences were seen in the complexity of exercise cognitions. Males appear to think in black and white (positive versus negative), balancing the positive aspects and the negative aspects of exercising in a decisional balance-like approach. Females appear to have much more elaborate cognitive maps and as such the female decision to exercise is not such a straightforward procedure. As the number of dimensions determined the number of distinct clusters, there were only two main groupings for the male sample and five main groupings for the female sample.

Figures 11.3 and 11.4 show the clustering of items with the level of specificity increasing from the right-hand side to the left-hand side of the diagram. This complexity concerns several issues. Females grouped cardiovascular health factors together in a separate cluster. Although males tended to have a cardiovascular health grouping, this grouping was not pronounced enough to form a separate cluster and suggests that it was not a foremost belief structure for males. Females make the distinction between 'sport' and 'exercise' and appear to recognise the benefits of unstructured, moderate (effortless) activity. King et al. (1992) reported similar results where gender differences existed only for vigorous but not moderate intensity activity.

Interestingly, alcohol has different connotations for males and females. Males appear to associate alcohol with social enjoyment and exercise while females recognise alcohol as a CHD risk factor, which is associated with lack of exercise. The male sample grouped the competitive concepts of 'winning', 'losing' and 'compete' together with the positive aspects of a

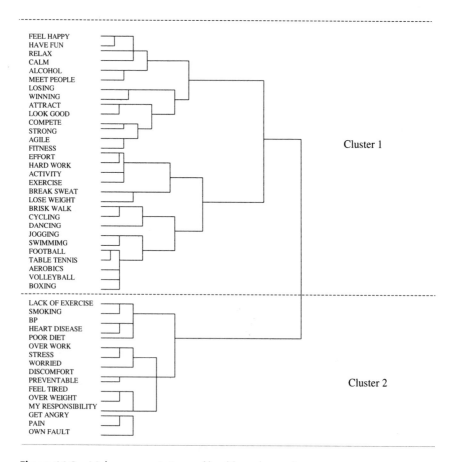

Figure 11.3   Male representations of health and exercise

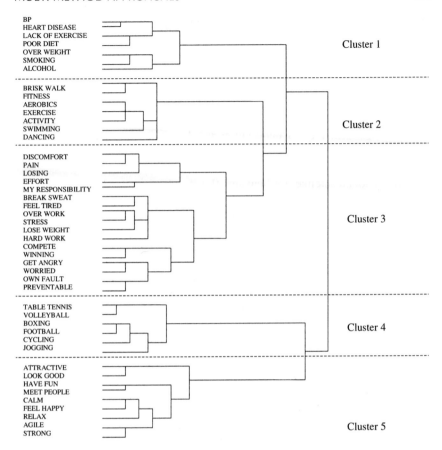

Figure 11.4   Female representation of health and exercise

healthy lifestyle, and in particular with the psychosocial aspects associated with a healthy, sporty lifestyle. Females, however, grouped these cards with the negative aspects of an unhealthy lifestyle. This may reflect the notion of males exercising for competitive reasons. Discourse analytic research by Drew (1996) revealed very similar results with females showing a strong concern for appearance while males talked more about performance factors. It is important to highlight this congruence between conclusions reached by these different methodological approaches.

Advantages of MDS

There are many different methods by which researchers can obtain some kind of spatial representation of psychological data: For example, factor analysis, hierarchical clustering schemes, multidimensional scaling, and parametric mapping. However, the use of MDS has several advantages over the use of such conventional multidimensional data analysis methods such as factor analysis.

1. The MDS model is based on distances between points whereas the factor analysis model is based on the angles between vectors. Both models generally use Euclidean space, but MDS has the advantage in that it is easier to interpret distances between points than angles between vectors.

2. In most social science applications the standard factor analytic methods have led to representation of a large number of solutions. Such results cannot be easily represented in a visual manner. In fact they are usually presented in the very same form as the original data, namely as a large matrix of numbers. This high dimensionality characteristic of factor analysis is in part a consequence of the rigid assumptions of linearity upon which the standard factor analytic methods have been based. The MDS approach does not contain this assumption and as such normally provides more readily interpretable, visual solutions of lower dimensionality.

3. Data for MDS, when collected by direct judgement of dissimilarities, are subject less to experimenter bias (although whether this is viewed as an advantage will depend upon one's epistemological stance) and most likely to contain structures relevant to the individual. Data for factor analysis generally contain scores for each stimulus on a highly subjective, and often conceptually incomplete, list of verbal descriptors. Within MDS the adjective descriptors are best used to help understand the multidimensional space obtained from the similarity judgements, not to derive one. In addition, research designed to collect similarity data for MDS analysis generates a large amount of information and generally yields stable spaces with only a few participants.

4. The appeal of MDS over conventional multivariate techniques is strengthened by the fact that no prior knowledge of the attributes of the stimuli to be scaled is required. Rather, the attributes provide a space that reveals dimensions relevant to the subjects. Conventional methods are often used to assess constructs that are behaviour specific. This can present a problem for these methods when the participants have no prior knowledge of the behaviour. This is the case, for example, in assessing exercise-specific self-efficacy in sedentary individuals with no prior exercise experience.

One disadvantage of MDS is that such a study can be time consuming and expensive. Although the total time taken depends on the number and nature of the stimuli, MDS studies generally take longer to complete than traditional quantitative methods of data collection. In addition, from a practical viewpoint, the collection of qualitative data may require specialised research assistance.

To summarise, MDS techniques may be particularly useful for measuring subjective beliefs concerning exercise adherence as they help systematise data where the organising concepts and the underlying dimensions are not well developed. They are low in experimenter contamination and they do not require prior knowledge of the attributes of the stimuli to be studied. The use of MDS techniques to analyse qualitative data may lead to a more complete representation of individual beliefs and perceptions than the use of conventional multivariate analytical techniques.

EXPLORATORY VERSUS CONFIRMATORY ANALYSIS: TESTING EA MODELS

Techniques such as MDS permit the quantification of qualitative data while still maintaining the complexity of the material. However, models of exercise adherence are still not subjected to direct assessment and as such these models are derived from *exploratory* techniques. Also, as these techniques are correlational in nature, they can never be used to imply causality. However, the resulting themes and suggested models can be assessed subsequently through *confirmatory* techniques allowing causal statements with regard to sport and exercise adherence behaviour. Such techniques can include confirmatory factor analysis (CFA) or path analysis (PA), both of which are special examples of a more general technique, referred to as structural equation modelling (SEM).

Structural Equation Modelling: Application and Advantages for Sport and Exercise Adherence Research

Structural equation modelling, as already mentioned, is a *confirmatory* rather than *exploratory* technique. Models are estimated, tested, and even modified through the use of SEM (Ullman, 1996). In this respect models are tested in an *a priori* manner. Some of the major goals for SEM are to test a specific hypothesis regarding a model, to modify existing models or to assess a set of related models. All of these make it an obvious choice for adherence research, given the fact that the question of adherence is complex and multidimensional in nature. As Ullman (1996) points out:

When the phenomena of interest are complex and multidimensional SEM is the *only* analysis that allows complete and simultaneous (*quantitative*) tests of all relationships', [p. 712, italics and parenthesis added].

In very simple terms, SEM allows the assessment of the model's ability to produce results consistent with observed data. In this way direct assessment of a specific model (or models) of adherence are possible. From this point specifics of the model can be ascertained.

Perhaps the greatest advantage of employing SEM in sport and exercise research is that it allows assessment and comparison of the many models used to explain sport and exercise behaviour. Through such an application of SEM techniques it may be possible to assess the applicability of models which have generally been taken from areas outside sport and exercise science. For example, many models of adherence behaviour have been generalised to explain adherence behaviour in sport and exercise. These have included such models as the health belief model (Becker & Mainman, 1975), the theory of planned behaviour (Ajzen, 1985, 1988, 1991) and the transtheoretical model of change (Prochaska & DiClemente, 1983; Prochaska, DiClemente, Velicer & Rossi, 1993; Prochaska, Velicer, DiClemente, & Fava, 1988). However, as noted by Biddle (see Chapter 5) with respect to the theory of planned behaviour, these models usually explain small amounts of adherence behaviour in sport and exercise. Through the use of SEM techniques the applicability of particular adherence models can be assessed. Moreover, it may be that certain models generalise to different populations or types of sport and exercise adherence but not to others. SEM may help to elucidate these issues in the future, as well as the use of problematic self-selection in adherence research, which has been mentioned earlier in this chapter.

From the preceding example, using MDS and cluster analysis to examine health and exercise beliefs with regards to adherence behaviour, different representations of exercise were suggested for males and females (Figures 11.3, 11.4). From these data possible models can be proposed. Structural equation modelling can then be used to assess such models. If one of the goals of sport and exercise research is to identify barriers to participation, the importance of specific models of behaviour for particular populations, in this case males and females are obviously crucial to the achievement of this goal. Thus, through a combination of exploratory techniques such as those outlined in previous sections, variables can be identified which are related to sport and exercise adherence. From this the promotion of particular adherence models can be presented. SEM affords a confirmatory test of these models, if that is indeed the intended goal of the research.

Although the potential for SEM within adherence research appears promising, it is not without its drawbacks. Apart from the usual issues of multivariate normality, linearity of relationships and other parametric assumptions, perhaps the biggest practical problem is that of sample size; a problem common in much of the research in this area (Perkins & Epstein, 1988). As with many statistical techniques variance (or more appropriately, covariances) become unstable with small sample sizes (Tabachnick & Fidell, 1996). The necessary sample size is open to some debate; however, the general rule of thumb applied to techniques such as Factor Analysis are also applicable with SEM. It is generally recommended that for every measure (or parameter estimate) that the sample includes 10 participants, although in general for small to medium models it is recommended that a minimum sample of 200 be used (Tabachnick & Fidell, 1996). No doubt any model of exercise behaviour would be rather complex and contain many parameter estimates; consequently sample sizes would be far in excess of this recommended number. For this reason SEM may hold more promise for health and exercise research than those involved with elite sport.

Another problem with the use of SEM is the potential for misuse. As is often the case when behavioural scientists apply statistical procedures without giving due consideration to the limitations and assumptions of such techniques, results and therefore conclusions can often be meaningless. Thus, if SEM is to be a useful tool for exercise research then these aspects of SEM should be acknowledged. There are several excellent recent references that discuss the use of SEM in social science. As it is not the purpose of this chapter to present a review of the procedures involved in SEM, interested readers may wish to consult a specialist text (e.g., Byrne, 1994; Kelloway, 1996; Schumaker, 1996).

CONCLUSIONS

The need for alternative approaches to research in sport and exercise sciences (Martens, 1987) and in particular the need for qualitative studies concerning exercise adherence (Dishman, 1988) has been highlighted. Traditionally, both qualitative and quantitative research is run as separate distinct entities often with one group having no knowledge of the other. The time has now come to promote an integrated approach to adherence research. By combining true qualitative techniques to identify issues specifically related to adherence with more traditional (positivistic) quantitative techniques a more complete understanding of the factors relating to adherence may be possible. However, it is important to emphasise that as qualitative and quantitative approaches stem from opposing epistemological stances, each approach must be evaluated using paradigm-appropriate judgements (Lincoln, 1992). It is too often the case that qualitative research is evaluated within a quantitative framework and is thus considered inferior because it does not adhere to quantitative rules.

From the discussion presented in this chapter it is clear that the potential exists to quantifiably test exploratory derived models of adherence in sport and exercise using structural equation modelling. This is not to say that exploratory techniques such as those mentioned are redundant. On the contrary, such techniques are an essential prerequisite, providing valuable insight into the underlying constructs relating to adherence in sport and exercise settings. In conjunction with 'true' qualitative methods such as grounded theory, exploratory procedures, such as MDS, may direct the promotion of specific models of adherence. It could be argued that it is in fact premature to suggest (or indeed test) adherence models when it is unclear what this construct actually represents, and what the components of these models should comprise. At this stage in our understanding, adherence research must arguably employ a combination of exploratory methods as outlined in this chapter. Once this has been achieved, then it may be appropriate to use SEM to examine the validity of adherence models in sport and exercise. However, irrespective of the approach adopted methodological rigour is imperative.

REFERENCES

Addison, R.B. (1992). Grounded hermeneutic research. In B.F. Crabtree, & W.L. Miller (eds). *Doing qualitative research* (pp. 110–124). London: Sage.

Ajzen, I. (1985). From intentions to actions: A theory of planned behaviour. In J. Kuhl and J. Beckmann (eds.), *Action-control: From cognition to behaviour* (pp. 11–39). Heidelberg: Springer.

Ajzen, I. (1988). *Attitudes, personality, and behaviour.* Chicago: Dorsey Press.

Ajzen, I. (1991). The theory of planned behaviour. *Organisational Behaviour and Human Decision Process,* **50**, 179–211.

Baron, R.M. & Kenny, D.A. (1986). The moderator-mediator variable distinction in social psychological research: Conceptual, strategic, and statistical consideration. *Journal of Personality and Social Psychology,* **51**, 1173–1182.

Becker, M.H., & Mainman, L.A. (1975). Sociobehavioural determinants of compliance with health care and medical recommendations. *Medical Care,* **13**, 10–24.

Brewer, B.W. (1994). Review & critique of models of psychological adjustment to athletic injury. *Journal of Applied Sport Psychology,* **6**, 89–100.

Brewer, B. (1998). Adherence to sport injury rehabilitation programmes. *Journal of Applied Sport Psychology*, **10**, 70–82.

Byrne, B.M. (1994). Structural Equation Modelling with EQS and EQS for Windows: *Basic concepts, applications, and programming*. London: Sage.

Carroll, J.D. & Chang, J.J. (1970). Analysis of individual differences in multidimensional scaling via an N-way generalisation of Eckart-Young decomposition. *Psychometrika*, **48**, 157–169.

Charmaz, K. (1990). 'Discovering' chronic illness: Using grounded theory. *Social Science and Medicine*, **30**, 1161–1172.

Clarke, P. (1996a). Determining the complexity of health behaviour. Paper presented at 10th European Health Psychology Society Conference, Royal College of Surgeons, Dublin, 4–6 September 1996.

Clarke, P. (1996b). Using multidimensional scaling procedures to help predict exercise behaviour. Paper presented at the British Association of Sport and Exercise Sciences Conference, Lilleshall Centre, 7–9 September, 1996.

Côté, J., Salmela, J.H., Baria, A. & Russell, S. (1993). Organizing and interpreting unstructured qualitative data. *The Sport Psychologist*, **7**, 127–137.

Cox, B.D. (1987). *The health and lifestyle survey: preliminary report*. London: Health Promotion Research Trust.

Denzin, N. K. & Lincoln, Y. S. (eds). (1998a). *The landscape of qualitative research: Theories and Issues*. London: Sage.

Denzin, N. K. & Lincoln, Y. S. (eds). (1998b). *Collecting and interpreting qualitative materials*. London: Sage.

Denzin, N.K. & Lincoln, Y.S. (eds). (1998c). *Strategies of qualitative inquiry*. London: Sage.

Dishman, R.K. (ed.), (1988). *Exercise Adherence: Its impact on public health*. Champaign, IL: Human Kinetics.

Drew, S. (1996). Perceptions of the body and motivations for physical activity. Paper presented at the British Association of Sport & Exercise Science, Lilleshall Centre, 7–9 September, 1996.

Duda, J.L., Smart, A.E., & Tappe, M.K. (1989). Predictors of adherence in the rehabilitation of athletic injuries: An application of personal investment theory. *Journal of Sport and Exercise Psychology*, **11**, 367–381.

Fields, J., Murphey, M., Horodyski, M., & Stopka, C. (1995). Factors associated with adherence to sport injury rehabilitation college-age recreational athletes. *Journal of Sport Rehabilitation*, **4**, 172–180.

Fisher, A.C., Domm, M.A., & Wuest, D.A. (1988). Adherence to sports injury rehabilitation programmes. *The Physician and Sportsmedicine*, **16**, 47–52.

Ford, I.W., Gordon, S, & Horsley, C. (1993). Providing social support for injured athletes: The perspective of elite coaches. *Sports Coach*, October–December, 13–19.

Glaser, B., & Strauss, A. (1967). *The discovery of grounded theory*. Chicago, IL:Aldine.

Godin, G. (1993). The theories of reasoned action and planned behaviour: Overview of findings, emerging research problems, and usefulness for exercise promotion. *Journal of Applied Sport Psychology*, **5**, 141–157.

Gordon, S., Milios, D., & Grove, J.R. (1991). Psychological aspects of the recovery process from sport injury: The perspective of sports physiotherapist's. *The Australian Journal of Science & Medicine in Sport*, **23**, 53–60.

Gould, D., Jackson, S., & Finch, L. (1993). Sources of stress in national champion figure skaters. *Journal of Sport & Exercise Psychology*, **15**, 134–159.

Gould, D., Udry, E., Bridges, D., Beck, L. (1997a). Stress sources encountered when rehabilitating from season-ending ski injuries. *The Sport Psychologist*, **11**, 361–378.

Gould, D., Udry, E., Bridges, D., Beck, L. (1997b). Coping with season-ending injuries. *The Sport Psychologist*, **11**, 379–399.

Guttman, L. (1965). The structure of inter-relations among intelligence tests. In *Proceedings of the 1964 Invitational Conference on Testing Problems* (pp. 25–36). Princeton, N.J.: Educational Testing Service.

Health Education Authority and Sports Council. (1992). *Allied Dunbar National Fitness. Survey: Main findings*. London: Sports Council and HEA.

Henwood, K. & Pigeon, N. (1992). Qualitative research and psychological theorising. *British Journal of Psychology*, **83**, 83–111.

Henwood, K. & Pigeon, N. (1995). Grounded theory and psychological research. *The Psychologist*, March, 115–119.

Johnston, L.H. (1997). The temporal and situational context of athletes' emotional responses following injury. Unpublished Doctoral Dissertation, University of Birmingham, Birmingham, England.

Johnston, L.H. & Carroll, D. (1998). The context of emotional responses to athletic injury: A qualitative analysis. *Journal of Sport Rehabilitation*, **7**, 206–220.

Kelloway, E.K. (1996). *Using LISERAL for structural equation modelling: A researcher's guide*. London: Sage.

King, A.C., Blair, S.N., Bild, D.E., Dishman, R.K., Dubbert, P.M., Marcus, B.H., Oldridge, N.B., Paffenbarger, R.S. Jr., Powell, K., & Yeager, K.K. (1992). Determinants of physical activity and interventions in adults. *Medicine and Science in Sports and Exercise*, **24**, S221–S236.

Kruskal, J.B. & Wish, M. (1978). *Multi-dimensional Scaling*. London: Sage.

Lalljee, M., Lamb, R., & Carnibella, G. (1993). Lay prototypes of illness: their content and use. *Psychology and Health*, **8**, 33–49.

Levy, I.M. (1988). Formulation and sense of the NAIRS athletic injury surveillance system. *American Journal of Sports Medicine*, **16** (Suppl. 1), 132–134.

Lincoln, Y.S. (1992). Sympathetic connections between qualitative methods and health research. *Qualitative Health Research*, **2**, 375–391.

Marlow, C. & Bull, S.J. (1998). A conceptual framework for the study of factors affecting adherence to training. *Journal of Sports Sciences* (Abstract), **16**, 92–93.

Martens, R. (1987). Science, knowledge, and sport psychology. *The Sport Psychologist*, **1**, 29–55.

Naea DeValle, M., & Norman, P. (1992). Causal attributions, health locus of control beliefs and lifestyle changes among pre-operative coronary patients. *Psychology and Health*, **7**, 201–211.

Norman, P. (1991). Causal beliefs for coronary heart disease. Paper presented at the British Psychological Society Health Psychology Section Conference, Nottingham.

O'Reilly, P. (1988). Methodological issues in social support and social network research. *Social Science and Medicine*, **26**, 863–873.

Perkins, K.A. & Epstein, L.H. (1988). Methodology in exercise adherence research. In R. K. Dishman (ed.), *Exercise adherence: Its impact on public health* (pp. 399–426). Champaign, IL: Human Kinetics.

Pope, C. & Mays, N. (1995). Reaching the parts other methods cannot reach: An introduction to qualitative methods in health and health services research. *BritishMedical Journal*, **311**, 42–45.

Prochaska, J.O., & DiClemente, C.C. (1983). Stages and processes of self-change of smoking: Towards an integrative model of change. *Journal of Consulting and Clinical Psychology*, **51**, 390–395.

Prochaska, J.O., DiClemente, C.C., Velicer, W.F., & Rossi, J. (1993). Standardized, individualised, interactive and personalized self help programs for smoking cessation. *Health Psychology*, **12**, 399–405.

Prochaska, J.O., Velicer, W.F., DiClemente, C.C., & Fava, J.L. (1988). Measuring processes of change: Applications to the cessation of smoking. *Journal of Consulting and Clinical Psychology*, **56**, 520–528.

Qualitative Solutions & Research Pty Ltd. (1997). QSR NUD*IST 4 User Guide (2nd edn). London: Sage.

Richards, T., J. & Richards, L. (1998). Using computers in qualitative research. In N. K.Denzin, & Y. S. Lincoln (eds). *Collecting & interpreting qualitative materials* (pp. 211, 245). London: Sage.

Rose, J.M.C., & Jevne, R.F.J. (1993). Psychosocial processes associated with athletic injuries. *The Sport Psychologist*, **7**, 309–328.

Rosenberg, S., & Kim, M.P. (1975). The method of sorting as a data-gathering procedure in multivariate research. *Multivariate Behavioural Research*, **10**, 489–502.

Scanlan, T.K., Stein, G.L., & Ravizza, K. (1989). An in-depth study of former elite figure skaters: II. Sources of enjoyment. *Journal of Sport and Exercise Psychology*, **11**, 65, 83.

Schumaker, R.E. (1996). *A beginners guide to structural equation modelling*. Hillsdale, NJ: Lawrence Erlbaum.

Smith, A. (1996). Psychological Impact of Injuries in Athletes. *Sports Medicine*, **22**, 391–405.

Strauss, A., & Corbin, J. (1990). *Basics of qualitative research: Grounded theory procedures and techniques*. London: Sage.

Strauss, A., & Corbin, J. (1998). Grounded theory methodology: An overview. In N.K. Denzin, & Y.S. Lincoln (eds). *Strategies of Qualitative Inquiry* (pp. 158–183). London: Sage.

Tabachnick, B.G. & Fidell L.S. (eds) (1996). *Using multivariate statistics* (3rd edn). New York: Harper Collins.

Udry, E., Gould, D., Bridges, D., Beck, L. (1997). Down but not out: Athlete responses to season ending injuries. *Journal of Sport and Exercise Psychology*, **19**, 229–248.

Udry, E., Gould, D., Bridges, D., Tuffey, S. (1997). People helping people? Examining social ties of athletes coping with burnout and injury stress. *Journal of Sport and Exercise Psychology*, **19**, 368–395.

Ullman, J.B. (1996). Structural Equation Modelling. In B. G. Tabachnick & L. S. Fidell (eds.). *Using Multivariate Statistics* (3rd edn). New York: Harper Collins.

Wallston, K.A,. Wallston, B.S., & DeVellis, R. (1978). Development of the multidimensional health locus of control (MHLC) scales. *Health Education Monographs*, **6**, 160–170.

Weller, S.C. & Romney, A.K. (1990). *Systematic data collection* (2nd edn.). London: Sage.

Wiese, D.M., Weiss, M.R., & Yukelson, D.P. (1991). Sport psychology in the training room: A survey of athletic trainers. *The Sport Psychologist*, **5**, 15–24.

Wiese-Bjornstal, D.M., & Smith, A.M. (1993). Counseling strategies for enhanced recovery of injured athletes within a team approach. In D. Pargman (ed.). *Psychological bases of sport injuries* (pp. 149–183). Morgantown, WV: Fitness Information Technology.

Wiese-Bjornstal, D.M., Smith, A.M., & LaMott, E.E. (1995). A model of psychological response to athletic injury and rehabilitation. *Athletic Training; Sports Health Care Perspectives*, **1**, 16–30.

Yardley, D. & Savage, D. (1998). A Rationale for A Constructionist Grounded Theory Research Model. Paper presented at the Fourth European Personal Construct Association Conference, 6–9th April, 1998, Chester, England.

AUTHOR INDEX

Pate, R.R. 75, 78
Paton, L. 89–90
Patrick, K. 48, 51
Patterson, C.H. 224
Paxton, R. 217
Pell, J. 83
Pender, N.J. 48, 49
Perkins, K.A. 186, 283
Perri, M.G. 100
Peterson, L. 207, 208
Petitpas, A. 226
Petruzello, S.J. 2
Pierce, E.F. 97
Pope, C. 265
Porras, J.I. 206
Prochaska, J.O. 19–20, 23, 26–7, 29, 30, 31, 36, 37, 38, 51, 77–8, 156, 184, 282

Quaglietti, S. 83, 84, 99
Quinn, A.M. 148, 151, 157, 158, 160

Rabinowitz, F.E. 211
Ravizza, K. 172, 174–5, 176
Reed, B.D. 50
Reed, G. 31, 33, 40
Reid, D. 47
Rejeski, W.J. 160
Rendall, E.O. 153
Reynolds, K.D. 118
Richards, T. 270
Rickli, R.E. 89
Rider, S. 184
Rigsby, L. 87
Rives, K. 160
Roberts, G.C. 119
Robison, J.I. 3
Rodgers, W. 178
Rogers, C. 223, 224, 248, 250
Rogers, R.W. 152, 153
Rollnick, S. 52
Romney, A.K. 181
Rose, J.M.C. 240, 266, 273
Rosenberg, S. 275
Rosenthal, R. 50, 65
Rossi, J. 29
Rovario, S. 83

Ruscher, S.M. xvii
Rushall, B.S. 210
Ryan, R.M. 133

Sallis, J.F. 77, 139, 183
Sarrazin, P. 120, 121, 122
Satterfield, M.J. 146, 160
Scanlan, T.K. 137, 241, 266
Schaffer, N.D. 209
Schumaker, R.E. 283
Schwandt, T.A. 243
Scott, J. 92
See Tai, S. 66
Sexton, T.L. 223, 224, 225, 229, 231
Shambrook, C.J. 175, 177–8, 180–1, 183, 184, 189
Shank, R.H. 148, 153, 154, 155, 157, 158
Sharratt, M.T. 88
Shaw, B.F. 209
Shelbourne, K.D. 160
Shephard, R.J. 51, 54, 100
Shropshire, J. 12
Silva, J.M.III. 221
Simkin, A.J. 89
Simon, H.B. 86
Singer, R.N. 221, 222, 228
Sinyor, D. 93
Sloane, R. 224
Smith, A. 274
Smith, B. 246, 247
Smith, E. 89
Smith, E.L. 89
Smith, F. 48
Smith, P. 48, 56
Smith, R.A. 3, 50
Smith, R.E. 169
Southwell, M. 249
Spink, K.S. 6, 7
Sports Council 96, 277
Spray, C.M. 123, 124
Startup, M. 208, 210
Steenbarger, B.N. 229, 231
Stenstrom, C.H. 88
Stephens, T. 3
Steptoe, A. 50
Stevens, W. 62
Stockport Leisure Services 54, 60

SUBJECT INDEX

Indexes compiled by Liz Granger

Related titles of interest...

Experiencing Sport
Edited by JOHN KERR
0471 975311   272pp   April 1999   Paperback

Training in Sport
Applying Sport Science
Edited by BRUCE ELLIOTT
0471 978701   440pp   January 1999   Hardback

Understanding Psychological Preparation for Sport
Theory and Practice of Elite Performers
LEW HARDY, GRAHAM JONES and DANIEL GOULD
0471 957879   320pp   1996   Paperback

Sports Psychology
Theory, Applications and Issues
T. MORRIS and J. SUMMERS
0471 335495   672pp   1995 Paperback